T0351090

Neural Machine Translation

Deep learning is revolutionizing how machine translation systems are built today. This book introduces the challenge of machine translation and evaluation – including the historical, linguistic, and applied context – then develops the core deep learning methods used for natural language applications. Code examples in Python give readers a hands-on blueprint for understanding and implementing their own machine translation systems. The book also provides extensive coverage of machine learning tricks, issues involved in handling various forms of data, model enhancements, and current challenges and methods for analysis and visualization. Summaries of the current research in the field make this a state-of-the-art textbook for undergraduate and graduate classes, as well as an essential reference for researchers and developers interested in other applications of neural methods in the broader field of human language processing.

PHILIPP KOEHN is a leading researcher in the field of machine translation and professor of computer science at Johns Hopkins University. In 2010, he authored the textbook *Statistical Machine Translation* (Cambridge University Press). He received the Award of Honor from the International Association for Machine Translation and was one of three finalists for the European Inventor Award of the European Patent Office in 2013. Koehn also works actively in the technology industry as Chief Scientist for Omniscien Technologies and as a consultant for Facebook.

Neural Machine Translation

Philipp Koehn
Johns Hopkins University

Shaftesbury Road, Cambridge CB2 8EA, United Kingdom

One Liberty Plaza, 20th Floor, New York, NY 10006, USA

477 Williamstown Road, Port Melbourne, VIC 3207, Australia

314–321, 3rd Floor, Plot 3, Splendor Forum, Jasola District Centre, New Delhi – 110025, India

103 Penang Road, #05–06/07, Visioncrest Commercial, Singapore 238467

Cambridge University Press is part of Cambridge University Press & Assessment, a department of the University of Cambridge.

We share the University's mission to contribute to society through the pursuit of education, learning and research at the highest international levels of excellence.

www.cambridge.org
Information on this title: www.cambridge.org/9781108497329

DOI: 10.1017/9781108608480

© Philipp Koehn 2020

This publication is in copyright. Subject to statutory exception and to the provisions of relevant collective licensing agreements, no reproduction of any part may take place without the written permission of Cambridge University Press & Assessment.

First published 2020

A catalogue record for this publication is available from the British Library

Library of Congress Cataloging-in-Publication data
Names: Koehn, Philipp, author.
Title: Neural machine translation / Philipp Koehn, Center for Speech and
    Language Processing, Department of Computer Science, Johns Hopkins University.
Description: First edition. I New York : Cambridge University Press, 2020. I
    Includes bibliographical references and index.
Identifiers: LCCN 2019046120 (print) I LCCN 2019046121 (ebook) I
    ISBN 9781108497329 (hardback) I ISBN 9781108608480 (epub)
Subjects: LCSH: Machine translation. I Neural networks (Computer science)
Classification: LCC P308 .K638 2020 (print) I LCC P308 (ebook) I
    DDC 418/.020285–dc23
LC record available at https://lccn.loc.gov/2019046120
LC ebook record available at https://lccn.loc.gov/2019046121

ISBN   978-1-108-49732-9   Hardback

Cambridge University Press & Assessment has no responsibility for the persistence or accuracy of URLs for external or third-party internet websites referred to in this publication and does not guarantee that any content on such websites is, or will remain, accurate or appropriate.

for Leo, Phianna, and Trishann

Contents

Preface

A decade after the publication of my textbook *Statistical Machine Translation*, translation technology has changed drastically. As in other areas of artificial intelligence, deep neural networks have become the dominant paradigm, bringing with them impressive improvements of translation quality but also new challenges.

What you are holding in your hands started out four years ago as a chapter of an envisioned second edition of that textbook, but the new way of doing things expanded so dramatically, and so little of previous methods is still relevant, that the text has grown into a book of its own. Besides the chapter on evaluation, there is very little overlap between these two books. For the novice reader interested in machine translation, this is good news. We all started anew a few years ago, so you are not far behind in learning about the state of the art in the field.

While machine translation is a specific application of natural language processing, and the book limits itself to this application, the concepts presented here are nevertheless the key underpinnings to address many other language problems. The models and methods for text classification, sentiment detection, information extraction, summarization, question answering, dialog systems, and so on are surprisingly similar, and this book will serve as a useful introduction to the broader field. Even more distant tasks such as speech recognition, game playing, computer vision, and even self-driving cars are built on the same principles.

This book benefited from the insight and feedback of a great many people. At my research lab at Johns Hopkins University and its Center for Language and Speech Processing, I would especially like to thank my colleagues Kevin Duh, Matt Post, Ben Van Durme, Jason Eisner, and David Yarowsky, Sanjeev Khudanpur, Najim Dehak, Dan Povey, Raman Arora, Mark Dredze, Paul McNamee, Hynek Hermansky, Tom Lippincott, Shinji Watanabe, as well as my PhD students Rebecca Knowles, Adi Renduchitala, Gaurav Kumar, Shuoyang Ding, Huda Khayrallah, Brian Thompson, Becky Marvin, Kelly Marchisio, and Xutai Ma. Thanks also to my former home, the University of Edinburgh, where the group around Barry Haddow, Lexi Birch, Rico Sennrich, and Ken Heafield were pioneers in the world of neural machine translation. There are many fellow researchers with whom I had fruitful discussions that broadened my view, and while it is impossible to list them all, I would like to explicitly thank Holger Schwenk, Marcin Junczys-Dowmunt, Chris Dyer, Graham Neubig, Alexander Fraser, Marine Carpuat, Lucia Specia, Jon May, George Foster, and Collin Cherry. This book also benefited from my exposure to practical deployments of machine translation technology. I have worked with Facebook to make machine translation technology available for the next hundred languages and would like to thank Paco Guzmán, Vishrav Chaudhary, Juan Pino, Ahmed Kishky, Benxiong Wu, Javad Dousti, Yuqing Tang, Don Husa, Denise Diaz, Qing Sun, Hongyu Gong, Shuohui, Ves Stoyanov, Xian Li, James Cross, Liezl Puzon, Dmitriy Genzel, Fazil Ayan, Myle Ott, Michael Auli, and Franz Och. My long-standing collaboration with Omniscien Technology, led by Dion Wiggins and Gregory Binger, gave me an appreciation of the changing currents of the commercial machine translation market. I received valuable feedback to early drafts of this book from Achim Ruopp, Kelly Marchisio, Kevin Duh, Mojtaba Sabbagh-Jafari, Parya Razmdide, Kyunghyun Cho, Chris Dyer, and Rico Sennrich.

Reading Guide

The whole book is divided into three parts. Part I gives a gentle introduction to the problem of machine translation, its history, and how the technology is used in the world. It concludes with a chapter on evaluation, an embattled aspect of the field. Part II, in five short chapters, explains neural networks, the design of basic machine translation models, and core aspects of training and decoding. Part III both covers essential aspects to build state-of-the-art models and touches on the research frontier of open challenges and unsolved problems.

The core concepts of the book are introduced in four ways: in an informal description, a formal mathematical definition, graphical illustrations, and example code (in Python and PyTorch). The hope is that the reader will understand the foundational knowledge behind neural machine translation and also be able to implement state-of-the-art models and modify existing toolkits in novel ways.

Who should read this book
This book is mainly conceived as a textbook for undergraduate and graduate university classes. It may be used in a course on natural language processing (with additional material on other applications in that subject area) or in a course just focused on machine translation (where some aspects of statistical machine translation—such as word alignment, simpler translation models, and decoding algorithms—should be introduced as well). Since the book covers material up to the state of the art in the field at the time of this writing, it also serves as a reference for researchers in the field.

For the eager reader
You may jump ahead to Chapter 5 where the core technical part begins. While Part II (Chapters 5–9) contains all the basic concepts for neural machine translation, including a code guide to implement such models, the final (and largest) part of the book contains many essential topics that are required to build state-of-the-art systems. Especially Chapter 10, Section 12.3, and Section 14.1 are required reading. This is a fast-moving field, so Chapter 11 on alternative architectures where I introduce the Transformer model will keep you apace with the present technology.

Material for lecturers

Additional information about this book can be found on its website, www.statmt.org/nmt-book. The author teaches a class based on the book at Johns Hopkins University and the course web page at http://mt-class .org/jhu will be useful for the reader. The further reading sections at the end of most chapters are mirrored on the site www.statmt.org/survey, where future papers will be discussed as well.

Part I
Introduction

Chapter 1
The Translation Problem

Imagine that you are a translator. You are asked to translate from German to English and you come across the word *Sitzpinkler*. Its literal meaning is *someone who pees sitting down*, but its intended meaning is *wimp*. The implication is that a man who sits down to pee is not a real man.

But there is more going on here. This word was popularized on a comedy show that coined several other terms in this fashion. One is *Warmduscher, someone who takes a warm shower,* or even *Frauenver-steher, someone who understands women.* In fact, a whole fad emerged to come up with new terms like this. All these terms are used as insults, but not as real serious insults. They are used very much in jest, a slight mocking.

These terms are also firmly a reflection of the current zeitgeist, when the expectations of what it means to be a man are changing. Using such terms is a light-hearted commentary on this change. It is not really unmanly to sit down to pee, although it is something that women do and hence a man who wants to be a traditional "real" man loses some of his identity this way. As you can see, there is a lot going on here.

So, what is a translator going to do? Probably use *wimp* and move on. This example demonstrates that translation is basically impossible. The meaning of words in a language are tied to their prior use in a specific culture. *Four score and seven years* is not just any way to say *87 years*. And *I have a dream* implies much more than just announcing a vision of the future. Words carry not only an explicit meaning but also an undercurrent of implications that often does not have any equivalent in another language and another culture.

Figure 1.1 Ten translators translate the same short French sentence—*Sans se démonter, il s'est montré concis et précis.*—in 10 different ways. Human evaluators also disagree for each translation if it is correct or wrong.

Assessment Correct/Wrong	Translation
1/3	*Without fail, he has been concise and accurate.*
4/0	*Without getting flustered, he showed himself to be concise and precise.*
4/0	*Without falling apart, he has shown himself to be concise and accurate.*
1/3	*Unswayable, he has shown himself to be concise and to the point.*
0/4	*Without showing off, he showed himself to be concise and precise.*
1/3	*Without dismantling himself, he presented himself consistent and precise.*
2/2	*He showed himself concise and precise.*
3/1	*Nothing daunted, he has been concise and accurate.*
3/1	*Without losing face, he remained focused and specific.*
3/1	*Without becoming flustered, he showed himself concise and precise.*

goals of translation

1.1 Goals of Translation

There are many different ways to translate a sentence. See Figure 1.1 for an example (from a study on a computer aided translation tool). Ten translators translated the same short French sentence—*Sans se démonter, il s'est montré concis et précis.*—in 10 different ways. There is the challenge of the French phrase *Sans se démonter*, which does not seem to have a nice equivalent, so translators make choices from very literal translations that are awkward English (say, *Without dismantling himself*) to fairly free translations (*Unswayable*), to just dropping this phrase. But there is also a lot of variance for the rest of the sentence. In fact, no two translations are the same. And this is by far the most typical outcome when several translators translate the same sentence. In this study, the translations were also evaluated by four human assessors each as either correct and wrong. For most translations, there is disagreement.

Translation is always an approximation. Translators have to make choices, and different translators make different choices. The main competing goals are **adequacy** and **fluency**. Adequacy means retaining the meaning of the original text. Fluency requires producing output text that reads just like any well-written text in the target language.

Often, these two goals are in conflict. To closely maintain the meaning of the original sentence may make a translation clumsy. Different genres of text make different trade-offs here. Translations of literature are more concerned with style, that text flows well, so it may completely change some of the meaning to maintain the overall spirit of a text. Think about the translation of song lyrics. It is more important that the translated song sounds right and carries across the same emotion.

However, when translating an operations manual or a legal text, concerns about fluency are secondary. It is fine to produce wooden and awkward phrases when this is the only way to express the same facts.

Consider an example that may show up in a newspaper article: the phrase *about the same population as Nebraska*. Let's say you want to translate this into Chinese. Very few people in China will have any idea of how many people live in Nebraska. So, you may want to change *Nebraska* to the name of a Chinese city or province that the reader will be familiar with. This was the whole intention of the author—to provide a concrete example that is meaningful to the reader.

A more subtle example is a foreign phrase that literally translates to *the American newspaper the New York Times*. For any American reader this would come across at least as odd. It is well known that the *New York Times* is an American newspaper, so what is the reason to point this out? It is likely the original phrase did not intend to place special emphasis on the American nature of the paper. It is just there to inform the readers who may not know the paper. Consider the converse. A literal translation from German may be *Der Spiegel reported*, which leaves most American readers unsure about the reliability of the source. So, a professional translator may decide to render this as *the popular German news weekly Der Spiegel reported*.

A goal of translation is to be invisible. At no point should a reader think *This is translated really well/badly* or even worse *What did this say in the original?* Readers should not notice any artifacts of translation and should be given the illusion that the text was originally written in their own language.

1.2 Ambiguity

ambiguity

If there is one word that encapsulates the challenge of natural language processing with computers, it is **ambiguity**. Natural language is ambiguous on every level: word meaning, morphology, syntactic properties and roles, and relationships between different parts of a text. Humans are able to deal with this ambiguity somewhat by taking in the broader context and background knowledge, but even among humans there is a lot of misunderstanding. Sometimes the speaker is purposely ambiguous to not make a firm commitment to a particular interpretation. In that case, the translation has to retain that ambiguity.

1.2.1 Word Translation Problems

word translation problems

The first obvious example of ambiguity is that some words have strikingly different meanings. Consider the example sentences:

- *He deposited money in a* **bank** *account with a high* **interest** *rate.*
- *Sitting on the* **bank** *of the Mississippi, a passing ship piqued his* **interest***.*

The words *bank* and *interest* have different meanings in these two sentences. A *bank* may be the shore of a river or a financial institution, while *interest* may mean curiosity or have the financial meaning of a fee charged for a loan.

How could computers ever know the difference? Well, how do humans know the difference? We consider the surrounding words and the overall meaning of the sentence. In the examples, the word *rate* following *interest* is already a very strong indicator. Computers have to take this context into account as well.

1.2.2 Phrase Translation Problems

phrase translation problems

The next challenge is that meaning is not always compositional. This prevents us from cleanly breaking up the translation problem into small subproblems. The clearest examples for this are idiomatic phrases such as *It's raining cats and dogs*. This will not translate well word for word into any other language. A good German translation may be *es regnet Bindfäden*, which translates literally to English as *it rains strings of yarn* (the rain droplets are so close that they string together).

You may sometimes be able to track down an idiom through its origin story or the metaphor it builds on, but in practice human users of language just memorize these and do not think too much about them.

1.2.3 Syntactic Translation Problems

syntactic translation problems

The classic example for syntactic ambiguity is prepositional phrase attachment. There is a difference between *eating steak with ketchup* and *eating steak with a knife*, in the first case the noun in the prepositional phrase is connected to the object *steak* while in the second case it is connected to the verb *eating*. However, this problem often does not matter much for translation, since the target language may allow for the same ambiguous structure, so there is no need to resolve it.

However, languages often differ in their sentence structure in ways that matter for translation. One of the main distinctions between languages is if they use word order or morphology to mark the relationships between words. English mostly relies on word order, the standard sentence structure is subject–verb–object. Other languages, like German, allow the subject or object at the beginning of the sentence, and they use morphology, typically changes to word endings, to make the distinction clear.

Consider the following short German sentence, with possible translations for each word below it.

das	*behaupten*	*sie*	*wenigstens*
that	claim	they	at least
the		she	

There is a lot going on here.

- The first word *das* could mean *that* or *the*, but since it is not followed by a noun, the translation *that* is more likely.

- The third word *sie* could mean *she* or *they*.
- The verb *behaupten* means *claim,* but it is also morphologically inflected for plural. The only possible plural subject in the sentence is *sie* in the interpretation of *they*.

So, the closest English translation *they claim that at least* requires the reordering from object–verb–subject word order to subject–verb–object word order. Google Translate translates this sentence as *at least, that's what they say,* which avoids some of the reordering (*that* is still in front of the verb). This is also a common choice of human translators who would like to retain the emphasis on *that* by placing it early in the English sentence.

1.2.4 Semantic Translation Problems

semantic translation problems

Translation becomes especially tricky when meaning is expressed differently in different languages or, even worse, requires some inference over several distant literal items or may even be just implied.

Consider the problem of **pronominal anaphora**. Pronouns are used to refer to other mentions, typically prior to the occurrence of the pronoun but not always. Here is one example:

pronominal anaphora

I saw the movie, and **it** *is good.*

This is straightforward example where *it* refers to *movie*. When translating this sentence into languages such as German or French, we also have to find a pronoun for the translation of *it*. However, German and French have gendered nouns. Not all things are of neutral gender as in English, they may be masculine, feminine, or neutral, with apparently arbitrary assignment (*moon* is male in German but female in French, *sun* is female in German but male in French). In our example, a good translation for movie is *Film* in German, which has masculine gender. Hence the pronoun *it* has to be rendered as the masculine pronoun *er* and not the feminine *sie* or the neutral *es*.

So there is quite a lot of inference required: the co-reference between the English pronoun *it* and the English noun *movie*, the decision of translating *movie* into *Film*, the acquisition of the knowledge that *Film* is a masculine noun, and the use of all this information when translating *it* into *er*. So, a lot of information needs to tracked, and the hard problem of co-reference resolution (detecting which entities in a text refer to the same thing) has to be solved.

Let us consider an even more difficult example that involves co-reference resolution.

Whenever I visit my uncle and his daughters, I can't decide who is my

favorite **cousin**.

The English word *cousin* is gender neutral, but there is no gender neutral translation of the word into German. Compare that to the strong preference in English for the gendered nouns *brother* and *sister* opposed to the gender neutral *sibling* which is very unusual in certain circumstances (*I'll visit my sibling this weekend* sounds rather odd).

In this case, there is even more complex inference required to detect that the cousin is female—because it is the daughter of my uncle. This **world knowledge** requires **world knowledge** about facts of family relationships, in addition to the need for co-reference resolution (*cousin* and *daughters* are connected) and knowledge of grammatical gender of German nouns.

discourse Finally, let us look at problems posed by **discourse** relationships. Consider the two examples:

Since *you suggested it, I now have to deal with it.*

Since *you suggested it, we have been working on it.*

Here, the English discourse connective *since* has two different senses. In the first example, it is equivalent to *because*, marking a **causal relationship** **causal** relationship between the two clauses. In the second example, **temporal relationship** it has a **temporal** sense. The word will be translated differently for these different senses into most languages. However, detecting the right sense requires information about how the two clauses relate to each **discourse structure** other. Analyzing the **discourse structure** of a document, i.e., how all the sentences hang together, is an open and very hard research problem in natural language processing.

Moreover, discourse relationships may not even be marked by discourse connectives like *since*, *but*, or *for example*. Instead, they may be revealed through the choice of grammatical sentence structure. To give one example:

Having said that, I see the point.

The first clause here has a grammatical form that is used to mark a **concession** **concession**. We could also use the word *although* there. When translating this into other languages, this implicit encoding of the **concession** relationship may need to be made explicit with a discourse connective.

1.3 The Linguistic View
linguistics

The examples in the previous section suggest that the problem of translation requires not only several levels of abstractions over natural language but also ultimately commonsense reasoning informed by knowl- **AI hard** edge about the world, making machine translation an **AI hard** problem. In other words, solving machine translation ultimately requires

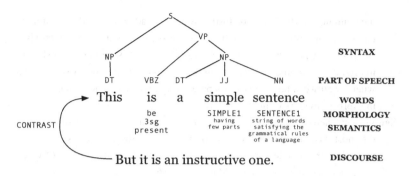

Figure 1.2 Levels of abstraction used in natural language processing.

solving the core problem of **artificial intelligence**. Translating speech acts ultimately requires understanding what these speech acts mean in the world.

    Let us be a more explicit about the types of abstraction that have been developed over the decades in natural language processing research. See Figure 1.2, which shows various types of linguistic annotation for the sentence *This is a simple sentence*.

artificial intelligence

Words: While breaking up speech acts into sentences and words seems uncontroversial, it is actually not totally obvious. Consider the case of languages that do not separate words by spaces (such as Chinese), where breaking up a sentence into words requires linguistic tools.

word

Parts of speech: We like to distinguish between nouns, verbs, determiners, etc. Parts of speech fall into two main classes: content words (also called open class words), which describe objects, actions, and properties of the world, and function words, which provide the glue to make the relationships between these words clear. Languages differ quite a bit in the type of open class words that exist (for instance, Chinese does not have determiners, which are admittedly kind of useless).

part of-speech

Morphology: The endings of words may be changed to clarify some of their syntactic or semantic properties. We distinguish between inflectional morphology (e.g., *dog* and *dogs*, *eats* and *eating*), which accounts for count, gender, case, tense, etc., and derivational morphology, which changes the part of speech of a word (*eat, eater, eatery*). For the task of translation it is sometimes useful to break up words into **stems** (which carry the dictionary meaning) and **morphemes** (which carry inflectional or derivational information), for example, *eats* → *eat + s*.

morphology

stem

morpheme

Syntax: We can understand the meaning of a sentence by understanding the connections between its words. Sentences may have multiple clauses (such as the main clause and a relative clause), each clause has at its center a verb, which requires arguments such as subjects and objects, and additional adjuncts such as adverbs (say, *quickly*) temporal phrases (say, *for five minutes*). Subjects and objects are typically noun phrases that break up into

syntax

syntax tree

dependency structure

the main noun, which may be further refined by adjectives and determiners but also relative clauses. A core property of natural language is its recursive structure, so a good way to represent this structure is a **syntax tree**, as shown in Figure 1.2. Another way to represent syntax is by **dependency structure**, where each word has a link to its parent (e.g., the object noun *sentence* to the verb *is*, in our example).

semantics

lexical semantics

AMR

abstract meaning representation

Semantics: There are several levels of semantics that could be considered. At the most basic level, **lexical semantics** addresses the different senses of a word. In our example, the meaning of *sentence* is detected as SENTENCE1, which has the definition *string of words satisfying the grammatical rules of a language*, opposed to, say, a prison sentence. But we may also describe the meaning of the entire sentence. One formalism to do this is **abstract meaning representation (AMR)**. For our example sentence, this looks like this:

```
(b / be
  :arg0 (t / this)
  :arg1 (s / sentence
          :mod (s2 / simple)))
```

Compared to syntax structure, it contains mostly only content words and pronouns, and defines their relationships in form of semantic roles (such as actor, patient, temporal modifier, quantity, etc.). There is much disagreement about the correct formalisms to use for higher-level semantics, and even AMR is a work in progress.

discourse

Discourse: Finally, discourse deals with the relationship between clauses (or elementary discourse units) in a text. It attempts to define the structure of a text, for instance to aid applications such as summarization. There is not much consensus about the right formalisms here and even trained human annotators cannot agree very well on which discourse relationships to assign to a given text.

interlingua

One vision for machine translation is shown in Figure 1.3, initially proposed by Vauquois (1968). The ultimate goal is to analyze a source sentence into its meaning, hopefully in a language-independent meaning representation called **interlingua**, and then to generate the target sentence from that interlingua representation. The research strategy toward this goal is to start with simple lexical transfer models and then move on to more complex intermediate representations at the level of syntax and language-dependent semantics.

Before the advent of neural machine translation, the field of statistical machine translation made great strides along this path. The best performing systems for language pairs such as Chinese–English and German–English were syntax-based systems that generated

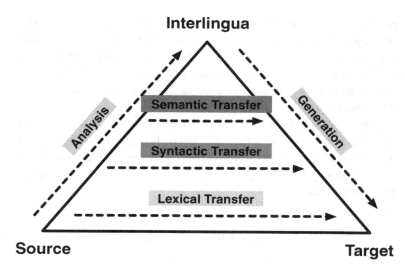

Figure 1.3 The Vauquois triangle. The linguistic vision to analyze the meaning of a source sentence into a language-independent meaning representation and then the generation of the target sentence.

syntax structures during the translation process. With neural machine translation, we are currently back to the level of lexical transfer, but there is a plausible argument to be made that once we mastered that level, we can make another climb up the Vauquois triangle.

1.4 The Data View

data

During the twenty-first century, machine translation research has been firmly grounded in the paradigm that it is futile to write down all the necessary dictionaries and rules that govern language and translation. Instead, all information should be automatically acquired from large amounts of translation examples.

There are two main types of text **corpora** (a corpus is a collection   corpus
of text): monolingual and parallel. If we acquire large amounts of text in a single language, we can learn a lot from it, i.e., the words used in the language, how these words are used, the structure of sentences, and so on. There is even the dream to learn how to translate purely from large amounts of monolingual text, called **unsupervised machine**   unsupervised machine
translation. But better resources to learn how to translate are parallel   translation
corpora, also called bi-texts, that typically come in the form of sentence pairs, a source sentence and its translation.

1.4.1 Adequacy

adequacy

Let us take a look at how data will help us solve translation problems, beginning with adequacy, i.e., matching the meaning of the source sentence. To start, take the German word *Sicherheit*, which has three main possible translations into English: *security*, *safety*, and *certainty*. The distinction between *security* and *safety* is arguably subtle, but in most cases, only one of the choices is a correct translation. For instance *job security* and *job safety* mean very different things—the former is concerned with not losing a job, the second with not getting harmed while working.

So, how is a computer to know which translation to use? The first stab is to count in a parallel corpus, how often *Sicherheit* was translated into each of the three choices. Here is what an analysis of a corpus drawn from the parliamentary proceedings of the European Parliament reveals:

$$Sicherheit \rightarrow security: 14{,}516$$

$$Sicherheit \rightarrow safety: 10{,}015$$

$$Sicherheit \rightarrow certainty: 334$$

So, without other further information, the best bet is *security*, but *safety* is a close second, so we would be wrong very many times.

Can we do better? Yes, by doing what a human would do, i.e., considering the broader context the word is used in. This includes at least the surrounding words. Even just one neighboring word may be sufficient to detect the right word sense in the source language, allowing for the correct translation into the target language. Here some examples, of a preceding noun (which in German is merged into a compound).

$$Sicherheitspolitik \rightarrow security\ policy: 1{,}580$$

$$Sicherheitspolitik \rightarrow safety\ policy: 13$$

$$Sicherheitspolitik \rightarrow certainty\ policy: 0$$

$$Lebensmittelsicherheit \rightarrow food\ security: 51$$

$$Lebensmittelsicherheit \rightarrow food\ safety: 1{,}084$$

$$Lebensmittelsicherheit \rightarrow food\ certainty: 0$$

$$Rechtssicherheit \rightarrow legal\ security: 156$$

$$Rechtssicherheit \rightarrow legal\ safety: 5$$

$$Rechtssicherheit \rightarrow legal\ certainty: 723$$

In case of *Sicherheitspolitik* and *Lebensmittelsicherheit*, the data indicate clear preferences, even though *safety policy* and *food security* are valid concepts (policies to ensure that products are safe to use and having enough food to eat on a regular basis, respectively).

What this example illustrates is twofold: contextual information can make predictions of the correct translation of words highly reliable, but there will be always be some error, e.g., always translating *Sicherheit-spolitik* into *security policy* will miss the few cases where *safety policy* is the right translation. Hence the engineering mantra of data-driven machine translation research is not to achieve perfect translation, but to drive down error rates.

1.4.2 Fluency

fluency

Text corpora help not only with finding the right translation for words but also with arranging these words in the right way to ensure fluent output. This involves selecting the right word order, the right function words, and sometimes even different phrasing from what a too literal translation would dictate. To know what constitutes fluent language, we need only consult large amounts of target language corpora, which are much more plentiful than parallel corpora.

Such corpora will tell us, say, that *the dog barks* is a much better word order than *barks dog the*, just because the first sequence of words will have been observed many more times than the latter. Or, to give another example: suppose we would like to find the right preposition to connect the words *problem* and *translation*, describing the type of problem that is concerned with translation.

Here is what looking up the phrase with a Google search reveals; the occurrence counts for possible choices are:

> *a problem for translation:* 13,000
>
> *a problem of translation:* 61,600
>
> *a problem in translation:* 81,700

So a slight preference for *problem in translation*. Actually, the most common way to phrase this concept is *translation problem* (235,000 counts).

Fluency also involves picking the right content words when there are several possible synonyms available. The source context may already give us some preference based on counts in a parallel corpus, but a much larger monolingual corpus may be also helpful. Consider the Google search counts for different choices for the verb in the following synonymous sentences:

> *police disrupted the demonstration:* 2,140
>
> *police broke up the demonstration:* 66,600
>
> *police dispersed the demonstration:* 25,800
>
> *police ended the demonstration:* 762
>
> *police dissolved the demonstration:* 2,030

police stopped the demonstration: 722,000

police suppressed the demonstration: 1,400

police shut down the demonstration: 2,040

So *stopped* wins out, even if it is synonymous with the 1,000 times less likely *ended*.

1.4.3 Zipf's Law

Zipf's law

sparsity

The biggest obstacle to data-driven methods is **sparsity**. And it is worse than you may think. Naively, when handed a billion-word corpus for English that may have 100,000 different valid words, the numbers suggest that each word occurs on average 10,000 times, seemingly fairly rich statistics to learn about their usage in the language. Unfortunately, this conclusion is far off the mark.

Consider again the corpus of parliamentary proceedings of the European Parliament. Its most frequent words are shown in Figure 1.4. The most frequent word is *the*, which occurs 1,929,379 times, accounting for 6.5% of the 30-million-word corpus. But on the other extreme, there is a large tail of words that occur rarely: 33,447 words occur only once, for instance *cornflakes*, *mathematicians*, and *Bollywood*.

The distribution of words in a corpus is highly skewed. One of the few mathematical laws in natural language processing, Zipf's law, states that the frequency f of a word (or its count in a corpus) multiplied with its rank r when words are sorted by frequency is a constant k:

$$f \times r = k. \tag{1.1}$$

Figure 1.5 illustrates this law with real numbers from the English Europarl corpus. The single points at the left of the chart show the

Figure 1.4 The most frequent words in a version of the English Europarl corpus that consists of 30 million words.

any word		nouns	
Frequency in text	Token	Frequency in text	Content word
1,929,379	*the*	129,851	*European*
1,297,736	,	110,072	*Mr*
956,902	.	98,073	*commission*
901,174	*of*	71,111	*president*
841,661	*to*	67,518	*parliament*
684,869	*and*	64,620	*union*
582,592	*in*	58,506	*report*
452,491	*that*	57,490	*council*
424,895	*is*	54,079	*states*
424,552	*a*	49,965	*member*

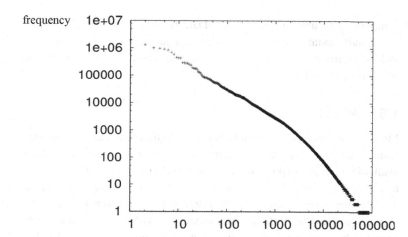

Figure 1.5 Validation of Zipf's law on the Europarl corpus. The *y*-axis is the frequency of each word, the *x*-axis the rank of the word based on the frequency. The graph is plotted in log-scale.

most frequent words as single dots (single-digit rank, frequency around a million) and the singletons (words occurring once) at the right as a stretched out line. The overall curve is close to a line, as Zipf's law predicts, since the graph is plotted using log-scale axis:

$$f \times r = k$$
$$f = \frac{k}{r} \qquad (1.2)$$
$$\log f = \log k - \log r.$$

Zipf's law predicts that no matter how big a corpus is, there will be very many rare words in it. Gathering larger corpora will increase the frequency of words but also reveal previously unseen words with low counts. Moreover, for many aspects of machine translation, such as disambiguation from context, word occurrences are not enough, since we rely on the co-occurrence of words with relevant context words to inform our models.

Zipf's law is often cited as the strongest argument against purely data-driven methods. These may need to be augmented with relevant generalizations obtained from linguistic understanding. A human needs to be told only once *a yushinja is a new kind of fish* to be able to use this made-up word in all kinds of different ways. The data-driven methods that I discuss in this book are not able to match this performance. Yet.

1.5 Practical Issues

Machine translation is a very accessible field. Anybody who can read this book will be able to build a machine translation system that is comparable to the state of the art. Data resources are widely shared, benchmarks established by evaluation campaigns are easily accessible, and as is currently common, newly developed methods are available in open source tool kits.

1.5.1 Available Data

available data

Most of translated content (think books or commercial publications) are constricted by copyright, but there is still a vast reservoir of publicly available parallel corpora. International and governmental institutions that openly publish their content on the web provide a plentiful source.

The first corpus used for data-driven machine translation is the Hansard corpus, the parliamentary proceedings of Canada that are published in both French and English. Similarly, the European Union has also published a lot of content in its 24 official languages. Its parliamentary proceedings have been prepared as a parallel corpus (Europarl[1]) to train machine translation systems and are widely used. The topics discussed in the Parliament are broad enough, so that the Europarl corpus is sufficient to build, for instance, a decent news translation system.

The website OPUS[2] collects parallel corpora from many different sources, such as open source software documentation and localization, governmental publications, and religious texts. The Bible is available as a parallel corpus for the widest range of languages, although its size and often archaic language use makes it less useful for modern applications.

An ongoing effort called Paracrawl makes parallel corpora crawled from all over the web available. However, since it collects data indiscriminately, the quality of the data varies. Paracrawl does provides a quality score for each sentence pair.

The overall picture of available data is that for the biggest languages, such as French, Spanish, German, Russian, and Chinese, plentiful data are available, but for most languages data are rather scarce. Especially when moving beyond the most common languages into so-called low-resource languages, lack of training data is a serious constraint. Even for languages such as many widely spoken Asian languages there is a serious lack of available parallel corpora.

1.5.2 Evaluation Campaigns

evaluation campaigns

Compared with other problems in natural language processing, machine translation is a relatively well-defined task. The research field lacks ideological battles but is rather characterized by a friendly competitive spirit.

---

[1] www.statmt.org/europarl.
[2] http://opus.nlpl.eu.

One reason for this is that it is not sufficient to claim that your machine translation is better, you have to demonstrate that by participating in open shared evaluation campaigns. There are currently two such annual campaigns organized by academic institutions.

The **Conference for Machine Translation (WMT) evaluation campaign**[3] is organized as part of the Conference for Machine **WMT** Translation. It takes place alongside one of the major conferences of the of the Association for Computational Linguistics. It started out as a shared task for a few languages based on the Europarl corpus but has also recently embraced a broad pool of languages such as Russian and Chinese and often features low-resource languages. Besides the main WMT news translation task, specialized tasks on, say, biomedical translation, translation of closely related languages, or evaluation metrics take place under the same umbrella.

The **IWSLT evaluation campaign** has been focused on the integra- **IWSLT** tion of speech recognition and machine translation and features transla- tion tasks for transcriptions of spoken content (such as TED talks) but **TED talks** also end-to-end speech translation systems.

In addition, the American **National Institute for Standards in Technology** (NIST) organizes shared tasks, typically related to ongoing **NIST** Defense Advanced Research Projects Agency (DARPA) or Intelligence **DARPA** Advanced Research Projects Activity (IARPA) funded research pro- **IARPA** grams and not following a regular schedule. Its early Chinese and Arabic machine translation shared tasks were very influential. In recent years the focus has shifted toward low-resource languages.

There is also an evaluation campaign organized by the Chinese Workshop on Machine Translation that covers Chinese and Japanese.

1.5.3 Tool Kits

tool kits

There is an extensive proliferation of tool kits available for research, development, and deployment of neural machine translation systems. At the time of writing, the number of tool kits is multiplying, rather than consolidating. So, it is quite hard and premature to make specific recommendations.

Some of the currently broadly used tool kits currently are:

- OpenNMT (based on Torch/pyTorch): `http://opennmt.net`   **OpenNMT**
- Sockeye (based on MXNet): `https://github.com/awslabs/sockeye`

  Sockeye
- Fairseq (based on pyTorch): `https://github.com/pytorch/fairseq`

  Fairseq

---

[3] `www.statmt.org/wmt19`.

Marian

- Marian (stand-alone implementation in C++): `https://marian-nmt` `.github.io`

transformer

- Google's Transformer (based on Tensorflow): `https://github.com/` `tensorflow/models/tree/master/official/transformer`

T2T

- T2T (based on Tensorflow): `https://github.com/tensorflow/` `tensor2tensor`

All tool kits but Marian rely on general deep learning frameworks (Tensorflow, PyTorch, MXNet), which are also developed in a very dynamic environment. For instance, the initially popular tool kit Nematus has been abandoned since its underlying framework Theano is not actively developed anymore. Neural machine translation is computationally expensive, so it is common practice to train and deploy models on graphical processing units (GPUs). Consumer-grade GPUs that cost a few hundred dollars and can be installed in regular desktop machines are sufficient (at the time of writing, nVidia's RTX-2080 is one of the best options).

Chapter 2
Uses of Machine Translation

The goal of current machine translation research is not to achieve perfect translation but to drive down error rates of machine translation systems. So, if machine translation is nonperfect and error prone, what is it good for? Or to cite Church and Hovy (1993), what are good applications for **crummy translation**?

crummy translation

2.1 Information Access

information access

Google Translate has more than anything brought machine translation to a wider audience. It brings translation directly to users where they need it. You are trying to find some information on the internet, you come across a web page in a foreign language, say a Finnish page that addresses the problem you have with your computer or a French page that explains how to buy tickets to the Parisian metro—and with a click of a button (*translate this page*), you get its content rendered in English or any other language you are more familiar with (Figure 2.1).

Google Translate opens up the web across all languages. It is even more valuable for translating English content into other languages. English is still a dominant language on the internet (consider, for instance, the various sizes of Wikipedia), and some highly valuable content, such as advanced scientific information, is just not available in other languages.

Cross-lingual information access from the internet also clearly sets user expectations of the technology. The user initiates the translation. Hence the user knows that it is done by a machine and is ready to

Figure 2.1 Automatic translation of web pages. Information about the Paris Metro in French and the machine translation into English. (Courtesy of RATP, www.ratp.fr/visite-paris/francais/preparez-votre-sejour-paris-les-horaires.)

attribute mistranslations and disfluent language to the limitations of the technology and not to shortcomings of the publisher of the information.

Machine translation for information access is also the driving force behind much of the research funding in the United States. One of these funding programs (the recent DARPA LORELEI) poses as a prototypical challenge: a humanitarian disaster in a foreign country where aid workers need access to life-saving information but do understand the language that the affected population speaks, writes in, or tweets in.

There are many commercial use cases along these lines. A patent lawyer needs to keep track about what claims are made in patents published in Chinese. News reporters need to understand developments in foreign countries. A hedge fund manager needs access to any information published in any language that affects the profitability of companies.

Even low-quality machine translation may be useful. It is sufficient to get the general gist of a document to be able to decide if it is relevant or not. Only relevant documents need to then be passed on to a language specialist who can take a closer look at them.

There is one big problem with such information access. If any of the meaning of the original document is distorted during translation, it is up to the user to detect this. This may be possible given clues from bad language and semantic implausibility. But bad translations may mislead the user. Misinformation due to mistranslation is a significant concern with neural machine translation, which sometimes prefers fluency over adequacy to the point of completely distorting the output so it has no confidence score relation to the input. The development of **confidence scores** that indicate how reliable a translation is becomes an important factor if decisions are made solely on the machine translation.

2.2 Aiding Human Translators

Translation is a large industry, but machine translation quality is not computer aided translation high enough that customers would pay a large amount of money for it.

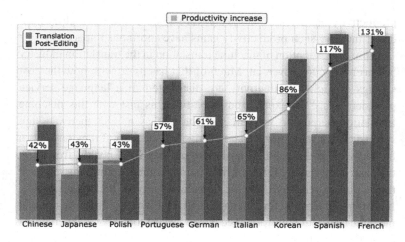

Figure 2.2 Increase in translator productivity when using machine translation (measured in words per hour). Study from Autodesk (Plitt and Masselot, 2010) on several language pairs with an in-house machine translation system.

High-quality translation requires professional translators who are native speakers of the target language and ideally also experts in the subject matter. The bulk of the translation industry consists of many so-called **language service providers** that often outsource their work to freelance translators.

    While machine translation cannot compete with professional translators on the basis of quality, it is a tool that can be used by translators to become more productive. The work style of translators, who once relied on pen and paper, had already changed in the 1990s when **translation memory tools** became common. Think of these tools as searchable parallel corpora. When confronted with a sentence to translate, the tool searched its database of previous translations to find the most similar sentence and presented it with its translation. When professional translators regularly work for the same client, they become much faster when translating repetitive content, such as annual reports, legal contracts, and product descriptions that contain a lot of re-used text.

    The adoption of machine translation by professional translators has been a very long slog, which is still not completed. For some types of translation jobs, machine translation is not a useful tool, such as marketing messages that have to home in on the nuances of the targeted local culture. Other examples are literature and poetry. But for many more conventional translation jobs, machine translation is able to help.

    The crudest form of collaboration between machine and human is to provide professional translators with the raw output of the machine translation system and task them to correct it. This is called **postediting machine translation**. Figure 2.2 presents a study that compared translation speeds of professional translators when postediting machine translation and when translation from scratch. In this particular study,

language service provider

translation memory

postediting

productivity increases of 42–131% were achieved. In the multibillion-dollar industry such productivity gains have enormous impact.

However, adoption of machine translation in the translation industry has been very controversial. Much of that has to do with how the cost savings of higher productivity are distributed. If a language service provider says, "We expect you to be twice as fast with this machine translation output, so we will pay you half as much," then it is not surprising that translators react negatively, especially if they have been burned with bad machine translation and had little benefit from it in the past. High-quality machine translation requires optimizing machine translation systems to a specific domain, e.g., type of content or style. It is often not feasible for language service providers to achieve optimal machine translation performance due to lack of tools, data, expertise, or computing resources.

Another major hurdle for the adoption of machine translation is that postediting machine translation is just much less enjoyable than translation from scratch. Being the clean-up crew after a machine messed up (and made the same mistakes over and over again) is not the same as being a creative author of novel text inspired by a foreign language document. There is also the valid concern that the future trajectory of the job of a translator is to be ever more rushed to churn out translations at a faster pace with less and less regard for polished language.

adaptive machine translation
interactive machine translation

There have been efforts to make machine translation more **adaptive** and **interactive**. Adaptive means machine translation systems learn from the translator. While a translator is translating a document, sentence by sentence, the created sentence pairs constitute new training material for machine translation system. This is the best for training a machine, since it covers the right content in the correct style. From a technical point of view, we need to build machine translation systems that can be quickly updated and tuned to incoming training sentence pairs.

interactive translation
prediction

Interactive machine translation, also called **interactive translation prediction** is a different type of collaboration where the machine translation system makes suggestions to the translator and updates those suggestions when a translator deviates from them. So, instead of providing a static machine translation of a source sentence, the machine makes predictions in response to the professional translator's choices.

Figure 2.3 illustrates this work mode in the open source CAS-MACAT workbench. The tool suggests to continue the German translation with *ausbrach, zum ersten*. The figure also shows a translation option array that contains alternative word and phrase translations for the source sentence.

Creating good user interfaces for translators is an open challenge. Machine translation can provide endless amounts of additional

Figure 2.3 Screenshot from the CASMACAT workbench, a tool for translators. The top left English sentence is being translated into German in the top left text box. Interactive translation prediction suggests to continue the translation with *ausbrach, zum ersten*. The source word *erupted* is highlighted as the correspondence for the next predicted target word. Part of the source sentence is shaded, since it has been already translated. Below the editing text box, translation alternatives are shown for each of the source words and phrases.

information, such as alternative translations, confidence scores, and tracking of consistency of term use. But overwhelming a translator with information overload is quite distracting. The ideal tool would quickly provide the translator with the exact answers to questions that arise during translation (e.g., What translation for this technical term is used by this manufacturer?) but be otherwise unobtrusive.

However, what questions a translator may have at any given time is not easy to detect. Research projects have used key logging and eye tracking to closely monitor translator behavior. One lesson of these studies is that translators use very different work styles from each other. But even armed with these detailed data, it is not easy to figure out what a translator is wrestling with when he or she stares at the screen for a minute without any detectable activity.

2.3 Communication

communication

A third broad application area for machine translation is communication. Directly facilitating a dialog between two speakers of different languages poses a number of new challenges. It may be combined with other technologies such as speech processing to fit seamlessly into a natural way of communication. Machine translation for communication also has to be fast. The translation process may even have to start before the speaker ends a sentence to avoid pauses.

Skype Translator

Skype Translator

One of the most ambitious projects in this area is Microsoft's integration of machine translation into **Skype**. The idea is that you can carry on a translated conversation over Skype, maybe you are speaking in English and your friend is speaking in Spanish.

The speech is already being passed through computers, so they can do additional processing. Looking closely at this problem reveals that there are three distinct steps: (1) speech recognition of the input utterance, i.e., transcription into text; (2) machine translation; and (3) speech synthesis of the translation. Ideally, speech synthesis would also reproduce the emphasis and emotional aspects of the original speech, maybe even in the voice of the original speaker. However, for most practical applications in this area, speech synthesis is often completely dropped. It is easier to read an often imperfect translation as text on a screen, rather than to listen to it.

Spoken language typically has a smaller vocabulary than written language. However, there is a mismatch between readily available parallel corpora of text translation and the type of language used in communication: the much more frequent use of pronouns *I* and *you* and corresponding verb inflections, more frequent questions, ungrammatical utterances with disfluencies and restarts, more colloquial language, use of slang, and so on. In fact, it is rather shocking, how ungrammatical and incoherent casually spoken language is—you may want to avoid looking at a faithful transcripts of your daily speech. Developers of dialog translation systems found it useful to use the Open Subtitle corpus (Lison and Tiedemann, 2016) which contains translations of subtitles for movies and television to train their models.

Chat Translator

chat

Communication does not imply speech. Machine translation has also been successfully integrated into **chat** forums, where users type in their questions and responses. Chat forums range from free-flowing entertainment to customer support. Still, most of the concerns about different language use apply here too. Chat text has additional quirks, such as emoticons, slang acronyms, and frequent misspellings.

In terms of quality demands, the bar is not as high as for machine translation for publication. If the machine translation system makes mistakes, the partners in the communication will likely spot it and try to clarify what was meant. They may also get horribly offended.

Travel Translator

travel translator

The need for translation becomes immediately obvious when you travel to a foreign country. The idea of a **travel translator** was famously popularized by the *Hitchhiker's Guide to the Galaxy* where such a translator existed in the form of a fish called a "Bablefish," which you placed in your ear and so it could translate the sounds waves coming in.

Figure 2.4 Sign in German and translation with Google image translator. (Courtesy of Uwe Vogel, www.oldskoolman.de/ bilder/freigestellte- bilder/schilder/ vorsicht-hochspannung.)

Today's tools are more intrusive than that. The typical format is a handheld device or maybe just a phone app. The actual technology needed to power such a device is similar to the speech and chat applications discussed earlier. If the device does speech translation, a useful feature is to also show the spoken original language text on the screen, so the speaker can verify if he or she was correctly understood.

Given the imperfections of the technology and the added problem of noisy environments and limited computational resources on a device (computing in the cloud is an option but adds additional delays), the most robust versions of a travel translator work on a text basis, with speech recognition only as an add-on.

There is one additional interesting angle for a travel translator: **image translation**. Imagine you are in a restaurant and are handed a menu with indecipherable text, maybe even written in obscure symbols. Just use the camera of your travel translator app and it translates the text in the captured image into your language. The earliest versions of such a phone app were quite simplistic in their translation component—they just used a dictionary for translation but had nice added gimmicks, such as mimicking the font of the original text in the translation (Figure 2.4 provides an example).

image translation

Lecture Translator

On the topic of speech translation, the earliest efforts aimed at translating speeches or university **lectures**, deployed at the Karlsruhe Institute of Technology (Fügen et al., 2007; Dessloch et al., 2018). It had to address all the main challenges of chaining speech recognition and machine translation as well as assume better acoustic conditions and a more formal speaking style.

lecture translation

In these efforts, first attempts were made of not just passing on the speech transcript to the machine translation component but to aim at a closer integration, such as passing n-best lists with alternative translations or the scored word lattice that encodes other possible paths of recognized utterances. The machine translation system then can use additional context to disambiguate uncertainties inherent in the speech signal. Not too much has come from this work. Just processing the 1-best transcription is often as good as it gets and keeps the processing pipeline simple.

Some of the other interesting integration challenges is that written text contains punctuation that needs to be inserted at some point or dropped from the input text for machine translation systems. In text, numbers are written as digits (e.g., *15*) while speech recognition will detect the actual spoken words (e.g., *fifteen*).

Sign Language Translator

sign language translation

A final interesting translation challenge to mention in this context is **sign language translation**. Deaf communities spontaneously develop hand gestures and facial expressions to match what can be communicated with spoken language. There are several broadly accepted standards such as American Sign Language (ASL). Sign language has interesting properties such as pointing to a point in space and then later referring back to that point as means of establishing co-reference.

Translating sign language from video is an interesting challenge that goes well beyond machine translation and requires complex image recognition. There has been some successful work of translating written forms of sign language, but overall this is still an exciting open problem.

2.4 Natural Language Processing Pipelines

natural language processing

As machine translation, natural language processing in general has recently become mature enough to be used in many practical applications. Some of these applications, such as text search (think Google) have been successful well before machine translation, some are currently hotbeds of activity, such as requests to personal assistants (think Amazon's Echo), while others are still visions for the future, such as customer support dialog systems, complex question answering, or making convincing arguments.

It is a challenge is to take the broad vision of machines that talk like humans and turn them into practical applications for which measurable progress can be tracked. For instance, humans have to be able perform them consistently to the point that we can benchmark machine performance against human performance. Compared to other applications of natural language processing, machine translation is a relatively well defined task for which we can measure progress, even though professional translators disagree on the exact translation for sentences. Other tasks such as summarization of the content of documents, making a coherent case for a point of view, or open-ended chat are less well defined.

Machine translation may be part of a bigger natural language processing application. Consider the case of **cross-lingual information retrieval**. What if we carry out a Google search not only over English web pages but also over web pages in any other language that may have content relevant for us? This requires some form of query translation, web page translation, or both. The US funding agency Intelligence Advanced Research Projects Activity (IARPA) has recently started such a cross-lingual information retrieval project with the added difficulty of low resource data conditions (i.e., languages such as Swahili, Tagalog, and Somali).

cross-lingual information retrieval

Taking it a step further, **cross-lingual information extraction** not only requires finding the relevant information in a collection of text but also has to distill core facts that follow a schema. For instance, a query over a collection of multilingual news articles may be *find me a list of mergers and acquisitions in the last month*. We expect the system to return not only the relevant stories but also a formatted table that includes the names of companies involved, date of the event, monetary payments or stock conversions, etc.

cross-lingual information extraction

Each of these applications may make special demands on the capability of machine translation systems. Consider query translation, where the input sentence may just be a word or two. We cannot rely anymore on the sentence context for disambiguation, but we may be able to make use of the search history of the user. There may also different demands due to, say, the need for high recall, e.g., finding all relevant documents. A translation system's preferred translation choice for a particular word in a foreign document may not match the query term, but a translation into the query term may be possible. We still want this document returned, possibly with a confidence score cautioning about the reliability of the translation.

2.5 Multimodal Machine Translation

In the processing pipelines discussed in this chapter, machine translation is still a self-contained component with text as input and text as output. There has been also growing interest in multimodal machine translation, where the input is not just text but also additional information in other modalities. The most prominent task is **image caption translation**. The caption itself may be ambiguous, but the image has the relevant content to point to one specific interpretation. An example is the caption *The girl wears a hat* (Figure 2.5) when translated into German. German makes a distinction between hats that are worn as a fashion item or protection against the sun (German *Hut*), opposed

multimodal machine

image caption translation

Figure 2.5 Translating the caption *The girl wears a hat* into German: since it is a winter hat, the caption translates as *Mütze* instead of *Hut*. The image makes that distinction clear.

to winter hats worn to keep the head warm (German *Mütze*). The image in the example makes the distinction clear.

A big practical multimodal translation challenge is **video subtitle translation**. Again, the video context may provide important clues that should be taken into account, and there is also the benefit of a longer consistent story to provide context.

video subtitle translation

Subtitle translation has its own unique challenges, such as the practical limitations of screen space for the caption and reading time of the viewer. The translated caption cannot be too long and may have to drop some information to still be readable. A particular annoyance is that subtitles of longer utterances are often broken up into pieces that go over multiple subtitle screens, and thus have to be joined before translation and split again in appropriate ways to match what is on the screen.

Coming back to speech translation, we may also devise a translation component that is not just pipelined after speech recognition but also using the original speech signal as input. Important nuances such as emphasis may be essential for the proper interpretation of input speech and may have consequences for translation. So, for multimodal machine translation, we have to build new neural architectures that also allow us to pay attention to the input beyond the sequence of input words.

Chapter 3
History

Both neural networks and machine translation research have a long and storied history. Both share the experience of several boom-and-bust cycles. Each such cycle is characterized by some breakthrough of methods and some practical progress, at least in terms of proof-of-concept, but then also have overly optimistic expectations that inevitably led to disappointment and, on several occasions, to long dark periods of winter where all research activity withered and came to standstill.

The long-running jocular answer in machine translation to the question, "When will we reach *fully automated high quality machine translation?*" is five years. Similarly, due to artificial intelligence, half **artificial intelligence** of the current jobs are thought to become obsolete any day now. This is a great pitch for research funding and venture capital investment, but eventually five years pass, and broken promises do not make for a good long-term strategy.

Over the last 20 years, at least, machine translation researchers have learned these hard lessons and restrained themselves to more modest expectations. The promise is that machine translation is already *good enough* for many applications and that the expected increased quality that would be coming over the next years would lead to more widespread use and new applications. But *solving* the task of machine translation has not been not in the cards.

It is only a slightly exaggerated characterization to say that the recent wave of young and excitable deep-learning researchers moved in, showed improvements through their methods, declared success, and moved to bigger and better things. Caution was blown to the wind, and

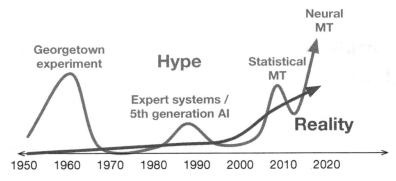

Figure 3.1 Machine translation (MT) hype cycle. For most of its history the expectations of machine translation quality have either over- or underestimated the real progress in quality, forming boom-and-bust cycles for research and development. Nevertheless machine translation has become a practical reality over the last 20 years. (Note: chart based on my subjective impressions, not hard facts.)

phrases like *near human* or *human parity* were uttered and made their way into the popular press.

Whatever the perception, there has been indeed good solid progress in the quality of machine translation systems that are available to real users. Arguably, this progress has been more incremental and mainly due to the slow mastery of new methods rather than singular break-throughs that get all the attention. Figure 3.1 is an attempt to contrast the history of hype with reality in machine translation over its history.

With this in mind, it is instructive to revisit the history of these research fields. There are lessons to be learned about the advancements and limitations of the methods over time and also how this research evolved in the ecosystem of funding agencies, by commercial developers, and through acceptance by users.

3.1 Neural Networks

neural network

3.1.1 The Biological Inspiration

biological inspiration

Let us first take a look how research in neural networks evolved.[1] It starts with the term *neural*, expressing inspiration from neurons in the brain. Figure 3.2 illustrates the core elements of a real neuron—the human brain has about 100 million of them. Each neuron receives as input signals from other neurons via its dendrites. If the combined signals

---

[1] A more detailed history is presented by Andrey Kurenkov at
www.andreykurenkov.com/writing/ai/a-brief-history-of-
neural-nets-and-deep-learning.

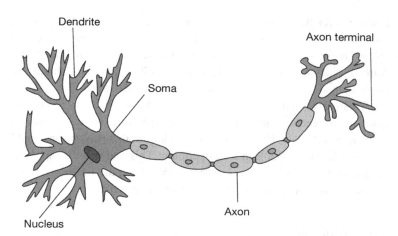

Dendrite

Axon terminal

Soma

Axon

Nucleus

Figure 3.2 Neuron in the brain: the neuron receives signals from its dendrites and, based on the strength of those signals, passes a signal to other neurons through its axon. ("Neuron Hand-tuned.svg" by Quasar Jarosz is licensed under CC BY-SA 3.0.)

are strong enough, the neuron becomes activated and passes a signal via its axon to the various axon terminals that are connected to other dendrites of other neurons.

From this biological inspiration, **artificial neural networks (ANN)**, as they are sometimes called to clarify the distinction, take the idea of combining inputs (by a weighted sum), an activation function, and an output value. But artificial neurons and natural neurons are quite different. The activation in artificial neurons is represented as a real number, while natural neurons have activation in the form of binary spikes at different frequencies. Artificial neurons are connected in orderly architectures and grouped into layers that are processed in a sequence of steps, while natural neurons have much more complex connection patterns. Artificial neural networks typically learn their weights by supervised training, while natural neurons evolve without being given the right answer directly.

ANN

artificial neural network

So, it is not surprising that some researchers are uncomfortable with drawing any parallels to the brain and avoid the term *neural networks*. But the term has stuck, even despite current rebranding efforts to *deep learning*.

3.1.2 Perceptron Learning

perceptron learning

The first neural network models were called **perceptrons**, proposed by Rosenblatt (1957), drawing on earlier ideas from McCulloch and Pitts (1943). Perceptrons consist of only a single processing layer, essentially a list of neurons, each with the same number of binary inputs and one binary output. Rosenblatt also proposed a crude learning algorithm.

He showed that perceptrons could learn basic mathematical operations, such as Boolean AND and OR. Nevertheless he had great ambitions for these models, which were expected to "be able to walk, talk, see, write, reproduce itself, and be conscious of its existence" (New Navy Device, 1958). Given the limitations of computer hardware, the actual applications were too ambitious, but still hardware implementations of perceptrons were experimented with.

This early excitement about these new kinds of electronic brains came to a screeching halt with the publication of the book *Perceptrons* (Minsky and Papert, 1969). The authors showed that perceptrons could not even learn the Boolean XOR operation. This and other disappointments brought neural network research into disrepute for more than a decade, commencing the first winter of research activity.

3.1.3 Multiple Layers

multiple layers

Marvin Minsky, a leading researcher in artificial intelligence, has already pointed out in his book that XOR could be modeled with multiple layers of processing. However, the originally proposed learning algorithm did not work for multilayer perceptrons.

What makes multilayer neural networks work trainable is the backpropagation algorithm. It was proposed several times, dating back to the 1960s, but during the neural winter not much attention was paid to it, and even researchers who worked out the details did not find the courage to publish them, since nobody was interested anymore. Backpropagation was finally popularized by Rumelhart et al. (1986). This gave neural network research new momentum, strengthened by the seminal paper by Hornik et al. (1989) that showed that any mathematical function could be approximated with neural networks with a sufficient number of layers.

In the following years, neural network research exploded and networks were trained for various classification problems, such as handwritten digit recognition, surpassing the quality of any previous method (LeCun et al., 1989). Most of the refinements that I discuss in this book were proposed: convolutional neural networks, recurrent neural networks, long short-term memory cells, and so on.

Ambitious tasks like speech recognition were tackled, with some success. But generally, researchers found it hard to train neural networks with several layers, especially recurrent neural networks that process sequential data. While neural networks were seen as potentially useful, they gained the reputation of being too complex and too hard to train.

This brought about a second winter, starting in the late 1990s, during which other machine learning methods were proposed and used. Natural language processing, for instance, went through methods such as naive Bayes, decision trees, random forests, maximum entropy models, support vector machines, and Bayesian graphical models.

3.1.4 Deep Learning

deep learning

Researchers Geoffrey Hinton, Yan LeCun, and Yoshua Bengio now tell
the legends of their time as the "deep learning conspiracy" during this
second cold winter in Canada in the first decade of the new millennium,
surviving on funding rations from the Canadian government. Nobody
would listen to them but they made slow progress on training multilayer
neural networks, deliberately rebranded as deep learning. They were
finally recognized with the Turing Award, the highest honor in computer
science, in 2019.

The group developed better weight initialization methods and activation functions, and showed progress on the handwriting recognition
task, which got some attention at last. The real breakthrough came with
raw brute-force computing power in the form of graphical processing
units (GPUs), i.e., graphics cards sold in high volumes to computer
game players.

They showed progress on speech recognition and computer vision.
The real trigger point for the current wave of neural network research
was their 2012 submission to the Image classification task ImageNet,
where their convolutional neural network blew away the competition,
outperforming the second best system by an error rate of 15.3%
versus 26.2%.

Chris Manning, a leading natural language processing researcher and
professor at Stanford said in his presidential address at the Annual Meeting of the Association for Computational Linguistics in 2015: "Deep
Learning waves have lapped at the shores of computational linguistics for
several years now, but 2015 seems like the year when the full force of the
tsunami hit the major Natural Language Processing (NLP) conferences"
(Manning, 2015).

Now neural networks are everywhere again. Even the term **artificial intelligence** (AI) is again proudly used almost synonymously
to celebrate the current wave of progress. Revolutions are reported in
fields as diverse as image processing (deep fakes), warehouse automa-
tion, and healthcare. A visible recent success story, for instance, is
Google's AlphaGo, which won a Go match against the best Go player
in the world in 2017. Self-driving cars seem to be just a few months
away.

artificial intelligence

AI

3.2 Machine Translation

3.2.1 Code Breaking

code breaking

Efforts to build machine translation systems started almost as soon
as electronic computers came into existence. Computers were used
in Britain to crack the German Enigma code in World War II, and

decoding language codes seemed like an apt metaphor for machine translation. Warren Weaver, one of the pioneering minds in machine translation, wrote in 1947:

> When I look at an article in Russian, I say: 'This is really written in English, but it has been coded in some strange symbols. I will now proceed to decode.' (Weaver 1947, 1949)

The emergence of electronic brains created all kinds of expectations, and some researchers hoped to solve the problem of machine translation early on. Major funding went into the field.

Some of the principles of machine translation that were established in the early days remain valid today. Not only are we still talking about *decoding* a foreign language and using such modeling techniques as the noisy-channel model, it also appears that the funding for the field of machine translation is still driven by the same motivation as code breaking. Governments, especially that of the United States, seem to be most willing to tackle the languages of countries that are taken to be a threat to national security, be it militarily or economically.

direct translation
transfer methods
interlingua

Many approaches were explored, ranging from simple **direct translation** methods that map input to output with basic rules, through more sophisticated **transfer** methods that employ morphological and syntactic analysis, and up to **interlingua** methods that use an abstract meaning representation.

3.2.2 The ALPAC Report and Its Consequences

ALPAC report

The early days were characterized by great optimism. Promises of imminent breakthroughs were in the air, and the impression was created that mechanical translation (as it was then called) would soon be solved. In the **Georgetown experiment**, the translation of Russian to English was demonstrated, suggesting that the problem was almost solved. On the other hand, sceptics made the claim that some problems, especially those related to semantic disambiguation, are impossible to solve by automatic means.

Georgetown experiment

The flurry of activity surrounding machine translation came to a grinding halt with the issue of the **ALPAC report** in 1966. US funding agencies commissioned the Automatic Language Processing Advisory Committee to carry out a study of the realities of machine translation and the need to translate Russian documents from the Soviet Union, their Cold War rival.

The study showed, among other things, that post-editing machine translation output was not cheaper or faster than full human translation. It established that only about $20 million was spent on translation

in the United States annually. Very little Russian scientific literature was deemed worth translating, and there was no shortage
of human translators. The committee suggested that there was no
advantage in using machine translation systems. Funding should rather
go into basic linguistic research and the development of methods to
improve human translation.

Funding for machine translation in the United States stopped
almost entirely as a consequence. While the ALPAC report may
have unfairly considered only the goal of high-quality translation, the
experience shows the dangers of over-promising the abilities of machine
translation systems.

3.2.3 First Commercial Systems

commercial systems

Despite sharply reduced research efforts, the foundations of commercial
translations were nevertheless laid in the decade after the ALPAC report.
One early fully functioning system is the **Météo** system for translating   Météo
weather forecasts, which was developed at the University of Montreal.
It has been operating since 1976.

Systran was founded in 1968. Its Russian–English system has been   Systran
used by the US Air Force since 1970. A French–English version was
bought by the European Commission in 1976, and thereafter systems
for more European language pairs were developed. Other commercial
systems that came to the market in the 1980s were the **Logos** and   Logos
METAL systems.   METAL

The Pan American Health Organization in Washington has successfully developed and widely used a system for translating Spanish to
English and back since the 1970s. In the late 1980s, Japanese computer
companies built translation systems for Japanese and English. During
the 1990s, the more widespread use of desktop computer systems led
to the development of **computer aided translation** systems for human   computer aided translation
translators by companies such as **Trados**.

3.2.4 Research in Interlingua-Based Systems

A research trend in the 1980s and 1990s was the focus on the development of systems that use **interlingua** to represent meaning independent   interlingua
of a specific language. Syntactic formalism grew more sophisticated,
including reversible grammars that may be used for both analysis and
generation. The notion of representing meaning in a formal way tied
together several strands of research both from artificial intelligence and
computational linguistics.

One example in the development of interlingua-based systems is
the CATALYST project at Carnegie Mellon University (CMU), which

was developed for the translation of technical manuals of Caterpillar Tractor. Another example is the Pangloss system that was developed at New Mexico State University, the University of Southern California, and CMU. The development of interlingua systems was also an important element in the large German Verbmobil project (1993–2000).

The attraction of developing such systems is easy to see. Translating involves expressing meaning in different languages, so a proper theory of meaning seems to address this problem at a more fundamental level than the low-level mapping of lexical or syntactic units. The problem of representing meaning in a formal way is one of the grand challenges of artificial intelligence, with interesting philosophical implications about the nature of knowledge.

3.2.5 Data-Driven Methods

data-driven methods

Since language translation is burdened with so many decisions that are hard to formalize, it may be better to learn how to translate from past translation examples. This idea is also motivation for **translation memory** systems for human translators that store and retrieve matching translation examples for a given new input text.

translation memory

example-based translation

Early efforts based on this idea are **example-based translation** systems, which have been built especially in Japan since the 1980s. These systems try to find a sentence similar to the input sentence in a parallel corpus and make the appropriate changes to its stored translation.

In the late 1980s, the idea of statistical machine translation was born in the labs of IBM Research in the wake of successes of statistical methods in speech recognition. By modeling the translation task as a statistical optimization problem, the Candide project put machine translation on a solid mathematical foundation.

The emergence of statistical machine translation was groundbreaking. In retrospect it seems that the world was not quite ready for it. Throughout the 1990s, most researchers still focused on syntax-based and interlingua systems, which were tied in with work in semantic representations. Most of the original researchers at IBM left the field and found fortunes on Wall Street instead.[2]

While research on statistical methods for machine translation continued throughout the 1990s to some degree (their success in the German

---

[2] An interesting character in this story is Robert Mercer, one of the pioneers of statistical machine translation. He left the field to start one of the first hedge funds dedicated to a data-driven approach to equity trading, called Renaissance Technology. This become wildly successful and made him and his partners billionaires. He recently came to broader prominence as one of the main boosters of right-wing political causes in the United States, such as Steve Bannon and Breitbart, and one of the early and most important backers of Donald Trump's presidential campaign.

Verbmobil project is one highlight), the approach gathered full steam only around the year 2000. A number of factors contributed to this.

In 1998, participants at a Johns Hopkins University workshop reimplemented most of the IBM methods and made the resulting tools widely available. **DARPA** (Defense Advanced Research Projects Agency), the leading funding agency in the United States, showed great interest in statistical machine translation and funded the large TIDES (2000–2004), GALE (2005–2010), and BOLT (2011–2016) programs. The US response to the events of September 11, 2001 also played a role in the renewed interest in the automatic translation of foreign languages, especially Arabic.

Other factors in the rise of statistical methods were the increase in computing power and data storage, along with the increasing availability of digital text resources as a consequence of the growth of the internet.

3.2.6 An Open Research and Development Environment

The barrier of entry for research in statistical machine translation was lowered by a number of factors. Parallel corpora started to be shared by research groups that collected them from the internet, such as the Canadian Hansard corpus and the Europarl corpus. Software was made available open source. Especially the open source **Moses** system, developed first at the University of Edinburgh and then enhanced and extended by a larger group of developers after the 2006 Johns Hopkins University workshop, became the most broadly used tool kit. Computers became fast enough, so that by the mid-aughts, anyone with some technical skills could download freely available tools and data to build a machine translation system on a typical home computer.

Several evaluation campaigns brought the research field together. The NIST (National Institute of Standards and Technology) evaluation workshop followed the goals of DARPA-funded research programs and initially focused on translation from Chinese and Arabic into English. The Workshop for Machine Translation (WMT) was initially based on the Europarl corpus, but then branched out to news translation for mostly European language pairs, funded by EU projects such as Euro-Matrix (2006–2009), EuroMatrixPlus (2009–2012), and EU-BRIDGE (2012–2015). The International Workshop on Spoken Language Translation (IWSLT) combined speech recognition and machine translation, initially limited to constraint tasks such as travel conversations.

Hundreds of research papers were published every year on statistical machine translation by around 2010. The field advanced by better machine learning methods, such as parameter tuning (MERT), discriminative training, and minimum Bayes risk, often inspired by

DARPA

open source

Moses

their successful use in the related field of speech recognition. The other direction of advancement was the development of more sophisticated linguistic models. Morphology was handled by preprocessing or factored translation models. Syntax-based models became the state of the art for Chinese–English and German–English. Attempts were made to incorporate semantics into these models, including the development of a new semantic formalism called abstract meaning representation (AMR).

3.2.7 Reaching Users

Statistical machine translation systems were developed in a large number of academic and commercial research labs. Some of these efforts led to the founding of new companies. Language Weaver was the first company, founded in 2002, that fully embraced the new paradigm and promised *translation by numbers*. Commercial statistical machine translation systems started also to be developed by large software companies such as IBM, Microsoft, and Google, sometimes replacing existing rule-based efforts.

Traditional machine translation companies, such as the historic market leader Systran, were integrating statistical methods into their systems. Internet users translated web pages using systems hosted by Google, Yahoo, Microsoft, and others. Google Translate became a tool known to most users of the internet, expanding to over 100 languages today.

The proliferation of open source software and widely available parallel corpora also triggered the start up of several companies that sell customized machine translation systems to end users. Asia Online (now Omniscien Technology), Safaba (later acquired by Amazon), Iconic Translation Machines, KantanMT, and many others started by using the open source Moses tool kit and enriched it into products for the marketplace.

Machine translation was also integrated into tools for professional translators. SDL, the developer of the dominant translation tool Trados, bought Language Weaver. Several new tools for translators were developed centered around machine translation, such as Matecat, CASMACAT, Unbabel, and Lilt. Also, machine translation as a travel app on smartphones arrived. Machine translation was no longer a parlor trick but a tool as natural as a web browser.

By the mid-2010s, machine translation research and ever wider adoption benefited from healthy research funding, on the order of tens of millions of dollars per year, especially from the European Union and the US government, but also increasingly in China. Nevertheless, there were also increasingly skeptical voices, claiming that a plateau in terms of quality improvements has been reached.

3.2.8 The Neural Turn

Already during the previous wave of neural network research in the 1980s and 1990s, machine translation was in the sight of researchers exploring neural methods (Allen, 1987; Waibel et al., 1991). In fact, the models proposed by Forcada and Ñeco (1997) and Castaño et al. (1997) are striking similar to the current neural machine translation approaches. However, none of these models was trained on data sizes large enough to produce reasonable results for anything but toy examples. The computational complexity involved by far exceeded the computational resources of that era, and hence the idea was abandoned for almost two decades.

During this hibernation period, data-driven approaches such as statistical machine translation rose from obscurity to dominance and made machine translation a useful tool for many applications, from information gisting to increasing the productivity of professional translators.

The modern resurrection of neural methods in machine translation started with the integration of neural language models into traditional statistical machine translation systems. The pioneering work by Schwenk (2007) showed large improvements in public evaluation campaigns. However, these ideas were adopted only slowly, mainly due to computational concerns. The use of GPUs for training also posed a challenge for many research groups that simply lacked such hardware or the experience to exploit it.

Moving beyond the use in language models, neural network methods crept into other components of traditional statistical machine translation, such as providing additional scores or extending translation tables (Schwenk, 2012; Lu et al., 2014), reordering (Li et al., 2014; Kanouchi et al., 2016) and preordering models (de Gispert et al., 2015), and so on. The joint translation and language model by Devlin et al. (2014) was influential since it showed large quality improvements on top of a very competitive statistical machine translation system.

More ambitious efforts aimed at pure neural machine translation, abandoning existing statistical approaches completely. Early steps were the use of convolutional models (Kalchbrenner and Blunsom, 2013) and sequence-to-sequence models (Cho et al., 2014; Sutskever et al., 2014). These were able to produce reasonable translations for short sentences but fell apart with increasing sentence length. The addition of the attention mechanism finally yielded competitive results (Bahdanau et al., 2015). With a few more refinements, such as byte pair encoding and back-translation of target-side monolingual data, neural machine translation became the new state of the art.

Within a year or two, the entire research field of machine translation went neural. To give some indication of the speed of change: at the shared task for machine translation organized by WMT, only one pure neural machine translation system was submitted in 2015. It was competitive but underperformed traditional statistical systems. A year later, in 2016, a neural machine translation system won in almost all language pairs. In 2017, almost all submissions were neural machine translation systems.

At the time of writing, neural machine translation research is progressing at rapid pace. There are many directions that are and will be explored in the coming years, ranging from core machine learning improvements such as deeper models to more linguistically informed models. More insight into the strength and weaknesses of neural machine translation is being gathered and will inform future work.

Chapter 4
Evaluation

For the most time of its history, machine translation had the reputation of being terrible and useless. Claims that fully automatic high-quality machine translation would be reached in, say, just five years have been repeatedly proven wrong. But over the last decade or so, machine translation has actually become useful. Google Translate is taken as granted for internet searches, and the profession of human translators is wrestling with *how* and not *if* to make use of machine translation technology.

At the time of writing, we appear to have entered another period of hype and hyperbole, even with claims of having reached "human parity" in some data conditions (Figure 4.1). At the same time, hilarious and calamity-causing machine translation errors make it into the popular press.

All these discussions ultimately raise the question of how to evaluate whether machine translation is of good quality. From an engineering perspective, as we embark on considering different machine translation methods, evaluation is also a crucial step. To check if we are making progress, we need to be able to measure quality, ideally with a single score. How to arrive at such a score is still an open research question, although some best practices have been established, and in general there is broad consensus on how to track quality gains.

4.1 Task-Based Evaluation

task-based evaluation

Among vendors of machine translation technology, the phrase *good enough* is commonly used. It is an admission that machine translation technology today and in the foreseeable future is not perfect and will

41

Figure 4.1 Headlines on
progress of machine
translation in 2018.

Facebook's AI Just Set A New Record In Translation And Why It Matters

Linguists, update your resumes because Baidu thinks it has cracked fast AI translation

Microsoft AI translates news as well as humans, takes on Google Translate

SDL Cracks Russian to English Neural Machine Translation

make mistakes. However, the technology, as it is today, is still useful for a wide range of tasks where perfect quality is not required.

What constitutes good enough depends on the task. Another phrase overheard from discussions by vendors of machine translation technology is: *Quality is what the customer says it is.* Ultimately, the success of machine translation is determined if it helps accomplish the broader task, and the people working on the task are the best judge.

4.1.1 Real-World Tasks

real-word tasks

Take the example of a web search to fix a problem you have with your computer. You type in the error message that you get and all you receive is a web page in Finnish. A click on the translate button of your favorite web browser brings up an English translation. Flawed as it may be, it gives you sufficient information to fix your problem. This is a success story for machine translation.

This example also demonstrates that machine translation in the real world is not an end goal. It is a processing step in a larger task. The task in this example could be called information gathering.

While tasks like information gathering may be the most common current use of machine translation today, they are also impractical to be turned into an evaluation metric for machine translation researchers and developers. Each instance of a task (e.g., finding out what to do in case of a computer error message based on a translation of a Finnish web page) requires a lot preparation to set up and trained evaluators. The task also has to be easy enough that the evaluator would do well when given a perfect translation, but also hard enough to be impossible with just the raw Finnish text. And after all this preparation and work by the evaluator, we end up just with a single data point, when we really need hundreds or thousands.

4.1.2 Content Understanding

To turn real-world tasks into benchmarks for machine translation quality, we need to narrow them down into small bites that can be posed to an evaluator repeatedly with sufficient frequency. The example of information gathering comes down to the question of whether the evaluator can grasp the essential meaning from the translation.

A first stab at narrowing down this task is to turn it into a question-answering exercise. We present the evaluator with the machine translation of a document and then pose a question about the content. While this idea is frequently suggested, there have not been any large-scale studies that used this evaluation protocol. There is still significant work involved in picking documents and designing questions that are neither too easy nor too hard.

As part of the WMT evaluation campaign, the manual evaluation of machine translation systems in 2010 narrowed down this idea even further. It asked only one question about the translation of a sentence: *What does this translation mean?* First, an evaluator was asked to rewrite the machine translation (which was shown without the source sentence) into a fluent sentence in the output language. Then, a second evaluator assessed if the corrected translation was actually correct, having access to source sentence, the corrected target translation, and a human reference translation.

Table 4.1 shows the percent of sentence translations that were corrected successfully for different language pairs. The best results

Table 4.1 Content understanding evaluation. A first evaluator attempts to fix the translation without access to source or reference translation. A second evaluator judges the edited translation as correct or not (with access to the source sentence). A human reference translation is judged the same way. Results from the WMT 2010 evaluation campaign (Callison-Burch et al., 2010).

Language Pair	Best System (%)	Reference (%)
French–English	70	91
Spanish–English	71	98
German–English	80	98
Czech–English	60	100
English–French	54	91
English–Spanish	58	83
English–German	80	94
English–Czech	56	97

were obtained for German–English (80%), the worst for English–French (54%). However, the second evaluators were much more lenient for German translations than for French translations, reflected by the judgments given to human reference translations (98% and 91%, respectively).

When properly calibrated with trained and consistent human evaluators, the numbers resulting from such an evaluation are quite intuitive. They indicate how much of the translated content is understandable. We may also view them as an answer to the question of how often machine translation could be corrected by a monolingual speaker of the target language alone, reducing the skill level needed by a human posteditor in a computer aided translation scenario.

4.1.3 Translator Productivity

productivity

If machine translation is used to increase the productivity of professional translators, then content understanding is not the right measure. A translation may be understandable but still require a lot of effort to edit into an acceptable high-quality translation. On the other hand, a translation may have a glaring translation error that is easy to fix, say the omission of the word *not*.

The metric that matters is how much time professional translators spend on postediting the machine translation output. Measuring translator productivity is a well-established standard in the language service industry. Just to give a general ideal, translation speeds of 500–1,000 words per hour (or 3–7 seconds per word) are common for high-quality translations of specialized translators.

In fact, productivity increase is often touted as a metric by vendors of machine translation solutions who promise 50%, 100%, or even 200% productivity increase with their technology. Recall Figure 2.2 for such an assessment of machine translation technology. In that study of productivity, the translator translated between 42% (for Chinese) and 131% (for French) more words per hour when postediting machine translation.

Sanchez-Torron and Koehn (2016) carried out a study that measured translator productivity using machine translation systems of different qualities. A group of translators were randomly assigned sentences that were translated with any of the systems. When using the best system's translation as a draft, this group of translators spend on average 4.06 seconds per word. With the worst system's translations, it took them 5.03 seconds per word. See also the plot in Figure 4.2.

There are a number of confounding variables that make such a measurement difficult. When translating a document, translators spend

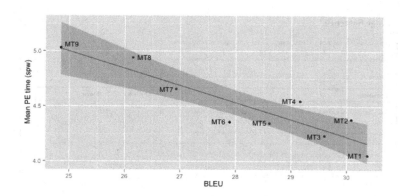

Figure 4.2 Postediting speed for different machine translation systems. The worst system's translations (MT9) took on average 5.03 seconds per word to edit. The best system's translations (MT1) took 4.06 seconds per word to edit.

more time on the initial sentences when they have to familiarize themselves with the content. They have to make translation decisions for ambiguous words that get repeated later. Individual translators also differ quite dramatically in their personal translation speeds. In this study, the fastest translator spend 2.86 seconds per word while the slowest required 6.36 seconds per word.

The variance added by differently qualified translators and other effects requires large evaluation sets to achieve statistically significant results. When translators are recruited over crowd-sourcing platforms, quality control also becomes a major issue, adding to the complexity and the cost of any such evaluation.

4.2 Human Assessments

human assessment

Let us now turn to human assessment protocols that are frequently employed in evaluations of machine translation systems. They are not as informative as the task-based evaluation methods just outlined, but they can be done at scale with reasonable cost.

4.2.1 Adequacy and Fluency

The first idea for assessing the quality of machine translation may be to show qualified bilingual speakers of source and target languages several sentences along with their machine translations and ask the human translators if the translations are correct. Manual evaluations using such a harsh correctness standard—Is the translation perfect or not?—have been done, although usually only on short sentences, where there is at least a reasonable chance that often enough no mistakes are made by the machine translation system.

A more common approach is to use a graded scale when eliciting judgments from human evaluators. Moreover, correctness may be too

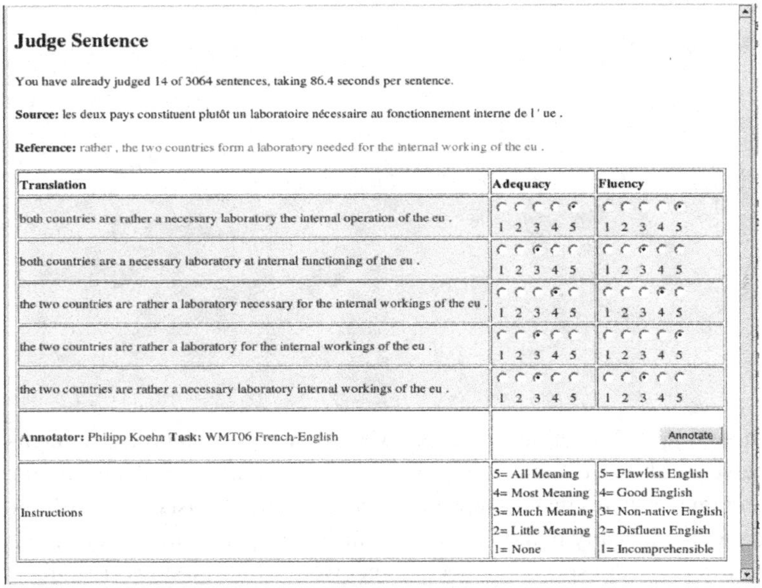

Figure 4.3 Evaluation tool to elicit judgments of translation quality. Five different system outputs are presented, to be scored on a scale of 1–5 for fluency (good English) and adequacy (correct meaning).

broad a measure. It is therefore more common to use the two criteria of fluency and adequacy:

fluency

Fluency: Is the output good fluent English? This involves both grammatical correctness and idiomatic word choices.

adequacy

Adequacy: Does the output convey the same meaning as the input sentence? Is part of the message lost, added, or distorted?

See Figure 4.3 for an example from an evaluation tool that elicits fluency and adequacy judgments from a human annotator. The annotator is given the following definitions of adequacy and fluency:

Adequacy		Fluency	
5	all meaning	5	flawless English
4	most meaning	4	good English
3	much meaning	3	non-native English
2	little meaning	2	disfluent English
1	none	1	incomprehensible

These definitions are very vague, and it is difficult for evaluators to be consistent in their application. Also, some evaluators may generally be more lenient when assigning scores (say, giving an average of 4) than others (say, giving an average of 2) for the same translations.

For example, in the evaluation presented by Koehn and Monz (2005) the average fluency judgment per judge ranged from 2.33 to 3.67, the

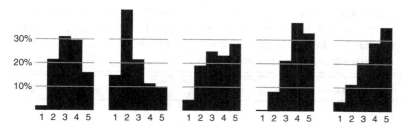

Figure 4.4 Histograms of adequacy judgments by different human evaluators in the WMT 2006 evaluation. Different evaluators use the scale 1–5 in remarkably different ways. The same is true for fluency judgments.

average adequacy judgment per judge ranged from 2.56 to 4.13. See also Figure 4.4 for the judgments given out by the five most prolific judges (more than 1,000 judgments each).

Judging adequacy is tricky. The human mind is quite adept at filling in missing information. Consider the following: If you first read the system output, you may be very puzzled by its meaning, which becomes clear only after reading the reference translation (or input sentence). But if you first read the reference or input sentence and then read the system output, you may not notice that the system output is incomprehensible but may come to the conclusion that the gist of the meaning can be found in there. The latter may also be the case if you have sufficient domain knowledge that helps you understand the meaning of the sentence.

4.2.2 Ranking

Recent evaluation campaigns have shown that judgments of fluency and adequacy are closely related. This may be not completely surprising, since a sentence in garbled English typically also brings across less meaning. But the similarity between the two criteria may also point to the difficulty that humans have in distinguishing the two criteria. So, we may just ask for a simple quality judgment.

Instead of judging fluency and adequacy on an absolute scale, it is typically easier to **rank** two or more systems against each other on a sentence-by-sentence basis. In the case of two systems, the question, "Is system output A better than system output B, or worse, or indistinguishable?" is typically answered by human evaluators in a more consistent manner than questions about adequacy or fluency.

In a way, the annotator interface shown in Figure 4.3 already presents an implicit a ranking of tasks. The translations of different systems are shown, and an evaluator will likely try to assign higher scores to better translations.

What makes one human evaluation method better than another? One consideration is how reliable evaluators can perform the task. We can

ranking

Table 4.2 Inter-evaluator agreement in the WMT 2007 evaluation campaign. $p(A)$ is the ratio of agreement, $p(E)$ is the ratio of agreement by chance. The Kappa coefficient is better for sentence ranking than for adequacy and fluency judgments.

Evaluation type	$p(A)$	$p(E)$	Kappa
Fluency	0.400	0.2	0.250
Adequacy	0.380	0.2	0.226
Sentence ranking	0.582	0.333	0.373

measure *inter-annotator agreement* between multiple evaluators with the Kappa coefficient, which is defined as

$$K = \frac{p(A) - p(E)}{1 - p(E)}, \tag{4.1}$$

where $p(A)$ is proportion of times that the evaluators agree and $p(E)$ is the proportion of time that they would agree by chance. For instance, on a 5-point scale, chance agreement is $p(E) = \frac{1}{5}$. On the ranking task, chance agreement is $p(E) = \frac{1}{3}$, given the choices of either one of the two systems being better or their being tied.

Table 4.2 shows Kappa coefficients for fluency and adequacy assessments on a 5-point scale and sentence ranking, based on evaluator data from the WMT 2007 evaluation campaign. The value for sentence ranking (0.373) is significantly higher for sentence ranking than for adequacy and fluency judgments. This piece of evidence convinced the organizers of this evaluation campaign to move toward sentence ranking, making it the official method for the following decade.

The ranking method gives straightforward statistics on which system is preferred over another. We count the number of times system S_1 is ranked higher than system S_2 as win(S_1, S_2) and the converse as loss(S_1, S_2). If wins are higher than losses, S_1 is deemed better.

The nature of evaluation campaigns with multiple systems participating creates the desire to derive a ranking from pairwise statistics. **expected win** This can be computed as the **expected win** of a system against any of the other n systems.

$$\text{expected-wins}(S_j) = \frac{1}{n} \sum_{k, k \neq j} \frac{\text{win}(S_j, S_k)}{\text{win}(S_j, S_k) + \text{loss}(S_j, S_k)}. \tag{4.2}$$

There are some fine points about handling ties. These could be either ignored or counted as half wins and half losses.

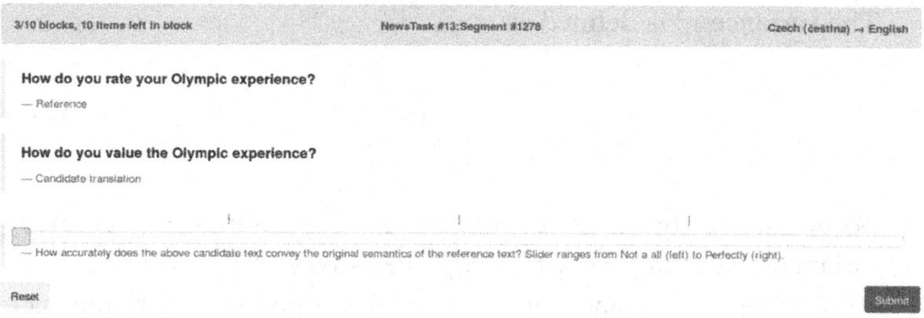

Figure 4.5 Direct assessment using a continuous scale along a slider. Not giving annotators a handful of possible scores for a translation (say, the scores from 1 to 5), allows for more graded distinctions and easier normalization of the scores of different evaluators.

4.2.3 Continuous Scale

The most recent development in human assessment of machine translation systems in evaluation campaigns is called **direct assessment**. The name reflects a return to assessment of a single translated sentence at a time, in contrast to the ranking approach just described. Its main contribution, however, is the use of a 100-point scale that is presented to the human assessor as an unlabeled continuous slider. See Figure 4.5 for a screenshot of direct assessment in action.

    A 100-point scale addresses the core deficiencies of judgments on a 1–5 scale that I discussed earlier. Human evaluators will differ in their quality expectations and hence some will tend to give higher scores and some will give lower scores. They also differ how much of the scale they use. As discussed, some evaluators will never assign a translation a score of 1 or 5.

    With a 100-point scale, it is possible to address these issues. Quality expectation can be measured with the **mean** score of all quality judgments of an evaluator. The utilized range of the scale that is reflected in the **variance** of the scores.

    We would therefore like to **normalize** the judgments. Ideally, all evaluators use scores around the same average. The average $\bar{x}$ of a set of judgments $\{x_1, \ldots, x_n\}$ of an evaluator is defined as

$$\bar{x} = \frac{1}{n} \sum_{i=1}^{n} x_i. \tag{4.3}$$

    If we want all judges to have the same average, say 50, then we need to adjust the individual scores x_i by adding in an adjustment value $50 - \bar{x}$.

direct assessment

mean

variance

normalization of judgments

The variance s^2 is defined as

$$s^2 = \frac{1}{n-1} \sum_{i=1}^{n} (x_i - \bar{x})^2. \tag{4.4}$$

To normalize for variance, we divide mean-normalized scores by the variance s^2. Putting everything together, say, with the goal of a mean score of 50 and a variance of 10, then we adjust scores x_i for each individual evaluator using his or her personal mean score $\bar{x}$ and variance s^2 by computing

$$x_i^{\text{norm}} = 50 + \sqrt{10} \times \frac{(x_i - \bar{x})}{s^2}. \tag{4.5}$$

When deploying direct assessment in evaluation campaigns, translations are randomly selected from the different machine translation system outputs. After normalizing scores for the different human evaluators, we compute the average score for translations from each machine translation system.

Compared to pairwise ranking of output from different machine translation systems, direct assessment scales better. If we compare n systems, then there are $\frac{n(n-1)}{2}$ pairs to be considered. In evaluation campaigns with 10 or even 20 systems participating, it is hard to collect sufficient judgments for any one system pair. Direct assessment, on the other hand, scales linearly with the number of systems.

Direct assessment is often done by showing a human reference translation alongside the machine translation. This allows the evaluation task to be done by a monolingual speaker of the target language. However, the human reference translations may bias the evaluation. If the quality of the human reference translation is bad, the evaluation will not be reliable.

So, we may instead show the source sentence alongside the machine translation output. While this requires at least some degree of evaluator fluency of the source language, it does have the added benefit that we can also evaluate the human reference translation in the same way we evaluate machine translations. This gives us some indication how far away we are from parity with human performance.

4.2.4 Crowd-Sourcing Evaluations

crowd-sourcing

Any human evaluation requires a significant amount of labor. Fortunately, this is not a particularly difficult task for anybody who is fluent in the target language. So, it is popular to outsource this task to crowd workers via platforms such as Mechanical Turk.

For instance, in the WMT 2018 evaluation campaign, hundreds of crowd workers contributed to the evaluation effort. They were tasked with making direct assessment judgments of a single machine translated sentence at a time, given either the reference translation or the source sentence. The work is broken up into so-called human intelligence tasks (HIT). Each HIT consists of 100 sentence translation assessments, which takes about half an hour to finish.

A crucial step in crowd sourcing is quality control. Since anybody can sign up for these tasks without engaging in a long-term work relationship, there is a temptation to game the system and do the task as quickly as possible without actually deploying human intelligence. Therefore, when setting up a task it is important to include quality-control checks.

For the task of direct assessment of 100 sentences, 60 are normal assessments (showing the translation of a machine translation system), and 40 are 10 blocks consisting of

(1) a system's translation
(2) a repetition of the system's translation
(3) the human-generated reference translation
(4) a degraded version of system's translation, such as replacing a phrase with a phrase randomly drawn from elsewhere in the test set

Note that the reference translation can be shown only in source-based direct assessment, or when are two different human reference translations.

The 100 items are shuffled randomly. We would expect that a diligent evaluator would, compared to the system's original machine translation (1), give

- the repeated translation (2) roughly the same score
- the human-generated reference translation (3) a better score
- the degraded translation (4) a worse score

For each annotator, we can check if any of this is the case. This may be done by standard significance tests that check if annotator gives significantly worse scores to the degraded translation (4) compared to the system's translation (1). In the WMT 2018 evaluation campaign, evaluations from annotators who did not meet this case with a p-value of 0.05 were discarded. Only 10% of Chinese and 22% of Russian evaluators were deemed reliable, compared to 42% for English.

Hence, when human evaluation is done frequently, it is a good idea to build up a pool of trusted evaluators to increase the ratio of reliable assessments.

4.2.5 Human Translation Edit Rate

human translation edit rate

Arguably, an evaluation method that asks to assess sentence translation HTER is more reflective of how informative machine translation is, not of how much work is needed to correct it. To repeat the striking example, a translation that misses a *not* will likely be judged quite negatively by a human evaluator, but it is quick to fix.

So, instead we may do evaluation by postediting, as already suggested as a task-based evaluation method in Section 4.1.3. As I remarked then, measuring postediting time requires instrumented postediting tools that track keyboard activity, so instead we may just resort to counting the number of words a human posteditor changed. We do not have to concern ourselves with the tools used, we just compare the original machine translation with the postedited version, and compute the human translation edit rate (more on the computation of the rate in Section 4.3.3).

Human translation edit rate (HTER) was used in the IWSLT evaluation campaign. Here, translations from different machine translation systems were randomly distributed to human posteditors. Then, for each machine translation system, its translations were compared against their postedited versions.

A few interesting observations: the edit rate between a machine translation and its postedited version is dramatically lower than between the machine translation and an independently produced human reference translation. To give a typical example, the Romanian–Italian system from Kyoto University in the 2017 IWSLT evaluation campaign (Cettolo et al., 2017) has a edit rate of 29.3% of its translations against their postedited version, which can be roughly interpreted as 3 in 10 words having been changed by the human posteditor. When compared against an independently produced human reference translation, the edit rate was 60.6%.

Because output from other participating systems was also postedited, we can compare the output from Kyoto University's system against any of these postedited translations. They may be more similar than its own postedited version. In fact, when taking the closest match for each sentence, the edit rate drops to just 22.7%. This is surprising. One explanation is that machine translation output from different systems in evaluation campaigns tend to be similar to each other, so this is a consequence of some posteditors performing fewer edits than others.

4.3 Automatic Metrics

automatic metrics

When it comes to evaluating machine translation systems, we tend to put most trust into the judgment of human evaluators who look at the output of several systems, examine it sentence by sentence, assess each sentence, and conclude with an overall score for each system.

This method, however, has one major disadvantage. It takes a lot of time, and if the evaluators expect to be paid, also a lot of money.

The typical machine translation researcher, on the other hand, would like to carry out evaluations very frequently and cheaply, often many times per day to examine different system configurations.

Therefore, we need an automatic method for assessing the quality of machine translation output. Ideally, we would like a computer program to tell us quickly whether our system got better after a change, or not. This is the objective of **automatic machine translation evaluation**. The main trick here is to provide a human-generated **reference translation** and compare the system output against the reference translation.

reference translation

Much progress has recently been made in this field, to the point that machine translation researchers trust automatic evaluation metrics and design their systems based on the rise and fall of automatic evaluation scores. However, automatic evaluation metrics are under constant debate and their true value in distinguishing better and worse systems is often called into question. We will come back to this discussion in Section 4.4.1. Let us first get a better understanding of automatic evaluation methods.

4.3.1 BLEU

BLEU

All automatic machine translation evaluation metrics in practical use for guiding research are based on the comparison of the system output to a gold standard reference translation. How to make such a comparison is actually a problem.

There are two major challenges. First, the inherent ambiguity of the translation task. Since even two professional translators will almost always produce two different translations for the same sentence, perfectly matching a single human reference translation is too high a bar to reach for machine translation. Second, we not only have to deal with matching words but also with word order. Some word order differences are legitimate, some are not.

Because of these challenges, simple methods such as counting the number of correct words (which ignores word order) or word error rate (used in speech recognition and requires the same word order) will not work well.

Researchers at IBM developed a metric that is a compromise between ignoring and requiring matching word order. They called their metric BLEU, which is French for *blue*, the corporate color of IBM. Almost everybody pronounces it *blue*. It is the acronym for *bilingual evaluation understudy*, a name that clearly suggests that it is not as good as the lead character for the role of evaluator, the human assessor, but a substitute.

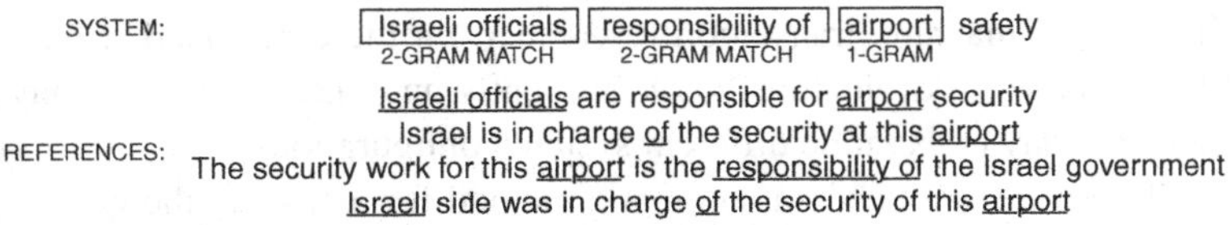

SYSTEM: | Israeli officials | | responsibility of | | airport | safety
                  2-GRAM MATCH   2-GRAM MATCH   1-GRAM

                    Israeli officials are responsible for airport security
                        Israel is in charge of the security at this airport
REFERENCES:
     The security work for this airport is the responsibility of the Israel government
                  Israeli side was in charge of the security of this airport

Figure 4.6 Additional *n*-gram matches by using multiple reference translations, accounting for variability in acceptable translations.

The idea behind BLEU is that it counts not only the number of words in the translation that match the reference but also the larger-order *n*-gram matches. So it rewards correct word order, since it increases the likelihood that there will be matching word pairs (bigrams), or even sequences of three or four words (trigrams and 4-grams).

There are a couple more refinements to this basic idea. The first is to use multiple reference translations. Since it is hard to match a single human reference translation, the idea is to have multiple human reference translations and if the machine translation has *n*-gram matches with any of them, that is good enough (Figure 4.6 provides an example).

The second refinement addresses the problem that BLEU is a precision **precision** metric, meaning we compute the ratio of the *n*-grams in the machine translation that match the reference translation, not the other way around. A way to game such a metric is to not produce any output at all in difficult cases. Often precision in metrics is paired with recall **recall**, which would compute the ratio of the *n*-grams in the reference translation that match the machine translation. They can be combined f-measure into a metric called the **f-measure**:

$$\text{precision} = \frac{\text{matches}}{\text{total in machine translation}} \tag{4.6}$$

$$\text{recall} = \frac{\text{matches}}{\text{total in reference translation}} \tag{4.7}$$

$$\text{f-measure} = 2 \times \frac{\text{precision} \times \text{recall}}{\text{precision} + \text{recall}} \tag{4.8}$$

$$= \frac{\text{matches}}{(\text{total in machine translation} + \text{total in reference translation})/2}. \tag{4.9}$$

In the case of BLEU, the idea of using multiple reference translation makes the use of recall complicated, so instead BLEU opts for the explicit use of a brevity penalty. It is based on the ratio between the number of words in the machine translation and reference translation and kicks in if this ratio is below 1 (i.e., the machine translation is too short).

The BLEU metric is defined as

$$\text{BLEU} = \text{brevity-penalty}$$

$$\times \exp \sum_{i=1}^{4} \log \frac{\text{matching } i\text{-grams}}{\text{total } i\text{-grams in machine translation}}$$

$$\text{brevity-penalty} = \min \left(1, \frac{\text{output-length}}{\text{reference-length}}\right). \qquad (4.10)$$

BLEU scores are computed from statistics over an entire test set of typically thousands of sentence pairs. The use of multiple reference translation has fallen out of fashion, but it is still used occasionally.

4.3.2 Synonyms and Morphological Variants

synonym
morphological variants

Automatic machine translation evaluation struggles with the challenge of turning a fundamentally semantic task (*does the meaning of the system output match a human reference translation*) into a surface-level word-matching task. Whether changes to words and word order make little difference or fundamentally change the meaning of a sentence is a hard problem.

The **METEOR** metric introduced a couple of novel ideas. One **METEOR** perceived flaw of BLEU is that it gives no credit at all to near matches. Recall that one of our example system outputs used the noun *responsibility*, but the reference used the adjective *responsible*. Both carry the same meaning, but since the words are not the same, BLEU counts this as an error. By stemming the two words, i.e., reducing them to their morphological stem *respons*, we are able to match them.

Another way to detect near misses is using synonyms, or semantically closely related words. Consider the reference translations in Figure 4.6. Translators varied in their use of *security* and *safety*, as well as *responsibility* and *charge*. These different word choices may be irrelevant in bringing across the meaning of the sentences and should not be penalized.

METEOR incorporates the use of stemming and synonyms by first matching the surface forms of the words and then backing off to stems and finally semantic classes. The latter are determined using Wordnet, a popular ontology of English words that also exists for other languages.

The main drawback of METEOR is that its method and formula for computing a score is much more complicated that BLEU's. Linguistic resources such as morphological stemmers and synonym databases are required. The matching process involves computationally expensive word alignment. There are many more parameters—such as the relative weight of recall to precision and the weight for stemming or synonym matches—that have to be tuned.

4.3.3 TER

The BLEU metric is fairly simple, but the computed number for any system output and reference translation does not have a intuitive interpretation. In speech recognition, the quality of a transcription of an audio recording is measured by the word error rate (WER), which counts the number of added, deleted, and substituted words. Reporting, say, that a system has a 7% word error rate gives a good intuitive sense about the quality of the system.

There is one big problem for adopting word error rate for machine translation. Consider the following example:

- **MT:** *A spokesperson announced today: "The plan will go forward."*
- **Reference:** *"The plan will go forward," a spokesperson announced today.*

A near-perfect match, but the computed word error rate for this example is terrible. Since words have to be match in sequence, it will match up the machine translation as follows:

> ~~A spokesperson announced today:~~ *"The plan will go forward."*
>
> *a spokesperson announced today.*

So, it would count the main clause *A spokesperson announced today* first as a 4-word deletion, and then as a 4-word insertion, thus 8 word errors for a 9-word sentence (ignoring punctuation).

Translation error rate (TER), sometimes also called translation edit rate, adds a shift operation to the addition, deletion, and substitution of words. Moving any sequence of words is counted as 1 error. For our example, this means that there is only 1 error for a 9-word translation, thus a TER score of $\frac{1}{9} = 11\%$.

TER scores not only are quite intuitive but are also a much better metric when scoring a single sentence. The computation of BLEU scores has as a factor 4-gram precision, but the translation of a sentence may not have any 4-gram match, resulting in a BLEU score of 0. While TER is not as widely used as BLEU, it is the preferable metric for sentence-level evaluation.

There is, however, one drawback: the computation of TER scores is NP-complete. While word error rate has a well-known dynamic programming solution with worst-case quadratic run time, there are just too many shifts to consider to efficiently compute the optimal TER match between machine translation and reference. Snover et al. (2006)

propose a greedy hill-climbing algorithm to compute TER. Initially, it computes WER between machine translation and reference. Then it considers all possible shifts and checks which reduces WER the most. The best shift operation is adopted. This process is iterated: finding the best shift operation, applying it to the translation, keeping count, until all possible shift operations would lead to a worse score.

This is a heuristic search solution to the problem, so it is not guaranteed to find the optimal match and still has a fairly long runtime.

4.3.4 CHARACTER

Among the problems raised for word-matching metrics such as BLEU and TER are the failure to give partial credit for morphological variants and not rewarding important content word matches higher than less-relevant function words. CHARACTER, computation of translation edit rate on the character level, is an elegant solution to these problems. Morphological variants are similar in spelling and thus still have many character-level matches. Content words are typically longer than function words, so they count more.

character translation edit rate

Given the computational challenges for TER, computing it at the character level dramatically increases the runtime. However, this has a fairly simple solution: limiting shift operations to word sequence movements, i.e., do not break up words during moves. There is also a refinement to the score computation for shifts: to bring their cost in line with word deletion, insertion, and substitution costs (which involve many character edits), the cost of a shift is calculated as the average word length of the reference translation.

CHARACTER has been shown to be especially suitable for morphologically rich target languages. However, like many other metrics that have been recently proposed, it has not been widely adopted.

4.3.5 Bootstrap Resampling

bootstrap resampling

If we make a change to our machine translation system, we measure system performance before and after the change by translating a test set of a few thousand sentences and computing BLEU, METEOR, TER, or CHARACTER scores. If the changed system yields a better score, we would like to conclude that the change was indeed an improvement.

However, the old system is likely better for some sentences, and the new system better for others. What if we would have run this evaluation on a different test set? The result may be reversed.

It is common practice in science to measure not just the resulting scores of an experiment but also **statistical significance**. In our case, we

statistical significance

Figure 4.7 Confidence interval in a normal distribution. With probability $q = 0.95$ (shaded part under the graph), the true score lies in an interval around the sample score (here $\bar{x} = 37.2$).

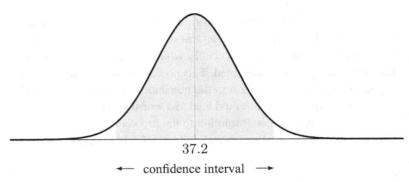

37.2

$\longleftarrow$ confidence interval $\longrightarrow$

may be interested in answers to two questions. If we perform a **pairwise**

pairwise comparison **comparison** of two systems, how sure are we that one is better than the other? If we get, say, a BLEU score for our system, what **confidence**

confidence interval **interval** do we expect scores to fall in when we would have selected a test set of the same type (same level of difficulty and domain) but with different test sentences?

Statistical significance testing provides us with the tools to answer such questions. These answers come in the form of, say: *System A is better than system B with 95% probability (p-level 0.05)*. For many simple measures, such as human judgment scores on a per-sentence basis, there are well-established tools to compute the level of statistical significance. However, for the metrics just discussed, which rely on complex calculations on the similarity between machine translation and reference, these computations do not apply.

One method for computing statistical significance for complex metrics is called **bootstrap resampling**. Let us first consider the case of estimating confidence intervals. Pairwise comparison is very similar.

Consider the following: Let us say that we are using a test set of 2,000 sentences that we sampled from a large collection of available test sentences. We then proceed to compute the BLEU score for this set. But how likely is that score to be representative of the true BLEU score computed on a test of near-infinite size?

If we were to repeatedly sample test sets of 2,000 sentences, and compute the BLEU score on each of them, we would get a distribution of scores that looks like the bell curve in Figure 4.7. With enough test set samples, say 1,000, we can then empirically determine the 95% confidence interval. By ignoring the 25 highest and 25 lowest BLEU scores, we are left with an interval that contains 95% of the scores.

To restate the argument: if we pick one of the test set samples at random, then there will be a 95% probability it will be in the interval between the extreme tails of the distribution. Hence a truly representative test set sample will also have a 95% probability of being in this interval.

Of course, taking 1,000 test sets of 2,000 sentences means translating 2 million sentences, and if we were able to do that, we could most likely come up with a tighter confidence interval. So instead we apply the following trick. We sample the 1,000 test sets from the *same* 2,000 sentences of the initial test set, with replacement. Since we are allowed to take the same sentences more than once, we will come up with 1,000 different test sets, and therefore 1,000 different test scores. We then move on and compute the confidence interval, as if these sets were truly independent samples.

We will not go into the theoretical arguments about bootstrap resampling here; the reader is referred to Efron and Tibshirani (1993). Intuitively, bootstrap resampling uses the variability in the test sets to draw conclusions about statistical significance. If the system translated most parts of the test set with very similar performance, then we are more likely to trust the resulting score, as opposed to a test set translation with parts that have widely different performance.

The application of bootstrap resampling to the pairwise comparison of different systems is straightforward. We compute both systems' scores on the resampled test set and check which system is better. If one system is better on at least 950 samples, then it is deemed to be statistically significantly better at the $p \leq 0.05$ level.

4.4 Metrics Research

metrics research

4.4.1 The Evaluation Debate

evaluation debate

The use of automatic evaluation metrics in machine translation is under constant debate in the research community. It seems to be hard to believe that simplistic metrics such as the BLEU score and the other metrics that I introduced in the previous section properly reflect differences in meaning between system output and reference translations (or input, for that matter).

The main points of **critique** are as follows:

- BLEU ignores the relative relevance of different words. Some words matter more than others. One of the most glaring examples is the word *not*, which, if omitted, will cause very misleading translations. Names and core concepts are also important words, much more so than, e.g., determiners and punctuation, which are often irrelevant. However, all words are treated the same way by the metrics we presented here.
- BLEU operates on only a very local level and does not address overall grammatical coherence. System output may look good on an *n*-gram basis, but very

Figure 4.8 Correlation between an automatic metric (here: NIST score) and human judgment (fluency, adequacy). (Illustration by George Doddington.)

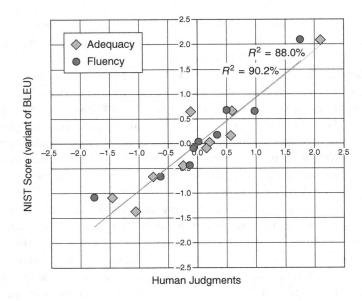

muddled beyond that. There is a suspicion that this biases the metric in favor of machine translation systems, which are good at producing good n-grams but are less able to produce grammatically coherent sentences.

- The actual BLEU scores are meaningless. Nobody knows what a BLEU score of 30% means, since the actual number depends on many factors, such as the number of reference translations, the language pair, the domain, and even the tokenization scheme used to break up the output and reference into words.
- Recent experiments computed so-called human BLEU scores, where a human reference translation was scored against other human reference translations. Such human BLEU scores are barely higher (if at all) than BLEU scores computed for machine translation output, even though the human translations are of much higher quality.

Many of these arguments were brought up when BLEU was initially introduced to a skeptical audience, and all of them also apply broadly to any other automatic evaluation metric. There are counterarguments. The most convincing argument is shown in Figure 4.8. The graph plots system performance as measured by automatic scores against human judgment scores for submissions to the 2002 machine translation evaluation on Arabic–English, organized by NIST.

In this analysis, systems with low automatic scores also received low human judgment scores, and systems with high automatic scores also received high human judgment scores. What this shows is a high **correlation** between human and automatic scores. This is what we expect from a good automatic evaluation metric, and this is what evaluation metrics should be assessed on.

4.4.2 Evaluation of Evaluation Metrics

evaluation of evaluation metrics

The introduction of BLEU birthed a cottage industry for automatic evaluation metrics. The steady supply of human judgment data from evaluation campaigns such as the Conference of Machine Translation (WMT) makes it possible to check if a newly proposed metric correlates better with human judgment than traditional metrics such as BLEU.

The most widely used method for computing the correlation between two metrics is the **Pearson correlation coefficient**. Formally, we are faced with a set of data points $\{(x_i, y_i)\}$ that contain values for two variables x, y. The Pearson correlation coefficient r_{xy} between the two variables is defined as

Pearson correlation coefficient

$$r_{xy} = \frac{\sum_i (x_i - \bar{x})(y_i - \bar{y})}{(n-1)\, s_x\, s_y}. \qquad (4.11)$$

To compute the coefficient r_{xy} we first need to compute the sample means $\bar{x}, \bar{y}$ and the sample variances s_x, s_y of the two variables x and y:

$$\bar{x} = \frac{1}{n} \sum_{i=1}^{n} x_i$$

$$s_x^2 = \frac{1}{n-1} \sum_{i=1}^{n} (x_i - \bar{x})^2. \qquad (4.12)$$

What counts as a good correlation between perfect correlation ($r_{xy} = 1$) and total independence between the variables ($r_{xy} = 0$) is anybody's guess. Figure 4.9 gives a typical interpretation of the correlation coefficient. If our goal is to compare different automatic evaluation metrics with respect to their correlation with a manual metric, the answer is straightforward: a higher correlation is better.

Correlation	Negative	Positive
Small	−0.29 to −0.10	0.10 to 0.29
Medium	−0.49 to −0.30	0.30 to 0.49
Large	−1.00 to −0.50	0.50 to 1.00

Figure 4.9 Typical interpretation of the correlation coefficient r_{xy}.

Figure 4.10 Examples of lack of correlation between BLEU and manual judgment. Manually postedited machine translation is scored low by BLEU, but high by humans, both in terms of adequacy (a) and fluency (b). A rule-based system receives a much lower BLEU score than a comparable statistical system that is trained and evaluated on the Europarl corpus (c).

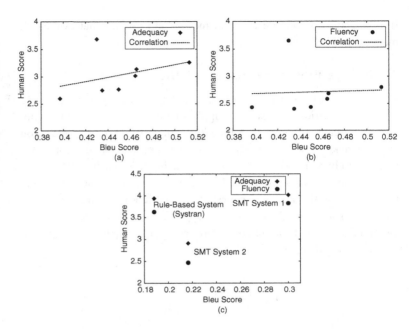

4.4.3 Evidence of Shortcomings of Automatic Metrics

shortcomings

These kind of correlation studies carried out on data from evaluation campaigns have revealed exceptions to the correlation of manual and automatic scores for some special cases.

In the 2005 NIST evaluations on Arabic–English, one of the submissions was a system that was improved by human postediting. The postediting was done by monolingual speakers of the target language with no knowledge of the source language. The postediting effort led to only small increases in the automatic BLEU score but to large improvements in both fluency and adequacy judgments in the manual evaluation (Figure 4.10a,b).

Second, in an experiment comparing a commercial rule-based machine translation system with two instances of a statistical system (one trained on the full data set, the other on 1/64 of it), the automatic BLEU score failed to reflect the human judgment. The worse statistical system, although given much lower judgments by humans, still achieved a higher BLEU score than the rule-based system. Human evaluators scored the rule-based system and the better statistical system similarly; the BLEU scores, however, were 18% and 30%, respectively (Figure 4.10c).

The WMT 2006 evaluation campaign confirmed the latter result—again a rule-based system participated along with a range of statistical systems. Interestingly, the correlation of scores was much higher when the systems were tested on out-of-domain test data. While the rule-based system was not developed for a specific domain, the statistical systems were trained on Europarl data, but the out-of-domain test data set was political and economic commentary. This finding seems to suggest that part of the explanation for the lack of correlation is that automatic scores are overly literal and reward the right choice of jargon much more strongly than human evaluators.

The state of the current debate on automatic evaluation metrics evolves around a general consensus that automatic metrics are an essential tool for system development of statistical machine translation systems but not fully suited to computing scores that allow us to rank systems of different types against each other. Developing evaluation metrics for this purpose is still an open challenge to the research community.

4.4.4 Novel Metrics

The development of automatic evaluation metrics is a well-defined task. **novel metrics** Given the human judgment data from years of evaluation campaigns, the challenge is to come up with an automatic metric that correlates well with these data. In fact, there has been an annual shared task[1] to develop such automatic metrics alongside the main WMT translation shared task. Over the years, dozens of new metrics have been proposed.

Some of the innovations are as follows:

- The idea of assigning partial scores to matches of synonyms or words with the same morphological stems pioneered by METEOR can be applied to any other word-matching metric. For instance, the BLEU score has been extended to the variant BLEU-S, where partial credit is given to n-grams that match under such relaxed conditions.
- Given a clear set of inputs and outputs, the triplets of source sentence, machine translation, and reference translation on one side and the human judgment score on the other side, we have straightforward data conditions suitable for a machine learning approach. We can train a metric on past human judgment data and apply them to any new test set. A variety of such metrics have been proposed. A currently popular metric is BEER, which combines word, subword, and character-based features with word order features.
- Most evaluation metrics focus on matching words between machine translation and reference. For language pairs such as Japanese–English with large word order differences, this focus may be misplaced. Correct word order should be directly measured and taken into account. To address this, metrics such as RIBES have been proposed, which count the number of word pairs that are in correct order.

---

[1] See www.statmt.org/wmt19/metrics-task.html.

- Since the comparison between machine translation and reference is essentially a semantic matching task, deeper linguistic representations may be more useful. Metrics that match syntactic tree structures and semantic properties such as semantic roles have been proposed (e.g., MEANT).
- Finally, the wave of deep learning has also reached metrics research. Instead of matching word tokens, we may match word embeddings instead. Or, machine translation and reference translation are both converted into sentence embeddings, which are then compared. Such metrics require pretrained embeddings, e.g., sentence embeddings trained on large amounts of monolingual text.

interpretability It is worth noting that correlation with human judgment is not the only criterion to judge a metric by. I already argued that **interpretability** is a positive property of a metric. For instance, the inability to communicate what a BLEU score of, say, 34.2 means is a problem for machine translation research. TER scores that can be roughly characterized as *ratio of words that need to be changed* are much more intuitive.

resources Some metrics require additional **resources**, either linguistic tools (syntactic and semantic parsers, part-of-speech taggers, morphological stemmers, synonym matchers) or data (prior judgment data, monolingual and parallel data) that may not readily exist for any language and may also be domain dependent. Any metric that requires training is more expensive to use and suspect to idiosyncrasies of data conditions, either of the training data or of the test sets that it is applied to. The

computation cost **computation cost** of using a metric may also be a concern when it is used as part of automatic system optimization.

So while it is somewhat surprising that despite over a decade of metrics research, the go-to metric is still the BLEU score, which was the first automatic metric commonly used in data-driven machine translation research, some of these concerns indicate why this is so. There is also the

credibility problem of **credibility** of trusting a new metric. Researchers who report scores with only a relatively new metric will be asked how their claimed system improvements also lead to higher BLEU scores. Reporting scores in multiple metrics does not further the cause for new metrics, since most readers will home in on the familiar scores.

Part II
Basics

Chapter 5
Neural Networks

A neural network is a machine learning technique that takes a number of inputs and predicts outputs. In many ways, they are not very different from other machine learning methods but have distinct strengths.

5.1 Linear Models

linear model

Linear models are a core element of statistical machine translation. A potential translation x of a sentence is represented by a set of features $h_j(x)$. Each feature is weighted by a parameter λ_j to obtain an overall score. The following formula sums up the model:

$$\text{score}(\lambda, x) = \sum_j \lambda_j \, h_j(x). \qquad (5.1)$$

Graphically, a linear model can be illustrated by a network, where feature values are **input nodes**, arrows are **weights**, and the score is an output node (Figure 5.1).

input node

weight

output node

Training methods assign a weight value λ_j to each feature $h_j(x)$, related to their importance in contributing to scoring better translations higher. In statistical machine translation, this is called **tuning**.

tuning

However, linear models do not allow us to define more complex relationships between the features. Let us say that we find that for short sentences the language model is less important than the translation model, or that average phrase translation probabilities higher than 0.1 are similarly reasonable but any value below that is really terrible. The first hypothetical example implies dependence between features, and

Figure 5.1 A linear model as a network. Feature values are input nodes, arrows are weights, and the score is an output node.

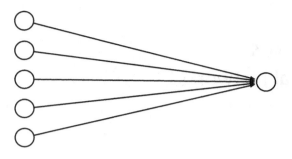

the second example implies a nonlinear relationship between the feature value and its impact on the final score. Linear models cannot handle these cases.

A commonly cited counterexample to the use of linear models is XOR, i.e., the boolean operator $\oplus$ with the truth table $0 \oplus 0 = 0$, $1 \oplus 0 = 1$, $0 \oplus 1 = 1$, and $1 \oplus 1 = 0$. For a linear model with two features (representing the inputs), it is not possible to come up with weights that give the correct output in all cases. Linear models assume that all instances, represented as points in the feature space, are linearly separable. This is not the case with XOR and may not be the case for the types of features we use in machine translation.

5.2 Multiple Layers

multiple layers

Neural networks modify linear models in two important ways. The first is the use of multiple layers. Instead of computing the output value directly from the input values, **hidden layers** are introduced. They are **hidden layer** called hidden because we can observe inputs and outputs in training instances but not the mechanism that connects them — this use of the concept *hidden* is similar to its meaning in hidden Markov models (Figure 5.2).

The network is processed in two steps. First, a linear combination of weighted input nodes is computed to produce each hidden node value. Then a linear combination of weighted hidden nodes is computed to produce each output node value.

At this point, let us introduce mathematical notations from the neural network literature. A neural network with a hidden layer consists of

- a vector of input nodes with values $\vec{x} = (x_1, x_2, x_3, \ldots x_n)^T$;
- a vector of hidden nodes with values $\vec{h} = (h_1, h_2, h_3, \ldots h_m)^T$;
- a vector of output nodes with values $\vec{y} = (y_1, y_2, y_3, \ldots y_l)^T$;
- a matrix of weights connecting input nodes to hidden nodes $U = \{u_{j \leftarrow k}\}$;
- a matrix of weights connecting hidden nodes to output nodes $W = \{w_{i \leftarrow j}\}$.

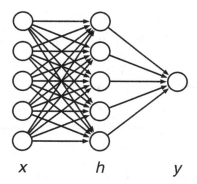

Figure 5.2 A neural
network with a hidden layer.

$$x \qquad h \qquad y$$

The computations in a neural network with a hidden layer, as sketched out so far, are

$$h_j = \sum_k u_{j\leftarrow k} x_k \quad \text{and} \tag{5.2}$$

$$y_i = \sum_j w_{i\leftarrow j} h_j. \tag{5.3}$$

Note that we sneaked in the possibility of multiple output nodes y_k, although the figures so far showed only one.

5.3 Nonlinearity

nonlinear

If we carefully think about the addition of a hidden layer as in Equations 5.2 and 5.3, we realize that we have not gained anything so far that will model more complex input/output relationships. We can easily do away with the hidden layer by multiplying out the weights:

$$
\begin{aligned}
y_i &= \sum_j w_{i\leftarrow j} h_j \\
&= \sum_j w_{i\leftarrow j} \sum_k u_{j\leftarrow k} x_k \\
&= \sum_{j,k} w_{i\leftarrow j} u_{j\leftarrow k} x_k \qquad (5.4) \\
&= \sum_k x_k \left(\sum_j w_{i\leftarrow j} u_{j\leftarrow k} \right).
\end{aligned}
$$

Hence, a salient element of neural networks is the use of a **nonlinear activation function**. After computing the linear combination of weighted feature values $s_j = \sum_k u_{j\leftarrow k} x_k$, we obtain the value of a node

activation function
nonlinear

Figure 5.3 Typical activation functions in neural networks.

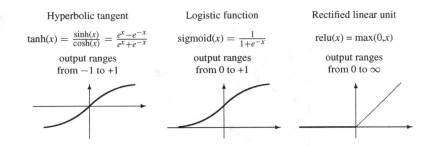

only after applying such a function $h_j = f(s_j)$. Instead of Equation 5.2, we have

$$h_j = f\left(\sum_k u_{j\leftarrow k} x_k\right). \tag{5.5}$$

Popular choices for nonlinear activation functions are the **hyperbolic tangent** $\tanh(x)$ and the **logistic function** $\text{sigmoid}(x)$. See Figure 5.3 for more details on these functions. A good way to think about these activation functions is that they segment the range of values for the linear combination s_j into

hyperbolic tangent
tangent
logistic function

- a segment where the node is turned off (values close to 0 for tanh, or -1 for sigmoid);
- a transition segment where the node is partly turned on;
- a segment where the node is turned on (values close to 1).

A different popular choice is the activation function for the **rectified linear unit** (ReLU). It does not allow for negative values and floors them at 0, but does not alter the value of positive values. It is simpler and faster to compute than $\tanh(x)$ or $\text{sigmoid}(x)$.

rectified linear unit
ReLU

You could view each hidden node as a feature detector. For a certain configurations of input node values, it is turned on, for others it is turned off. Advocates of neural networks claim that the use of hidden nodes obviates (or at least drastically reduces) the need for feature engineering: Instead of manually detecting useful patterns in input values, training of the hidden nodes discovers them automatically.

We do not have to stop at a single hidden layer. The currently fashionable name **deep learning** for neural networks stems from the fact that often better performance can be achieved by deeply stacking together layers and layers of hidden nodes.

deep learning

5.4 Inference

inference

Let us walk through neural network **inference** (i.e., how output values are computed from input values) with a concrete example. Consider the

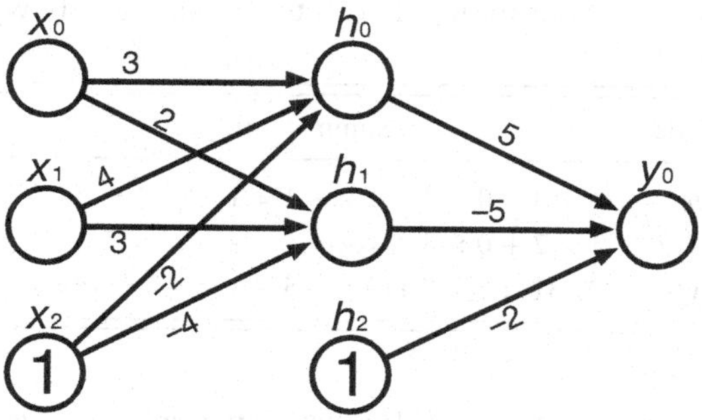

Figure 5.4 A simple neural network with bias nodes in input and hidden layers.

neural network in Figure 5.4. This network has one additional innovation that we have not presented so far: bias units. These are nodes that always have the value 1. Such bias units give the network something to work with in the case when all input values are 0. Otherwise, the weighted sum s_j would be 0 no matter the weights.

Let us use this neural network to process some input, say the value 1 for the first input node x_0 and 0 for the second input node x_1. The value of the bias input node (labeled x_2) is fixed to 1. To compute the value of the first hidden node h_0, we have to carry out the following calculation:

$$h_0 = \text{sigmoid}\left(\sum_k x_k u_{0 \leftarrow k}\right)$$

$$= \text{sigmoid}\,(1 \times 3 + 0 \times 4 + 1 \times -2) \qquad (5.6)$$

$$= \text{sigmoid}\,(1)$$

$$= 0.73.$$

The calculations for the other nodes are summarized in Table 5.1. The output value in node y_0 for the input $(0,1)$ is 0.743. If we expect binary output, we would understand this result as the value 1, since it is over the threshold of 0.5 in the range of possible output values $[0;1]$.

Here, the output for all possible binary inputs:

Input x_0	Input x_1	Hidden h_0	Hidden h_1	Output y_0
0	0	0.119	0.018	$0.183 \to 0$
0	1	0.881	0.269	$0.743 \to 1$
1	0	0.731	0.119	$0.743 \to 1$
1	1	0.993	0.731	$0.334 \to 0$

Our neural network computes XOR. How does it do that? If we look at the hidden nodes h_0 and h_1, we notice that h_0 acts like the Boolean OR: Its value is high if at least of the two input values is 1 ($h_0 = 0.881, 0.731, 0.993$, for the three configurations), it otherwise has a low value (0.119). The other hidden node h_1 acts like the Boolean

Table 5.1 Calculations for Input (1,0) to the Network shown in Figure 5.4.

Layer	Node	Summation	Activation
Hidden	h_0	$1 \times 3 + 0 \times 4 + 1 \times -2 = 1$	0.731
Hidden	h_1	$1 \times 2 + 0 \times 3 + 1 \times -4 = -2$	0.119
Output	y_0	$0.731 \times 5 + 0.119 \times -5 + 1 \times -2 = 1.060$	0.743

AND; has only a high value (0.731) if both inputs are 1. XOR is effectively implemented as the subtraction of the AND from the OR hidden node.

Note that the nonlinearity is key here. Since the value for the OR node h_0 is not that much higher for the input of $(1,1)$ opposed to a single 1 in the input (0.993 versus 0.881 and 0.731), the distinct high value for the AND node h_1 in this case (0.731) manages to push the final output y_0 below the threshold. This would not be possible if the values of the inputs would be simply summed up as in linear models.

As mentioned before, recently the use of the name **deep learning** for neural networks has become fashionable. It emphasizes that often higher performance can be achieved by using networks with multiple hidden layers. Our XOR example hints at where this power comes from. With a single input/output layer network it is possible to mimic basic Boolean operations such as AND and OR since they can be modeled with linear classifiers. XOR can be expressed as x AND $y - x$ OR y, and our neural network example implements the Boolean operations AND and OR in the first layer and the subtraction in the second layer. For functions that require more intricate computations, more operations may be chained together, and hence a neural network architecture with more hidden layers may be needed. It may be possible (with sufficient training data) to build neural networks for any computer program, if the number of hidden layers matches the depth of the computation. There is a line of research under the banner **neural Turing machines** that explores what kind of architectures are needed to implement basic algorithms (Gemici et al., 2017). For instance, a neural network with two hidden layers is sufficient to implement an algorithm that sorts n-bit numbers.

neural Turing machines

5.5 Back-Propagation Training

Training neural networks requires the optimization of weight values so that the network predicts the correct output for a set of training examples. We repeatedly feed the input from the training examples into the network, compare the computed output of the network with the correct output from the training example, and update the weights. Typically, several

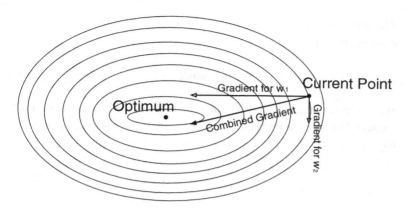

Figure 5.5 Gradient descent training. We compute the gradient in regard to every dimension. In this case the gradient with respect to weight w_2 is smaller than the gradient with respect to the weight w_1, so we move more to the left than down (note: arrows point in negative gradient direction, pointing to the minimum).

passes over the training data are carried out. Each pass over the data is called an **epoch**.

epoch

The most common training method for neural networks is called **back-propagation**, since it first updates the weights to the output layer and propagates back error information to earlier layers. Whenever a training example is processed, an error term is computed for each node in the network, which is the basis for updating the values for incoming weights.

back-propagation

The formulas used to compute updated values for weights follows principles of **gradient descent** training. The error for a specific node is understood as a function of the incoming weights. To reduce the error given this function, we compute the gradient of the error function with respect to each of the weights and move against the gradient to reduce the error.

gradient descent

Why is moving alongside the gradient a good idea? Consider that we optimize multiple dimensions at the same time. If you are looking for the lowest point in an area (maybe you are looking for water in a desert), and the ground falls off steep to the west of you and also slightly south of you, then you would go in a direction that is mainly west and only slightly south. In other words, you go alongside the gradient (Figure 5.5).

In the following two sections, I derive the formulas for updating weights for the example network. If you are less interested in the *why* and more in the *how*, you can skip these sections and continue reading when I summarize the update formulas in Section 5.5.3.

5.5.1 Weights to the Output Nodes

Let us first review and extend our notation. At an output node y_i, we first compute a linear combination of weight and hidden node values:

$$s_i = \sum_j w_{i \leftarrow j} h_j. \qquad (5.7)$$

The sum s_i is passed through an activation function such as sigmoid to compute the output value y:

$$y_i = \text{sigmoid}(s_i). \tag{5.8}$$

We compare the computed output values y_i against the target output values t_i from the training example. There are various ways to compute an error value E from these values. Let us use the L2 norm:

$$E = \sum_i \frac{1}{2}(t_i - y_i)^2. \tag{5.9}$$

As stated earlier, our goal is to compute the gradient of the error E with respect to the weights $w_{i \leftarrow j}$ to find out in which direction (and how strongly) we should move the weight value. We do this for each weight $w_{i \leftarrow j}$ separately. We first break up the computation of the gradient into three steps, essentially unfolding Equations 5.7 to 5.9:

$$\frac{\partial E}{\partial w_{i \leftarrow j}} = \frac{\partial E}{\partial y_i} \frac{\partial y_i}{\partial s_i} \frac{\partial s_i}{\partial w_{i \leftarrow j}}. \tag{5.10}$$

Let us now work through each of these three steps.

- Since we defined the error E in terms of the output values y_i, we can compute the first component as follows:

$$\frac{\partial E}{\partial y_i} = \frac{\partial}{\partial y_i} \frac{1}{2}(t_i - y_i)^2 = -(t_i - y_i). \tag{5.11}$$

- The derivative of the output value y_i with respect to s_i (the linear combination of weight and hidden node values) depends on the activation function. In the case of sigmoid, we have:

$$\frac{\partial y_i}{\partial s_i} = \frac{\partial \text{ sigmoid}(s_i)}{\partial s_i} = \text{sigmoid}(s_i)(1 - \text{sigmoid}(s_i)) = y_i(1 - y_i). \tag{5.12}$$

To keep our treatment below as general as possible and not commit to the sigmoid as an activation function, we will use the shorthand y_i' for $\frac{\partial y_i}{\partial s_i}$ below. Note that for any given training example and any given differentiable activation function, this value can always be computed.

- Finally, we compute the derivative of s_i with respect to the weight $w_{i \leftarrow j}$, which turns out to be quite simply the value of the hidden node h_j:

$$\frac{\partial s}{\partial w_{i \leftarrow j}} = \frac{\partial}{\partial w_{i \leftarrow j}} \sum_j w_{i \leftarrow j} h_j = h_j. \tag{5.13}$$

Where are we? In Equations 5.11 to 5.13, we computed the three steps needed to compute the gradient for the error function given the unfolding laid out in Equation 5.10. Putting it all together, we have

$$\frac{\partial E}{\partial w_{i \leftarrow j}} = \frac{\partial E}{\partial y_i} \frac{\partial y_i}{\partial s_i} \frac{\partial s}{\partial w_{i \leftarrow j}} \quad (5.14)$$
$$= -(t_i - y_i) \; y_i' \; h_j.$$

Factoring in a **learning rate** μ gives us the following update formula   learning rate
for weight $w_{i \leftarrow j}$. Note that we also remove the minus sign, since we move against the gradient toward the minimum:

$$\Delta w_{i \leftarrow j} = \mu (t_i - y_i) \; y_i' \; h_j.$$

It is useful to introduce the concept of an **error term** δ_i. Note that   error – term
this term is associated with a node, while the weight updates concern weights. The error term has to be computed only once for the node, and it can be then used for each of the incoming weights:

$$\delta_i = (t_i - y_i) \; y_i'. \quad (5.15)$$

This reduces the update formula to:

$$\Delta w_{i \leftarrow j} = \mu \; \delta_i \; h_j. \quad (5.16)$$

5.5.2 Weights to the Hidden Nodes

The computation of the gradient and hence the update formula for hidden nodes is quite analogous. As before, we first define the linear combination z_j (previously s_i) of input values x_k (previously hidden values h_j) weighted by weights $u_{j \leftarrow k}$ (previously weights $w_{i \leftarrow j}$):

$$z_j = \sum_k u_{j \leftarrow k} x_k. \quad (5.17)$$

This leads to the computation of the value of the hidden node h_j:

$$h_j = \text{sigmoid}(z_j). \quad (5.18)$$

Following the principles of gradient descent, we need to compute the derivative of the error E with respect to the weights $u_{j \leftarrow k}$. We decompose this derivative as before:

$$\frac{\partial E}{\partial u_{j \leftarrow k}} = \frac{\partial E}{\partial h_j} \frac{\partial h_j}{\partial z_j} \frac{\partial z_j}{\partial u_{j \leftarrow k}}. \quad (5.19)$$

The computation of $\frac{\partial E}{\partial h_j}$ is more complex than in the case of output nodes, since the error is defined in terms of output values y_i, not values for hidden nodes h_j. The idea behind back-propagation is to track how the error caused by the hidden node contributed to the error in the next layer. Applying the chain rule gives us:

$$\frac{\partial E}{\partial h_j} = \sum_i \frac{\partial E}{\partial y_i} \frac{\partial y_i}{\partial s_i} \frac{\partial s_i}{\partial h_j}. \tag{5.20}$$

We have already encountered the first two terms, $\frac{\partial E}{\partial y_i}$ (Equation 5.11) and $\frac{\partial y_i}{\partial s_i}$ (Equation 5.12). To recap:

$$\begin{aligned}
\frac{\partial E}{\partial y_i} \frac{\partial y_i}{\partial s_i} &= \frac{\partial}{\partial y_i} \sum_{i'} \frac{1}{2} (t_i - y_{i'})^2 \; y_i' \\
&= \frac{\partial}{\partial y_i} \frac{1}{2} (t_i - y_i)^2 \; y_i' \\
&= -(t_i - y_i) \; y_i' \\
&= \delta_i.
\end{aligned} \tag{5.21}$$

The third term in Equation 5.20 is computed straightforwardly:

$$\frac{\partial s_i}{\partial h_j} = \frac{\partial}{\partial h_j} \sum_i w_{i\leftarrow j} h_j = w_{i\leftarrow j}. \tag{5.22}$$

Putting Equation 5.21 and Equation 5.22 together, Equation 5.20 can be solved as:

$$\frac{\partial E}{\partial h_j} = \sum_i \delta_i w_{i\leftarrow j}. \tag{5.23}$$

This gives rise to a quite intuitive interpretation. The error that matters at the hidden node h_j depends on the error terms δ_i in the subsequent nodes y_i, weighted by $w_{i\leftarrow j}$, i.e., the impact the hidden node h_j has on the output node y_i.

Let us tie up the remaining loose ends. The missing pieces from Equation 5.19 are the second term:

$$\begin{aligned}
\frac{\partial h_j}{\partial z_j} &= \frac{\partial \; \text{sigmoid}(z_j)}{\partial z_j} \\
&= \text{sigmoid}(z_j)(1 - \text{sigmoid}(z_j)) = h_j(1 - h_j) = h_j',
\end{aligned} \tag{5.24}$$

and third term:

$$\frac{\partial z_j}{\partial u_{j\leftarrow k}} = \frac{\partial}{\partial u_{j\leftarrow k}} \sum_k u_{j\leftarrow k} x_k = x_k. \tag{5.25}$$

Putting Equation 5.23, Equation 5.24, and Equation 5.25 together gives us the following gradient:

$$\frac{\partial E}{\partial u_{j \leftarrow k}} = \frac{\partial E}{\partial h_j} \frac{\partial h_j}{\partial z_j} \frac{\partial z_j}{\partial u_{j \leftarrow k}}$$
$$= \sum_i \left(\delta_i w_{i \leftarrow j} \right) \, h_j' \, x_k. \tag{5.26}$$

If we define an error term δ_j for hidden nodes analogous to output nodes:

$$\delta_j = \sum_i \left(\delta_i w_{i \leftarrow j} \right) \, h_j'. \tag{5.27}$$

then we have an analogous update formula:

$$\Delta u_{j \leftarrow k} = \mu \, \delta_j \, x_k. \tag{5.28}$$

5.5.3 Summary

We train neural networks by processing training examples, one at a time and update weights each time. What drives weight updates is the gradient toward a smaller error. Weight updates are computed based on error terms δ_i associated with each non-input node in the network.

For output nodes, the error term δ_i is computed from the actual output y_i of the node for our current network and the target output t_i for the node:

$$\delta_i = (t_i - y_i) \, y_i'. \tag{5.29}$$

For hidden nodes, the error term δ_j is computed via back-propagating the error term δ_i from subsequent nodes connected by weights $w_{i \leftarrow j}$:

$$\delta_j = \sum_i \left(\delta_i w_{i \leftarrow j} \right) \, h_j'. \tag{5.30}$$

Computing y_i' and h_j' requires the derivative of the activation function, to which the weighted sum of incoming values is passed.

Given the error terms, weights $w_{i \leftarrow j}$ (or $u_{j \leftarrow k}$) from each proceeding node h_j (or x_k) are updated, tempered by a learning rate μ:

$$\Delta w_{i \leftarrow j} = \mu \, \delta_i \, h_j$$
$$\Delta u_{j \leftarrow k} = \mu \, \delta_j \, x_k. \tag{5.31}$$

Once weights are updated, the next training example is processed. There are typically several passes over the training set, called epochs.

5.5.4 Example

Given the neural network in Figure 5.4, let us see how the training example $(1,0) \rightarrow 1$ is processed.

Let us start with the calculation of the error term δ for the output node y_0. During inference (recall Table 5.1), we computed the linear combination of weighted hidden node values $s_0 = 1.060$ and the node value $y_0 = 0.743$. The target value is $t_0 = 1$:

$$\delta = (t_0 - y_0)\, y_0' = (1 - 0.743) \times \text{sigmoid}'(1.060)$$
$$= 0.257 \times 0.191 = 0.049. \tag{5.32}$$

With this number, we can compute weight updates, such as for weight $w_{0 \leftarrow 0}$:

$$\Delta w_{0 \leftarrow 0} = \mu\, \delta_0\, h_0 = \mu \times 0.049 \times 0.731 = \mu \times 0.036. \tag{5.33}$$

Since the hidden node h_0 leads only to one output node y_0, the calculation of its error term δ_0 is not more computationally complex:

$$\delta_j = \sum_i (\delta_i u_{i \leftarrow 0})\, h_0' = (\delta \times w_{0 \leftarrow 0}) \times \text{sigmoid}'(z_0)$$
$$= 0.049 \times 5 \times 0.197 = 0.049. \tag{5.34}$$

Table 5.2 summarizes the updates for all weights.

Table 5.2 Weight Updates (with Unspecified Learning Rate μ) for the Neural Network Shown in Figure 5.4 (Reprinted Here) for the Training Example $(1,0) \rightarrow 1$.

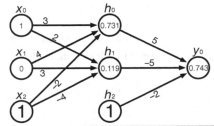

Node	Error Term	Weight Updates
	$\delta = (t_0 - y_0)\,\text{sigmoid}'(s_0)$	$\Delta w_{0 \leftarrow j} = \mu\, \delta\, h_j$
y_0	$\delta = (1 - 0.743) \times 0.191 = 0.049$	$\Delta w_{0 \leftarrow 0} = \mu \times 0.049 \times 0.731 = 0.036$
		$\Delta w_{0 \leftarrow 1} = \mu \times 0.049 \times 0.119 = 0.006$
		$\Delta w_{0 \leftarrow 2} = \mu \times 0.049 \times 1 = 0.049$
	$\delta_j = \delta\, w_{i \leftarrow j}\, \text{sigmoid}'(z_j)$	$\Delta u_{j \leftarrow i} = \mu\, \delta_j\, x_i$
h_0	$\delta_0 = 0.049 \times 5 \times 0.197 = 0.048$	$\Delta u_{0 \leftarrow 0} = \mu \times 0.048 \times 1 = 0.048$
		$\Delta u_{0 \leftarrow 1} = \mu \times 0.048 \times 0 = 0$
		$\Delta u_{0 \leftarrow 2} = \mu \times 0.048 \times 1 = 0.048$
h_1	$\delta_1 = 0.049 \times -5 \times 0.105 = -0.026$	$\Delta u_{1 \leftarrow 0} = \mu \times -0.026 \times 1 = -0.026$
		$\Delta u_{1 \leftarrow 1} = \mu \times -0.026 \times 0 = 0$
		$\Delta u_{1 \leftarrow 2} = \mu \times -0.026 \times 1 = -0.026$

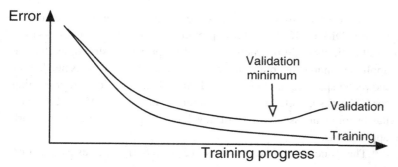

Error

Validation
minimum

Validation

Training

Training progress

Figure 5.6 Training progress over time. The error on the training set continuously decreases. However, on a validation set (not used for training), at some point the error increases. Training is stopped at the validation minimum before such overfitting sets in.

5.5.5 Validation Set

Neural network training proceeds for several epochs, i.e., full iterations over the training data. When to stop? When we track training progress, we see that the error on the training set continuously decreases. However, at some point **overfitting** sets in, where the training data are memorized and not sufficiently generalized.

overfitting

We can check this with an additional set of examples, called the **validation set**, that is not used during training (Figure 5.6). When we measure the error on the validation set at each point of training, we see that at some point this error increases. Hence we stop training when the minimum on the validation set is reached.

validation set

5.6 Exploiting Parallel Processing

5.6.1 Vector and Matrix Operations

We can express the calculations needed for handling neural networks as vector and matrix operations.

vector
matrix

- Forward computation: $\vec{s} = W \vec{h}$.
- Activation function: $\vec{y} = \text{sigmoid}(\vec{s})$.
- Error term: $\vec{\delta} = (\vec{t} - \vec{y})\,\text{sigmoid}'(\vec{z})$.
- Propagation of error term: $\vec{\delta}_i = W^T \vec{\delta}_{i+1} \cdot \text{sigmoid}'(\vec{z}_i)$.
- Weight updates: $\Delta W = \mu\, \vec{\delta}\, \vec{h}$.

Executing these operations is computationally expensive. If our layers have, say, 200 nodes, then the matrix operation $W\vec{h}$ requires $200 \times 200 = 40,000$ multiplications. Such matrix operations are also common in another highly used area of computer science: graphics processing. When rendering images on the screen, the geometric properties of 3-dimensional objects have to be processed to generate the color values of the 2-dimensional image on the screen. Since there is high demand for fast graphics processing—for instance for the use in realistic-looking computer games—specialized hardware has become common-place: **graphics processing units (GPUs)**.

GPU
graphics processing unit

These processors have a massive number of cores (for example, the NVIDIA GTX 1080ti GPU provides 3,584 thread processors) but a rather lightweight instruction set. GPUs provide instructions that are applied to many data points at once, which is exactly what is needed for the vector space computations listed earlier in this section. Programming for GPUs is supported by various libraries, such as CUDA for C++, and has become an essential part of developing large-scale neural network applications.

tensor   The general term for scalars, vectors, and matrices is **tensors**. A tensor may also have more dimensions: a sequence of matrices can be packed into a 3-dimensional tensor. Such large objects are actually frequently used in today's neural network tool kits.

5.6.2 Mini Batches

Each training example yields a set of weight updates Δw_i. We may first process all the training examples and only afterward apply all the updates. But neural networks have the advantage that they can immediately learn from each training example. A training method that updates

online learning   the model with each training example is called **online learning**. The online learning variant of gradient descent training is called **stochastic**

stochastic gradient descent   **gradient descent**.

Online learning generally takes fewer passes over the training set (called **epochs**) for convergence. However, since training constantly changes the weights, it is hard to parallelize. So, instead, we may want to process the training data in batches, accumulate the weight updates, and then apply them collectively. These smaller sets of training examples are

mini batch   called **mini batches** to distinguish this approach from **batch training**
batch training   where the entire training set is considered one batch.

There are other variations for organizing the processing of the training set, typically motivated by restrictions of parallel processing. If we process the training data in mini batches, then we can parallelize the computation of weight update values Δw, but have to synchronize their summation and application to the weights.

Hogwild   Finally, a scheme called **Hogwild** runs several training threads that immediately update weights, even though other threads still use the weight values to compute gradients. While this clearly violates the safeguards typically taken in parallel programming, it does not hurt in practical experience.

5.7 Hands On: Neural Networks in Python

There are many tool kits that support implementation of neural networks, often based on Python, currently the most popular scripting language.

In the following chapters, I will go over how to implement neural machine translation models. You can type the following commands in the interactive Python interpreter and inspect what they compute.

5.7.1 Data Structures and Functions in Numpy

Let us start with the inference and training I described in this chapter. For now, we do not use any dedicated neural network tool kit. However, we do the advanced math library **numpy**, which supports computation with vectors, matrices, and other tensors.

```
import math
import numpy as np
```

In computer science, the typical data structure to represent vectors, matrices, and higher-order tensors is an array. Numpy has its own array data structures for which it defines basic tensor operations such as addition and multiplication.

Here is how we represent the parameters for our example feed-forward neural network, which computes XOR, i.e., the weight matrices W and W_2 and the bias vectors b and b_2.

```
W  = np.array([[3,4],[2,3]])
b  = np.array([-2,-4])
W2 = np.array([5,-5])
b2 = np.array([-2])
```

The sigmoid that we use as activation function is not already provided by Numpy, so we need to define it ourselves. The function operates element-wise on vectors, so we need to signal this to numpy with @np.vectorize. We define the sigmoid function $\text{sigmoid}(x) = \frac{1}{1+e^{-x}}$ and its derivative sigmoid'(x).

```
@np.vectorize
def sigmoid(x):
    return 1 / (1 + math.exp(-x))

@np.vectorize
def sigmoid_derivative(x):
    return sigmoid(x) * ( 1 - sigmoid(x) )
```

The input and output pair from our example was $(1,0) \rightarrow 1$. So, we need to define these as well as vectors, thus as numpy arrays.

```
x = np.array([1,0])
t = np.array([1])
```

5.7.2 Forward Computation

Now, we have all the pieces in place to carry out inference in our neural network. Using matrix and vector representations the computation from the input to the hidden layer is

$$s = Wx + b$$
$$h = \text{sigmoid}(s).$$

(5.35)

The computation from the hidden layer to the output layer is

$$z = W_2 h + b_2$$
$$y = \text{sigmoid}(z).$$

(5.36)

Numpy makes it very easy to translate this into Python code. For the multiplication of a weight matrix with a vector, we need the dot product. Note that the default multiplication (*) is performed element-wise.

```
s = W.dot(x) + b
h = sigmoid( s )

z = W2.dot(h) + b2
y = sigmoid( z )
```

You can check the value of the computed output.

```
>>> y
array([0.7425526])
```

Now is also a good time to inspect the computed intermediate values, such as the hidden layer. The numbers should match what we showed in this chapter's tables.

5.7.3 Backward Computation

The next step is training via back-propagation. Recall that we start with the computed error and compute gradients of the weights with respect to the error. These gradients are then scaled with a learning rate and used to update parameters.

So, first we need to compute the error between the computed output y and the target value t. We used the L2 norm for this, i.e., $E = \frac{1}{2}(t-y)^2$.

```
error = 1/2 * (t - y)**2
```

We also need to set the learning rate μ. This is typically a small number like 0.001 but here we just use 1.

```
mu = 1
```

We went over quite a bit of math to derive formulas for the gradients $\frac{\partial E}{\partial W}$, $\frac{\partial E}{\partial b}$, $\frac{\partial E}{\partial W_2}$, and $\frac{\partial E}{\partial b_2}$. Our update formulas simplified this a bit by first computing an error terms δ_2 and δ_1 and then using them for the weight updates.

For the updates of parameters between the hidden layer and the final layer, our formulas first compute δ_2, and then the weight updates for W_2 and b_2 are

$$\delta_2 = (t - y) \, \text{sigmoid'}(z)$$
$$\Delta W_2 = \mu \, \delta_2 \, h \tag{5.37}$$
$$\Delta b_2 = \mu \, \delta_2.$$

Each equation can be formulated as one line in Python.

```
delta_2 = ( t - y ) * sigmoid_derivative( z )
delta_W2 = mu * delta_2 * h
delta_b2 = mu * delta_2
```

The update formulas for the parameters connecting the input layer to the hidden layer are quite similar, partly due to our introduction of the concept of an error term δ. The value for the this error term δ_1 for first layer is computed partly based on the value for the error term δ_2 for the second layer. This is back-propagation of the error in action:

$$\delta_1 = W \, \delta_2 \cdot \text{sigmoid'}(s)$$
$$\Delta W = \mu \, \delta_1 \, h \tag{5.38}$$
$$\Delta b = \mu \, \delta_1.$$

Also, the Python code is quite similar.

```
delta_1 = delta_2 * W2 * sigmoid_derivative( s )
delta_W = mu * np.array([ delta_1 ]).T * x
delta_b = mu * delta_1
```

5.7.4 Repeated Use of the Chain Rule

Let us take another view at the backward pass, which will also serve as a segue to the next chapter. You may have already forgotten how we derived at the formulas for the weight updates, and your head may be hurting from the flashbacks to high school math.

However, it is actually simpler than you may believe. To derive weight updates through back-propagation, we rely heavily on the chain rule. Viewed from a high level, we have a computation chain, which is a sequence of function applications, such as matrix multiplication and activation functions.

Consider the part of the calculation that connects the target output vector t, hidden vector h, the weight matrix W_2, and the bias term b_2 to the error E:

$$E = \text{L2}(\text{sigmoid}(W_2 h + b_2), t). \tag{5.39}$$

Consider the computation chain from the parameter matrix W_2 to E. We first have a matrix multiplication, then a vector addition, then the sigmoid and finally the L2 norm. To compute $\frac{\partial E}{\partial W_2}$, we treat the other values (t, b_2, h) as constants. Abstractly, we have a computation of the form $y = f(g(h(i(x))))$, with the weight matrix W_2 as input value x and the error E as output value y.

To obtain the derivative, our go-to rule here is the chain rule. Let us play this through for the simpler example of just two chained functions $f(g(x))$:

$$\begin{aligned} F(x) &= f(g(x)) \\ F'(x) &= f'(g(x))\, g'(x). \end{aligned} \tag{5.40}$$

Using different notation to clarify what we take the derivative over:

$$\frac{\partial}{\partial x} f(g(x)) = \frac{\partial}{\partial g(x)} f(g(x)) \frac{\partial}{\partial x} g(x). \tag{5.41}$$

Let us be explicit about the intermediate variable $g(x)$ by naming it a:

$$\begin{aligned} a &= g(x) \\ \frac{\partial}{\partial x} f(g(x)) &= \frac{\partial}{\partial a} f(a) \frac{\partial}{\partial x} a. \end{aligned} \tag{5.42}$$

So, we need to compute the derivatives of the elementary functions f and g with respect to their inputs. We also need the values computed in the forward computation since we will plug them into these derivatives.

Let us now work through the computation chain, starting from the end. The last computation is the computation of the error:

$$E(y) = \frac{1}{2}(t - y)^2$$
$$\frac{\partial}{\partial y}E(y) = t - y.$$

(5.43)

Let us do this in Python.

```
d_error_d_y = t - y
```

Continue on to the next step backward, the sigmoid activation function. It processed the intermediate value z. Since we are trying to compute gradients backward, we are still interested in the derivative of the error with respect to this value. So, this is where we now deploy the chain rule. Refer to Equation 5.42 with the substitutions $y \rightarrow a$, $z \rightarrow x$, sigmoid $\rightarrow g$, and $E \rightarrow f$ in mind:

$$y = \text{sigmoid}(z)$$
$$\frac{\partial}{\partial z}y = \text{sigmoid}'(z)$$
$$\frac{\partial}{\partial z}E(\text{sigmoid}(z)) = \frac{\partial}{\partial y}E(y)\frac{\partial}{\partial z}y.$$

(5.44)

We already computed $\frac{\partial}{\partial y}E(y)$ in the previous step. So, we reuse that and multiply it with the derivative of the sigmoid, applied to the input value z at this step.

This is how it looks in Python.

```
d_y_d_z = sigmoid_derivative( z )
d_error_d_z = d_error_d_y * d_y_d_z
```

Let us take a closer look at one more step to get a good feeling for how the gradient computation progresses backward through the computation chain. The computation that computes z is $W_2 h + b_2$. Here we are interested in several gradients. One each for the parameters W_2 and b_2 to apply weight updates and one for the hidden layer values h to proceed with the backward computation.

Let us look at just the derivatives for W_2:

$$z = W_2 h + b_2$$

$$\frac{\partial}{\partial W_2} z = h \tag{5.45}$$

$$\frac{\partial}{\partial W_2} E(\text{sigmoid}(z)) = \frac{\partial}{\partial z} E(\text{sigmoid}(z)) \frac{\partial}{\partial W_2} z.$$

Again, we already computed $\frac{\partial}{\partial z} E(\text{sigmoid}(z))$ in the previous step, so we can reuse it here.

```
d_z_d_W2 = h
d_error_d_W2 = d_error_d_z * d_z_d_W2
```

The gradient d_error_d_W2 that we computed at this point matches delta_W2 (see the previous section) since the learning rate μ is 1. We can check this by comparing the computed values by our code.

```
>>> d_error_d_W2
array([0.03597961, 0.00586666])
>>> delta_W2
array([0.03597961, 0.00586666])
```

The computations for the other gradients for the forward step $z = W_2 h + b_2$ follow the same logic.

```
d_z_d_b2 = 1
d_error_d_b2 = d_error_d_z * d_z_d_b2

d_z_d_h = W2
d_error_d_h = d_error_d_z * d_z_d_h
```

The computations for the layer connecting the input x to the hidden values h matches closely with what we just presented in detail.

```
d_s_d_h = sigmoid_derivative( s )
d_error_d_s = d_error_d_h * d_s_d_h

d_W_d_s = x
d_error_d_W = np.array([ d_error_d_s ]).T *
d_W_d_s

d_b_d_s = 1
d_error_d_b = d_error_d_s * d_b_d_s
```

Further Readings

A good introduction to modern neural network research is the textbook *Deep Learning* (Goodfellow et al., 2016). There is also a book on neural network methods applied to the natural language processing in general (Goldberg, 2017).

Chapter 6

Computation Graphs

For our example neural network from Section 5.5, we painstakingly worked out derivates for gradient computations needed by gradient descent training. After all this hard work, it may come as surprise that you will likely never have to do this again. It can be done automatically, even for arbitrarily complex neural network architectures. There are a number of tool kits that allow you to define the network, and it will take care of the rest. In this section, we will take a close look at how this works.

6.1 Neural Networks as Computation Graphs

First, we will take a different look at the networks we are building. We previously represented neural networks as graphs consisting of nodes and their connections (recall Figure 5.4), or by mathematical equations such as

$$h = \text{sigmoid}(W_1 x + b_1)$$
$$y = \text{sigmoid}(W_2 h + b_2).$$

(6.1)

These equations describe the feed-forward neural network that we use as our running example. We now represent this math in form of a **computation graph**. Figure 6.1 shows the computation graph for our network. The graph contains as nodes the parameters of the models (the weight matrices W_1, W_2 and bias vectors b_1, b_2), the input x, and the mathematical operations that are carried out between them (product, sum, and sigmoid). Next to each parameter, we show their values.

Figure 6.1 Two-layer
feed-forward neural network
as a computation graph,
consisting of the input value
x; weight parameters W_1,
W_2, b_1, b_2; and computation
nodes (product, sum,
sigmoid). To the right of each
parameter node, its value is
shown. To the left of input
and computation nodes, how
the input $(1,0)^T$ is processed
by the graph is shown.

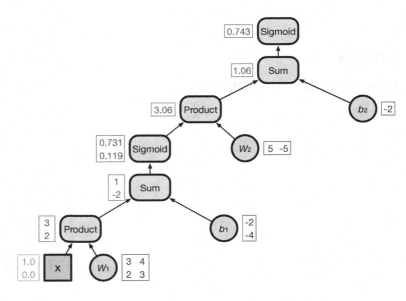

Neural networks, viewed as computation graphs, are any arbitrary
connected operations between an input and any number of parameters.
Some of these operations may have little to do with any inspiration from
neurons in the brain, so we are stretching the term *neural networks* quite
a bit here. The graph does not have to have a nice tree structure as in our
acyclical directed graph   example, but may be any **acyclical directed graph**, i.e., anything goes
as long there is a straightforward processing direction and no cycles.
Another way to view such a graph is as a fancy way to visualize a
sequence of function calls that take as arguments the input, parameters,
previously computed values, or any combination thereof, but have no
recursion or loops.

Processing an input with the neural network requires placing the
input value into the node x and carrying out the computations. In the
figure, we show this with the input vector $(1,0)^T$. The resulting numbers
should look familiar since they are the same as when previously worked
through this example in Section 5.4.

Before we move on, let us take stock of what each **computation**
computation node   **node** in the graph has to accomplish. It consists of the following:

- a function that executes its computation operation,
- links to input nodes,
- when processing an example, the computed value.

We will add two more items to each node in the following section.

6.2 Gradient Computations

So far, we showed how the computation graph can be used to process an input value. Now we will examine how it can be used to vastly simplify model training. Model training requires an error function and the computation of gradients to derive update rules for parameters.

The first of these is quite straightforward. To compute the error, we need to add another computation at the end of the computation graph. This computation takes the computed output value y and the given correct output value t from the training data and produces an error value. A typical error function is the L2 norm $\frac{1}{2}(t-y)^2$. From the view of training, the result of the execution of the computation graph is an error value.

Now, for the more difficult part—devising update rules for the parameters. Looking at the computation graph, model updates originate from the error values and propagate back to the model parameter. Hence we also call the computations needed to compute the update values the **backward pass** through the graph, opposed to the **forward pass** that computed output and error.

Consider the chain of operations that connect the weight matrix W_2 to the error computation:

gradient computation

Calculus Refresher

In calculus, the **chain rule** is a formula for computing the derivative of the composition of two or more functions. That is, if f and g are functions, then the chain rule expresses the derivative of their composition $f \circ g$ (the function that maps x to $f(g(x))$) in terms of the derivatives of f and g and the product of functions as follows:

$$(f \circ g)' = (f' \circ g) \cdot g'.$$

This can be written more explicitly in terms of the variable. Let $F = f \circ g$, or equivalently, $F(x) = f(g(x))$ for all x. Then one can also write $F'(x) = f'(g(x))g'(x)$.

The chain rule may be written, in Leibniz's notation, in the following way. If a variable z depends on the variable y, which itself depends on the variable x, so that y and z are therefore dependent variables, then z, via the intermediate variable of y, depends on x as well. The chain rule then states,

$$\frac{\partial z}{\partial x} = \frac{\partial z}{\partial y} \cdot \frac{\partial y}{\partial x}.$$

The two versions of the chain rule are related, if $z = f(y)$ and $y = g(x)$, then

$$\frac{\partial z}{\partial x} = \frac{\partial z}{\partial y} \cdot \frac{\partial y}{\partial x} = f'(y)g'(x) = f'(g(x))g'(x).$$

(adapted from Wikipedia)

chain rule

backward pass

forward pass

$$e = \text{L2}(y, t)$$
$$y = \text{sigmoid}(s)$$
$$s = \text{sum}(p, b_2)$$
$$p = \text{product}(h, W_2),$$

(6.2)

where h are the values of the hidden layer nodes, resulting from earlier computations.

To compute the update rule for the parameter matrix W_2, we view the error as a function of these parameters and take the derivative with respect to them, in our case $\frac{\partial \text{L2}(W_2)}{\partial W_2}$. Recall that when we computed this derivate we first broke it up into steps using the chain rule. We now do the same here:

$$\frac{\partial \text{L2}(W_2)}{\partial W_2} = \frac{\partial \text{L2}(\text{sigmoid}(\text{sum}(\text{product}(h, W_2), b_2)), t)}{\partial W_2}$$

$$= \frac{\partial \text{L2}(y, t)}{\partial y} \frac{\partial \text{sigmoid}(s)}{\partial s} \frac{\partial \text{sum}(p, b_2)}{\partial p} \frac{\partial \text{product}(h, W_2)}{\partial W_2}.$$

(6.3)

Note that for the purpose of computing an update rule for W_2, we treat all the other variables in this computation (the target value t, the bias vector b_2, the hidden node values h) as constants. This breaks up the derivative of the error with respect to the parameters W_2 into a chain of derivatives along the line of the nodes of the computation graph.

Hence all we have to do for gradient computations is to come up with derivatives for each node in the computation graph. In our example these are

$$\frac{\partial \text{L2}(y, t)}{\partial y} = \frac{\partial \frac{1}{2}(t - y)^2}{\partial y} = t - y$$

$$\frac{\partial \text{sigmoid}(s)}{\partial s} = \text{sigmoid}(s)(1 - \text{sigmoid}(s))$$

$$\frac{\partial \text{sum}(p, b_2)}{\partial p} = \frac{\partial p + b_2}{\partial p} = 1$$

$$\frac{\partial \text{product}(h, W_2)}{\partial W_2} = \frac{\partial W_2 h}{\partial W_2} = h.$$

(6.4)

If we want to compute the gradient update for a parameter such as W_2, we compute values in a backward pass, starting from the error term y (Figure 6.2).

To give more detail on the computation of the gradients in the backward pass, starting at the bottom of the graph:

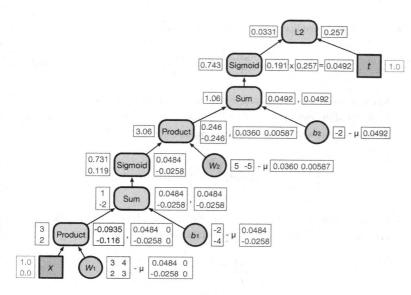

Figure 6.2 Computation graph with gradients computed in the backward pass for the training example $(0,1)^T \rightarrow 1.0$. Gradients are computed with respect to the input of the nodes, so some nodes that have two inputs also have two gradients. See text for details on the computations of the values.

- For the **L2** node, we use the formula   L2

$$\frac{\partial L2(y, t)}{\partial y} = \frac{\partial \frac{1}{2}(t - y)^2}{\partial y} = t - y. \tag{6.5}$$

The given target output value given as training data is $t = 1$, while we computed $y = 0.743$ in the forward pass. Hence the gradient for the L2 norm is $1 - 0.743 = 0.257$. Note that we are using values computed in the forward pass for these gradient computations.

- For the higher **sigmoid** node, we use the formula   sigmoid

$$\frac{\partial \text{sigmoid}(s)}{\partial s} = \text{sigmoid}(s)(1 - \text{sigmoid}(s)). \tag{6.6}$$

Recall that the formula for the sigmoid is $\text{sigmoid}(s) = \frac{1}{1 + e^{-s}}$. Plugging in the value for $s = 1.06$ computed in the forward pass into this formula gives us 0.191. The chain rule requires us to multiply this with the value that we just computed for the **L2** node, i.e., 0.257, which gives us $0.191 \times 0.257 = 0.0492$.

- For the higher **sum** node, we simply copy the previous value, since the derivate is 1:

$$\frac{\partial \text{sum}(p, b_2)}{\partial p} = \frac{\partial p + b_2}{\partial p} = 1. \tag{6.7}$$

Note that there are two gradients associated with the sum node. One with respect to the output of the **product** node and one with the b_2 parameter. In both cases, the derivative is 1, so both values are the same. Hence the gradient in both cases is 0.0492.

- For the higher **product** node, we use the formula

$$\frac{\partial \text{product}(h, W_2)}{\partial W_2} = \frac{\partial W_2 h}{\partial W_2} = h. \tag{6.8}$$

So far, we dealt with scalar values. Here we encounter vectors for the first time: the value of the hidden nodes $h = (0.731, 0.119)^T$. The chain rule requires us to multiply this with the previously computed scalar 0.0492:

$$\left(\begin{bmatrix} 0.731 \\ 0.119 \end{bmatrix} \times 0.0492 \right)^T = \begin{bmatrix} 0.0360 & 0.00587 \end{bmatrix}.$$

As for the sum node, there are two inputs and hence two gradients. The other gradient is with respect to the output of the lower **sigmoid** node:

$$\frac{\partial \text{product}(h, W_2)}{\partial h} = \frac{\partial W_2 h}{\partial h} = W_2. \tag{6.9}$$

Similarly to above, we compute

$$(W_2 \times 0.0492)^T = \left(\begin{bmatrix} 5 & -5 \end{bmatrix} \times 0.0492 \right)^T = \begin{bmatrix} 0.246 \\ -0.246 \end{bmatrix}.$$

Having all the gradients in place, we can now read of the relevant values for weight updates. These are the gradients associated with trainable parameters. For the W_2 weight matrix, this is the second gradient of the **product** node. So the new value for W_2 at time step $t + 1$ is

$$W_2^{t+1} = W_2^t - \mu \frac{\partial \text{product}(x, W_2^t)}{\partial W_2^t} = \begin{bmatrix} 5 & 5 \end{bmatrix} - \mu \begin{bmatrix} 0.0360 & 0.00587 \end{bmatrix}. \tag{6.10}$$

The remaining computations are carried out in very similar fashion, since they form simply another layer of the feed-forward neural network.

Our example did not include one special case: the output of a computation may be used multiple times in subsequent steps of a computation graph. So, there are multiple output nodes that feed back gradients in the back-propagation pass. In this case, we add up the gradients from these descendent steps to factor in their added impact.

Let us take a second look at what a node in a computation graph comprises:

- a function that computes its value,
- links to input nodes (to obtain argument values),
- when processing an example in the forward pass, the computed value,

- a function that executes its gradient computation,
- links to children nodes (to obtain downstream gradient values),
- when processing an example in the forward pass, the computed gradient.

From an object oriented programming view, a node in a computation graph provides a forward and backward function for value and gradient computations. As instantiated in an computation graph, it is connected with specific inputs and outputs and is also aware of the dimensions of its variables its value and gradient. During the forward and backward pass, these variables are filled in.

6.3 Hands On: Deep Learning Frameworks

In the next sections, we will encounter various network architectures. What all of these share, however, are the need for vector and matrix operations as well as the computation of derivatives to obtain weight update formulas. It would be quite tedious to write almost identical code to deal with each these variants. Hence a number of frameworks have emerged to support developing neural network methods for any chosen problem. At the time of writing, the most prominent ones are **PyTorch**,[1] **TensorFlow**,[2] **MXNet**,[3] and **DyNet**.[4] These libraries allow programming of neural networks in Python or other programming languages, while they hide the computation, including computation on GPUs.

deep learning framwork

Torch

Tensorflow

MX-Net

DyNet

6.3.1 Forward and Backward Computation in PyTorch

These frameworks are less geared toward ready-to-use neural network architectures, but provide efficient implementations of the vector space operations and computation of derivatives, with seamless support of GPUs. Our example from Chapter 5 can be implemented in a few lines of Python code, as shown in this section, using the example of PyTorch (other frameworks are quite similar).

You can execute the following commands on the Python command line interface if you first installed PyTorch (`pip install torch`).

```
import torch
```

[1] Pytorch, http://pytorch.org.
[2] TensorFlow, www.tensorflow.org.
[3] MXNet, http://mxnet.apache.org.
[4] DyNet, http://dynet.readthedocs.io.

PyTorch has its own data type for parameter vectors, matrices, and so on, called `torch.tensor`. Here is how we specify the parameters of our example neural network:

```
W = torch.tensor([[3,4],[2,3]], requires_grad=True,
    dtype=torch.float)
b = torch.tensor([-2,-4], requires_grad=True,
    dtype=torch.float)
W2 = torch.tensor([5,-5], requires_grad=True,
    dtype=torch.float)
b2 = torch.tensor([-2], requires_grad=True,
    dtype=torch.float)
```

The definition of these variables also includes the specification of their basic data type (`float`) and the indication that we are interested in computing gradients for them (`requires_grad=True`). More on that later.

To use our example neural network, we also need an input and output pair:

```
x = torch.tensor([1,0], dtype=torch.float)
t = torch.tensor([1], dtype=torch.float)
```

With the variables in place, it is straightforward to define the computation chain from input x to output y:

```
s = W.mv(x) + b
h = torch.nn.Sigmoid()(s)

z = torch.dot(W2, h) + b2
y = torch.nn.Sigmoid()(z)

error = 1/2 * (t - z) ** 2
```

As you can see, PyTorch has its own sigmoid function `torch.nn.Sigmoid()`, so we do not need to define it ourselves. The multiplications of tensors have different functions, depending on the type of tensors involved. The first multiplication is between the matrix W and the vector x, so the multiplication is named mv. Multiplication between two matrices is mm. The second multiplication is between two vectors W2 and h, and it is called `torch.dot`.

That was the forward computation, which looks very similar to what we did when we just used numpy in Section 5.7.2.

How about the backward computation? Here it is:

```
error.backward()
```

There is no need to derive gradients for each of the functions we use. All this is done automatically.

After running the backward pass, we can look them up for the variables for which we set `requires_grad`. For instance:

```
>>> W2.grad
tensor([-0.0360, -0.0059])
```

Note when playing with this: when you run this code multiple times, the gradients accummulate. You have to reset them with, e.g., `W2.grad.data.zero_()`.

6.3.2 Training Loop

During training, we present examples of input and output pairs to the model and update its parameters. This is typically done by two loops: one that loops through all given training examples. A completion of a pass through all training data is called an epoch. A second loop repeats such epochs for a certain number of times (typically 10 to 100 for neural machine translation) or until a convergence criteria is met (such as no improvements in model quality over the last iterations).

Figure 6.3 puts together the code snippets from the previous section and wraps them up in the loop over epochs and the loop over training examples. A lot of the code should look familiar.

Our training set consists of the four examples of binary XOR operations:

x	y	$x \oplus y$
0	0	0
0	1	1
1	0	1
1	1	0

We put them all into the array `training_data`. Each input and output is encoded as a PyTorch tensor. Note that we use the shorter notation to indicate their nature as floats by adding a period to each number instead of explicitly declaring the tensor as having the data type `torch.float`.

```
import torch
W = torch.tensor([[3,4],[2,3]], requires_grad=True, dtype=torch.float)
b = torch.tensor([-2,-4], requires_grad=True, dtype=torch.float)
W2 = torch.tensor([5,-5], requires_grad=True, dtype=torch.float)
b2 = torch.tensor([-2], requires_grad=True, dtype=torch.float)

training_data = [ [ torch.tensor([0.,0.]), torch.tensor([0.]) ],
                  [ torch.tensor([1.,0.]), torch.tensor([1.]) ],
                  [ torch.tensor([0.,1.]), torch.tensor([1.]) ],
                  [ torch.tensor([1.,1.]), torch.tensor([0.]) ] ]

mu = 0.1

for epoch in range(1000):
  total_error = 0

  for item in training_data:
    x = item[0]
    t = item[1]

    # forward computation
    s = W.mv(x) + b
    h = torch.nn.Sigmoid()(s)
    z = torch.dot(W2, h) + b2
    y = torch.nn.Sigmoid()(z)
    error = 1/2 * (t - y) ** 2
    total_error = total_error + error

    # backward computation
    error.backward()

    # weight updates
    W.data  = W  - mu * W.grad.data
    b.data  = b  - mu * b.grad.data
    W2.data = W2 - mu * W2.grad.data
    b2.data = b2 - mu * b2.grad.data

    W.grad.data.zero_()
    b.grad.data.zero_()
    W2.grad.data.zero_()
    b2.grad.data.zero_()

  print("error: ", total_error/4)
```

Figure 6.3 Basic implementation of training our example neural network over several epochs.

The code also tracks the mean error of the training examples over time. If you run the code, you will see that in the initial iteration an error of 0.0353 is reported, which is reduced in the final iteration to 0.0082. The changes are more pronounced at the beginning.

6.3.3 Batch Training

Note how we carry out the weight updates. We compute gradients for each training example and update the model immediately. A common strategy is to process training examples in batches and update the model only after all examples of a batch are processed.

You can change the code by moving everything after the comment `weight updates` out of the inner loop into the outer loop. It is easy like that since the gradients accumulate until they are explicitly zeroed out.

But there is also another way to implement batch updates. Instead of running back-propagation on each training example with

```
error.backward()
```

and letting the gradients accumulate, we can also run back-propagation on the accumulated error:

```
total_error.backward()
```

Since `total_error` adds up the computed `error` for all the training examples, this connects up all their computation graphs that end at `total_error`. However, all this does is concatenate all the individual computation graphs and runs the backward pass on each of them separately.

We can gain efficiencies by presenting a batch of examples to training at once:

```
x = torch.tensor([ [0.,0.], [1.,0.], [0.,1.], [1.,1.] ])
t = torch.tensor([ 0., 1., 1., 0. ])
```

The implementation of the forward pass has to be changed slightly, since the input is now a matrix (one dimension for the examples, one dimension for the values of each example). The hidden layer's values is also matrix for the same reason:

```
s = x.mm(W) + b
h = torch.nn.Sigmoid()(s)
z = h.mv(W2) + b2
y = torch.nn.Sigmoid()(z)
```

PyTorch has a handy function of taking the average of the individual error values computed for the training examples.

```
error = 1/2 * (t - y) ** 2
mean_error = error.mean()
mean_error.backward()
```

6.3.4 Optimizers

The code in Figure 6.3 is quite explicit and spells out in detail processing steps that are common to almost all neural network training scenarios. It makes sense to separate out at least four components: (1) the model, (2) the data, (3) the optimizer that defines how weights are changed, and (4) the training loop.

In PyTorch, a neural network model is defined as a class derived from `torch.nn.Module`. Here is how our example neural network is implemented in that fashion:

```
class ExampleNet(torch.nn.Module):

  def __init__(self):
    super(ExampleNet, self).__init__()
    self.layer1 = torch.nn.Linear(2,2)
    self.layer2 = torch.nn.Linear(2,1)
    self.layer1.weight = torch.nn.Parameter(torch.tensor([[3.,2.],[4.,3.]]))
    self.layer1.bias = torch.nn.Parameter(torch.tensor([-2.,-4.]))
    self.layer2.weight = torch.nn.Parameter(torch.tensor([[5.,-5.]]))
    self.layer2.bias = torch.nn.Parameter(torch.tensor([-2.]))

  def forward(self, x):
    s = self.layer1(x)
    h = torch.nn.Sigmoid()(s)
    z = self.layer2(h)
    y = torch.nn.Sigmoid()(z)
    return y
```

This code uses the built-in functionality of linear mappings that include a weight matrix and a bias vector. We provide here explicit values for them, although it is more common to randomly initialize them, which is done by default.

The forward computation is implemented in a function that is aptly called `forward`. It takes a batch of training examples and returns the computed value.

With the data structure in place, we can instantiate a neural network object and define the optimizer for it:

```
net = ExampleNet()
optimizer = torch.optim.SGD(net.parameters(), lr=0.1)
```

This uses stochastic gradient descent (SGD) for training, as we have done in our example so far. But using Adam or other update schemes, just requires the choice of a different optimizer here. The training loop illustrates how the optimizer is used:

```
for iteration in range(1000):
    optimizer.zero_grad()
    out = net.forward( x )
    error = 1/2 * (t - out) ** 2
    mean_error = error.mean()
    print("error: ",mean_error.data)
    mean_error.backward()
    optimizer.step()
```

Before processing training examples, gradients are set to zero (optimizer.zero_grad()). The forward pass is executed by calling the class function net.forward. The error is computed as before. After the backward pass, an optimizer step is triggered (optimizer.step()).

Chapter 7
Neural Language Models

Neural networks are a very powerful method for modeling conditional probability distributions with multiple inputs $p(d|a, b, c)$. They are robust to unseen data points—say, an unobserved (a,b,c,d) in the training data. Using traditional statistical estimation methods, we may address such a sparse data problem with back off and clustering, which require insight into the problem (what part of the conditioning context to drop first?) and arbitrary choices (how many clusters?).

N-gram language models reduce the probability of a sentence to the product of word probabilities in the context of a few previous words—say, $p(w_i|w_{i-4}, w_{i-3}, w_{i-2}, w_{i-1})$. Such models are a prime example for a conditional probability distribution with a rich conditioning context for which we often lack data points and would like to cluster information. In statistical language models, complex discounting and back-off schemes are used to balance rich evidence from lower-order models—say, the bigram model $p(w_i|w_{i-1})$—with the sparse estimates from high-order models. Now, we turn to neural networks for help.

7.1 Feed-Forward Neural Language Models

Figure 7.1 gives a basic sketch of a 5-gram neural network language model. Network nodes representing the context words have connections to a hidden layer, which connects to the output layer for the predicted word.

feed-forward neural network

Figure 7.1 Sketch of a
neural language model. We
predict a word W_i based on
its preceding words.

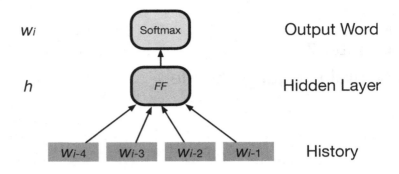

Figure 7.1 Sketch of a neural language model. We predict a word W_i based on its preceding words.

7.1.1 Representing Words

word representation

We are immediately faced with a difficult question: how do we represent words? Nodes in a neural network carry real-numbered values, but words are discrete items out of a very large vocabulary. We cannot simply use token IDs, since the neural network will assume that token 124,321 is very similar to token 124,322—while in practice these numbers are completely arbitrary. The same argument applies to the idea of using bit encoding for token IDs. The words $(1, 1, 1, 1, 0, 0, 0, 0)^T$ and $(1, 1, 1, 1, 0, 0, 0, 1)^T$ have very similar encodings but may have nothing to do with each other. While the idea of using such bit vectors is occasionally explored, it does not appear to have any benefits over what we consider next.

Instead, we will represent each word with a high-dimensional vector, one dimension per word in the vocabulary, and the value 1 for the dimension that matches the word, and 0 for the rest. The type of vectors **one hot vector** are called **one hot vector**. For instance:

- $dog = (0, 0, 0, 0, 1, 0, 0, 0, 0, \ldots)^T$,
- $cat = (0, 0, 0, 0, 0, 0, 0, 1, 0, \ldots)^T$,
- $eat = (0, 1, 0, 0, 0, 0, 0, 0, 0, \ldots)^T$.

These are very large vectors, and we will continue to wrestle with the impact of this choice to represent words. One stopgap is to limit the vocabulary to the most frequent, say, 20,000 words, and pool all the other words in an other token. We could also use word classes (either automatic clusters or linguistically motivated classes such as part-of-speech tags) to reduce the dimensionality of the vectors. We will revisit the problem of large vocabularies later.

To pool evidence between words, we introduce another layer between the input layer and the hidden layer. In this layer, each context word is individually projected into a lower-dimensional space. We use the same weight matrix for each of the context words, thus generating

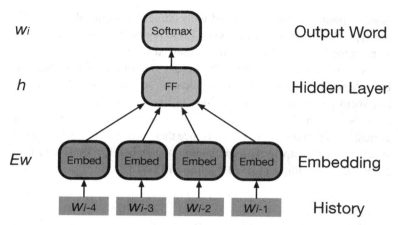

w_i

h

E_w

Figure 7.2 Full architecture of a feed-forward neural network language model. Context words $(w_{i-4}; w_{i-3}; w_{i-2}; w_{i-1})$ are represented in a one hot vector, then projected into continuous space as word embeddings (using the same weight matrix E for all words). The predicted word is computed as a one hot vector via a hidden layer.

a continuous space representation for each word, independent of its position in the conditioning context. This representation is commonly referred to as **word embedding**.

word embedding

Words that occur in similar contexts should have similar word embeddings. For instance, if the training data for a language model frequently contain the n-grams

- *but the cute dog jumped*
- *but the cute cat jumped*
- *child hugged the cat tightly*
- *child hugged the dog tightly*
- *like to watch cat videos*
- *like to watch dog videos*

then the language model would benefit from the knowledge that *dog* and *cat* occur in similar contexts and hence are somewhat interchangeable. If we would like to predict from a context where *dog* occurs but we have seen this context only with the word *cat*, then we would still like to treat this as positive evidence. Word embeddings enable generalizing between words (clustering) and hence having robust predictions in unseen contexts (back off).

7.1.2 Neural Network Architecture

neural network architecture

Figure 7.2 shows the architecture of the fully fledged feed-forward neural network language model, consisting of the context words as the one hot vector input layer, the word embedding layer, the hidden layer and predicted output word layer.

The context words are first encoded as one hot vectors. These are then passed through the embedding matrix E, resulting in a vector of floating point numbers, the word embedding. This embedding vector has typically on the order of 500 or 1,000 nodes. Note that we use the same embedding matrix E for all the context words.

Also note that mathematically there is not all that much going on here. Since the input to the multiplication to the matrix E is a one hot vector, most of the input values to the matrix multiplication are zeros. So, practically, we are selecting the one column in the matrix that corresponds to the input word ID. Hence there is no use for an activation function here. In a way, the embedding matrix is a lookup table $E(w_j)$ for word embeddings, indexed by the word ID w_j:

$$E(w_j) = E \, w_j. \tag{7.1}$$

Mapping to the hidden layer in the model requires concatenation of all context word embeddings $E(w_j)$ as input to a typical feed-forward layer, say, using tanh as activation function:

$$h = \tanh\left(b_h + \sum_j H_j E(w_j)\right). \tag{7.2}$$

The output layer is interpreted as a probability distribution over words. As before, first the linear combination s_i of weights w_{ij} and hidden node values h_j is computed for each node i:

$$s = W \, h. \tag{7.3}$$

To ensure that it is indeed a proper probability distribution, we use the **softmax** activation function to ensure that all values add up to one:

$$p_i = \text{softmax}(s_i, \vec{s}) = \frac{e^{s_i}}{\sum_j e^{s_j}}. \tag{7.4}$$

What we described here is close to the neural probabilistic language model proposed by Bengio et al. (2003). This model had one more twist, it added direct connections of the context word embeddings to the output word, adding in the word embeddings $E(w_j)$ for each word w_j after a linear transform with a weight matrix U_j. So, Equation 7.3 is replaced by

$$s = W \, h + \sum_j U_j \, E(w_j). \tag{7.5}$$

Their paper reports that having such **direct connections** from context words to output words speeds up training, although does not ultimately improve performance. We will encounter the idea of short-cutting hidden layers again a bit later when I discuss deeper models with more hidden layers. They are also called **residual connections**, **skip connections**, or even **highway connections**.

softmax (margin note beside equation 7.4 paragraph)

direct connection (margin note)

residual connection (margin note)
skip connection (margin note)
highway connection (margin note)

7.1.3 Training

We train the parameters of a neural language model (word embedding matrix, weight matrices, bias vectors) by processing all the n-grams in the training corpus. For each n-gram, we feed the context words into the network and match the network's output against the one hot vector of the correct word to be predicted. Weights are updated using back-propagation (I will go into details in the next section).

Language models are commonly evaluated by perplexity, which is related to the probability given to proper English text. A language model that likes proper English is a good language model. Hence the training objective for language models is to increase the likelihood of the training data.

During training, given a context $\mathbf{x} = (w_{n-4}, w_{n-3}, w_{n-2}, w_{n-1})$, we have the correct value for the 1 hot vector $\vec{y}$. For each training example $(\mathbf{x}, \vec{y})$, the training objective is defined based on negative log-likelihood as

$$L(\mathbf{x}, \vec{y}; W) = -\sum_{k} y_k \log p_k. \qquad (7.6)$$

Note that only one value y_k is 1, the others are 0. So this really comes down to the probability p_k given to the correct word k. Defining the training objective this way allows us to update all weights, including the one that lead to the wrong output words.

7.2 Word Embeddings

Before we move on, it is worth reflecting the role of word embeddings in neural machine translation and many other natural language processing tasks. We introduced them here as compact encoding of words in relatively high-dimensional space, say 500 or 1,000 floating point numbers. In the field of natural language processing, at the time of this writing, word embeddings have acquired the reputation of having an almost magical quality.

Consider the role they play in the neural language models just described. They represent context words to enable prediction the next word in a sequence.

Recall part of our earlier example:

- *but the cute dog jumped*
- *but the cute cat jumped*

Since *dog* and *cat* occur in similar contexts, their influence on predicting the word *jumped* should be similar. It should be different from words such as *dress*, which is unlikely to trigger the completion *jumped*.

The idea that words that occur in similar contexts are semantically similar is a powerful idea in lexical semantics.

At this point in the argument, researchers love to cite John Rupert Firth: "You shall know a word by the company it keeps." Or, as Ludwig Wittgenstein put it a bit more broadly: "The meaning of a word is its use."

Meaning and semantics are quite difficult concepts with largely unresolved definitions. The idea of **distributional lexical semantics** is to define words by their distributional properties, i.e., in which contexts they occur. Words that occur in similar contexts (*dog* and *cat*) should have similar representations. In vector space models, such as the word embeddings that we use here, similarity can be measured by a distance function, e.g., the cosine distance—the angle between the vectors.

distributional lexical semantics

If we project the high-dimensional word embeddings down to two dimensions, we can visualize word embeddings as shown in Figure 7.3. In this figure, words that are similar (*drama, theater, festival*) are clustered together.

But why stop there? We would like to have semantic representations so we can carry out semantic inference such as

- *queen = king + (woman – man)*
- *queens = queen + (kings – king)*

Figure 7.3 Word embeddings projected into two dimensions. Semantically similar words occur close to each other. (Illustration by James Le, used with permission).

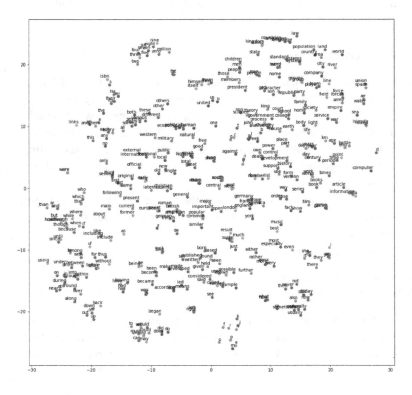

Indeed there is some evidence that word embedding allows just that (Mikolov et al., 2013d). However, we better stop here and just note that word embeddings are a crucial tool in neural machine translation.

7.3 Noise Contrastive Estimation

noise contrastive estimation

We discussed earlier the problem that computing probabilities with a neural language model is very expensive due to the need to normalize the output node values y_i using the softmax function. This requires computing values for all output nodes, even if we are interested only in the score for a particular n-gram. To overcome the need for this explicit normalization step, we would like to train a model that already has y_i values that are normalized.

One way is to include the constraint that the normalization factor $Z(x) = \sum_j e^{s_j}$ is close to 1 in the objective function. So, instead of the just the simple likelihood objective, we may include the L2 norm of the log of this factor. Note that if $\log Z(x) \simeq 0$, then $Z(x) \simeq 1$:

$$L(\mathbf{x}, \vec{y}; W) = -\sum_k y_k \log p_k - \alpha \log^2 Z(x). \qquad (7.7)$$

Another way to train a self-normalizing model is called noise contrastive estimation. The main idea is to optimize the model so that it can separate correct training examples from artificially created noise examples. This method needs less computation during training, since it does not require the computation of all output node values.

Formally, we are trying to learn the model distribution $p_m(\vec{y}|\mathbf{x}; W)$. Given a noise distribution $p_n(\vec{y}|\mathbf{x})$—in our case of language modeling a unigram model $p_n(\vec{y})$ is a good choice—we first generate a set of noise examples U_n in addition to the correct training examples U_t. If both sets have the same size $|U_n| = |U_t|$, then the probability that a given example $(\mathbf{x}; \vec{y}) \in U_n \cup U_t$ is predicted to be a correct training example is

$$p(\text{correct}|\mathbf{x}, \vec{y}) = \frac{p_m(\vec{y}|\mathbf{x}; W)}{p_m(\vec{y}|\mathbf{x}; W) + p_n(\vec{y}|\mathbf{x})}. \qquad (7.8)$$

The objective of noise contrastive estimation is to maximize $p(\text{correct}|\mathbf{x}, \vec{y})$ for correct training examples $(\mathbf{x}; \vec{y}) \in U_t$ and to minimize it for noise examples $(\mathbf{x}; \vec{y}) \in U_n$. Using log-likelihood, we define the objective function as

$$L = \frac{1}{2|U_t|} \sum_{(\mathbf{x}; \vec{y}) \in U_t} \log p(\text{correct}|\mathbf{x}, \vec{y})$$

$$+ \frac{1}{2|U_n|} \sum_{(\mathbf{x}; \vec{y}) \in U_n} \log (1 - p(\text{correct}|\mathbf{x}, \vec{y})). \qquad (7.9)$$

Returning the the original goal of a self-normalizing model, first note that the noise distribution $p_n(\vec{y}|\mathbf{x})$ is normalized. Hence the model distribution is encouraged to produce comparable values. If $p_m(\vec{y}|\mathbf{x}; W)$ would generally overshoot—i.e., $\sum_{\vec{y}} p_m(\vec{y}|\mathbf{x}; W) > 1$—then it would also give too high values for noise examples. Conversely, generally undershooting would give too low values to correct translation examples.

Training is faster, since we only need to compute the output node value for the given training and noise examples—there is no need to compute the other values, since we do not normalize with the softmax function.

Given the definition of the training objective L, we have now a complete computation graph that we can implement using standard deep learning tool kits, as we have done before. These tool kits compute the gradients $\frac{\partial L}{\partial W}$ for all parameters W and use them for parameter updates via gradient descent training (or its variants).

7.4 Recurrent Neural Language Models

recurrent neural language model The feed-forward neural language model described in this chapter is able to use longer contexts than traditional statistical back-off models, since it has more flexible means to deal with unknown contexts—namely, the use of word embeddings to make use of similar words, and the robust handling of unseen words in any context position. Hence it is possible to condition on much larger contexts than traditional statistical models. In fact, large models, say, 20-gram models, have been reported to be used.

Alternatively, instead of using a fixed context word window, **RNN** **recurrent neural networks** may condition on context sequences of **recurrent neural network** any length. The trick is to reuse the hidden layer that was used when predicting word w_n as an additional input to predicting word w_{n+1} (Figure 7.4).

Initially, the model does not look any different from the feed-forward neural language model that we have discussed so far. The inputs to the network is the first word of the sentence w_1 and a second set of neurons

Figure 7.4 Recurrent neural language models. After predicting Word 2 in the context of following Word 1, we reuse the hidden layer (alongside the correct Word 2) to predict Word 3. Again, the hidden layer of this prediction is reused for the prediction of Word 4.

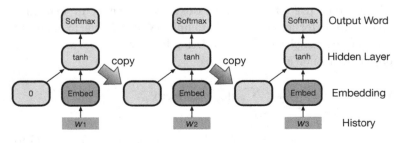

that, at this point, indicate the start of the sentence. The word embedding of w_1 and the start-of-sentence neurons first map into a hidden layer h_1, which is then used to predict the output word w_2.

This model uses the same architecture as before: words (input and output) are represented with one hot vectors; word embeddings and the hidden layer use, say, 500 real valued neurons. We use a tanh activation function at the hidden layer and the softmax function at the output layer.

Things get interesting when we move to predicting the third word w_3 in the sequence. One input is the directly preceding (and now known) word w_2, as before. However, the neurons in the network that we used to represent the start of the sentence are now filled with values from the hidden layer of the previous prediction of word w_2.

In the previous feed-forward architecture (Equation 7.2), on the path to predict the ith word, we computed the hidden state h_i from the word embeddings $E(w_{i-j})$ of the previous, say, three words. This uses a shared word embedding matrix E and a weight matrix H_j for each of the previous words, plus a bias term b_h:

$$h_i = \tanh\left(b_h + \sum_{1 \le j \le 3} H_j E(w_{i-j})\right). \qquad (7.10)$$

Now, we change this to a recursive definition, where we combine the single directly preceding word w_{i-1} with the previous hidden state h_{i-1}. We add a weight matrix V to parameterize the mapping from the previous hidden state h_{i-1}:

$$h_i = \tanh\left(b_h + HE(w_{i-1}) + Vh_{i-1}\right). \qquad (7.11)$$

In a way, the neurons in the hidden state h_{i-1} encode the previous sentence context. They are enriched at each step with information about a new input word and are hence conditioned on the full history of the sentence. So even the last word of the sentence is conditioned in part on the first word of the sentence. Moreover, the model is simpler: it has less weights than a 3-gram feed-forward neural language model.

How do we train such a model with arbitrarily long contexts?

One idea: At the initial stage (predicting the second word from the first), we have the same architecture and hence the same training procedure as for feed-forward neural networks. We assess the error at the output layer and propagate updates back to the input layer. We could process every training example this way, essentially by treating the hidden layer from the previous training example as fixed input the current example. However, this way, we never provide feedback to the representation of prior history in the hidden layer.

Figure 7.5

Back-propagation through time. By unfolding the recurrent neural network over a fixed number of prediction steps (here: 3), we can derive update formulas based on the training objective of predicting all output words and back-propagation of the error via gradient descent.

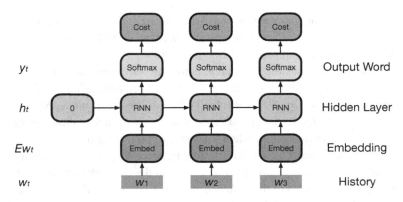

y_t Output Word

h_t Hidden Layer

Ew_t Embedding

w_t History

back-propagation through time   The **back-propagation through time** training procedure (Figure 7.5) unfolds the recurrent neural network over a fixed number of steps, by going back over, say, five word predictions.

Back-propagation through time can be applied for each training example (here called time step), but this is computationally quite expensive. Each time, computations have to be carried out over several steps. Instead, we can compute and apply weight updates in mini-batches (recall Section 5.6.2). First, we process a larger number of training examples (say, 10 to 20, or the entire sentence), and then update the weights.

Given modern compute power, fully **unfolding the recurrent** **unfolding** **neural network** has become more common. While recurrent neural networks have in theory arbitrary length, given a specific training example, its size is actually known and fixed, so we can fully construct the computation graph for each given training example, define the error as the sum of word prediction errors, and then carry out back-propagation over the entire sentence. This does require that we can quickly build **dynamic computation graph** computation graphs—so-called **dynamic computation graphs**—which are currently supported by some tool kits better than others.

7.5 Long Short-Term Memory Models

Consider the following step during word prediction in a sequential language model:

After much economic progress over the years, the **country** → *has*

The directly preceding word *country* will be the most informative for the prediction of the word *has*, all the previous words are much less relevant. In general, the importance of words decays with distance. The hidden state in the recurrent neural network will always be updated with the most recent word, and its memory of older words is likely to diminish over time.

But sometimes, more distant words are much more important, as the following example shows:

The **country** *which has made much economic progress over the years still* → *has*

In this example, the inflection of the verb *have* depends on the subject *country* which is separated by a long subordinate clause.

Recurrent neural networks allow modeling of arbitrarily long sequences. Their architecture is very simple. But this simplicity causes a number of problems.

- The hidden layer plays double duty as memory of the network and as continuous space representation used to predict output words.
- While we may sometimes want to pay more attention to the directly previous word and sometimes pay more attention to the longer context, there is no clear mechanism to control that.
- If we train the model on long sequences, then any update needs to back propagate to the beginning of the sentence. However, propagating through so many steps raises concerns that the impact of recent information at any step drowns out older information. This problem is called **vanishing gradients**.[1]   **vanishing gradient**

The rather confusingly named **long short-term memory (LSTM)** neural network architecture addresses these issues. Its design is quite elaborate, although it is not very difficult to use in practice. Mathematically, it changes the simple state progression that takes the previous time step's state and new input to compute a new hidden state. Instead of a simple linear transform with an activation functions, it strings together a series of computations with intermediate results that are named **gates** and **states** in allusion to digital circuity design.

LSTM
long short-term memory

A core distinction of the basic building block of LSTM networks, the so-called **cell**, is an explicit memory state. The memory state in the cell is motivated by digital memory cells in ordinary computers. Digital memory cells offer operations to read, write, and reset. While a digital memory cell may store just a single bit, a LSTM cell stores a real number.

cell (LSTM)

Furthermore, the read/write/reset operations in a LSTM cell are regulated with real numbered parameters, which are called **gates** (Figure 7.6).

gate

- The **input gate** parameter regulates how much new input changes the memory state.

input gate

---

[1] Note that there is a corresponding **exploding gradient** problem, where over long distance, gradient values become too large. This is typically suppressed by **clipping** gradients, i.e., limiting them to a maximum value set as a hyper parameter.

exploding gradient

gradient clipping

Figure 7.6 A cell in a long short-term memory model neural network. As recurrent neural networks, it receives input from the previous layer and the output value from the previous time step $t-1$. The memory state m is updated from the input state i, and the earlier value of the memory state m^{t-1}. Various gates channel information flow in the cell toward the output value o.

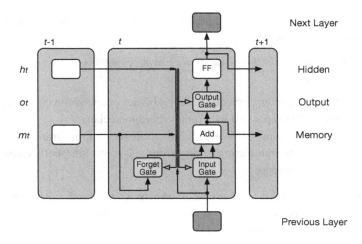

forget gate
- The **forget gate** parameter regulates how much of the prior memory state is retained (or forgotten).

output gate
- The **output gate** parameter regulates how strongly the memory state is passed on to the next layer.

Formally, marking the input, memory, and output values with the time step t, we define the flow of information within a cell as follows:

$$\text{memory}^t = \text{gate}_{\text{input}} \times \text{input}^t + \text{gate}_{\text{forget}} \times \text{memory}^{t-1}$$
$$\text{output}^t = \text{gate}_{\text{output}} \times \text{memory}^t. \tag{7.12}$$

The hidden node value h^t passed on to the next layer is the application of an activation function f to the output value:

$$h^t = f(\text{output}^t). \tag{7.13}$$

An LSTM layer consists of a vector of LSTM cells, just as traditional layers consist of a vector of nodes. The input to the LSTM layer is computed in the same way as the input to a recurrent neural network node. Given the node values for the preceding layer x^t and the values for the hidden layer from the previous time step h^{t-1}, the input value is the typical combination of matrix multiplication with weights W^x and W^h and an activation function g:

$$\text{input}^t = g\left(W^x x^t + W^h h^{t-1}\right). \tag{7.14}$$

But how are the gate parameters set? They actually play a fairly important role. In particular contexts, we would like to give preference to recent input ($\text{gate}_{\text{input}} \simeq 1$), rather than retain past memory (gate$_{forget} \simeq 1$) or pay less attention to the cell at the current point in time (gate$_{output} \simeq 0$). Hence this decision has to be informed by a broad view of the context.

How do we compute a value from such a complex conditioning context? Well, we treat it like a node in a neural network. For each gate $a \in$ (input, forget, output) we define matrices W^{xa}, W^{ha}, and W^{ma} to compute the gate parameter value by the multiplication of weights and node values in the previous layer x^t, the hidden layer h^{t-1} at the previous time step, and the memory states at the previous time step memory^{t-1}, followed by an activation function h:

$$\text{gate}_a = h\left(W^{xa}x^t + W^{ha}h^{t-1} + W^{ma}\text{memory}^{t-1}\right). \qquad (7.15)$$

LSTMs are trained the same way as recurrent neural networks, using back-propagation through time or fully unrolling the network. While the operations within a LSTM cell are more complex than in a recurrent neural network, all the operations are still based on matrix multiplications and differentiable activation functions. Hence we can compute gradients for the objective function with respect to all parameters of the model and compute update functions.

7.6 Gated Recurrent Units

LSTM cells add a large number of additional parameters. For each gate alone, multiple weight matrices are added. More parameters lead to longer training times and risk overfitting. As a simpler alternative, **gated recurrent units** (GRUs) have been proposed and used in neural translation models. At the time of this writing, LSTM cells seem to be making a comeback in neural machine translation, but both are still commonly used.

GRU cells have no separate memory state, just a hidden state that serves both purposes (Figure 7.7). Also, there are only two gates. These gates are predicted, as before, from the input and the previous state:

$$\text{update}_t = g(W_{update} \text{ input}_t + U_{update} \text{ state}_{t-1} + \text{bias}_{update})$$
$$\text{reset}_t = g(W_{reset} \text{ input}_t + U_{reset} \text{ state}_{t-1} + \text{bias}_{reset}). \qquad (7.16)$$

The first gate is used in the combination of the input and previous state. This combination is identical to traditional recurrent neural network, except that the previous states impact is scaled by the reset gate. Since the gate's value is between 0 and 1, this may give preference to the current input:

$$\text{combination}_t = f(W \text{ input}_t + U(\text{reset}_t \circ \text{state}_{t-1})). \qquad (7.17)$$

gated recurrent unit
GRU

Figure 7.7 Gated recurrent
unit (GRU). A simplification of
LSTM cells. It has only one
internal state that is
communicated to the
outside.

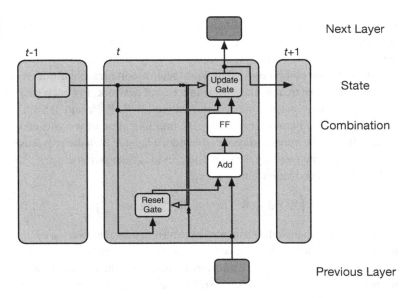

Then, the update gate is used for an interpolation of the previous
state and the just computed combination. This is done as a weighted
sum, where the update gate balances between the two:

$$\text{state}_t = (1 - \text{update}_t) \circ \text{state}_{t-1}$$
$$+ \text{update}_t \circ \text{combination}_t) + \text{bias}. \tag{7.18}$$

In one extreme case, the update gate is 0, and the previous state is
passed through directly. In another extreme case, the update gate is 1,
and the new state is mainly determined from the input, with as much
impact from the previous state as the reset gate allows.

It may seem a bit redundant to have two operations with a gate each
that combine prior state and input. However, these play different roles.
The first operation yielding combination$_t$ (Equation 7.17) is a classic
recurrent neural network component that allows more complex computations in the combination of input and output. The second operation
yielding the new hidden state and the output of the unit (Equation 7.18)
allows for bypassing of the input, enabling long-distant memory that
simply passes through information and, during back-propagation, passes
through the gradient, thus enabling long-distance dependencies.

7.7 Deep Models

deep model

The currently fashionable term **deep learning** for the latest wave of
neural network research has a real motivation. Large gains have been

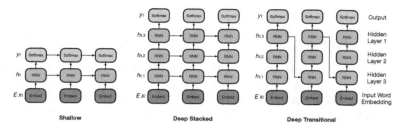

Figure 7.8 Deep recurrent neural networks. The input is passed through a few hidden layers before an output prediction is made. In deep stacked models, the hidden layers are also connected horizontally, i.e., a layer's values at time step t depends on its value at time step $t-1$ as well as the previous layer at time step t. In deep transitional models, the layers at any time step t are sequentially connected. The first hidden layer is also informed by the last layer at time step $t-1$.

seen in tasks such as vision and speech recognition due to stacking multiple hidden layers together.

More layers allow for more complex computations, just as having sequences of traditional computation components (Boolean gates) allows for more complex computations such as addition and multiplication of numbers. While this has been generally recognized for a long time, modern hardware finally enabled to train such deep neural networks on real-world problems. And we learned from experiments in vision and speech that having a handful, and even dozens, of layers does give increasingly better quality.

How does the idea of deep neural networks apply to the sequence prediction tasks common in language? There are several options; Figure 7.8 gives two examples. In shallow neural networks, the input is passed to a single hidden layer, from which the output is predicted. Now, a sequence of hidden layers is used. These hidden layers $h_{t,i}$ may be **deeply stacked**, so that each layer acts like the hidden layer in the   **deeply stacked** shallow recurrent neural network. Its state is conditioned on its value at the previous time step $h_{t-1,i}$ and the value of previous layer in the sequence $h_{t,i-1}$.

$$
\begin{aligned}
h_{t,1} &= f_1(h_{t-1,1}, x_t) & \text{first layer} \\
h_{t,i} &= f_i(h_{t-1,i}, h_{t,i-1}) & \text{for } i > 1 \quad (7.19) \\
y_t &= f_{i+1}(h_{t,I}) & \text{prediction from last layer } I.
\end{aligned}
$$

Or the hidden layers may be directly connected in **deep transitional**   **deep transition** networks, where the first hidden layer $h_{t,1}$ is informed by the last hidden layer at the previous time step $h_{t-1,I}$, but all other hidden layers are not connected to values from previous time steps:

$$h_{t,1} = f_1(h_{t-1,I}, x_t) \qquad\qquad \text{first layer}$$

$$h_{t,i} = f_i(h_{t,i-1}) \qquad\qquad\quad \text{for } i > 1 \qquad (7.20)$$

$$y_t = f_{i+1}(h_{t,I}) \qquad \text{prediction from last layer } I.$$

In all these equations, the function f_i may be a feed-forward layer (matrix multiplication plus activation function), an LSTM cell, or a GRU cell.

Experiments with using neural language models in traditional statistical machine translation have shown benefits with three to four hidden layers (Luong et al., 2015a).

While modern hardware allows training of deep models, they do stretch computational resources to their practical limit. Not only are there more computations in the neural network, convergence of training is typically slower. Adding skip connections (linking the input directly to the output or the final hidden layer) sometimes speeds up training, but we still have training times that are several times longer than with shallow networks.

7.8 Hands On: Neural Language Models in PyTorch

We introduced the use of PyTorch to implement neural networks models at the end of the last chapter. The use of automatic gradient computation and library classes for basic neural network building blocks as well as optimizers significantly reduce the amount of code that needs to be written.

Let us take a look in this section on how to implement a neural language model as a recurrent neural network.

recurrent neural network

7.8.1 Recurrent Neural Networks

One difference between recurrent neural networks and the feed-forward neural network that we implemented at the end of the last chapter is that the structure of the computation graph depends on the size of the sentence that is being processed. Longer sentences require much larger computation graphs.

However, once we know a sentence to be processed, we know its length and can lay out how its computation graph needs to be constructed. We will handle this by implementing a class that carries out a single word prediction and then loops over the sentence to build it out for the whole sentence.

The class that makes a single word prediction in the recurrent neural network may be implemented as follows:

```
class RNN(torch.nn.Module):
  def __init__(self, vocab_size, hidden_size):
    super(RNN, self).__init__()
    self.hidden_size = hidden_size
    self.embedding = torch.nn.Embedding(vocab_size, hidden_size)
    self.gru = torch.nn.GRU(hidden_size, hidden_size)
    self.out = torch.nn.Linear(hidden_size, vocab_size)
    self.softmax = torch.nn.LogSoftmax(dim=1)

  def forward(self, input, hidden):
    embedded = self.embedding(torch.tensor([[input]])).view(1, 1, -1)
    output, hidden = self.gru(embedded, hidden)
    output = self.softmax(self.out(output[0]))
    return output, hidden

  def initHidden(self):
    return torch.zeros(1, 1, self.hidden_size)
```

The code defines member variables and a `forward` function, as we have seen before. It also has a special function to create the initial hidden state called `initHidden`. This specific implementation makes good use of PyTorch's existing neural network building blocks:

- an embedding step `torch.nn.Embedding` that maps vocabulary ID numbers to embedding vectors,
- a gated recurrent unit `torch.nn.GRU` as the core of the recurrent network that takes in a previous hidden state and a new input word and computes a new hidden state and an output prediction,
- an additional feed-forward layer `torch.nn.Linear` to process the output state into a prediction over output words,
- a softmax activation function `torch.nn.LogSoftmax` to turn the prediction over output words into a proper probability distribution.

These basic computation steps are defined during initialization of the recurrent neural network class, since they also instantiate parameter vectors (with initial random values) and hence stay associated with the object no matter how often the `forward` function is called.

The actual forward function just calls these steps in sequence.

7.8.2 Handling Text

Usually in natural language processing, there is a good amount of preprocessing and data preparation work needed to get training and test data in shape. We will limit ourselves to some basic steps here. We presume that the training data for a language model is stored in a file, one sentence per line.

One key data structure that we need to define is the vocabulary that maps word strings like *dog* into ID numbers like *73*. For this, we implement a `Vocabulary` class:

```
class Vocabulary:
  def __init__(self):
    self.word2id = {"<s>": 0, "</s>": 1}
    self.id2word = {0: "<s>", 1: "</s>"}
    self.n_words = 2

  def getID(self, word):
    if word not in self.word2id:
      self.word2id[word] = self.n_words
      self.id2word[self.n_words] = word
      self.n_words += 1
    return self.word2id[word]
```

There are two special word tokens, <s> for the start of a sentence and </s> for the end of a sentence. We give them the special ID numbers 0 and 1, respectively. Two Python dictionary data structures allow for the mapping from words to IDs and from IDs to words.

The function getID also maps a word into an ID, but with the additional ability to add any new words to the vocabulary. We will call this function when loading the training data. After that, the vocabulary stays fixed.

In the example code, we do not address the case when during test time words are encountered that are not in the vocabulary. For this, typically a special unknown word token is added to the dictionary and used instead of the actual word. Your may want to add this to your implementation.

With the vocabulary object in place, we can read in a training corpus. As stated before, we assume the data are already split into one sentence per line. We carry out basic tokenization with the function tokenizeString and remove any characters that are not Latin letters or the three punctuation characters period, exclamation mark, and question mark. This makes the code ready to use while in practice, tokenization would be handled externally with, possibly language-specific tools:

```
def tokenizeString(s):
  s = re.sub(r"([.!?])", r" \1", s)
  s = re.sub(r"[^a-zA-Z.!?]+", r" ", s)
  return s

def readCorpus(file):
  lines = open(file, encoding='utf-8').read().strip().split('\n')
  text_corpus = ["<s> " + tokenizeString(l) + " </s>" for l in lines]
  return text_corpus
```

The function readCorpus(file) reads in a text file and returns an array of sentences, each being a string. The following code calls the functions of this section to read in an example text file:

```
text_corpus = readCorpus("example.txt")
vocab = Vocabulary()
numbered_corpus = [[vocab.getID(word) for word in
sentence.split(' ')] for sentence in text_corpus]
```

After running this code, we have the training data in place for neural network training, as an array of sentences, each being an array of words in their numbered ID representation.

7.8.3 Training Loop

With all the basic objects and data structures in place, we can now implement the training loop. It starts with the setting of hyper parameters and instantiating class objects:

```
criterion = torch.nn.NLLLoss()
hidden_size = 256
learning_rate = 0.01
rnn = RNN(vocab.n_words, hidden_size)
optimizer = torch.optim.SGD(rnn.parameters(), lr=learning_rate)
```

This code sets the size of the hidden layer to 256 neurons and sets a learning rate of 0.01. It also instantiates a recurrent neural network object rnn and defines a loss function torch.nn.NLLLoss(), i.e., negative log likelihood. The goal of the language model is to predict the correct given words with high probability, or likelihood. The log keeps the numbers in a reasonable range, and negation allows us to treat this as a loss (a positive value that we want to drive down).

With this loss function as training criterion in place, we set basic stochastic gradient descent (torch.optim.SGD) as update method. Stochastic gradient descent sticks to the same learning rate during training and scales gradients with this learning rate to compute parameter updates.

Let's get to the finish line and implement the training loop. As before, we will take several passes over the training data, so we need a loop over epochs, and we will loop over each training sentence:

```
for epoch in range(10):
  total_loss = 0
  for sentence in numbered_corpus:
    optimizer.zero_grad()
    sentence_loss = 0
    hidden = rnn.initHidden()
    for i in range(len(sentence)-1):
      output, hidden = rnn.forward( sentence[i], hidden )
      word_loss = criterion( output, torch.tensor([sentence[i+1]]))
      sentence_loss += word_loss
    total_loss += sentence_loss.data.item();
    sentence_loss.backward()
    optimizer.step()
```

Processing each sentence is framed by standard stuff, like resetting the optimizer, defining a variable for the loss at the beginning, and adding up total training loss, triggering the backward pass and optimizer at the end. The interesting part is how we process the words of any given sentence.

The recurrent neural network needs a hidden state, so we initialize it with our function `rnn.initHidden`. Then we loop over the words of the sentence. For each word, we call the forward function `rnn.forward` to extend the computation graph. But the processing of each word also makes a prediction `output`, which we check against the actual next word `sentence[i+1]`. Recall that the prediction `output` is a probability distribution over all words in the vocabulary. The negative log likelihood computation pulls out only the value assigned to the correct word.

The loss for each word (`word_loss`) is added up into `sentence_loss`. Only once the entire sentence is processed and hence the entire computation graph is built, we carry out the backward pass, starting with `sentence_loss`.

7.8.4 Suggestions

I presented the complete code for training neural network language models. This is a nice starting point for various possible extensions to practice your deep learning coding skills. Here some suggestions.

Report Loss: Add some print statements that track `word_loss`, `sentence_loss`, and `total_loss`. Think about what is a reasonable way to normalize these raw scores so they can be interpreted in a reasonable way. Which ones are the most informative? Are there other ways to aggregate scores? For fine-grained tracking, also add the reporting for the best predictied word (`torch.argmax(output, dim=1)`), the correct given word, and the probability predicted to the correct given word.

Process Batches: Currently, the code processes one sentence at a time. As discussed, it is more efficient to process batches of multiple sentences. Change the code so that it can process training batches. Note: the size of the computation graph will be determined by the length of the largest sentence in the batch.

Validation Set: Tracking training loss will not indicate when overfitting sets in. Add a validation set and compute the loss on the validation set at regular intervals. Typically early stopping is triggered when the loss on the validation set does not reach a new minimum after a given number of checks.

Generate Text: After a training run, use the model to generate new text. In other words, let the model make word predictions and feed the last predicted word (and the hidden state) to the RNN `forward` function. Generate a given number of sentences. You can also try this on a character-based version of the language model, i.e., where each letter is generated separately, which will be computationally less expensive. For the latter, how often are valid words in the language generated?

Train on GPU: You will not be able to train a language model on CPU on large data sets in reasonable time. Modify the code, so it runs on a GPU. This requires that the GPU is declared as a device (set `torch.device`) and the parameters are stored in GPU memory (`to(device)`) so that the execution of the computation graph forward and backward steps are done on GPU.

Deeper Models: Section 7.7 discusses deeper architectures for neural language models. Implement some of them.

The website `https://pytorch.org/` will be an essential source of information for this.

7.9 Further Readings

The first vanguard of neural network research tackled language models. A prominent reference for neural language model is Bengio et al. (2003), who implement an n-gram language model as a feed-forward neural network with the history words as input and the predicted word as output. Schwenk et al. (2006) introduce such language models to machine translation (also called "continuous space language models"), and use them in reranking, similar to the earlier work in speech recognition. Schwenk (2007) proposes a number of speed ups. The implementation was made available as a open source tool kit (Schwenk, 2010), which also supports training on a GPU (Schwenk et al., 2012).

By first clustering words into classes and encoding words as pair of class and word-in-class bits, Baltescu et al. (2014) reduce the computational complexity sufficiently to allow integration of the neural network language model into the decoder. Another way to reduce computational complexity to enable decoder integration is the use of noise contrastive estimation by Vaswani et al. (2013), which roughly self-normalizes the output scores of the model during training, hence removing the need to compute the values for all possible output words. Baltescu and Blunsom (2015) compare the two techniques—class-based word encoding with normalized scores versus noise-contrastive estimation without normalized scores—and show that the latter gives better performance with much higher speed.

As another way to allow straightforward decoder integration, Wang et al. (2013) convert a continuous space language model for a short list of 8,192 words into a traditional *n*-gram language model in ARPA (SRILM) format. Wang et al. (2014) present a method to merge (or "grow") a continuous space language model with a traditional *n*-gram language model to take advantage of both better estimates for the words in the short list and the full coverage from the traditional model.

Finch et al. (2012) use a recurrent neural network language model to rescore *n*-best lists for a transliteration system. Sundermeyer et al. (2013) compare feed-forward with long short-term neural network language models, a variant of recurrent neural network language models, showing better performance for the latter in a speech recognition reranking task. Mikolov (2012) reports significant improvements with reranking *n*-best lists of machine translation systems with a recurrent neural network language model.

Neural language models are not deep learning in the sense that they use a lot of hidden layers. However, Luong et al. (2015a) show that having three to four hidden layers improves over having just the typical single layer.

language model in machine translation *Language models in neural machine translation:* Traditional statistical machine translation models have a straightforward mechanism to integrate additional knowledge sources, such as a large out of domain language model. It is harder for end-to-end neural machine translation. Gülçehre et al. (2015) add a language model trained on additional monolingual data to this model, in form of a recurrently neural network that runs in parallel. They compare the use of the language model in reranking (or rescoring) against deeper integration where a gated unit regulates the relative contribution of the language model and the translation model when predicting a word.

Chapter 8
Neural Translation Models

We are finally prepared to look at actual translation models. We have already done most of the work by getting familiar with recurrent neural language models. The neural machine translation model that we will study now is a straightforward extension of that model, with one refinement: an alignment model.

8.1 Encoder–Decoder Approach

encoder–decoder

Our first stab at a neural translation model is a straightforward extension of the language model. Recall the idea of a recurrent neural network to model language as a sequential process. Given all previous words, such a model predicts the next word. When we reach the end of the sentence, we now proceed to predict the translation of the sentence, one word at a time (Figure 8.1).

To train such a model, we simply concatenate the input and output sentences and use the same method to train a language model. For decoding, we feed in the input sentence, and then go through the predictions of the model until it predicts an end-of-sentence token.

How does such a network work? Once processing reaches the end of the input sentence (having predicted the end-of-sentence marker $</s>$), the hidden state encodes its meaning. In other words, the vector holding the values of the nodes of this final hidden layer is the **input sentence embedding**. This is the **encoder** phase of the model. Then this hidden state is used to produce the translation in the **decoder** phase.

sentence embedding

encoder
decoder

Clearly, we are asking a lot from the hidden state in the recurrent neural network here. During encoder phase, it needs to incorporate all

Figure 8.1 Sequence-to-sequence encoder–decoder model. Extending the language model, we concatenate the English input sentence *the house is big* with the German output sentence *das Haus ist groß*. The central recurrent state (after processing the end-of-sentence token </s>) contains the embedding of the entire input sentence.

information about the input sentence. It cannot forget the first words toward the end of the sentence. During the decoder phase, not it need to have enough information to predict each next word, and there needs to be some accounting for what part of the input sentence has been already translated and what still needs to be covered.

In practice, the proposed models works reasonable well for short sentences (up to, say, 10–15 words), but fails for long sentences. Some minor refinements to this model have been proposed, such using the sentence-embedding state as input to all hidden states of the decoder phase of the model. This makes the decoder structurally different from the encoder and reduces some of the load from the hidden state during decoding, since it no longer needs to remember the input. Another idea is to reverse the order of the output sentence, so that the last words of the input sentences are close to the last words of the output sentence.

However, in the following section, we will embark on a more significant improvement of the model, by explicitly modeling the alignment of output words to input words.

8.2 Adding an Alignment Model

alignment

The first successful neural machine translation model was the sequence-to-sequence encoder–decoder model with attention. That is a mouthful, but it is essentially the model described in the previous section, with an explicit alignment mechanism. In the deep learning world, this alignment **attention** is called **attention**. We are using the words *alignment* and *attention* interchangeably here.

Since the attention mechanism does add a bit of complexity to the model, we are now slowly building up to it, by first taking a look at the encoder, then the decoder, and finally the attention mechanism.

8.2.1 Encoder

encoder

The task of the encoder is to provide a representation of the input sentence. The input sentence is a sequence of words, for which we first

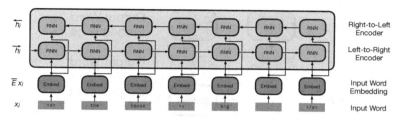

Figure 8.2 Neural machine translation model, part 1: input encoder. The encoder consists of two recurrent neural networks, running right to left and left to right (bidirectional recurrent neural network). The encoder states are the combination of the two hidden states of the recurrent neural networks.

consult the embedding matrix. Then, as in the basic language model described previously, we process these words with a recurrent neural network. This results in hidden states that encode each word with its left context, i.e., all the preceding words. To get the right context, we also build a recurrent neural network that runs right-to-left, or more precisely, from the end of the sentence to the beginning.

Figure 8.2 illustrates the model. Having two recurrent neural networks running in two directions is called a **bidirectional recurrent neural network**. Mathematically, the encoder consists of the embedding lookup for each input word x_j, and the mapping that steps through the hidden states $\overleftarrow{h}_j$ and $\overrightarrow{h}_j$

$$\overleftarrow{h}_j = f(\overleftarrow{h}_{j+1}, \bar{E}\,x_j) \tag{8.1}$$

$$\overrightarrow{h}_j = f(\overrightarrow{h}_{j-1}, \bar{E}\,x_j). \tag{8.2}$$

bidirectional recurrent neural network

In the equations above, we used a generic function f for a cell in the recurrent neural network. This function may be a typical feed-forward neural network layer—such as $f(x) = \tanh(Wx + b)$—or the more complex GRUs or LSTMs cells. The original paper proposing this approached used GRUs (Cho et al., 2014), but lately LSTMs have become more popular.

Note that we could train these models by adding a step that predicts the next word in the sequence, but we are actually training them in the context of the full machine translation model. Limiting the description to the decoder, its output is a sequence of word representations that concatenate the two hidden states ($\overleftarrow{h}_j$, $\overrightarrow{h}_j$).

8.2.2 Decoder

decoder

The decoder is also a recurrent neural network. It takes some representation of the input context (more on that in the Section 8.2.3) and the

Figure 8.3 Neural machine translation model, part 2: output decoder. Given the context from the input sentence and the embedding of the previously selected word, new decoder states and word predictions are computed.

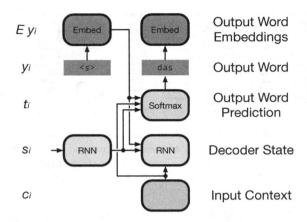

$E\,y_i$ — Output Word Embeddings

y_i — Output Word

t_i — Output Word Prediction

s_i — Decoder State

c_i — Input Context

previous hidden state and output word prediction and generates a new hidden decoder state and a new output word prediction (Figure 8.3).

Mathematically, we start with the recurrent neural network, which maintains a sequence of hidden states s_i that are computed from the previous hidden state s_{i-1}, the embedding of the previous output word Ey_{i-1}, and the input context c_i (which we still have to define):

$$s_i = f(s_{i-1},\ Ey_{i-1}, c_i). \tag{8.3}$$

Again, there are several choices for the function f that combines these inputs to generate the next hidden state: linear transforms with activation function, GRUs, LSTMs, etc. Typically, the choice here matches the encoder. So, if we use LSTMs for the encoder, then we also use LSTMs for the decoder.

From the hidden state we now predict the output word. This prediction takes the form of a probability distribution over the entire output vocabulary. If we have a vocabulary of, say, 50,000 words, then the prediction is a 50,000-dimensional vector, each element corresponding to the probability predicted for one word in the vocabulary.

The prediction vector t_i is conditioned on the decoder hidden state s_{i-1} and, again, the embedding of the previous output word Ey_{i-1} and the input context c_i:

$$t_i = \text{softmax}\big(W(Us_{i-1} + VEy_{i-1} + Cc_i) + b\big). \tag{8.4}$$

Note that we repeat the conditioning on Ey_{i-1} since we use the hidden state s_{i-1} and not s_i. This separates the encoder state progression from s_{i-1} to s_i from the prediction of the output word t_i.

The softmax is used to convert the raw vector into a probability distribution, where the sum of all values is 1. Typically, the highest value in the vector indicates the output word token y_i. Its word embedding Ey_{i-1} informs the next time step of the recurrent neural network.

During training, the correct output word y_i is known, so training proceeds with that word. The training objective is to give as much probability mass as possible to the correct output word. The cost function that drives training is hence the negative log of the probability given to the correct word translation:

$$\text{cost} = -\log t_i[y_i]. \tag{8.5}$$

Ideally, we want to give the correct word the probability 1, which would mean a negative log probability of 0, but typically it is a lower probability, hence a higher cost. Note that the cost function is tied to individual words, the overall sentence cost is the sum of all word costs.

During inference on a new test sentence, we typically chose the word y_i with the highest value in t_i, i.e., the most likely translation. We use its embedding Ey_i for the next inference steps. But we will also explore beam search strategies where the next likely translations are selected as y_i, creating a different conditioning context for the next words. More on that later.

8.2.3 Attention Mechanism

attention

We currently have two loose ends. The encoder gave us a sequence of word representations $h_j = (\overleftarrow{h_j}, \overrightarrow{h_j})$ and the decoder expects a context c_i at each step i. We now describe the attention mechanism that ties these ends together.

The attention mechanism is hard to illustrate using our typical neural network graphs, but Figure 8.4 gives at least an idea what the input and output relations are. The attention mechanism is informed by all input word representations $(\overleftarrow{h_j}, \overrightarrow{h_j})$ and the previous hidden state of the decoder s_{i-1}, and it produces a context state c_i.

The motivation is that we want to compute an association between the decoder state (which contains information where we are in the output sentence production) and each input word. Based on how strong this association is or, in other words, how relevant each particular input word is to produce the next output word, we want to weight the impact of its word representation.

Mathematically, we first compute this association with a feed-forward layer (using weight matrices W_a, U_a and weight vector v_a):

$$a(s_{i-1}, h_j) = v_a^T \tanh(W_a s_{i-1} + U_a h_j). \tag{8.6}$$

The output of this computation is a scalar value, indicating how important input word j is to produce output word i.

Figure 8.4 Neural machine translation model, part 3: attention model. Associations are computed between the last hidden state of the decoder and the word representations (encoder states). These associations are used to compute a weighted sum of encoder states. The resulting input context informs the next hidden state of the decoder.

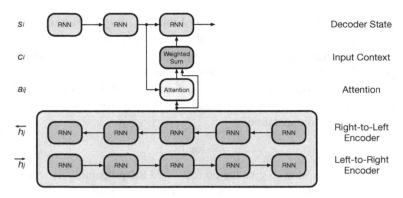

We normalize this attention value, so that the attention values across all input words j add up to one, using the softmax:

$$\alpha_{ij} = \frac{\exp(a(s_{i-1}, h_j))}{\sum_k \exp(a(s_{i-1}, h_k))}. \tag{8.7}$$

Now we use the normalized attention value to weigh the contribution of the input word representation h_j to the context vector c_i and we are done:

$$c_i = \sum_j \alpha_{ij} h_j. \tag{8.8}$$

Simply adding up word representation vectors (weighted or not) may at first seem an odd and simplistic thing to do. But it is very common practice in deep learning for natural language processing. Researchers have no qualms about using sentence embeddings that are simply the sum of word embeddings and other such schemes.

8.3 Training

training

With the complete model in hand, we can now take a closer look at training. One challenge is that the number of steps in the decoder and the number of steps in the encoder varies with each training example. Sentence pairs consist of sentences of different length, so we cannot have the same computation graph for each training example but instead have to dynamically create the computation graph for each of them. This **unrolling** technique is called **unrolling** the recurrent neural networks, which were discussed in regard to language models (recall Section 7.4).

The fully unrolled computation graph for a short sentence pair is shown in Figure 8.5. Note a couple of things. The error computed from this one sentence pair is the sum of the errors computed for each

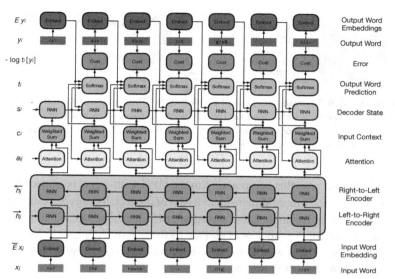

Figure 8.5 Fully unrolled computation graph for a training example with seven input tokens <s> the house is big </s> and six output tokens das Haus is groß</s>. The cost function (error) is computed for each output word individually and summed up across the sentence. When walking through the decoder states, the correct previous output words are used as conditioning context.

word. When proceeding to the next word prediction, we use the correct word as conditioning context for the decoder hidden state and the word prediction. Hence the training objective is based on the probability mass given to the correct word, given a perfect context. There have been some attempts to use different training objectives, such as the bleu score, but they have not yet been shown to be superior.

Practical training of neural machine translation models requires GPUs, which are well suited to the high degree of parallelism inherent in these deep learning models (just think of the many matrix multiplications). To increase parallelism even more, we process several sentence pairs (say, 100) at once. This implies that we increase the dimensionality of all the state tensors.

To given an example. We represent each input word in a specific sentence pair with a vector h_j. Since we already have a sequence of input words, these are lined up in a matrix. When we process a batch of sentence pairs, we again line up these matrices into a three-dimensional tensor.

Similarly, to give another example, the decoder hidden state s_i is a vector for each output word. Since we process a batch of sentences, we line up their hidden states into a matrix. Note that in this case it is not helpful to line up the states for all the output words, since the states are computed sequentially.

Recall the first computation of the attention mechanism:

$$a(s_{i-1}, h_j) = v_a^T \tanh(W_a s_{i-1} + U_a h_j). \qquad (8.9)$$

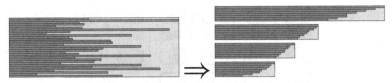

Figure 8.6 To make better use of parallelism in GPUs, we process a batch of training examples (sentence pairs) at a time. We convert a batch of training examples into a set of mini batches that have similar length. This wastes less computation on filler words (light gray).

We can pass this computation to the GPU with a matrix of decoder states s_{i-1} and a three-dimensional tensor of input encodings h_j, resulting in a matrix of attention values (one dimension for the sentence pairs, one dimension for the input words). Due to the massive reuse of values in W^a, U^a, and v^a as well as the inherent parallelism of this computation, GPUs can show their true power.

You may feel that we just created a glaring contradiction. First, we argued that we have to process one training example at a time, since sentence pairs typically have different lengths, and hence computation graphs have different sizes. Then, we argued for batching, say, 100 sentence pairs together to better exploit parallelism. These are indeed conflicting goals (Figure 8.6).

When batching training examples together, we have to consider the maximum sizes for input and output sentences in a batch and unroll the computation graph to these maximum sizes. For shorter sentences, we fill the remaining gaps with non-words and keep track of where the **mask**   valid data are with a **mask**. This means, for instance, that we have to ensure that no attention is given to words beyond the length of the input sentence and no errors and gradient updates are computed from output words beyond the length of the output sentence.

To avoid wasted computations on gaps, a nice trick is to sort the sentence pairs in the batch by length and break them up into **mini batch**   **mini-batches** of similar length.[1]

To summarize, training consists of the following steps:

- Shuffle the training corpus (to avoid undue biases due to temporal or topical order).
- Break up the corpus into maxi-batches.
- Break up each maxi-batch into mini-batches.

---

[1] There is a bit of confusion of the technical terms here. Sometimes the entire training corpus is called a *batch*, as used in the contrast between *batch* updating and *online* updating. In that context, smaller batches with a subset of them are called *mini-batches* (recall Section 5.6.2). Here, I use the term *batch* (or *maxi-batch*) for such a subset and the term *mini-batch* for a subset of the subset.

- Process each mini-batch, gather gradients.
- Apply all gradients for a maxi-batch to update the parameters.

Typically, training neural machine translation models takes 5–15 epochs (passes through entire training corpus). A common stopping criterion is to check the progress of the model on a validation set (which is not part of the training data) and halt when the error on the validation set does not improve. Training longer would not lead to any further improvements and may even degrade performance due to overfitting.

8.4 Deep Models

deep model

Learning the lessons from other research fields such as vision or speech recognition, recent work in machine translation has also looked at deeper models. Simply put, this involves adding more intermediate layers into the baseline architecture.

The core components of neural machine translation are the encoder, which takes input words and converts them into a sequence of contextualized representations, and the decoder, which generates an output sequence of words. Both are recurrent neural networks.

Recall that we already discussed how to build deeper recurrent neural networks for language modeling (see Section 7.7). We now extend these ideas to the recurrent neural networks in the encoder and the decoder.

What all these recurrent neural networks have in common is that they process an input sequence into an output sequence, and at each time step t, information from a new input x_t is combined with the hidden state from the previous time step h_{t-1} to predict a new hidden state h_t. From that hidden state, additional predictions may be made (output words y_t in the case of the decoder, the next word in the sequence in the case of language models), or the hidden state is used otherwise (via the attention mechanism in case of the encoder).

8.4.1 Decoder

decoder

Figure 8.7 shows part of the decoder in neural machine translation, using a particular deeper architecture. We see that instead of a single hidden state s_t for a given time step t, we now have a sequence of hidden states $s_{t,1}, s_{t,2}, \ldots, s_{t,I}$ for a given time step t.

There are various options for how the hidden states may be connected. In Section 7.7 I presented two ideas: (1) in stacked recurrent neural networks a hidden state $s_{t,i}$ is conditioned on the hidden state from a previous layer $s_{t,i-1}$ and the hidden state at the same depth from a previous time step $s_{t-1,i}$ and (2) in deep transition recurrent neural networks, the first hidden state $s_{t,1}$ is conditioned on the last hidden

Figure 8.7 Deep decoder. Instead of a single recurrent neural network layer for the decoder state, a deep model consists of several layers. Shown here is a combination of a deep transition and stacked RNNs. The figure omits the word prediction, word selection, and output word embedding steps, which are identical to the original architecture, shown in Figure 8.3.

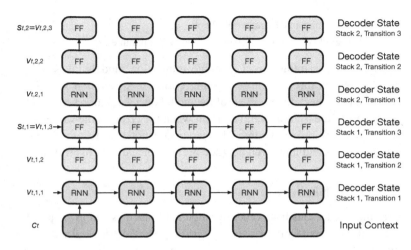

state from the previous time step $s_{t-1,i}$ and the input, while the other hidden layers $s_{t,1}$ $(i > 1)$ are just conditioned on the previous layer $s_{t,i-1}$.

Figure 8.7 combines these two ideas. Some layers are both stacked (conditioned on the previous time step $s_{t-1,i}$ and previous layer $s_{t,i-1}$), while others are deep transitions (conditioned only on the previous layer $s_{t,i-1}$.

Mathematically, we can break this out into the stacked layers $s_{t,i}$:

$$s_{t,1} = f_1(x_t, s_{t-1,1})$$
$$s_{t,i} = f_i(s_{t,i-1}, s_{t-1,i}) \quad \text{for } i > 1, \tag{8.10}$$

and the deep transition layers $v_{i,i,j}$.

$$v_{t,i,1} = g_{i,1}(\text{in}_{t,i}, s_{t-1,i}) \quad \text{in}_{t,i} \text{ is either } x_t \text{ or } s_{t,i-1}$$
$$v_{t,i,j} = g_{i,j}(v_{t,i,j-1}) \qquad \qquad \text{for } j > 1 \tag{8.11}$$
$$s_{t,i} = v_{t,i,J}.$$

The function $f_i(s_{t,i-1}, s_{t-1,i})$ is computed as a sequence of function calls $g_{i,j}$. Each of the functions $g_{i,j}$ may be implemented as feed-forward neural network layer (matrix multiplication plus activation function), LSTM cell, or GRU. In any case, each function $g_{i,j}$ has its own set of trainable model parameters.

8.4.2 Encoder

encoder

Deep recurrent neural networks for the encoder may draw in the same ideas as the decoder, with one addition: in the baseline neural translation model, we used bidirectional recurrent neural networks to condition on

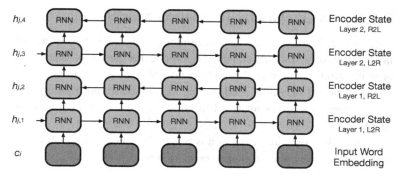

Figure 8.8 Deep alternating encoder, combining the idea of a bidirectional recurrent neural network previously proposed for neural machine translation (Figure 8.2) and the stacked recurrent neural network (Figure 8.2). This architecture may be further extended with the idea of deep transitions, as shown for the decoder (Figure 8.7).

both left and right contexts. We want to do the same for any deep version of the encoder.

Figure 8.8 shows one idea how this could be done, called an **alternating recurrent neural network**. It looks basically like a stacked recurrent neural network, with one twist: the hidden states at each layer $h_{t,i}$ are alternately conditioned on the hidden state from the previous time step $h_{t-1,i}$ or the next time step $h_{t+1,i}$.

alternating recurrent neural network

Mathematically, we formulate this as even-numbered hidden states $h_{t,2i}$ being conditioned on the left context $h_{t-1,2i}$ and odd-numbered hidden states $h_{t,2i+1}$ conditioned on the right context $h_{t+1,2i}$:

$$h_{t,1} = f(x_t, h_{t-1,1})$$
$$h_{t,2i} = f(h_{t,2i-1}, h_{t-1,2i}) \qquad (8.12)$$
$$h_{t,2i+1} = f(h_{t,2i}, h_{t+1,2i+1}).$$

As before in the encoder, we can extend this idea by having deep transitions.

Note that deep models are typically augmented with direct connections from the input to the output. In the case of the encoder, this may mean a direct connection from the embedding to the final encoder layer or connections at each layer that pass the input directly to the output. Such **residual connections** help with training. In early stages, the deep architecture can be skipped. Only when a basic functioning model has been acquired, the deep architecture can be exploited to enrich it. We typically see the benefits of residual connections in early training stages (faster initial reduction of model perplexity), and less so as improvement in the final converged model.

residual connection

8.5 Hands On: Neural Translation Models in PyTorch

Since neural translation models are in many ways extensions of neural language models, it should come as no surprise that their implementation is quite similar. The encoder and decoder models are similar to the recurrent neural networks used in language models, and training also steps through every output word to build up a dynamic computation graph.

The code shown in this section is adapted from the official PyTorch tutorial on sequence-to-sequence translation models.[2]

8.5.1 Encoder

encoder

The encoder is almost unchanged from the the recurrent neural network presented in Section 7.8.1:

```
class Encoder(torch.nn.Module):
  def __init__(self, vocab_size, hidden_size, max_length=MAX_LENGTH):
    super(Encoder, self).__init__()
    self.hidden_size = hidden_size
    self.max_length = max_length
    self.embedding = torch.nn.Embedding(vocab_size, hidden_size)
    self.gru = torch.nn.GRU(hidden_size, hidden_size)

  def forward(self, input, hidden):
    embedded = self.embedding(torch.tensor([[input]])).view(1, 1, -1)
    output, hidden = self.gru(embedded, hidden)
    return output, hidden
```

We dropped only the softmax computation here, since the encoder does not actually predict words. Note that this implementation returns the output of the gated recurrent unit and not the hidden state. In the simpler model described throughout most of this chapter, a feed-forward step is used instead, and its hidden state used as refinement of input representation.

We add one additional function to this class, the processing of an entire input sentence:

```
  def process_sentence(self, input_sentence):
    hidden = torch.zeros(1, 1, self.hidden_size)
    encoder_outputs = torch.zeros(self.max_length, self.hidden_size)
    for i in range(len(input_sentence)):
      embedded = self.embedding(torch.tensor([[input_sentence[i]]])).
view(1, 1, -1)
      output, hidden = self.gru(embedded, hidden)
      encoder_outputs[i] = output[0, 0]
    return encoder_outputs
```

[2] Sean Roberton, NLP from scratch: Translation with a sequence to sequence network and attention, PyTorch, https://pytorch.org/tutorials/intermediate/seq2seq_translation_tutorial.html.

The returned encoder representation for the entire input sentence `encoder_outputs` is a matrix, or a sequence of vector representations for words. The loop walks through the length of the sentence and stores the output state of the GRU in this matrix. This loop is quite similar to the training loop of the recurrent neural language model from the last chapter, except it does not compute any losses. Of course, we are just producing intermediate states here and not something that can be evaluated. This also means that the output state is not predicting the next word but is used downstream by the decoder.

8.5.2 Decoder

decoder

The decoder is at its heart also a recurrent neural network, but extended to handle the input sentence, which also involves computing attention and weighting the output states of the encoder. The full code for the decoder is given in Figure 8.9. Let us highlight here some key parts of the implementation.

The encoder takes into account not only the previous output word and hidden state but also the encoder outputs, as reflected in the arguments of the `forward` step. The length of the source sentence is also needed to mask attention:

```
def forward(self,
            prev_output_id,
            prev_hidden,
            encoder_output,
            input_length):
```

The previous output word is mapped into an embedding `prev_output`, as usual. Now comes the attention computation. It consists of two steps: the computation of attention weights and the application of these weights to weigh the contributions of the representations of the encoded input words.

We follow Equation 8.6 in the computation of attention scores:

$$a(s_{i-1}, h_j) = v_a^T \tanh(W_a s_{i-1} + U_a h_j).$$

This requires the linear transforms W_a and U_a as well as an additional parameter vector v_a:

```
self.Wa = torch.nn.Linear(hidden_size, hidden_size, bias=False)
self.Ua = torch.nn.Linear(hidden_size, hidden_size, bias=False)
self.va = torch.nn.Parameter(torch.FloatTensor(1,hidden_size))
```

```
class Decoder(torch.nn.Module):
  def __init__(self, vocab_size, hidden_size, max_length=MAX_LENGTH):
    super(Decoder, self).__init__()
    self.hidden_size = hidden_size
    self.vocab_size = vocab_size
    self.max_length = max_length

    self.gru = torch.nn.GRU(2 * hidden_size, hidden_size)
    self.embedding = torch.nn.Embedding(vocab_size, hidden_size)
    self.Wa = torch.nn.Linear(hidden_size, hidden_size, bias=False)
    self.Ua = torch.nn.Linear(hidden_size, hidden_size, bias=False)
    self.va = torch.nn.Parameter(torch.FloatTensor(1,hidden_size))

    self.out = torch.nn.Linear(3 * hidden_size, vocab_size)

  def forward(self,
                prev_output_id,
                prev_hidden,
                encoder_output,
                input_length):
    prev_output = self.embedding(torch.tensor([prev_output_id])).unsqueeze(1)

    m = torch.tanh(self.Wa(prev_hidden) + self.Ua(encoder_output))
    attention_scores = m.bmm(self.va.unsqueeze(2)).squeeze(-1)
    attention_scores = self.mask(attention_scores, input_length)
    attention_weights = torch.nn.functional.softmax( attention_scores, -1 )

    context = attention_weights.unsqueeze(1).bmm(encoder_output.unsqueeze(0))

    rnn_input = torch.cat((prev_output, context), 2)
    rnn_output, hidden = self.gru(rnn_input, prev_hidden)

    output = self.out(torch.cat((rnn_output, context, prev_output), 2))
    output = torch.nn.functional.log_softmax(output[0], dim=1)
    return output, hidden

  def mask(self, scores, input_length):
    s = scores.squeeze(0)
    for i in range(self.max_length-input_length):
      s[input_length+i] = -float('inf')
    return s.unsqueeze(0)

  def initHidden(self):
    return torch.zeros(1, 1, self.hidden_size)
```

Figure 8.9 Decoder in the neural translation model. The decoder computes attention over the encoder states and makes a prediction for one output word at the time.

The `forward` function implements the given equation. In the following, this is broken up into two steps for clarity:

```
m = torch.tanh(self.Wa(prev_hidden) + self.Ua(encoder_output))
attention_scores = m.bmm(self.va.unsqueeze(2)).squeeze(-1)
```

The attention scores are converted into weights by taking the softmax. Since the scores are computed for the maximum input sequence length, we need to mask the values that do not correspond to actual words:

```
attention_scores = self.mask(attention_scores, input_length)
attention_weights = torch.nn.functional.softmax( attention_scores, -1 )
```

The attention weights are applied to the encoder outputs to compute the input context:

```
context = attention_weights.unsqueeze(1).bmm(encoder_output.unsqueeze(0))
```

The state progression of the recurrent hidden state is similar to the encoder, except that it is conditioned not only on the previous hidden state but also on the previous output word:

```
rnn_input = torch.cat((prev_output, prev_hidden), 2)
rnn_output, hidden = self.gru(rnn_input, prev_hidden)
```

Finally, with both the input context and the information from the recurrent hidden state in place, we can make predictions for the next target word:

```
output = self.out(torch.cat((rnn_output, context, prev_output), 2))
output = torch.nn.functional.log_softmax(output[0], dim=1)
```

8.5.3 Training

With all the essential pieces in place, training should look very familar. We start with reading in the parallel corpus[3] (in two parts, the source side and the target side):

```
source_text_corpus = readCorpus("Tanzil.20k.de-en.de")
target_text_corpus = readCorpus("Tanzil.20k.de-en.en")
source_vocab = Vocabulary()
target_vocab = Vocabulary()
source_numbered_corpus = [[source_vocab.getIndex(word) for word in
sentence.split(' ')] for sentence in source_text_corpus]
target_numbered_corpus = [[target_vocab.getIndex(word) for word in
sentence.split(' ')] for sentence in target_text_corpus]
```

---

[3] Available at Tanzil, http://opus.nlpl.eu/Tanzil.php, here using the first 20,000 lines.

We need to set some hyper parameters, specifically the loss function, size of hidden states, and the learning rate:

```
criterion = torch.nn.NLLLoss()
hidden_size = 256
learning_rate = 0.01
```

With all this at hand, we can instantiate the encoder and decoder. Note that we have two models here, and hence have to define two optimizers, one for each:

```
encoder = Encoder(source_vocab.n_words, hidden_size)
decoder = Decoder(target_vocab.n_words, hidden_size)
encoder_optimizer = torch.optim.SGD(encoder.parameters(), lr=learning_rate)
decoder_optimizer = torch.optim.SGD(decoder.parameters(), lr=learning_rate)
```

Next, the training loop. It starts with opening the loops over epochs and training examples, and resetting the optimizer:

```
for epoch in range(100):
  for source_sentence, target_sentence in zip(source_numbered_corpus,
                                               target_numbered_corpus):
    encoder_optimizer.zero_grad()
    decoder_optimizer.zero_grad()
```

We defined a handy function to compute encoder states, so we just call this here:

```
encoder_output = encoder.process_sentence( source_sentence )
```

Now, we are ready to step through the words of the target sentence. This is essentially identical to the language model training loop, except that the forward function takes the additional `encoder_output` as an argument:

```
sentence_loss = 0
hidden = decoder.initHidden()
for i in range(len(target_sentence)-1):
  output, hidden = decoder.forward( target_sentence[i],
                                    hidden,
                                    encoder_output
                                    len(source_sentence) )
  word_loss = criterion( output, torch.tensor([target_sentence[i+1]]))
  sentence_loss += word_loss
```

Finally, we execute the backward pass and trigger the optimizers:

```
sentence_loss.backward()
encoder_optimizer.step()
decoder_optimizer.step()
```

8.6 Further Readings

The attention model has its roots in a sequence-to-sequence model. Cho et al. (2014) use recurrent neural networks for the approach. Sutskever et al. (2014) use a LSTM network and reverse the order of the source sentence before decoding.

The seminal work by Bahdanau et al. (2015) adds an alignment model (so-called attention mechanism) to link generated output words to source words, which includes conditioning on the hidden state that produced the preceding target word. Source words are represented by the two hidden states of recurrent neural networks that process the source sentence left to right and right to left. Luong et al. (2015b) propose variants to the attention mechanism (which they call the "global" attention model) and also a hard-constraint attention model ("local" attention model), which is restricted to a Gaussian distribution around a specific input word.

To explicitly model the trade-off between source context (the input words) and target context (the already produced target words), Tu et al. (2016a) introduce an interpolation weight (called "context gate") that scales the impact of the (1) source context state and (2) the previous hidden state and the last word when predicting the next hidden state in the decoder.

Deep Models

There are several variations for adding layers to the encoder and the decoder of the neural translation model. Wu et al. (2016) first use the traditional bidirectional recurrent neural networks to compute input word representations and then refine them with several stacked recurrent layers. Shareghi et al. (2016) alternate between forward and backward recurrent layers. Miceli Barone et al. (2017b) show good results with four stacks and two deep transitions each for encoder and decoder as well as alternating networks for the encoder. There are a large number of variations (including the use of skip connections, the choice of LSTM versus GRU, number of layers of any type) that still need to be explored empirically for various data conditions.

Chapter 9
Decoding

Decoding is the process of generating a translation for a given input sentence. In machine learning, this is also called **inference**, but we will inference stick here to the term that has been established in machine translation research.

In deep learning, decoding is implemented as the forward pass through the computation graph. As during training, we predict one word at a time. However, we do not match output word predictions against the truth as presented in the training data. Instead, we generate the entire sequence of output words. Since there are many word choices given by the probability distribution of the model, there is an exponentially large space of possible output sequences.

In this chapter, we explore how to address the search problem to find the best sequence with beam search, and describe varies extensions of this basic algorithm.

9.1 Beam Search

beam search

Translating with neural translation models proceeds one step at a time. At each step, we predict one output word. We first compute a probability distribution over all words. We then pick the most likely word and move to the next prediction step. Since the model is conditioned on the previous output word (recall Equation 8.3), we use its word embedding in the conditioning context for the next step (Figure 9.1).

At each time step, we obtain a probability distribution over words. In the example, the word *the* received the highest probability, so we pick it as the output word. We use the chosen word as conditioning context

Figure 9.1 Elementary decoding step. The model predicts a word prediction probability distribution. We select the most likely word (*the*). Its embedding is part of the conditioning context for the next word prediction (and decoder state).

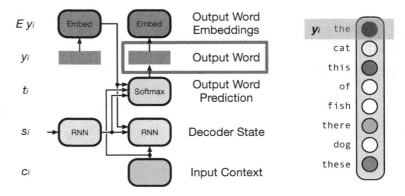

when computing the probability distribution for the next output word, pick the most probable word, and so on, until we produce the end-of-sentence symbol.

A real example of how a neural machine translation model translates a German sentence into English is shown in Figure 9.2. The model tends to give most, if not almost all, probability mass to the top choice, but the sentence translation also indicates word choice ambiguity, such as *believe* (68.4%) versus *think* (28.6%) or *different* (41.5%) versus *various* (22.7%). There is also ambiguity about grammatical structure, such as if the sentence should start with the discourse connective *but* (42.1%) or the subject *I* (20.4%).

This process suggests that we perform 1-best greedy search, always picking the most probable word. This makes us vulnerable to the so-called **garden-path problem**. Sometimes we follow a sequence of words and realize too late that we made a mistake early on. In that case, the best sequence consists initially of less probable words, which are redeemed by subsequent words in the context of the full output. Consider the case of having to produce an idiomatic phrase that is noncompositional. The first words of these phrases may be really odd word choices by themselves (e.g., *piece of cake* for *easy*). Only once the full phrase is formed is their choice redeemed.

Note that we are faced with the same problem in traditional statistical machine translation models—arguably even more so there since we rely on sparser contexts when making predictions for the next words. Decoding algorithms for these models keep a list of the *n*-best candidate **hypotheses** (partial translations), expand them, and keep the *n*-best expanded hypotheses. We can do the same for neural translation models.

When predicting the first word of the output sentence, we keep a **beam** of the top *n* most likely word choices. They are scored by their probability. Then, we use each of these words in the beam in the

(marginal notes) garden-path problem · hypothesis · beam

Input Sentence

ich glaube aber auch, er ist clever genug um seine Aussagen vage genug zu halten, so dass sie auf verschiedene Art und Weise interpretiert werden können.

Output Word Predictions

Best		Alternatives
but	(42.1%)	*however* (25.3%), *I* (20.4%), *yet* (1.9%), *and* (0.8%), *nor* (0.8%), ...
I	(80.4%)	*also* (6.0%), *,* (4.7%), *it* (1.2%), *in* (0.7%), *nor* (0.5%), *he* (0.4%), ...
also	(85.2%)	*think* (4.2%), *do* (3.1%), *believe* (2.9%), *,* (0.8%), *too* (0.5%), ...
believe	(68.4%)	*think* (28.6%), *feel* (1.6%), *do* (0.8%), ...
he	(90.4%)	*that* (6.7%), *it* (2.2%), *him* (0.2%), ...
is	(74.7%)	*'s* (24.4%), *has* (0.3%), *was* (0.1%), ...
clever	(99.1%)	*smart* (0.6%), ...
enough	(99.9%)	
to	(95.5%)	*about* (1.2%), *for* (1.1%), *in* (1.0%), *of* (0.3%), *around* (0.1%), ...
keep	(69.8%)	*maintain* (4.5%), *hold* (4.4%), *be* (4.2%), *have* (1.1%), *make* (1.0%), ...
his	(86.2%)	*its* (2.1%), *statements* (1.5%), *what* (1.0%), *out* (0.6%), *the* (0.6%), ...
statements	(91.9%)	*testimony* (1.5%), *messages* (0.7%), *comments* (0.6%), ...
vague	(96.2%)	*v@@* (1.2%), *in* (0.6%), *ambiguous* (0.3%), ...
enough	(98.9%)	*and* (0.2%), ...
so	(51.1%)	*,* (44.3%), *to* (1.2%), *in* (0.6%), *and* (0.5%), *just* (0.2%), *that* (0.2%), ...
they	(55.2%)	*that* (35.3%), *it* (2.5%), *can* (1.6%), *you* (0.8%), *we* (0.4%), *to* (0.3%), ...
can	(93.2%)	*may* (2.7%), *could* (1.6%), *are* (0.8%), *will* (0.6%), *might* (0.5%), ...
be	(98.4%)	*have* (0.3%), *interpret* (0.2%), *get* (0.2%), ...
interpreted	(99.1%)	*interpre@@* (0.1%), *constru@@* (0.1%), ...
in	(96.5%)	*on* (0.9%), *differently* (0.5%), *as* (0.3%), *to* (0.2%), *for* (0.2%), *by* (0.1%), ...
different	(41.5%)	*a* (25.2%), *various* (22.7%), *several* (3.6%), *ways* (2.4%), *some* (1.7%), ...
ways	(99.3%)	*way* (0.2%), *manner* (0.2%), ...
.	(99.2%)	*</s>* (0.2%), *,* (0.1%), ...
</s>	(100.0%)	

Figure 9.2 Word predictions of the neural machine translation model. Frequently, most of the probability mass is given to the top choice, but semantically related words may rank high, e.g., *believe* (68.4%) versus *think* (28.6%). The subword units *interpre@@* are explain in Section 12.3.

conditioning context for the next word. Due to this conditioning, we make different word predictions for each. We now multiply the score for the partial translation (at this point just the probability for the first word), and the probabilities from its word predictions. We select the highest scoring word pairs for the next beam (Figure 9.3).

This process continues. At each time step, we accumulate word **decoding** translation probabilities, giving us scores for each hypothesis. A sentence translation is complete when the end of sentence token is produced. At this point, we remove the completed hypothesis from the beam and reduce beam size by 1. Search terminates, when no hypotheses are left in the beam.

Search produces a graph of hypotheses, as shown in Figure 9.4. It starts with the start of sentence symbol *<s>* and its paths terminate

Figure 9.3 Beam search in neural machine translation. After committing to a short list of specific output words (the **beam**), new word predictions are made for each. These differ since the committed output word is part of the conditioning context to make predictions.

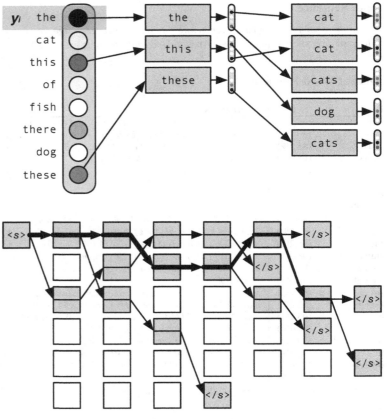

Figure 9.4 Search graph for beam search decoding in neural translation models. At each time step, the $n = 6$ best partial translations (called hypotheses) are selected. An output sentence is complete when the end of sentence token </s> is predicted. We reduce the beam after that and terminate when n full sentence translations are completed. Following the back pointers from the end-of-sentence tokens allows us to read them off. Empty boxes represent hypotheses that are not part of any complete path.

with the end of sentence symbol </s>. Given the compete graph, the resulting translations can be obtained by following the back-pointers. The complete hypothesis (i.e., one that ended with a </s> symbol) with the highest score points to the best translation.

When choosing among the best paths, we score each with the product of its word prediction probabilities. In practice, we get better results when we normalize the score by the output length of a translation, i.e., divide by the number of words. We carry out this normalization after search is completed. During search, all translations in a beam have the same length, so the normalization would make no difference.

Note that in traditional statistical machine translation, we were able to combine hypotheses if they share the same conditioning context for future feature functions. This not possible anymore for recurrent neural networks since we condition on the entire output word sequence from the beginning. As a consequence, the search graph is generally less diverse than search graphs in statistical machine translation models. It is really just a search tree where the number of complete paths is the same as the size of the beam.

9.2 Ensemble Decoding

A common technique in machine learning is to not just build one system for a given task, but multiple ones and then combine them. This is called an **ensemble** of systems. It is such a successful strategy that various methods have been proposed to systematically build alternative systems, for instance by using different features or different subsets of the data. For neural networks, one straightforward way is to use different initializations or stop at different points in the training process.

Why does it work? The intuitive argument is that each system makes different mistakes. When two systems agree, then they are more likely both right, rather than both make the same mistake. One can also see the general principle at play in human behavior, such as setting up committees to make decisions or the democratic voting in elections.

Applying ensemble methods to our case of neural machine translation, we have to address two subproblems: (1) generating alternate systems and (2) combining their output.

9.2.1 Generating Alternative Systems

Figure 9.5 shows two methods for the first subproblem, i.e., generating alternative systems. When training a neural translation model, we iterate through the training data until some stopping criterion is met. This is typically a lack of improvements of the cost function applied to a

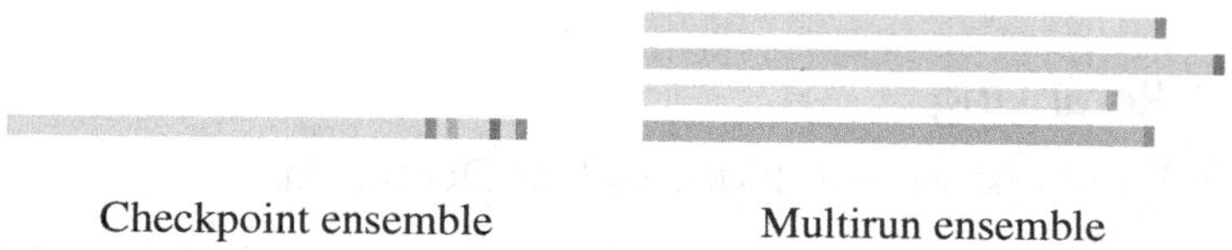

Checkpoint ensemble   Multirun ensemble

Figure 9.5 Two methods to generate alternative systems for ensembling: Checkpoint ensembling uses model dumps from various stages of the training process, while multirun ensembling starts independent training runs with different initial weights and order of the training data.

validation set (measured in cross-entropy) or the translation performance on that validation set (measured in BLEU).

During training, we dump out the model at fixed intervals (say, every 10,000 iteration of batch processing). Once training is completed, we can look back at the performance of the model these different stages. We then pick the, say, four models with the best performance on the validation set (typically translation quality is measured in BLEU). This **checkpoint ensemble** is called **checkpoint ensembling** since we select the models at different checkpoints in the training process.

multirun ensemble   **Multirun ensembling** requires building systems in completely different training runs. As mentioned before, this can be accomplished by using different random initialization of weights, which leads training to seek out different local optima. We also randomly shuffle the training data, so that presenting sentence pairs in different random order will also lead to different training outcomes.

Multirun ensembling usually works a good deal better, but it is also computationally much more expensive. Note that multirun ensembling can also build on checkpoint ensembling. Instead of combining the end points of training, we first apply checkpoint ensembling to each run, and then combine those ensembles.

9.2.2 Combining System Output

Neural translation models allow the combination of several systems fairly deeply. Recall that the model first predicts a probability distribution over possible output words, and then commits to one of the words. This is where we combine the different trained models. Each model predicts a probability distribution, and we then combine their predictions. The combination is done by simple averaging over the distributions. The averaged distribution is then the basis for selecting an output word (Figure 9.6).

There may be some benefit to weighing the different systems differently, although when they are just generated from different random starting points, they will all have very similar quality, so this is not typically done.

9.3 Reranking

reranking

9.3.1 Reranking with Right-to-Left Decoding

Let us take a look at an extension of the idea of ensembling: instead of building multiple systems with different random initialization, we can also build one set of systems as before, and then a second set of systems where we reverse the order of the output sentences. The second set of

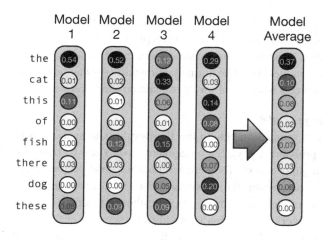

Figure 9.6 Combining predictions from a ensemble of models. Each model independently predicts a probability distribution over output words, which are averaged into a combined distribution.

systems is called **right-to-left** systems, although arguably this is not **right-to-left**
a good name since it makes no sense for languages such as Arabic or
Hebrew where the normal writing order is right to left.

The deep integration I described in the previous section does not
work anymore for the combination of left-to-right and right-to-left systems, since they produce the output sequence in a different direction. To
handle this, we have to resort to **reranking**. This involves several steps: **reranking**

- Use an ensemble of left-to-right systems to generate an n-best list of candidate
  translations for each input sentence.
- Score each candidate translation with the individual left-to-right and right-to-
  left systems.
- Combine the scores (simple average) of the different models for each candidate; select the candidate with the best score for each input sentence.

Scoring a given candidate translation with a right-to-left system
requires **forced decoding**, a special mode of running inference on an   **forced decoding**
input sentence, predicting a given output sentence. This mode is actually
much closer to training (where also an output translation is given) than
inference.

9.3.2 Reranking with Reverse Models

Traditional statistical machine translation systems combined several   **reverse model**
diverse model components, each of which contributed one of many
scores during decoding. One of these scoring components was based
on the Bayes rule that states:

$$p(y|x) = \frac{1}{p(x)} \, p(x|y) \, p(y). \tag{9.1}$$

Applied to the task of translation, this means that instead of directly estimating the translation probabilities $p(y|x)$, we instead use the reverse translation probability to translate from target to source $p(x|y)$ and a language model $p(y)$. The normalization with $\frac{1}{p(x)}$ can be ignored, since the sentence x is identical for all translation candidates y.

Language Model

The main motivation behind the Bayes rule is to sneak in a language model probability $p(y)$. Such language models can be trained on large monolingual corpora. They are essential for good performance for statistical machine translation systems. In neural machine translation, a language model can be trained as described in Chapter 7 as a recurrent neural network. Adding this as an additional scorer in ensemble decoding is straightforward, since it also predicts the probability of the next word given the previously produced output words.

Reverse Translation Model

Adding the reverse translation probability $p(x|y)$ is harder, since it is conditioned on the entire output sentence. This output sentence is available only upon completion of decoding. So, we have to go back to the method presented in the previous section: reranking. We first generate candidate translations with the original translation model $p(y|x)$, then score each candidate translation with the reverse translation model $p(x|y)$, and finally combine the score to find the best overall translation.

9.3.3 Increasing the Diversity of the *n*-Best List

diversity Beam search for neural machine translation models uses fairly small beam sizes, typically in the range of 5–20. This also means that the generated *n*-best lists are small—they are as big as the beam size (paths in the beam search never merge, so they have a search tree rather than a search lattice, as in traditional statistical machine translation models). Moreover, the translations in the *n*-best list are very similar to each other. For long sentences, they differ only in the last words. See Figure 9.7 for an example.

For reranking it is important to have a diverse set of translations to choose from. If all the candidate translations make the same mistake early on, there is no way to recover from that. There have been some attempts to generate more diverse *n*-best lists.

Monte Carlo Decoding

Instead of strictly selecting the best word prediction, we can roll the dice each time. We use a loaded dice. If the word translation prediction is, say, that the next word is *wanted* with an 80% probability, then we pick this

He never wanted to participate in any kind of confrontation.
He never wanted to take part in any kind of confrontation.
He never wanted to participate in any kind of argument.
He never wanted to take part in any kind of argument.
He never wanted to participate in any sort of confrontation.
He never wanted to take part in any sort of confrontation.
He never wanted to participate in any sort of argument.
He never wanted to take part in any sort of argument.
He never wanted to participate in any kind of controversy.
He never wanted to take part in any kind of controversy.
He never intended to participate in any kind of confrontation.
He never intended to take part in any kind of confrontation.
He never wanted to take part in some sort of confrontation.
He never wanted to take part in any sort of controversy.

Figure 9.7 Example of an *n*-best list for the translation of the German sentence *Er wollte nie an irgendeiner Art von Auseinandersetzung teilnehmen.* Most of the translations are very similar, there is no variation in sentence structure, only word choices.

word translation with an 80% chance. This still most likely produces the highest scoring translation, but if we repeat this process, we generate a longer list of diverse translations. Note that this is generally a less efficient decoding strategy.

Adding a Diversity Bias Term

Diversity in the beam is reduced if one single hypothesis generates too many of the surviving next hypotheses. To avoid this, we may add a penalty for the second best, third best, etc. prediction of each hypothesis, based on its rank in the *n*-best list. To give an example, instead of using the predicted probabilities 0.6, 0.2, 0.1, etc., we use $0.6 \times \beta^0$, $0.2 \times \beta^1$, $0.1 \times \beta^2$. The exact value for the bias term β has to be set by hand in the range between 0 and 1.

9.3.4 Learning Weights for Scoring Components

I just presented a number of models that all provide a score for a sentence pair, consisting of an input sentence and a candidate translation. In addition to the regular neural machine translation model that generates the *n*-best list of candidate translations, I presented a right-to-left model that translates a sentences by generating the last word of the output sentence first and the reverse translation model that motivates the use of a translation model trained in the opposite language direction and a language model.

So far, we proposed to just multiply the component scores f_i together (or rather add their log-scores together) to combine them:

$$\text{score}(y|x) = \sum_i f_i(y|x). \tag{9.2}$$

But what if some of the components are just better than others and should be given more weight? Mathematically, this implies a weight λ_i for each component:

$$\text{score}(y|x) = \sum_i \lambda_i f_i(y|x). \qquad (9.3)$$

This raises the question: how do we set the weights λ_i?

If there are only a handful of components f_i, then some intuition and experimentation may suffice. For any set of weights $\{\lambda_i\}$, we can rerank the n-best lists for all the input sentences on a development set, see what comes out of top, and score these top-ranked translations against a reference translation.

However, instead of manually trying out different weight settings, we can automate the process. Before we go into actual methods, let us be very clear about the experimental setup, as illustrated in Figure 9.8. We have to set a aside a **development set**, also called a **tuning set** of sentence pairs. Typically a few thousand sentences are used for this, hopefully representative of the type of test data that need to be generated.

For the input sentences in the tuning set, we generate n-best lists of candidate translations. For each candidate translation, we compute additional scores with the other components, and also a quality score. Computing a per sentence quality score is not straightforward for metrics such as BLEU, which is computed over the entire set and not as

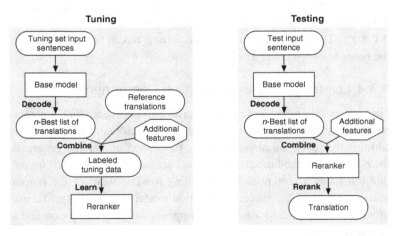

Figure 9.8 Reranking. To use features that cannot be computed during decoding (such as an right-to-left model or a reverse model in the other language direction), we first generate an n-best list of translations, score each translation with the additional features, and pick the one with best overall score. We may want to train feature weights to balance their contribution to rank high-quality translations on top.

an average over each score in the set. Typical stand-ins are (1) computing sentence-level BLEU scores (often with smoothing counts by adding one to each n-gram match count), (2) computing impact on the overall set level BLEU score if only the translation for the sentence in question is changed, or (3) computing the relevant statistics (n-gram match count, sentence length, reference length) and using these in the algorithm.

The resulting set of input sentences, their n-best list of translations, and component scores and quality scores for each of them are the labeled training data for the method to learn the weights of the reranker.

It's useful to compute the **Oracle score** for the development set and the n-best lists generated by the base model. It is the most optimistic score that we could reach if the highest quality translation comes out on top for every n-best list. While it is overly optimistic of what we can actually reach, it is nevertheless a useful upper bar to know. Especially, if the Oracle score is not very high, it is an indicator that either our base model is not very good or that its n-best list is not diverse enough.

Grid Search

If we have few scoring components and a set of reasonable weights for each of them (say: 0.1, 0.2, 0.5, 1, 2, 5, 10), then we can iterate over all the possible weights for all the components, rerank the n-best list, obtain the overall score, and see what weight setting is best. If we consider w possible weights for c components, then this requires c^w loops over the reranker, which is feasible if both c and w are relatively small (less than, say, 10). If we find a good weight setting, we may follow up with a finer grained grid search that explores weights in a small interval over the best-found weight setting.

Minimum Error Rate Training (MERT)

This method was a core element of training statistical machine translation systems for many years. If proceeds by optimizing one weight at a time. If we leave all the other weights fixed (starting with reasonable initial values for them), we can explore how different values impact the ranking of n-best lists, especially if a different translation comes out on top. A key insight is that small changes to the targeted weight do not make any difference. We can determine the threshold points for the weight values where there are actual changes to top-1 translations, resulting in a finite set of intervals that we have to explore. Hence we can actually exhaustively find the optimal value for a single weight (assuming that all the others are fixed). We do this for all weights, one at a time, possibly for multiple iterations until no single weight change leads to any improvement.

Pairwise Ranked Optimization (PRO)

We can turn the reranking challenge into a classification problem. By selecting two candidate translations from the n-best list, we have both their component scores and their quality scores. So we know which translation is better. This gives us a training example of the shape *score-difference* $\rightarrow$ {*better, worse*}. If we train a linear classifier that learns weights to do well on this classification task, then we can use these obtained weights in our reranker.

Note that reranking methods are not very common in today's neural machine translation systems, partly because they lack the elegance of a single comprehensive model and partly because they have not shown much gain over the limited number of components that have been considered. In contrast to this, reranking (also called parameter tuning), was a core step in statistical machine translation. Chapter 9 in the textbook *Statistical Machine Translation* (Koehn, 2010) includes a longer discussion that mostly still applies to neural machine translation.

9.4 Optimizing Decoding

optimizing decoding An important step in the training of traditional statistical machine translation systems is a tuning step where translation quality (typically measured in BLEU) is optimized based on a small tuning set of a few thousand sentence pairs. This draws a distinction between a generative model, which attempts to represent the training data accurately, and discriminative training, which aims to do well on the task. These approaches are not that different in neural machine translation. Neural machine translation models are directly optimized to predict the next word in a translation, which is pretty much the translation task.

Still, the single word prediction task may still fall short from the actual task of translating full sentences. The biggest concern is that the word prediction task is always performed given a perfect prefix. It is framed as a task given that all the previous word predictions were made the correct way. During actual test time, decoding may make bad decisions early on and then go completely off track. So maybe we want to optimize for the full sentence translation task instead.

Sentence Level Cost Function

There has been some work on changing the training objective from next-word prediction toward optimizing toward sentence-level scores. In this setup, during training, inference is run first on the full sentence (typically greedy search), then the cost is computed as a sentence-level quality score, for instance using a sentence-level BLEU score.

While the idea is straightforward, the actual execution of this idea is computationally expensive. Previously, we computed error feedback for every word in a way that was easy to parallelize over a batch of training examples. Now, we receive feedback just once per sentence, and we have less control over the target sentence length, which makes it harder to batch sentence pairs by length. At the time of writing, this technique has not found wide use.

Synthetic Training Data

If the goal is to produce translations that have high BLEU scores, we could create a tuning data set that consist of such translations. We first run the decoder on this tuning set, generate n-best lists, and then select the translation (or translations) with the highest score. We then train a neural machine translation model on these data, i.e., the original input sentence paired with the BLEU-best candidate from the n-best list.

What are the benefits of such synthetic translations compared to the actual reference translation, which would have the highest metric score? Simply put, the synthetic translations are more reachable by the model. They allow us to nudge the model toward better translations, rather than trying to shoot for the moon, i.e., reaching reference translations that are too far from what the current model would predict.

9.5 Directing Decoding

There are many occasions when we may want to override the best predictions of the decoding algorithm. In commercial scenarios, specific translation tasks often require adherence to pre-specified terminology. Maybe we use machine translation in an interactive environment where a translator can approve or reject choices of the machine translation system and we would need to respond with a translation that adheres to these decisions. We may also have a rule-based component that translates dates or quantities (e.g., dates from Western to Arabic calendars, temperatures from Celsius to Fahrenheit).

directing decoding

We may also want to direct the decoder to follow a specific word order, such as translating one part of the translation first or keeping specific phrases together.

9.5.1 XML Schema

XML

Such constraints to the decoding algorithm may be specified in a XML markup language. To give an example:

The <x translation="Router">router</x> is <wall/> a model <zone>Psy X500 Pro</zone>.

The XML tags specify to the decoder that

- the word *router* should be translated as *Router*
- the first part of the sentence, *The router is*, should be translated before the rest (`<wall/>`)
- the brand name *Psy X500 Pro* should be translated as a unit (`<zone>`, `</zone>`)

Integrating such a scheme into a traditional statistical machine translation decoding algorithm is straightforward, since that algorithm tracks alignment and coverage explicitly. Because each word is translated only once, specifying a translation for it with an XML tag simply overrides all existing translation options provided by the model. The decoder has no choice but to use it.

Enforcing such constraints on a neural machine translation decoder is much more difficult. There are no hard constraints on coverage and alignment—output words are only weakly linked via the attention mechanism to input words. So, if the attention mechanism is sufficiently focused on an input word with a specified translation, the decoding algorithm may chose to use the specified translations instead. But what is sufficient attention? And how do we ensure that the input word does not get translated again?

The XML scheme described in this chapter is implemented in the widely used statistical machine translation decoder Moses, but work in neural machine translation has so far addressed only the specification of word or phrase translations. Even that is still an open research challenge, but some ideas have been explored with some degree of success, measured both by the accuracy by which the specifications are followed and by the impact on overall translation quality.

9.5.2 Grid Search

grid search

Let us now take a look at one method to integrate translation constraints into neural machine translation decoding.

One concern is that satisfying a constraint comes at a cost — it typically forces the decoder to use low-probability word predictions and hence would generate hypotheses that would be pruned out by the beam search. Ad hoc measures to combat this are all flawed in different ways. If we make satisfying constraints free (i.e., not factoring in translation probabilities), then there is an incentive to first satisfy all the constraints, no matter if they really make sense only later in the sentence. Keeping all scoring but adding a constraint satisfaction bonus creates a new hyper parameter whose optimal value depends on each specific input sentence.

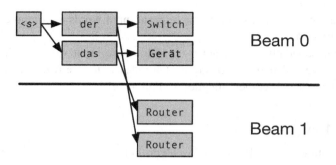

Beam 0

Beam 1

Figure 9.9 Grid search. Several beams are used to translate a sentence, based on the number of satisfied decoding constraints. When an hypothesis expansion satisfies a decoding constraint (here: producing the output word *Router*), it is placed in the next beam.

Hence came the idea to break up the beam depending on which constraints have been satisfied. Instead of a single beam that contains all hypothesis, we have a set of beams, one for each subset of constraints. Since we have now two dimensions (beams, hypotheses in beams), this is called a **grid** (Figure 9.9).

At any point in the search, we may want to start satisfying a constraint. This moves the subsequent hypothesis into a different beam. In that beam, the new hypothesis has to compete against other hypotheses that have satisfied the same constraints and hence are on a level playing field. An hypothesis that satisfies the constraints in a way that interferes the least with the underlying model will come out on top.

Upon conclusion of search, the best hypothesis in the beam where all constraints are satisfied points to the best translation.

9.5.3 Enforcing Attention

attention guided decoding

The grid search algorithm that we described so far only enforced that the output contains the translations that were specified. However, it did not consider that these translations should be placed at specific positions in the output and replace translations that the model would consider. So, the model may introduce these specified translations to replace the model's preferences for other output words or just in add them to its own full sentence translation.

Satisfying constraints should be guided by the attention mechanism, even if it is not a perfect means of alignment and coverage tracking. Attention to input words covered by a constraint should guide satisfying a constraint. We may enforce a limit on the minimum amount of attention that has to be paid to these input words in order to start constraint satisfaction.

Alternatively, we can consider the attention weight given to the relevant input words when satisfying a constraint as an additional cost factor. Hypotheses that cover a constraint when their attention is focused somewhere else should be penalized. A simple method is to add up the attention weight given to the relevant input words to compute this penalty cost.

Subsequently, we do not want to translate input words again for which we satisfied the constraint. One idea is to override the model predictions and set their attention weight to zero.

9.5.4 Evaluation

Evaluating how well a decoding algorithm performs when satisfying translation constraints is somewhat complex. When the specified output words are very unlikely according to the model, the decoder may get confused and generate very bad translations for the full sentence. This has been observed in practice. There are also types of errors specific to constraint decoding, such as the double decoding of input words covered by constraints and replacing the wrong output words.

Instead of hard enforcement of constraints, for some use cases we may instead want to balance the two goals of satisfying as many constraints as possible and achieving high translation quality. How to do this is still an open research question at the time of writing.

9.6 Hands On: Decoding in Python

Decoding is surprisingly independent from the specifics of the neural machine translation model and even the underlying tool kit used to implement it. The only interaction between decoding and the model is the call of the forward step to make one additional output word prediction. The decoding algorithm also needs to keep track of the hidden state of the model's decoder but does not need to know anything about what the state represents and how it is used within the model.

To illustrate the implementation of beam search, we provide code that could be attached to the neural machine translation model training from the previous section. Often, it makes sense to have training and decoder separated into two different executables. At the end of training, the best model is saved to disk. The decoder then loads this model to translate any input.

9.6.1 Hypothesis

A core data structure is the hypothesis, a node in the search tree, representing a partial translation. In our code, we just use it as a handy object to hold the four relevant facts about a search node: a link to the previous hypothesis, the corresponding hidden state in the model, the last generated output word, and the cost, i.e., the negative log-likelihood of the word translation probabilities of the path so far:

```python
class Hypothesis:
  def __init__(self,prev_hyp,state,word,cost):
    self.prev_hyp = prev_hyp
    self.state = state
    self.word = word
    self.cost = cost
```

9.6.2 Beam

The other data structure is the beam that holds a set of hypotheses. It is common to implement it as a class that internally handles adding hypotheses to the beam and other utility functions. For instance, it may hold useful information like the threshold value of the maximum cost for a new hypothesis to make it into the beam. A beam also has a maximum size, which it knows from the beginning:

```python
class Beam:
  def __init__(self,max_size):
    self.max_size = max_size
    self.hyp_list = []
    self.threshold = float('inf')
```

Adding an hypothesis to the beam is somewhat complex. We add only a hypothesis to the beam if would be among the top n hypotheses according to its cost. There are also a few special cases to consider. Let us walk through them.

First of all, the class function add takes a new hypothesis generated by the search algorithm:

```python
def add(self,new_hyp):
```

If the beam is not full yet, we can add it without any concern:

```python
if len(self.hyp_list) < self.max_size:
  self.hyp_list.append(new_hyp)
  return
```

Otherwise, we have to check if its cost is better than the cost of the worst hypothesis in the beam. There are fancy data structures to handle this, but let us be transparent and just search for the worst hypothesis on the beam explicitly:

```
self.threshold = 0
worst = 0
for i, hyp in enumerate(self.hyp_list):
  if hyp.cost > self.threshold:
    self.threshold = hyp.cost
    worst = i
```

This gives us the position `worst` of the worst hypothesis in the list `hyp_list` and its score `self.threshold`, which, as a side effect, is conveniently stored as a class variable.

We want to add the new hypothesis only if it has a better cost than the worst hypothesis. If that is indeed the case, we just overwrite the worst hypothesis:

```
if new_hyp.cost < self.threshold:
  self.hyp_list[worst] = new_hyp
```

Another useful class function deals with the size of the next beam. Recall that we reduce the beam size when one hypothesis reaches the end of the sentence. So the number of allowed extensions, i.e., the next size of the next beam, is the size of the current beam, minus the number of the hypotheses that end here. This is implemented in the following function:

```
def maxExtension(self):
  max_extension = len(self.hyp_list)
  for hyp in self.hyp_list:
    if hyp.word == END_OF_SENTENCE:
      max_extension -= 1
  return max_extension
```

9.6.3 Search

With the required data structures in place, we are ready for the beam search algorithm. It starts with a number of initializations, such as the declaration of the ID numbers of the start-of-sentence and end-of-sentence tokens, the maximum beam size:

```
START_OF_SENTENCE = 0
END_OF_SENTENCE = 1
MAX_BEAM = 12
```

Setting up the model requires encoding the given source sentence. We presume that the encoder and decoder have been instantiated already and their model parameters are loaded:

```
encoder_output = encoder.process_sentence( source_sentence )
```

Setting up beam search requires an initial beam that contains an initial hypothesis. The initial hypothesis consists of the initial decoder hidden state and the start-of-sentence token as word. It does not have a prior hypothesis (set to None) or cost (set to 0):

```
init_hyp = Hypothesis(None, decoder.initHidden(), START_OF_SENTENCE, 0)
beam = Beam( MAX_BEAM )
beam.add( init_hyp )
history = [ beam ]
```

We record the history of the beam search in the variable history.

We are ready to decode. The natural stop point of search is when the required number (MAX_BEAM) of hypotheses have reached the end-of-sentence token. But there is no guarantee that this token will ever be produced and weak translation models often get stuck in endless loops of generating the same output word or phrase over and over again. So, another stopping criterion would be to not produce a translation that is much longer than the input sentence. This is what we encode in the loop setup:

```
for position in range(len(source_sentence) * 2 + 5):
```

Before the real action starts, we need to determine how many hypotheses we need to generate for the new beam. Initially, this is MAX_BEAM but later we need to consult the previous beam to how many hypotheses have not reached the end of end-of-sentence token. If that is 0, then search has completed:

```
if position == 0:
  max_size = MAX_BEAM
else:
  max_size = beam.maxExtension()
  if max_size == 0:
    break
new_beam = Beam(max_size)
```

We now start extending hypothesis in the previous beam, unless they have reached the end of the sentence:

```
for hyp in beam.hyp_list:
  if hyp.word == END_OF_SENTENCE:
    continue
```

We consult the model for predictions for the next word:

```
output, hidden = decoder.forward( hyp.word,
                                   hyp.state,
                                   encoder_output,
                                   len(source_sentence) )
output = output[0].data
```

This gives us a distribution over output words. Recall that output is a mapping from all possible output word token IDs to a log-probability, as computed by the softmax. We now loop over this and create a new hypothesis if its cost (negative log-probability plus the cost of the original hypothesis) is below the threshold to make it into the beam:

```
for word in range(len(output)):
  cost = -output[word].item() + hyp.cost
  if cost < new_beam.threshold:
    new_hyp = Hypothesis( hyp, hidden, word, cost )
    new_beam.add( new_hyp )
```

At the end of all this, just a little bookkeeping: recording the new beam in the `history` and making the previous beam for the next iteration:

```
history.append( new_beam )
beam = new_beam
```

9.6.4 Report Best Translation

The search terminates with a search graph that contains all hypotheses, including full translations, i.e., hypothesis that end with an end-of-sentence token. Among these, we need to find the one with the best cost:

```
best = None
best_cost = float('inf')
for beam in history:
  for hyp in beam.hyp_list:
    if hyp.word == END_OF_SENTENCE and hyp.cost < best_cost:
      best_cost = hyp.cost
      best = hyp
```

We can read off the translation by following the back pointers of the best hypotheses, until we reach the initial hypothesis (that has no previous hypothesis):

```
hyp = best
translation = []
while hyp.prev_hyp != None:
  hyp = hyp.prev_hyp
  translation.insert( 0, target_vocab.id2word[ hyp.word ] )
print(' '.join(translation))
```

9.7 Further Readings

Beam Search Refinements

beam search

Hu et al. (2015b) modify the search in two ways. Instead of expanding all hypotheses of a stack of maximum size N, expand only the one best hypothesis from any stack at a time. To avoid only expanding the shortest hypothesis, a brevity penalty is introduced. Similarly, Shu and Nakayama (2018) do not generate a fixed number of hypotheses for each partial translation length but instead organize hypotheses in a single priority queue regardless of their length. They also use a length penalty (called progress penalty) and a prediction of the output length. Freitag and Al-Onaizan (2017) introduce threshold pruning to neural machine translation. Hypotheses whose score falls below a certain fraction of the best score are discarded, showing faster decoding while maintaining quality. Zhang et al. (2018c) explore recombination, a well-known technique in statistical machine translation decoding. They merge hypotheses that share the most recent output words and that are of similar length, thus speeding up decoding and reaching higher quality with fixed beam size. Zhang et al. (2018b) apply the idea of cube pruning to neural model decoding, by grouping together hypotheses with the same last output word into so-called "subcubes". States are expanded sequentially, starting with the highest scoring hypothesis from the highest scoring subcube, thus obtaining probabilities for subsequent hypotheses. For some hypotheses, states are not expanded when no promising new hypotheses would be generated from them.

One problem with beam search is that larger beam sizes lead to an earlier generation of the end-of-sentence symbol and thus shorter translations. Kikuchi et al. (2016) force the decoder to produce translations within a prespecified length range by ignoring other completed hypothesis. They also add a length embedding as an additional input feature to the decoder state progression. He et al. (2016b) add a word bonus for each generated word (they also propose to add lexical translation probabilities and an *n*-gram language model). Murray and Chiang (2018) learn the optimal value for this word bonus. Huang et al. (2017) add a bounded word reward that boosts hypothesis length up to an expected optimal length. Yang et al. (2018a) refine this reward and also change the stopping criteria for beam search so that sufficiently many long translations are generated.

Stochastic Search

stochastic search Monte-Carlo decoding was used by Ott et al. (2018a) to analyze the search space and by Edunov et al. (2018a) for back-translation.

Greedy Search

greedy search Cho (2016) proposes a variant of greedy decoding where noise is added to the hidden state of the decoder. Multiple passes are performed with different random noise and by picking the translation with the highest probability assigned by the nonnoisy model. Gu et al. (2017a) build on this idea to develop a trainable greedy decoding method. Instead of a noise term, they learn an adjustment term that is optimized on sentence-level translation quality (as measured by BLEU) using reinforcement learning.

Fast Decoding

Devlin (2017) obtains speed-ups with precomputation and the use of 16-bit floating point operations. Zhang et al. (2018b) remove the normalization in the softmax output word prediction, after adjusting the training objective to perform self-normalization. Hoang et al. (2018a) speed up decoding by batching several input sentences, refined k-best extraction with specialized GPU kernel functions, and use of 16-bit floating point operations. Iglesias et al. (2018) also show improvements with such batching. Argueta and Chiang (2019) fuse the softmax and k-best extraction computation. Senellart et al. (2018) build a smaller model with knowledge distillation that allows faster decoding.

fast decoding

Limiting Hypothesis Generation

Hu et al. (2015b) limit the computation of translation probabilities to words that are in the phrase table of a traditional phrase-based model for the input sentence, leading to several-fold speed-ups with little loss in quality. Extending this work, Mi et al. (2016) also consider top word translations and the most frequent words in the vocabulary filter for the prediction computation. Shi and Knight (2017) use dictionaries obtained from statistical alignment models and (unsuccessfully) locality sensitive hashing to speed up decoding.

limiting hypothesis generation

Limiting Search Space

Compared to statistical machine translation, neural machine translation may be less adequate, even if more fluent. In other words, the translation may diverge from the input in various ways, such as not translating part of the sentence or generating unrelated output words. Zhang et al. (2017a) propose to limit the search space of the neural decoder to the search graph generated by a phrase-based system. Khayrallah et al. (2017) extend this to the search lattice.

limiting search space

Reranking

Niehues et al. (2017) explore the search space considered during decoding. While they find that decoding makes very few search errors, better translation results could be obtained by picking other translations considered during beam search. Similarly, Blain et al. (2017) observe that very large beam sizes hurt 1-best decoding but generate higher scoring translations in the n-best list. Liu et al. (2016a) rerank the n-best list by training a model that generates the output starting with the last word of the sentence, called left-to-right decoding. Their approach was successfully used by Sennrich et al. (2016b) in their winning system in the WMT 2016 shared task. Hoang et al. (2017) propose using a model trained in the inverse translation direction and a language model.

reranking

Li and Jurafsky (2016) generate more diverse n-best lists by adding a bias term to penalize too many expansions of a single hypothesis. In a refinement, Li et al. (2016) learn the diversity rate with reinforcement learning, using as reward the generation of n-best lists that yield better translation quality after reranking. Stahlberg et al. (2017) use minimum Bayes risk to rerank decoding lattices. This method also allows the combination of SMT and NMT search graphs. Iglesias et al. (2018) show gains for minimum Bayes risk decoding for the Transformer model.

Niehues et al. (2016) attach the phrase-based translation to the input sentence and feed that into a neural machine translation decoder. Geng et al. (2018) extend this idea to multipass decoding. The output of a regular decoding pass is then used as additional input to a second decoding pass. This process is iterated for a fixed number of steps or stopped based on the decision of a so-called policy network. Zhou et al. (2017) propose a system combination method that combines the output of different translation systems (such as NMT and variants of SMT) that takes the form of multisource decoding, i.e., using multiple encoders, one for each system output, feeding into a single decoder that produces the consensus output.

decoding constraint ### Decoding Constraints

In practical deployment of machine translation, there is often a need to override model predictions with prespecified word or phrase translations, for instance to enforce required terminology or to support external components. Chatterjee et al. (2017) allow the specification of pre-defined translations for certain input words and modify the decoder to use them, based on input word attention. Hokamp and Liu (2017) modify the decoding algorithm to force the decoder to produce certain specified output strings. Each time such one of the output strings is produced, hypotheses are placed into a different beam, and final translations are picked from the beam, which contains hypotheses that produced all specified output. Related to this idea, Anderson et al. (2017) mark hypotheses with states in a finite state machine that indicate the subset of constraints (prespecified translations) that have been satisfied. Hasler et al. (2018) refine this approach by using a linear (not exponential) number of constraint satisfaction states and also remove attention from words whose constraints have been satisfied. Post and Vilar (2018) split up the beam into subbeams, instead of duplicating beams to prevent an increase in decoding time for sentences with such constraints. Hu et al. (2019) extends this work with a trie structure to encode constraints, thus improving the handling of constraints that start with the same words and also improve batching.

Song et al. (2019) replace the words with their specified translations in the input and aid the translation of such code-switched data with a pointer network that handles the copying of the specified translations. Dinu et al. (2019) also present the specified translations as input, but in addition to the original source words and using a source factor to label input tokens according to the three classes: regular input word, input word with specified translation, and specified translation.

Simultaneous Translation

simultaneous translation

Integrating speech recognition and machine translation for the real-time translation of spoken language, requires decoding algorithms that operate on an incoming stream of input words and the production of translations for them before the input sentence is complete, as much as that is possible. Satija and Pineau (2016) propose using reinforcement learning to learn the trade-off between waiting for input and producing output. Cho and Esipova (2016) frame the problem as predicting a sequence of read and write actions, i.e., reading an additional input word and writing out an output word. Gu et al. (2017b) optimize the decoding algorithm with reinforcement learning based on this frame-work. Alinejad et al. (2018) refine this with an prediction operation that predicts the next input words. Dalvi et al. (2018) propose a simpler static read-and-write approach that reads a certain number of input words ahead. Similarly, Ma et al. (2019b) use a wait-k strategy that reads a fixed number of words ahead and trains a prefix-to-prefix translation model. They argue that their model learns to anticipate missing content. Arivazhagan et al. (2019) integrate the learning of the size of the look-ahead window into the attention mechanism. Their training objective takes both prediction accuracy and look-ahead penalty into account. Similarly, Zheng et al. (2019) also train an end-to-end model that learns translation predictions and look-ahead (i.e., read) operations at the same time. For training, action sequences are generated from the training data with different look-ahead window sizes.

Lattice Decoding

In the case of speech translation off-line, i.e., for a stored audio file without any real-time requirements, tighter integration of the speech recognition component and the machine translation component may be attempted. A common strategy is to expose the full search graph of the speech recognition system in form of a word lattice, a method that also works for preserving ambiguity for word segmentation, morphological analysis, or differing byte pair encoding vocabularies. Zhang et al. (2019a) propose a novel attention mechanism over lattices. It excludes consideration of nodes in the lattice that cannot be in the same path

lattice decoding

for any given node and also incorporates the probabilities of nodes in the lattice.

interactive translation
prediction

Interactive Translation Prediction

Another special decoding scenario is the interactive translation by machines and humans. In this setup, the machine translation system offers up suggestions for word translations, one word at a time, which the human translator either accepts or modifies. Either way, the machine translation system has to propose extensions to the current partial translation. Knowles and Koehn (2016) show that neural methods make better predictions than traditional statistical methods with search lattice methods. Wuebker et al. (2016) and Peris et al. (2017b) also suggest force decoding the given partial translation and let the model make subsequent predictions. Knowles et al. (2019) carried out a study with professional translators, showing that interactive translation predictions allow some of them to translate faster. Peris and Casacuberta (2019) extend this technology to other sequence-to-sequence tasks, such as image captioning.

Part III
Refinements

Chapter 10
Machine Learning Tricks

Machine learning has a beautiful story to tell. Given a set of examples of a real world problem (in our case, translated sentence pairs), an algorithm automatically builds a model that represents the model so it can then make predictions. Deep learning promises that we do not even need to worry much about the specific properties of the problem (for instance, that sentences have verbs and nouns that play different roles). No, deep learning automatically discovers these and does away with the task of feature engineering. And all this just by the simple method of error back-propagation via gradient descent.

The unfortunate reality is that deep learning for complex problems such as machine translation requires a bag of tricks that addresses the many ways the basic learning algorithm may get off track. In this chapter, I first survey common pitfalls of machine learning and then go over methods that today's neural machine translation models use to address them.

This chapter reminds me of a conversation long ago with one of my graduate students who ventured deep into machine learning and whose thesis draft had a chapter on various machine learning tricks. I asked him why he listed all of those obscure and often counterintuitive methods, and he answered: "Because I use them all." The same is true today.

10.1 Failures in Machine Learning

machine learning failures

We painted a picture of gradient descent as walking down the hillside to a valley of minimum error. Even in this simple world—which ignores that we operated in a space with thousands, maybe even millions of

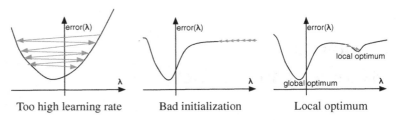

Too high learning rate   Bad initialization   Local optimum

Figure 10.1 Problems with gradient descent training that motivate some of the refinements detailed in this chapter. (a) A too high learning rate may lead to too drastic parameter updates, overshooting the optimum. (b) Bad initialization may require many updates to escape a plateau. (c) The existence of local optima trap training.

dimensions—a lot can go wrong. Some of the basic failures are pictured in Figure 10.1.

learning rate ### Learning Rate
The learning rate is a hyper parameter that defines how much the gradients are scaled to perform weight updates. In its simplest form, this is a fixed value that has to be set by hand. Setting the learning rate too high leads to updates that overshoot the optimum (Figure 10.1a). Conversely, a too low learning rate leads to slow convergence.

There are additional considerations about setting the learning rate. At the beginning of training, all the weights are far from optimal values, so we want to change them a lot. At later stages, updates are more nuanced, and we do not expect major changes. So, we may want to initially set the learning rate high, but decrease it over time. This general annealing idea is called **annealing**. Later in this chapter, we will explore more sophisticated methods that adjust the learning rate.

weight initialization ### Initialization of Weights
At the beginning of training, all weights are initialized to random values. Randomness is important so that the different hidden nodes start with different values and hence are able to learn different roles to play. If these values are very far from an optimum, we may need many update steps to reach it (Figure 10.1b). This is especially a problem with activation functions like sigmoid, which have only a short interval of significant change, and even more so with rectified linear units, which have gradients of zero for some interval. We obviously do not have a crystal ball to randomly set weights close to their optimal values, but at least they should be in a range of values that are easy to adjust, i.e., where changes to their values have an impact.

Local Optima

local optimum

Figure 10.1c gives a simple depiction of the problem of a local optimum. Instead of reaching the deep valley of the global optimum, training gets stuck in a little dip. Moving left or right would mean going uphill, so we will not leave it. The existence of local optima lead the search to get trapped and miss the global optimum.

Note that the depiction is a vast simplification of the problem. We usually operate with activation functions that are convex, i.e., they have a clear optimum that can be reached. However, we are operating with many parameters that span a highly dimensional space, and we also process many training examples (or batches of training examples) for which the error surface looks different every time.

Vanishing and Exploding Gradients

A specific problem of deep neural networks, especially recurrent neural networks, is the problem of vanishing and exploding gradients. A characteristics of these networks is a long path of computations that connects the input to the output of the computation. The error is measured at the output, but it has to be propagated all the way to the first parameters that operate on the input.

Recall that this happens by multiplication of the gradients of the computations along the path. If all of these gradients are above 1, we end up with a large number at the end (called **exploding gradients**). If all of these gradients are below 1, we end up close to zero (called **vanishing gradients**; see Figure 10.2). Hence we make either too extreme or practically no updates to the parameters for the early computations in the path.

exploding gradient
vanishing gradient

Note that this problem is especially acute for recurrent neural networks. Here, the long path of computations from input to output is packed with loops over the same calculations. Any increase or decrease of gradient values is accelerated in these loops.

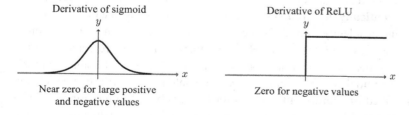

Derivative of sigmoid

Near zero for large positive and negative values

Derivative of ReLU

Zero for negative values

Figure 10.2 Vanishing gradients. If gradients are close to zero, no updates are applied to parameters, also for parameters upstream in the computation graph.

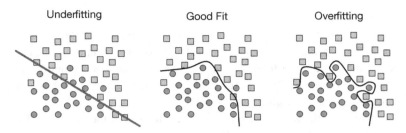

| Underfitting | Good Fit | Overfitting |

Figure 10.3 Underfitting and overfitting. With too few trainable parameters (low capacity), the model cannot match the data well (underfitting). Having too many parameters (high capacity) leads to memorizing the training data and insufficient generalization (overfitting).

Overfitting and Underfitting

The goal of machine learning is to learn the general principles of a problem based on representative examples. It does so by setting the values of the model parameters for a provided model architecture. The complexity of the model has to match the complexity of the problem. If the model has too many parameters and training runs long enough, the model will memorize all the training examples, but do poorly on

overfitting   unseen test examples. This is called **overfitting**. On the other hand, if the number of parameters is too small, the model will not be able to

underfitting   represent the problem. This is called **underfitting**.

Figure 10.3 shows a two-dimensional classification task. A too simple model that can only draw a line between the red circles and the green squares will not be able to learn the true curve separating the two classes. Having too much freedom to draw the curve leads to insufficient gener-

capacity   alization. The degree of freedom is called the **capacity** of the model.

10.2 Ensuring Randomness

randomness

The ideal view of machine learning is that we are starting in some random point in parameter space, encounter randomly **independent and identically distributed** training examples (meaning that they are drawn independently from the same underlying true probability distribution), and move closer to a model that resembles the truth. To come close to this ideal, it is important to avoid undue structure in the training data and the initial weight setting. There is a whole machine learning approach

maximum entropy training   called **maximum entropy training** that is based on the principle that absent concrete evidence, the model should be as random as possible (i.e., have maximum entropy).

10.2.1 Shuffling the Training Data

The training data used for neural machine translation typically come **shuffling training data** from several sources, say the European Parliament Proceedings or a collection of subtitle translations. These individual corpora have very specific characteristics that drive training into different directions. Each corpus may also have internally different characteristics, for instance a chronological sorted corpus that draws training data initially from older text and ends with the latest additions.

Since we are updating the weights one batch of training data at a time, they will be more affected by the last training examples seen. If the last part of the training data is all from one of the corpora, this biases the model unfairly to it. Note also that we typically stop training once performance on a validation set does not improve—measured by cross-entropy or translation quality such as the BLEU score. If parts of the training data are more helpful than others (or just more similar to the validation set), these performance measures may differ over the course of training, and training may be prematurely stopped just because a harmful stretch of training examples is encountered.

To balance out these effects, the training data are randomly shuffled at the beginning of training. It is common to reshuffle the training data each epoch (each full pass through the training data), but this may not be necessary due to the very large corpora used in neural machine translation.

10.2.2 Weight Initialization

initialization

Before training starts, weights are initialized to random values. The values are chosen from a uniform distribution. We prefer initial weights that lead to node values that are in the transition area for the activation function and not in the low or high shallow slope where it would take a long time to push toward a change. For instance, for the sigmoid activation function, feeding values in the range of, say, $[-1; 1]$ to the activation function leads to activation values in the range of $[0.269; 0.731]$.

For the sigmoid activation function, commonly used formulas for weights to the final layer of a network are

$$\left[-\frac{1}{\sqrt{n}}, \frac{1}{\sqrt{n}} \right], \tag{10.1}$$

where n is the size of the previous layer. For hidden layers, we chose weights from the range

$$\left[-\frac{\sqrt{6}}{\sqrt{n_j + n_{j+1}}}, \frac{\sqrt{6}}{\sqrt{n_j + n_{j+1}}} \right], \tag{10.2}$$

where n_j is the size of the previous layer, n_{j+1} size of next layer.

These formulas were first suggested by Glorot and Bengio (2010).

10.2.3 Label Smoothing

label smoothing

The predictions of the neural machine translation models are surprisingly confident. Often almost all the probability mass is assigned to a single word, with word prediction probabilities of over 99%. These peaked probability distributions are a problem for both decoding and training. In decoding sensible alternatives are not given enough credence, preventing successful beam search. In training, overfitting is more likely.

A common strategy for combating peaked distributions during decoding is to smooth them (Chorowski and Jaitly, 2017). As I described it so far, the prediction layer produces numbers for each word that are converted into probabilities using the softmax:

$$p(y_i) = \frac{\exp s_i}{\sum_j \exp s_j}. \tag{10.3}$$

temparature The softmax calculation can be smoothed with what is commonly called a **temperature** T:

$$p(y_i) = \frac{\exp s_i/T}{\sum_j \exp s_j/T}. \tag{10.4}$$

With higher temperature, the distribution becomes smoother, i.e., less probability is given to the most likely choice.

But the problem of peaked distributions is rooted in training where the truth assigns all probability mass to a single word, so the training objective is to optimize toward such distributions. To remedy this, we can present as truth not this perfectly peaked distribution but a smoothed distribution that spreads out some of the probability mass (say, 10% of it) to other words. This may be done uniformly (assigning all words the same probability), but may also take unigram word probabilities into account (relative counts of each word in the target side of the training data).

10.3 Adjusting the Learning Rate

adjusting the learning rate

Gradient descent training implies a simple weight update strategy: just follow the gradient downhill. Since the actual gradients have fairly large values, we scale the gradient with a learning rate—typically a very low number such as 0.001. Moreover, we may want to change the learning rate over time (starting with larger updates, and then refining weights with smaller updates), or adjust it for other reasons.

A simple **learning rate schedule** may reduce the learning rate after   learning rate schedule
each epoch, maybe cutting it in half. But more sophisticated method have been proposed and are in common use.

10.3.1 Momentum Term

Consider the case where a weight value is far from its optimum. Even if most training examples push the weight value in the same direction, it may still take a while for each of these small updates to accumulate until the weight reaches its optimum. A common trick is to use a **momentum term** to speed up training. This momentum term m_t gets updated at   momentum term
each time step t (i.e., for each training example). We combine the previous value of the momentum term m_{t-1} with the current raw weight update value Δw_t and use the resulting momentum term value to update the weights.

For instance, with a decay rate of 0.9, the update formula changes to

$$m_t = 0.9m_{t-1} + \Delta w_t$$
$$w_t = w_{t-1} - \mu\, m_t. \tag{10.5}$$

10.3.2 Adapting Learning Rate per Parameter

A common training strategy is to reduce the learning rate μ over time. At the beginning the parameters are far away from optimal values and have to change a lot, but in later training stages we are concerned with nuanced refinements, and a large learning rate may cause a parameter to bounce around an optimum.

Adagrad

Different parameters may be at different stages on the path to their optimal values, so a different learning rate for each parameter may be helpful. One such method, called **Adagrad**, records the gradients that   Adagrad
were computed for each parameter and accumulates their square values over time, and uses this sum to adjust the learning rate.

The Adagrad update formula is based on the sum of gradients of the error E with respect to the weight w at all time steps t, i.e., $g_t = \frac{\partial E_t}{\partial w}$. We divide the learning rate μ for this weight by the accumulated sum of gradients:

$$\Delta w_t = \frac{\mu}{\sqrt{\sum_{\tau=1}^{t} g_\tau^2}}\, g_t. \tag{10.6}$$

Intuitively, big changes in the parameter value (corresponding to big gradients g_t), lead to a reduction of the learning rate of the weight parameter.

Adam

Adam Combining the idea of momentum term and adjusting parameter update by their accumulated change is the inspiration of **Adam**, another method to transform the raw gradient into a parameter update.

First, there is the idea of momentum, which is computed as in Equation 10.5:

$$m_t = \beta_1 m_{t-1} + (1 - \beta_1)g_t. \tag{10.7}$$

Then, there is the idea of the squares of gradients (as in Adagrad) for adjusting the learning rate. Since raw accumulation runs the risk of becoming too large, and hence permanently depressing the learning rate, Adam uses exponential decay, just like for the momentum term:

$$v_t = \beta_2 v_{t-1} + (1 - \beta_2)g_t^2. \tag{10.8}$$

The hyper parameters β_1 and β_2 are set typically close to 1, but this also means that early in training the values for m_t and v_t are close to their initialization values of 0. To adjust for that, they are corrected for this bias:

$$\hat{m}_t = \frac{m_t}{1 - \beta_1^t}, \qquad \hat{v}_t = \frac{v_t}{1 - \beta_2^t}. \tag{10.9}$$

With increasing training time steps t, this correction goes away: $\lim_{t \to \infty} \frac{1}{1-\beta^t} \to 1$.

Having these pieces in hand (learning rate μ, momentum $\hat{m}_t$, accumulated change $\hat{v}_t$), the weight update per Adam is computed as:

$$\Delta w_t = \frac{\mu}{\sqrt{\hat{v}_t} + \epsilon} \hat{m}_t. \tag{10.10}$$

Common values for the hyper parameters are $\beta_1 = 0.9$, $\beta_2 = 0.999$ and $\epsilon = 10^{-8}$.

There are various other adaptation schemes. This is an active area of research. For instance, the second-order derivative gives some useful information about the rate of change (the square matrix with second Hessian matrix derivatives is called **Hessian matrix**). However, it is often expensive to compute, so other shortcuts are taken.

10.3.3 Batched Gradient Updates

One way to convert gradients into weight updates is to first process all the training examples, add up all the computed gradient values, and the use this sum to update parameters. However, this requires many passes over the training data for training to converge.

batched gradient updates

On the other extreme, as I described, we may process one training example at a time, and use its gradient immediately to update weights. This variant is called **stochastic gradient descent**, since it operates on a randomly sampled training example. This converges faster but has the disadvantage that the last seen training examples have a disproportionately higher impact on the final parameter values.

stochastic gradient descent

Given the efficiency gains of parallelization with as much computation as possible on modern GPU hardware, we typically batch together several sentence pairs, compute all their gradients for all their word predictions, and then use the sum over each batch to update parameters.

Note that it is not only the specifics of GPU design that leads us to process training examples in batches. We may also want to distribute training over several machines. To avoid communication overhead, each machine processes a batch of training examples and communicates gradients back to a parameter server for carry out the updates. This raises the problems that some machines are faster at processing their batch for various reasons, most having to do with underlying systems issues such as load on machines. Only when all machines have reported back their results, updates to the model are applied and new batches are issued.

In **asynchronous**, instead of waiting for all machines to report back their updates, each update is immediately applied and a new batch is issued. This training set up creates the problem that some machines operate on rather old parameter values. In practice, however, that does not seem to cause much of a problem. An alternative is not to wait for the stragglers and to discard their updates (Chen et al., 2016a).

asynchronous training

10.4 Avoiding Local Optima

The hardest problem for designing neural network architectures and optimization methods is to ensure that the model converges to the global optimum, or at least to a set of parameter values that give results close to this optimum on unseen test data. There is no real solution to this problem. It requires experimentation and analysis that is more craft than science. Still, this section presents a number of methods that generally help avoiding getting stuck in local optima.

avoiding local optima

10.4.1 Regularization

regularization

Large-scale neural machine translation models have hundreds of millions of parameters. But these models are also trained on hundreds of millions of training examples (individual word predictions). There are no hard rules for the relationship between these two numbers, but there is a general sense that having too many parameters and too few training examples leads to overfitting. Conversely a model with too few parameters and many training examples does not have enough capacity to learn the properties of the problem.

A standard technique in machine learning is **regularization**, which adds a term to the cost function to keep the model *simple*. By simple we mean parameter values that do not take on extreme values but rather have values close to zero, unless it is really necessary otherwise. A simple model also may not use all its parameters, i.e., sets their value to zero. There is a general philosophy behind the idea of keeping models simple. **Occam's razor** In this discussion **Occam's razor** is frequently invoked: if there are multiple explanations, prefer the simple one.

The complexity of a model is commonly measured with the L2 norm over the parameters. We add the L2 norm to the cost function, i.e., the sum of the squares of all parameters. So, the training objective is not only to match the training data as closely as possible but also to keep the parameters values small. Consider what happens when we compute the gradient of the L2 norm. We obtain a number relative to its current value. Gradient descent then reduces the parameter, unless there is evidence **weight decay** otherwise. So, adding the L2 norm can be understood as **weight decay**, where parameters that do not show any benefit are pushed towards zero.

Deep learning methods for machine translation typically may not include a regularization term in the cost function, but many techniques can be understood as a form of regularization by other means.

10.4.2 Curriculum Learning

The sentence pairs in the parallel corpus are presented to the learning algorithm in random fashion. There are good arguments for this randomness, as laid out above. But there is also a line of research that explores how to present the training data in different ways. This **curriculum learning** idea is called **curriculum learning**. Just students over their time in a elementary school or university are not bombarded with facts in random order, they start with the easiest concepts first, and then move to more complex issues.

For our problem of machine translation, this means that we may want to sort the training examples by easy to hard. First run an epoch on the easy examples, then add harder ones, and only in the final epochs run on the full training set. This is a simple idea, but there are a lot of difficult details.

First, how do we measure the difficulty of sentence pairs? We could take simple guidance such as preferring short sentences, maybe even creating artificial training data by extracting smaller segments from sentence pairs (similar to phrase pair extraction in statistical machine translation). We may use a pretrained neural machine translation system to score sentence pairs in the hope to discard outliers and poorly matched sentences.

Second, how exactly do we set up the curriculum? How many easy examples in the first epochs? How many epochs should we spend on each level of difficulty? These are decisions that are decided by experimentation to establish some rules of thumb, but the answers may differ a lot for different data conditions.

There are many open questions here at the time of writing, but we should note that the idea of training on different data sets in subsequent epochs is a common idea for adaptation, which I discuss at length in Chapter 13.

10.4.3 Dropout

While the last two sections discussed methods that help get training started, we now consider a different concern. What if training is well under way, but the current set of parameters are stuck in a region where some of the properties of the task have been learned, but the discovery of other properties would take it too far out of its comfort zone.

In machine translation, a vivid example of this is a model that has learned the language model aspects of the task, but is oblivious to the role of the input sentence and hence the translation aspects. Such a model produces beautiful output language, however it is completely unrelated to the input. Further training steps may just refine the model to make better use of distant words in the output sentence, but keep ignoring the input.

Various methods have been proposed to get training out of these local optima. One currently popular method is called **drop-out**. It sounds a bit **drop-out** simplistic and wacky. For each batch of training examples, some of the nodes in the network are randomly chosen to be ignored. Their values are set to 0, and their associated parameters are not updated. These dropped-out nodes may account for as much as 10%, 20% or even 50% of all the nodes. Training resumes for some number of iterations without the nodes (maybe just for just one batch), and then a different set of drop-out nodes are selected (Figure 10.4).

Figure 10.4 Dropout. For each batch of training examples, a different random set of nodes is removed from training, their values are set to 0 and their weights are not updated.

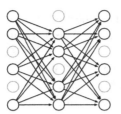 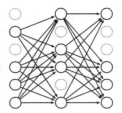 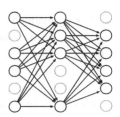

Obviously, the dropped-out nodes played some useful role in the model trained up to the point when they are ignored. But after that, other nodes have to pick up the slack. The end result is a more robust model where several nodes share similar roles.

One way to make sense of drop-out, is to view it as a form of ensemble learning. We can typically achieve large gains by not only training one model, but having multiple training runs, each producing a model and then merging their predictions during inference (see Section 9.2). Models make different mistakes, but when they agree they are more likely to be right. Removing nodes from the network creates effectively a different model that is trained on its own—at least for a while. So by masking out different subsets of nodes, we simultaneously train multiple models. While these share a lot of parameters and we do not explicitly merge multiple predictions, we avoid a lot of overhead by having a smaller set of parameters and fewer computation than when training a real ensemble.

10.5 Addressing Vanishing and Exploding Gradients

vanishing gradient
exploding gradient

Since gradients are computed over a long path of computations in the computation graph, these may misbehave, either becoming too small or too large. This is especially a problem for deep models with many layers or recurrent steps. When developing a neural network architecture, the behavior of gradients is important to keep in mind. There are also some general techniques that help address this problem.

10.5.1 Gradient Clipping

gradient clipping

If gradients become too large, a simple method is to just reduce their value. This method is called gradient clipping. The sum of all gradients for a parameter vector limited to a specified threshold. Typically, the L2 norm is used.

Formally, we define a hyper parameter τ for the threshold and check if the L2 norm of the gradient values for a parameter tensor (typically a weight matrix) exceeds it. If it does, we scale each gradient value by the ratio between the threshold τ and the L2 norm over all gradient values g_j. Thus each gradient g_i of the tensor, is adjusted by

$$g'_i = g_i \times \frac{\tau}{\max(\tau, L2(g))} = g_i \times \frac{\tau}{\max\left(\tau, \sqrt{\sum_j g_j^2}\right)}. \qquad (10.11)$$

Instead of choosing a fixed threshold, we may also dynamically detect unusual gradient values and discard these updates. In **adaptive gradient clipping**, we keep track of the mean and variance of gradient values, which allows us to detect gradient values that lie well outside the normal distribution. This is typically done by updating a moving average and moving standard deviation (Chen et al., 2018).

adaptive gradient clipping

10.5.2 Layer Normalization

layer normalization

Layer normalization addresses a problem that arises especially in the deep neural networks that we are using in neural machine translation, where computing proceeds through a large sequence of layers. For some training examples, average values at one layer may become very large, which feed into the following layer, also producing large output values, and so on. This is a problem with activation functions that do not limit the output to a narrow interval, such as rectified linear units.

The opposite problem is that for other training examples the average values at the same layers may be very small. This causes a problem for training. Recall from Equation 5.31 that gradient updates are strongly affected by node values. Too small node values lead to vanishing gradients and too large node values lead to exploding gradients.

To remedy this, the idea is to normalize the values on a per-layer basis. This is done by adding additional computational steps to the neural network. Recall that a feed-forward layer l consists of the the matrix multiplication of the weight matrix W with the node values from the previous layer h^{l-1}, resulting in a weighted sum s^l, followed by an activation function such as sigmoid:

$$s^l = W\, h^{l-1}$$
$$h^l = \text{sigmoid}(s^l). \qquad (10.12)$$

We can compute the mean μ^l and variance σ^l of the values in the weighted sum vector s^l by

$$\mu^l = \frac{1}{H} \sum_{i-1}^{H} s_i^l$$
$$\sigma^l = \sqrt{\frac{1}{H} \sum_{i-1}^{H} (s_i^l - \mu^l)^2}. \qquad (10.13)$$

Using these values, we normalize the vector s^l using two additional bias vectors g and b:

$$\hat{s}^l = \frac{g}{\sigma^l}(s^l - \mu^l) + b, \qquad (10.14)$$

where the difference subtracts the scalar average from each vector element.

The formula first normalizes the values in s^l by shifting them against their average value, hence ensuring that their average afterward is 0. The resulting vector is then divided by the variance σ^l. The additional bias vectors give some flexibility. They may be shared across multiple layers of the same type, such as multiple time steps in a recurrent neural network.

10.5.3 Shortcuts and Highways

shortcut connection
highway connection

The *deep* in deep learning implies models that go through several stages of computation (typically a sequence of layers). Obviously, passing the error information through these many stages is a challenge for the back-propagation algorithm. It is quite remarkable, that this works at all, considering the many computations that an input value has to travel to produce a output value, which is then matched against the true target value. All the parameters involved in this chain have to be adjusted. Given that we start with random values for all of them, it is amazing that training gets off the ground at all.

But deeper architecture may stretch this amazing ability too far. To avoid this problem, a common method is to add shortcuts to the architecture of these models. Instead of forcing input values though, say, 6 layers of processing, we add a connection that connects the input directly to the last layer. In early iterations of training, we expect the model to focus on these simpler paths (reflecting the learning of with simpler model architecture) but in later iterations to exploit the true power of the deep models.

residual connection
skip connection

These shortcuts have many names: **residual connections** and **skip connections** are commonly used. In their simplest form, a feed-forward layer,

$$y = f(x), \qquad (10.15)$$

is extended with just passing through the input (skipping the pass through the function f):

$$y = f(x) + x. \qquad (10.16)$$

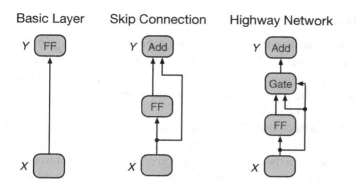

Figure 10.5 Shortcuts and highways. Left: basic connection between layer X and Y. Middle: in residual or skip connection, the input is added to the output of the processing between layers X and Y. Right: in highway networks, a gate value is learned that balances between processing

Note the effect on gradient propagation. The gradient for this computation is

$$y' = f'(x) + 1. \qquad (10.17)$$

The constant 1 implies that the gradient is passed through unchanged. So, even in a deep network with several layers, there is a direct path for error propagation from the last layer all the way to the input.

Taking this idea one step further, we may regulate how much information from $f(x)$ and x should impact the output y. In **highway networks**, this is regulated with a gate $t(x)$ (typically computed by a feed-forward layer).

$$y = t(x) f(x) + (1 - t(x)) x. \qquad (10.18)$$

Figure 10.5 shows these different designs for shortcut connections.

10.5.4 LSTM and Vanishing Gradients

vanishing gradient

I introduced long short-term memory cells in Section 7.5. One of the core motivations for these type of neural network elements is the vanishing gradient problem. Recurrent neural networks are especially prone to vanishing gradients, since the error is back-propagated through each step of the sequence that was processed. LSTM cells allow for shortcuts through the network, in the spirit of what I discussed in the previous section.

Specifically, the pass-through of memory connects the time steps of sequence processing. Recall Equation 7.12:

$$\text{memory}^t = \text{gate}_{\text{input}} \times \text{input}^t + \text{gate}_{\text{forget}} \times \text{memory}^{t-1}. \qquad (10.19)$$

For nodes for which the forget gate has values close to 1, the gradient is passed through to earlier steps nearly unchanged.

10.6 Sentence-Level Optimization

The cost function that we use to drive parameter updates so far has been defined at the word level. For each output word given in the parallel data, we first make a model prediction in the form of a distribution over output words. Then we compare how much probability was given to the given correct output word.

While this allows for many parameter updates, machine translation is a sequence prediction task. There is concern that predicting one word at a time, given the correct prefix of correct previous output words, is not a realistic learning objective for test time, when an entire output sequence has to be generated without the safety net of the correct prefix. In machine learning, this is called **exposure bias**, the problem that conditions seen at test time are never encountered during training. Should we not also at training time predict an output sequence and then compare that against the correct sequence?

10.6.1 Minimum Risk Training

When predicting an output sequence, word-by-word comparison against the given correct output sequence is not useful. If an additional word was generated at the beginning of the sequence, then all words are off by one position and none match, while the proposed sequence may be still a fine sentence translation. Also, consider the case of reordering—any deviation of the word order of the correct output sequence would be severely punished.

Comparing sentence translations for the purpose of evaluation has been extensively studied. This is essentially the long-standing problem of sentence-level automatic machine translation metrics. The oldest and still dominant metric is the BLEU score (see Section 4.3.1). It matches words and short word sequences between system output and reference translation, and includes a brevity penalty. But there are also other metrics, such as translation edit rate.

We previously used as cost function (or loss) cross-entropy on word predictions. We defined this as the negative of the predicted probability (according to the distribution t_i) assigned to the correct word y_i, as presented in Equation 8.5:

$$\text{loss} = -\log t_i[y_i]. \tag{10.20}$$

Another way to look at this, is that the model makes various predictions y for the ith output word, and we assign a loss value to each prediction, which happens to be 1 for the correct word and 0 for the incorrect words.

$$\text{loss} = -\log \sum_{y \in V} \delta(y = y_i) \, t_i[y]. \qquad (10.21)$$

This formulation allows us to use other quality measures beyond a 0/1 loss, which is what we have in mind for sentence-level optimization. Staying with word-level optimization for the moment, we may want to employ loss functions that give partial credits to near misses, such as morphological variants or synonyms. So, instead of the Kronecker delta δ that fires only when there is a match between y and y_i, we may use any other quality metric:

$$\text{loss} = -\log \sum_{y \in V} \text{quality}(y, y_i) \, t_i[y]. \qquad (10.22)$$

Since the quality score is weighted by the probability distribution t_i, the resulting loss function can be considered a computation of the **expected loss**. The method that optimizes to minimize the expected loss is called **minimum risk training**.

expected loss

minimum risk training

Now, we are predicting the full sequence **y**. Mathematically, this does not much change our definition of the loss:

$$\text{loss} = -\log \sum_{\mathbf{y'} \in V*} \text{quality}(\mathbf{y'}, \mathbf{y}) \, t(\mathbf{y'}). \qquad (10.23)$$

We can now use the BLEU score or any other evaluation metric as the quality score.

There are a number of computational challenges with this formulation. As written, the space of possible sequences $\mathbf{y'} \in V*$ is infinite but even with reasonable length constraints, the number of sequences is exponential with respect to the length. To keep matters manageable, we have to resort to sampling sequences that, combined, account for the bulk of the probability mass.

Sampling full-sequence translations can be done with beam search. While this aims to find the most probably translations, it suffers from lack of diversity. An alternative is **Monte Carlo search**. This works like repeated greedy search, with one distinction. Instead of choosing the most probable word from the distribution each time, we now choose the output word given its predicted probability.

Monte Carlo decoding

To give an example: if the model predicts the word *cat* with 17% probability, and the word *tiger* with 83% probability, we now roll a die and if the number 1 comes up, we choose cat, otherwise we choose tiger. This process generates each possible output sequence according to its sequence probability, given the model. We repeat this search multiple times and obtain multiple sentence translations. In the limit, the relative frequency of each output sequence approximates its probability—hence the required distribution t in Equation 10.23.

Note that while sampling the space of possible translations makes sentence-level optimization feasible, it is still more computationally expensive than traditional word-level optimization. We have to carry out a beam search or repeated Monte Carlo searches to collect one data point for computing back-propagation values. Previously, a single word prediction sufficed.

But there are clear benefits to sentence-level optimization. It more closely mirrors decoding during test time, when a sequence is predicted and scored. It also allows methods such as generative adversarial training.

10.6.2 Generative Adversarial Training

generative adversarial training   Coming from computer game playing research, generative adversarial networks (GANs) frame a task such as machine translation as a game **generator** between two players: the **generator** and the **discriminator**. The gen-**discriminator** erator makes predictions for the task, and the discriminator attempts to distinguish these predictions from actual training examples.

Applied to machine translation (Wu et al., 2017; Yang et al., 2018b), the generator is a traditional neural machine translation model that generates translations for input sentences and the discriminator attempts to tell them apart from real translations. Specifically, given a sentence pair (x, y) from the training data, the generator (i.e., the neural machine translation model) takes the input sentence x and produces a translation t for it. The discriminator aims to detect this translation pair (x, t) as coming from a machine, while classifying the sentence pair from the training data (x, y) as coming from a human.

During training, the discriminator receives a positive sample (x, y) and a negative sample (x, t) to improve its prediction ability. The ability to make the right decision for both of them is used as error signal for back-propagation training.

But the point of the discriminator is to also improve training of the generator. Typically, we train the generator to predict each word of the output sequence. Now, we combine this training objective with the objective to fool the discriminator. So, we have two objective functions. The importance of each objective is balanced with some weight λ, a hyper parameter, which has to be chosen by hand.

What makes this setup complex is that the signal from the discriminator can be computed only for a completed sentence translation t, while typical neural machine translation training is based on making correct individual word predictions. In machine learning, this type of problem

is framed as a **reinforcement learning** problem. Reinforcement learning
is defined as a setup where the error signal for training is obtained only
after a sequence of decisions. Good examples are games such as chess
and walking through a maze to avoid monsters and find the gold. In the
chess example, we only know if our moves are correct when the game
ended in our favor, but we do not get individual feedback for each step.

In the language of reinforcement learning, the generator is called
a **policy**, and the ability to fool the discriminator is called the **reward**.
A common solution to this problem is to sample different translations
based on our current neural machine translation model, as described in
the previous section. Given a set of sampled translations, we can compute
the reward, i.e., how well we can fool the discriminator, for each of them.
We use this as the training objective to update the model.

reinforcement learning

policy
reward

10.7 Further Readings

A number of key techniques that have been recently developed have
entered the standard repertoire of neural machine translation research.
Ranges for the random initialization of weights need to be carefully
chosen (Glorot and Bengio, 2010). To avoid overconfidence of the
model, label smoothing may be applied, i.e., optimization toward a target
distribution that shifts probability mass away from the correct given
target word toward other words (Chorowski and Jaitly, 2017). Distribut-
ing training over several GPUs creates the problem of synchronizing
updates. Chen et al. (2016a) compare various methods, including
asynchronous updates. Training is made more robust by methods such
as drop-out (Srivastava et al., 2014), where during training intervals a
number of nodes are randomly masked. To avoid exploding or vanishing
gradients during back-propagation over several layers, gradients are
typically clipped (Pascanu et al., 2013). Chen et al. (2018) present
briefly adaptive gradient clipping. Layer normalization (Lei Ba et al.,
2016) has similar motivations, by ensuring that node values are within
reasonable bounds.

Adjusting the Learning Rate

adjusting the learning rate

An active topic of research is optimization methods that adjust the
learning rate of gradient descent training. Popular methods are
Adagrad (Duchi et al., 2011), Adadelta (Zeiler, 2012), and currently
Adam (Kingma and Ba, 2015).

Sequence-Level Optimization

sentence-level optimization

Shen et al. (2016) introduce minimum risk training that allows for
sentence-level optimization with metrics such as the BLEU score. A set

of possible translation is sampled, and their relative probability is used to compute the expected loss (probability-weighted BLEU scores of the sampled translations). They show large gains on a Chinese–English task. Neubig (2016) also showed gains when optimizing toward smoothed sentence-level BLEU, using a sample of 20 translations. Hashimoto and Tsuruoka (2019) optimize toward the GLEU score (a variant of the BLEU score) and speed by training by vocabulary reduction. Wiseman and Rush (2016) use a loss function that penalizes the gold standard of falling off the beam during training. Ma et al. (2019c) also consider the point where the gold standard falls of the beam but record the loss for this initial sequence prediction and then reset the beam to the gold standard at that point. Edunov et al. (2018b) compare various word-level and sentence-level optimization techniques but see only small gains by the best-performing sentence-level minimum risk method over alternatives. Xu et al. (2019) use a mix of gold-standard and predicted words in the prefix. They use an alignment component to keep the mixed prefix and the target training sentence in sync. Zhang et al. (2019b) gradually shift from matching toward ground truth toward so-called word-level oracle obtained with Gumbel noise and sentence-level oracles obtained by selecting the BLEU-best translation from the n-best list obtained by beam search.

faster training **Faster Training**
Ott et al. (2018c) improve training speed with 16-bit arithmetic and larger batches that lead to less idle time due to less variance in processing batches on different GPU. They scale up training to 128 GPUs.

right-to-left training **Right-to-Left Training**
Several researchers report that translation quality for the right half of the sentence is lower than for the left half of the sentence and attribute this to the exposure bias: during training a correct prefix (also called teacher forcing) is used to make word predictions, while during decoding only the previously predicted words can be used. Wu et al. (2018) show that this imbalance is to a large degree due to linguistic reasons: it happens for right-branching languages like English and Chinese, but the opposite is the case for left-branching languages like Japanese.

adversarial training **Adversarial Training**
Wu et al. (2017) introduce adversarial training to neural machine translation, in which a discriminator is trained alongside a traditional machine translation model to distinguish between machine translation output and human reference translations. The ability to fool the discriminator is used as an additional training objective for the machine translation

model. Yang et al. (2018b) propose a similar setup, but add a BLEU-based training objective to neural translation model training. Cheng et al. (2018) employ adversarial training to address the problem of robustness, which they identify by the evidence that 70% of translations change when an input word is changed to a synonym. They aim to achieve more robust behavior by adding synthetic training data where one of the input words is replaced with a synonym (neighbor in embedding space) and by using a discriminator that predicts from the encoding of an input sentence if it is an original or an altered source sentence.

Knowledge Distillation

There are several techniques that change the loss function not only to reward good word predictions that closely match the training data but also to closely match predictions of a previous model, called the teacher model. Khayrallah et al. (2018a) use a general domain model as teacher to avoid overfitting to in-domain data during domain adaptation by fine-tuning. Wei et al. (2019) use the models that achieved the best results during training at previous checkpoints to guide training.

knowledge distillation

Chapter 11
Alternate Architectures

So far, we introduced a neural machine translation model that is based on recurrent neural networks. Recently, alternative architectures have been proposed that use other components in the neural network tool-box, such as convolutional neural networks, or self-attention. How to structure the architecture of neural machine translation model is still up for debate.

In this chapter, I first survey components of neural network architectures that have been applied to the translation problem, with special focus on attention mechanisms. I then explain in detail two recently emerged competitors to recurrent neural networks that have a structural different architecture, although all of them still maintain the general division of the model into an encoder that refines representation of the input and a decoder that produces the output string word by word.

11.1 Components of Neural Networks

While the original inspiration for neural networks were neurons in the brain, the principle idea of a computation graph allows for any arbitrary computation, as long as it is (at least partially) differentiable. This is a good argument for using the term *deep learning* instead of neural networks, since we are building models that deeply stack together trainable operations, without any appeals to biological validity.

Let us take a look at several such operations that are used in neural machine translation models today.

11.1.1 Feed-Forward Layer

feed-forward layer

The classic neural network component, introduced in Chapter 5, is the feed-forward layer. It consists of a matrix multiplication and an activation function.

Mathematically, an input vector x is multiplied with a matrix M, added to a bias vector b and then mapped with an element-wise activation function into an output y:

$$y = \text{activation}(Mx + b). \tag{11.1}$$

Since we will be using this basic component frequently, we will use the notation

$$y = FF_{\text{activation}}(x) = a(Mx + b). \tag{11.2}$$

Historic neural network designs consist of nothing more that several feed-forward layers (then called input layer, hidden layers, and output layer). Despite their simplicity, they have been demonstrated to be powerful tools for a wide range of machine learning problems. Whenever you have a fixed sized representation x that needs to be mapped into a different fixed sized representation y, a feed-forward layer is the first thing to try out.

Consider an example that is different from translation. Let us say, we have access to the preferences for movies for several people (ratings for the movies on a scale from, say, 1 to 5), and we want to predict their preferences for books (probability that they will like the book). Here the movie preferences of a specific person are encoded in the vector x and their book preferences in the vector y. A multilayer feed-forward neural network takes the input vector of movie preferences, processed through a number of hidden layers to produce book preference predictions as output.

affine transform   Feed-forward layers are also called **affine transforms**, a term that appeals to their geometrical properties, such that points connecting as straight lines in the original space are still straight lines in the output space.

11.1.2 Factored Decomposition

factored decomposition

One challenge to feed-forward layers are very large input and output vectors. The size of the weight matrix M is the product of the size of the input vector and the size of the output vector. This may be a very large number.

Recall our example for book and movie preferences: There are thousands of books and thousands of movies, so the matrix M will have

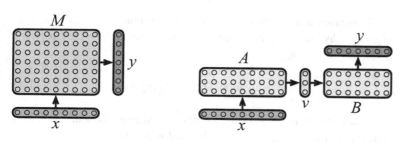

Figure 11.1 Factored decomposition. Instead of using a large matrix M to map between x and y, we first project x into a lower dimensional vector v and map to y.

millions if not billions of parameters that need to be learned. Given that we have access to only so many user preferences, there may be too many parameters to learn, leading to overfitting of the model.

So, we may want to reduce the highly dimensional vector x first into a lower dimensional vector v with a matrix A and then map that into the output space with a matrix B. Ignoring the activation function and bias term of the feed-forward layer for now, the computations involved are as follows:

$$v = Ax$$
$$y = Bv = BAx. \tag{11.3}$$

To illustrate the number of parameters involved here: if the vector x has 5,000 dimensions and y has 2,000 dimensions, but v has only 20 dimensions, then we reduced a matrix multiplication with $5,000 \times 2,000 = 10{,}000{,}000$ parameters into two matrix multiplications with $5,000 \times 20 = 100,000$ and $20 \times 2,000 = 40,000$ parameters, an almost 99% reduction (Figure 11.1).

There are several ways to think about the lower dimensional vector v. It captures the salient features that connect the properties in the input space and the output space. It is probably too much to expect, to stick with our example, that one of the neurons in vector v corresponds to a preference for drama and another one to a preference for science fiction. But the vector as a whole indeed encodes general properties, such as the genre of movies.

Word embeddings can be understood as the application of factored decompositions. Instead of working with representations with 10,000s or even 100,000s of dimensions, corresponding to the number of words in the vocabulary, we reduce these representations to more manageable 500 or 1,000 dimensions.

11.1.3 Basic Mathematical Operations

A number of basic mathematical operations are commonly used in computation graphs to combine multiple inputs or to reduce the size of representations.

Concatenation – We often have multiple input vectors to a processing step (say, an input word and the previous state). In a feed-forward layer, this may look like this:

$$y = \text{activation}(M_1 x_1 + M_2 x_2 + b). \tag{11.4}$$

Another way to view this is that first x_1 and x_2 are concatenated into a single vector x, which is then multiplied with a matrix M:

$$\begin{aligned} x &= \text{concat}(x_1, x_2) \\ y &= \text{activation}(Mx + b). \end{aligned} \tag{11.5}$$

In the case of inputs to a feed-forward layers, this seems like a trivial distinction with no practical impact. But when the multiple inputs are used for other purposes it makes sense to formulate this as an explicit concatenation operation.

Addition – A very common operation is to add up vectors, as long as they have the same dimension. This is done quite often in neural models, even if it seems overly simplistic. One still intuitive example is the addition of the output of a processing layer with a shortcut connection. This allows in early training stages for skipping the processing layer and then over time for learning adjustments.

A slightly less intuitive example is the bag of words model for sentence representation. If we have a sentence with words $w_1, \ldots, w_n$, we may add up all these vectors:

$$s = \sum_i^n w_i. \tag{11.6}$$

While it seems odd to just smash words together this way, it does have a lot of benefits. Sequences of words can have any length, but this way, we obtain a fixed-size representation s of the sentence.

The input vectors may be weighted. This is what we have done in our neural machine translation model where an attention mechanism computes a weight for each input word representation, before adding them all up.

Multiplication – Another elementary mathematical operation is multiplication. There are actually two ways to multiply two vectors. One is similar to the way we do addition, obtaining a new vector by element-wise multiplication. To illustrate this for two-dimensional vectors:

$$v \odot u = \begin{pmatrix} v_1 \\ v_2 \end{pmatrix} \odot \begin{pmatrix} u_1 \\ u_2 \end{pmatrix} = \begin{pmatrix} v_1 \times u_1 \\ v_2 \times u_2 \end{pmatrix}. \tag{11.7}$$

The other way is the dot product. Here, we obtain a single number by adding up the element-wise multiplications:

$$v \cdot u = \begin{pmatrix} v_1 \\ v_2 \end{pmatrix} \cdot \begin{pmatrix} u_1 \\ u_2 \end{pmatrix} = v_1 \times u_1 + v_2 \times u_2. \qquad (11.8)$$

To give one example, a simple form of the attention mechanism (see Section 11.2.1 for more details) computes the attention value a_{ij} between a decoder state s_{j-1} and the hidden representation of an input word h_i with the dot product $a_{ij} = s_{j-1} \cdot h_i$.

Maximum – When the goal is to reduce the dimensionality of representation, a simple maximum may suffice. Consider the case of image processing, where the goal is to detect certain types of objects, say, a human face. If any region of the image has a positive match, then this is a sufficient indication of the presence of a face in the image. So, if we have a vector where each element represents a different region of the image, then we check for the maximum value and return it. **maximum**

Max pooling layers take n-dimensional vectors (or $n \times m$-dimensional matrices) and reduce them into $\frac{n}{k}$-dimensional vectors (or $\frac{n}{k} \times \frac{m}{k}$-dimensional matrices), by applying the maximum operation to each group of k values. **max pooling**

Max out layers first branch out into different feed-forward layers and then take the element-wise maximum. To give a simple example, with two feed-forward layers (parameterized by W_1, b_1 and W_2, b_2): **max out**

$$\text{maxout}(x) = \max(W_1 x + b_1, W_2 x + b_2). \qquad (11.9)$$

The ReLu activation function can be understood as an example of a maxout layer, since it takes the maximum of a feed-forward layer and 0:

$$\text{ReLu}(x) = \max(Wx + b, 0). \qquad (11.10)$$

11.1.4 Recurrent Neural Networks

recurrent neural network

I described recurrent neural networks at length in Sections 7.4 to 7.7. Let us focus here on some properties of such models. In the most abstract form, they propagate a state s over time steps t by receiving an input x_t at each turn:

$$s_t = f(s_{t-1}, x_t). \qquad (11.11)$$

We explored various ways in which the state is computed; it may be as simple as a feed-forward layer, but more successful are gated recurrent units or long short-term memory cells.

Since we are processing word sequences as input and output in machine translation, this is a natural fit for the problem. It also matches some of our intuitions about language: humans process language word by word (by reading or listening) and produce language that way (one word at a time). Any linguist will tell you that language is structured recursively, but let us defer that notion to the next section. The most recent words are most relevant, and they are fewer computation steps away to the current state. Still, the entire prior sequence can influence the current state, so no information is discarded—in contrast to n-gram language models, which consider a limited history of $n - 1$ words.

However, recurrent neural networks pose computational problems. Since we are often processing sequences over dozens of words, they create very long computation chains. This means that gradient updates have to travel a long way during training. Also, it limits the ability to parallelize forward and backward computation. Both of these reasons have given recurrent neural networks the reputation of being hard to train, so researchers have been looking for alternatives.

11.1.5 Convolutional Neural Networks

convolutional neural network

Convolutional neural networks (CNNs) are common in image processing (Figure 11.2), and they have been essential to the recent deep learning revolution that started there. Their main benefit is to reduce the dimensionality of input spaces. Think about the millions of pixels of an image from which we may just want to predict if it contains a face.

There are good reasons why they should also be relevant for machine translation. Syntactic and semantic theories of language do not view language as a sequence of words, but as a recursive structure. The central word of a sentence is the verb, which has direct relationship to the subject and object noun, which may have further dependencies such as determiners and adjectives. The task of machine translation should not be viewed as mapping the words in the input language one

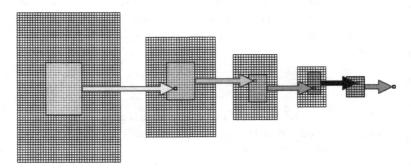

Figure 11.2 Convolutional neural networks in image processing: Regions of an image are reduced into increasingly smaller representations through a sequence of convolutional layers.

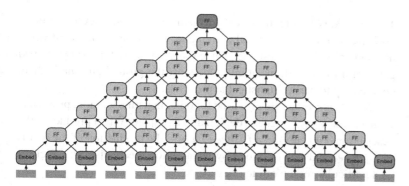

Figure 11.3 A convolutional neural network that computes a single sentence representation vector (top) from a sequence of word embeddings (bottom).

by one into the output language, but to take the meaning of the input sentence and express it in the output language. At the center of this is a single representation of the sentence meaning. How to obtain a **sentence embedding** is an active research topic in natural language processing. Convolutional neural networks are one means for it.

  sentence embedding

The key step of a convolutional neural network is to take a high-dimensional input representation (a vector, or in the case of images, a matrix) and map it to a lower-dimensional representation. This is usually done with a simple feed-forward layer. This is typically not done in one step, but in several. Also, no fixed hierarchical structure is imposed, but overlapping regions of the input are mapped at each step.

Convolutional neural networks for image processing reduce representations by kernels that map regions of, say, 50×50 pixels into scalar values. In natural language processing, we typically combine three or more neighboring words into a single vector. These steps are repeated, each time shrinking the representation into smaller matrices, as in the case of image processing, or fewer vectors in a sequence, as in processing a sentence (Figure 11.3).

Machine translation may use convolutional neural networks to encode the foreign sentence into a single vector and then decode this interlingual meaning representation into a full sentence in the target language.

11.2 Attention Models

attention model

Machine translation is a structured prediction task. By this we mean that the predictions made by machine translation models are not binary decisions or class assignments, but rather a bigger structure that has to be built in parts, i.e. a sentence translation that has to be constructed word by word. What is relevant for each individual word prediction varies, and sometimes it is really just a single word in the input sentence.

This motivates the attention mechanism that focuses the view of the input sentence to a few words, maybe even one. The addition of the attention mechanism to sequence-to-sequence recurrent neural networks helped get neural machine translation models off the ground and made them competitive to earlier statistical approaches.

Attention models are also used for other machine learning problems, such as describing the scene depicted in an image. When producing the description *a girl throws a frisbee to a boy*, the production of the words *girl, frisbee* and *boy* is guided by an attention mechanism that focuses on a particular region of the image.

11.2.1 Computing Attention

attention calculation

The attention mechanism was introduced in Section 8.2.3. There, we followed the original proposal by Bahdanau et al. (2015) where an attention value is computed by a feed-forward layer that takes the previous hidden state s_{i-1} and each input word embedding h_j as inputs:

$$a(s_{i-1}, h_j) = v_a^T \tanh(W_a s_{i-1} + U_a h_j). \tag{11.12}$$

This is not the only way to compute attention. Luong et al. (2015b) and Vaswani et al. (2017) propose models that use fewer parameters:

dot product
- Dot product: $a(s_{i-1}, h_j) = s_{i-1}^T h_j$
- Scaled dot product: $a(s_{i-1}, h_j) = \frac{1}{\sqrt{|h_j|}} s_{i-1}^T h_j$
- General: $a(s_{i-1}, h_j) = s_{i-1}^T W_a h_j$

local
- Local: $a(s_{i-1}) = W_a s_{i-1}$

Luong et al. (2015b) demonstrate good results with the dot product, which does not use any trainable parameters at all. The scaled dot product is used in the self-attention layers of the Transformer model, that discussed in Section 11.5.

Luong et al. (2015b) also proposed simplified processing in the decoder (Figure 11.4). It removes the redundant conditioning of the decoder state on the input context and the conditioning of the output word prediction on the previous output word embedding. Their variant has been mostly adopted in recent implementation of neural machine translation model, although still with the traditional feed-forward layer to compute attention.

11.2.2 Multihead Attention

multihead attention

Attention is computed as a single scalar value by which each input word representation is weighted. Given the centrality of attention to

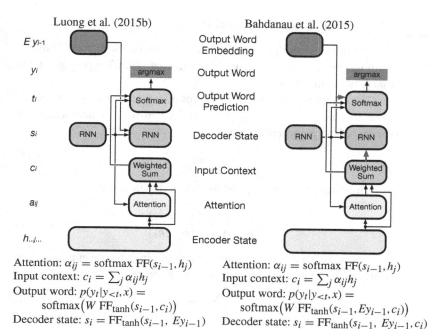

Attention: $\alpha_{ij} = $ softmax FF(s_{i-1}, h_j) Attention: $\alpha_{ij} = $ softmax FF(s_{i-1}, h_j)
Input context: $c_i = \sum_j \alpha_{ij} h_j$ Input context: $c_i = \sum_j \alpha_{ij} h_j$
Output word: $p(y_t | y_{<t}, x) = $ Output word: $p(y_t | y_{<t}, x) = $
$\quad$ softmax$\left(W \text{ FF}_{\text{tanh}}(s_{i-1}, c_i)\right)$ $\quad$ softmax$\left(W \text{ FF}_{\text{tanh}}(s_{i-1}, Ey_{i-1}, c_i)\right)$
Decoder state: $s_i = $ FF$_{\text{tanh}}(s_{i-1}, Ey_{i-1})$ Decoder state: $s_i = $ FF$_{\text{tanh}}(s_{i-1}, Ey_{i-1}, c_i)$

Figure 11.4 Decoder state progression proposed by Luong et al. (2015b) and Bahdanau et al. (2015). The decoder state computation is simplified, since typically GRU or LSTM cells are used.

connecting input and output, why not apply the general philosophy of having redundancy in neural networks? This is the motivation behind multihead attention (Vaswani et al., 2017).

In multihead attention, we compute a set of, say, 16 attention weights, each based on its own parameters. Formally, for each head k, we compute an association between the decoder state s_{i-1} (at time step i) and the encoder state h_j (for the jth input word), using the softmax of some parameterized function a^k:

$$\alpha_{ij}^k = \text{softmax } a^k(s_{i-1}, h_j). \tag{11.13}$$

We then average the attention weights:

$$\alpha_{ij} = \frac{1}{k} \sum_k \alpha_{ij}^k. \tag{11.14}$$

Multihead attention is a form of ensemble modeling. Each attention head has a slightly different take on the importance of input words, and their assessments are combined.

fine-grained attention

11.2.3 Fine-Grained Attention

But why just use a single scalar value to weight entire vectors? Why not learn weights for each element? **Fine-grained attention** proposes to do that (Choi et al., 2018).

The computation of attention values now returns a vector instead of a scalar value. Architecturally, this is still a feed-forward neural network (or any of the proposed variants):

$$a(s_{i-1}, h_j) = \text{FF}^k(s_{i-1}, h_j). \tag{11.15}$$

The softmax is now applied over each dimension d:

$$\alpha_{ij}^d = \frac{\exp a^d(s_{i-1}, h_j)}{\sum_k a^d(s_{i-1}, h_k)}. \tag{11.16}$$

The input context is now computed by a element-wise multiplication of the attention weights and the input word representation:

$$c_i = \sum_j \alpha_{ij} \times h_j. \tag{11.17}$$

self-attention

11.2.4 Self-Attention

Finally, a very different take at attention, motivated by the need to have an alignment between input words and output words. But how about also using this approach to refine the representation of input words in the encoder?

The representation of an input word mostly depends on itself, but it is also informed by the surrounding context. We previously modeled this with recurrent neural networks, which take the left or right context into account to refine each word representation. Instead, we now propose to use the attention mechanism for that.

Think about it this way: in a recurrent neural network, the hidden state is computed from the current word and the previous hidden state. It is a refinement of the current word representation, considering the previous context. Self-attention addresses the question: what is a better representation of this word, given all these other words? This starts with the question, how relevant are each of the words in the sentence? This is the attention part. Then the method uses these attention weights to refine the word representation.

Vaswani et al. (2017) define self-attention for a sequence of vectors h_j (of size $|h|$), packed into a matrix H, as

$$\text{self-attention}(H) = \text{softmax}\left(\frac{HH^T}{\sqrt{|h|}}\right) H. \tag{11.18}$$

Let us look at this equation in detail. The association between every word representation h_j any other context word h_k is done via the dot product between the packed matrix H and its transpose H^T, resulting in a vector of *raw association* values HH^T. The values in this vector are first scaled by the size of the word representation vectors $|h|$ and then by the softmax, so that their values add up to 1. The resulting vector of *normalized association* values is then used to weigh the context words.

Another way to put Equation 11.18 without the matrix H notation but using word representation vectors h_j is:

$$a_{jk} = \frac{1}{|h|} h_j h_k^T \qquad \text{raw association} \left(\frac{HH^T}{\sqrt{|h|}} \right)$$

$$\alpha_{jk} = \frac{\exp(a_{jk})}{\sum_\kappa \exp(a_{j\kappa})} \qquad \text{normalized association (softmax)}$$

$$\text{self-attention}(h_j) = \sum_k \alpha_{j\kappa} h_k \qquad \text{weighted sum.}$$

$$(11.19)$$

We describe the Transformer model, which makes use of self-attention, in detail in Section 11.5.

11.3 Convolutional Machine Translation

convolutional machine translation

The first end-to-end neural machine translation model of the modern era (Kalchbrenner and Blunsom, 2013) was actually not based on recurrent neural networks but based on convolutional neural networks.

Figure 11.5 shows their convolutional network architecture for encoding an input sentence. The basic building block of these networks is a convolutional kernel. It merges the representation of i input words into a single representation by using a matrix K_i. Applying the convolution to every sequence of input words reduces the length of the sentence representation by $i - 1$. Repeating this process leads to a sentence representation in a single vector.

The illustration shows an architecture with two convolutional K_i layers, followed by a final L_i layer, which merges the sequence of phrasal representations into a single-sentence representation. The size of the convolutional kernels K_i and L_i depends on the length of the sentences. The example shows a six-word sentence and a sequence of K_2, K_3, and L_3 layers. For longer sentences, bigger kernels are needed.

The hierarchical process of building up a sentence representation bottom-up is well grounded in linguistic insight in the recursive nature

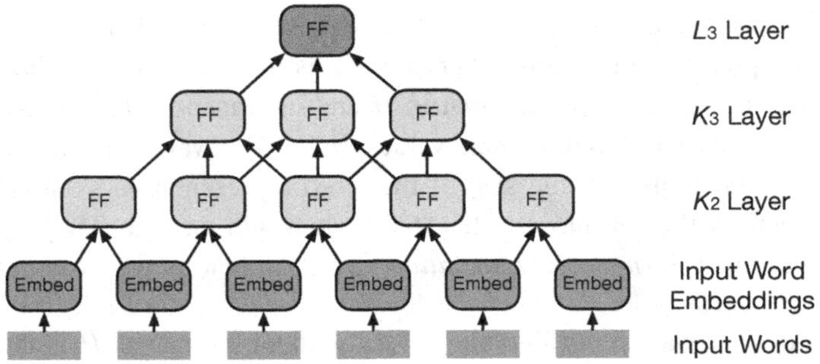

Figure 11.5 Encoding a sentence with a convolutional neural network. By always using two convolutional layers, the size of the convolutions differ (here K_2 and K_3). Decoding reverses this process.

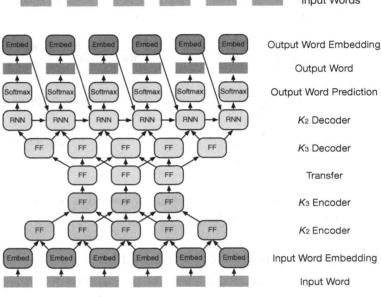

Figure 11.6 Refinement of the convolutional neural network model. Convolutions do not result in a single-sentence embedding but a sequence. The decoder is also informed by a recurrent neural network (connections from output word embeddings to final decoding layer).

of language. It is similar to chart parsing, except we are not committing to a single hierarchical structure. On the other hand, we are asking an awful lot from the resulting sentence embedding. It has to represent the meaning of an entire sentence of arbitrary length.

Generating the output sentence translation reverses the bottom-up process. One problem for the decoder is to decide the length of the output sentence. Kalchbrenner and Blunsom (2013) suggest addressing this problem is by adding a model that predicts output length from input length. This then leads to the selection of the size of the reverse convolution matrices.

Figure 11.6 provides a variation of this idea. The shown architecture always uses a K_2 and a K_3 convolutional layer, resulting in a sequence of phrasal representations, not a single-sentence embedding. There is an explicit mapping step from phrasal representations of input words to phrasal representations of output words, called the transfer layer.

The decoder of the model includes a recurrent neural network on the output side. Sneaking in a recurrent neural network here somewhat undermines the argument about better parallelization. However, the claim still holds true for encoding the input, and a sequential language model is just too powerful a tool to disregard.

While the just-described convolutional neural machine translation model helped set the scene for neural network approaches for machine translation, it could not be demonstrated to achieve competitive results compared to traditional approaches. The compression of the sentence representation into a single vector is especially a challenge for long sentences. However, the model was used successfully in reranking candidate translations generated by traditional statistical machine translation systems.

11.4 Convolutional Neural Networks with Attention

convolutional neural network with attention

Gehring et al. (2017) propose an architecture for neural networks that combines the ideas of convolutional neural networks and the attention mechanism. It is essentially the sequence-to-sequence attention that I described as the canonical neural machine translation approach, but with the recurrent neural networks replaced by convolutional layers.

I introduced convolutions in the previous section. The idea is to combine a short sequence of neighboring words into a single representation. To look at it in another way, a convolution encodes a word with its left and right context, in a limited window. Let us now describe in more detail what this means for the encoder and the decoder in the neural model.

11.4.1 Encoder

Figure 11.7 shows the convolutional layers used in the encoder. For each input word, the state at each layer is informed by the corresponding state in the previous layer and its two neighbors. Note that these convolutional layers do not shorten the sequence, because we have a convolution centered around each word, using padding (vectors with zero values) for word positions that are out of bounds.

Mathematically, we start with the input word embeddings Ex_j and progress through a sequence of layer encodings $h_{d,j}$ at different depths d until a maximum depth D:

$$h_{0,j} = E\,x_j$$
$$h_{d,j} = f(h_{d-1,j-k}, \ldots, h_{d-1,j+k}) \quad \text{for} \quad d > 0, d \leq D. \tag{11.20}$$

Gehring et al. (2017) use as function f a feed-forward layer, with a residual connection from the corresponding previous layer state $h_{d-1,j}$.

Figure 11.7 Encoder using stacked convolutional layers. Any number of layers may be used.

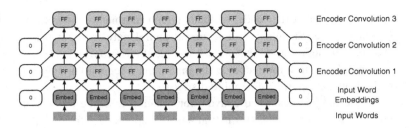

Note that even with a few convolutional layers, the final representation of a word $h_{D,j}$ may be informed by only a partial sentence context—in contrast to the bidirectional recurrent neural networks in the canonical model. However, relevant context words in the input sentence that help with disambiguation may be outside this window.

On the other hand, there are significant computational advantages to this idea. All words at one depth can be processed in parallel, even combined into one massive tensor operation that can be efficiently parallelized on a GPU.

11.4.2 Decoder

The decoder in the traditional model is, at its core, a recurrent neural network. Recall the state progression defined in Equation 8.3:

$$s_i = f(s_{i-1}, Ey_{i-1}, c_i). \tag{11.21}$$

where s_i is the decoder state, Ey_{i-1} the embedding of the previous output word, and c_i the input context.

The convolutional version of this does not have recurrent decoder states, i.e., the computation does not depend on the previous state s_{i-1}, but is conditioned on the sequence of the κ most recent previous words:

$$s_i = f(Ey_{i-\kappa}, \dots, Ey_{i-1}, c_i). \tag{11.22}$$

Furthermore, these decoder convolutions may be stacked, just as the encoder convolutional layers (Figure 11.8):

$$
\begin{aligned}
s_{1,i} &= f(Ey_{i-\kappa}, \dots, Ey_{i-1}, c_i) \\
s_{d,i} &= f(s_{d-1,i-\kappa-1}, \dots, s_{d-1,i}, c_i) \quad \text{for } d > 0, d \le \hat{D}.
\end{aligned}
\tag{11.23}
$$

The main difference between the canonical neural machine translation model and this architecture is the conditioning of the states of the decoder. They are computed in a sequence of convolutional layers and also always the input context.

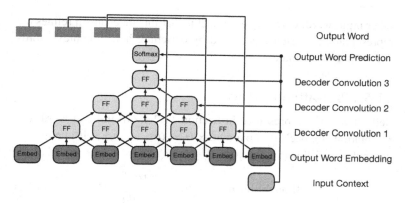

Figure 11.8 Decoder in convolutional neural network with attention. The decoder state is computed as a sequence of convolutional layers (here: 3) over the already predicted output words. Each convolutional state is also informed by the input context computed from the input sentence and attention.

Output Word

Output Word Prediction

Decoder Convolution 3

Decoder Convolution 2

Decoder Convolution 1

Output Word Embedding

Input Context

11.4.3 Attention

The attention mechanism for computing the input context c_i is essentially unchanged from the traditional recurrent neural translation model. Recall that is is based on an association $a(s_{i-1}, h_j)$ between the word representations computed by the encoder h_j and the previous state of the decoder s_{i-1} (refer back to Equation 8.6).

Since we still have such encoder and decoder states ($h_{D,j}$ and $s_{\hat{D},i-1}$), we use the same here. These association scores are normalized via softmax and used to compute a weighted sum of the input word representation (i.e., the encoder states $h_{D,j}$). A refinement is that the encoder state $h_{D,j}$ and the input word embedding x_j is combined via addition when computing the context vector. This is the usual trick of using residual connections to assist training with deep neural networks.

11.5 Self-Attention: Transformer

transformer

The critique of the use of recurrent neural networks is that they require a lengthy walk-through, word by word, of the entire input sentence, which is time-consuming and limits parallelization. The previous sections replaced the recurrent neural networks in our canonical model with convolutions. However, these have a limited context window to enrich representations of words. What we would like is some architectural component that allows us to use wide context and can be highly parallelized. What could that be?

In fact, we already encountered it: the attention mechanism. It considers associations between every input word and any output word and uses it to build a vector representation of the entire input sequence. The idea behind **self-attention** is to extend this idea to the encoder. Instead **self-attention** of computing the association between an input and an output word, self-attention computes the association between any input word and any other input word. One way to view it is that this mechanism refines the representation of each input word by enriching it with context words that help disambiguate it.

11.5.1 Self-Attention Layer

self-attention layer

Self-attention was presented in Section 11.2.4. Given input word representations h_j, packed into a matrix $H = (h_1, \ldots, h_j)$, self-attention is computed as follows:

$$\text{self-attention}(H) = \text{softmax}\left(\frac{HH^T}{\sqrt{|h|}}\right)H. \qquad (11.24)$$

This computation of self-attention is only one step in the self-attention layer used to encode the input sentence. There are four more steps that follow it:

- We combine self-attention with residual connections that pass the word representation through directly:

$$\text{self-attention}(h_j) + h_j. \qquad (11.25)$$

- Next up is a layer normalization step (described in Section 10.5.2):

$$\hat{h}_j = \text{layer-normalization}(\text{self-attention}(h_j) + h_j). \qquad (11.26)$$

- A standard feed-forward step with ReLU activation function is applied:

$$\text{relu}(W\hat{h}_j + b). \qquad (11.27)$$

- This is also augmented with residual connections and layer normalization:

$$\text{layer-normalization}(\text{relu}(W\hat{h}_j + b) + \hat{h}_j). \qquad (11.28)$$

Taking a page from deep models, we now stack several such layers (say, $D = 6$) on top of each other:

$$
\begin{aligned}
h_{0,j} &= Ex_j && \text{start with input word embedding} \\
h_{d,j} &= \text{self-attention-layer}(h_{d-1,j}) && \text{for } d > 0, d \leq D.
\end{aligned}
$$
$$(11.29)$$

The deep modeling is the reason behind the residual connections in the self-attention layer; such residual connections help with training since they allow a shortcut to the input, which may be utilized in early stages of training, before it can take advantage of the more complex interdependencies that deep models enable. The layer normalization step is one standard training trick that also helps especially with deep models (see Section 10.5.2 for details and Figure 11.9).

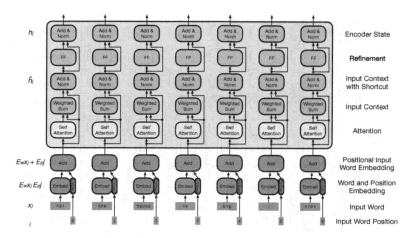

Figure 11.9 Encoder of the self-attentional transformer model. Instead of a recurrent neural network or a convolutional neural network, the attention mechanism is used to first mix the word embedding with the word embedding of related words and then refine this representation with a feed-forward layer.

11.5.2 Attention in the Decoder

The idea of self-attention is also used in the decoder. Now self-attention is computed between output words. The decoder also has more traditional attention. In total there are three sublayers:

- *Self-attention:* Output words are initially encoded by word embeddings $s_i = Ey_i$. We then perform exactly the same self-attention computation as described in Equation 11.18. However, the association of a word s_i is limited to words s_k with $k \leq i$, i.e., just the previously produced output words. Let us denote the result of this sublayer for output word i as $\tilde{s}_i$:

$$\text{self-attention}(\tilde{S}) = \text{softmax}\left(\frac{SS^T}{\sqrt{|h|}}\right) S. \qquad (11.30)$$

- *Attention:* The attention mechanism in this model follows very closely self-attention. The only difference is that, previously, we compute self-attention between the hidden states H and themselves. Now, we compute attention between the decoder states $\tilde{S}$ and the final encoder states H:

$$\text{attention}(\tilde{S}, H) = \text{softmax}\left(\frac{\tilde{S}H^T}{\sqrt{|h|}}\right) H. \qquad (11.31)$$

Using the same more detailed exposition as above for self-attention:

$$a_{ik} = \frac{1}{|h|}\tilde{s}_i h_k^T \qquad \text{raw association}\left(\frac{\tilde{S}H^T}{\sqrt{|h|}}\right)$$

$$\alpha_{ik} = \frac{\exp(a_{ik})}{\sum_\kappa \exp(a_{i\kappa})} \qquad \text{normalized association (softmax).} \qquad (11.32)$$

$$\text{attention}(\tilde{s}_i) = \sum_k \alpha_{jk} h_k \qquad \text{weighted sum}$$

Figure 11.10 Decoder of the self-attentional transformer model. The first part of the architecture is analog to the encoder: self-attention with a feed-forward step for refinement. Then, attention to the encoder states is computed and the representation is refined again.

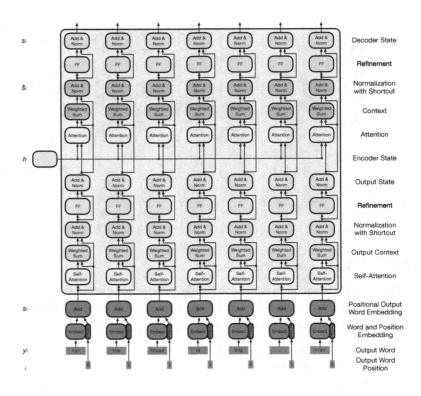

This attention computation is augmented by adding in residual connections, layer normalization, and an additional ReLU layer, just like the self-attention layer described earlier.

It is worth noting that, the output of the attention computation is a weighted sum over input word representations $\sum_k \alpha_{jk} h_k$. To this, we add the (self-attended) representation of the decoder state $\tilde{s}_i$ via a residual connection. This allows skipping over the deep layers, thus speeding up training.

- *Feed-forward layer:* This sublayer is identical to the encoder, i.e., relu $(W_s \hat{s}_i + b_s)$.

Each of the sublayers is followed by the add-and-norm step of first using residual connections and then layer normalization (as noted in the description of the attention sublayer). The steps of the decoder are visualized in Figure 11.10.

The full transformer model consists of several encoder and decoder layers, stacked on top of each other. The entire multilayer model is shown in Figure 11.11.

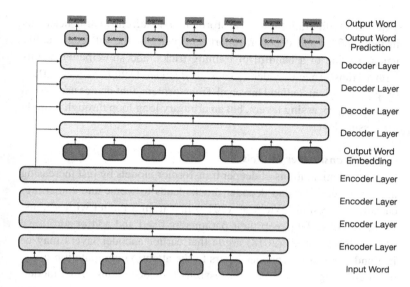

Figure 11.11 The full attention-based transformer model. The input is encoded with several layers of self-attention. The decoder computes attention-based representations of the output in several layers, initialized with the embeddings of the previous output words.

11.6 Further Readings

I presented a number of different architectures to recurrent neural network based machine translation. We may not have to choose between them, but use their best elements. We also do not have to use only single encoder or decoder architecture but can combine them, for instance having both a recurrent neural network encoder and self-attention encoder in parallel and combine their representations.

Convolutional Neural Networks
Kalchbrenner and Blunsom (2013) build a comprehensive machine translation model by first encoding the source sentence with a convolutional neural network and then generate the target sentence by reversing the process. A refinement of this was proposed by Gehring et al. (2017) who use multiple convolutional layers in the encoder and the decoder that do not reduce the length of the encoded sequence but incorporate wider context with each layer.

Self-Attention (Transformer)
Vaswani et al. (2017) replace the recurrent neural networks used in attentional sequence-to-sequence models with multiple self-attention layers, both for the encoder as well as the decoder. There are a number of additional refinements of this model: so-called multihead attention, encoding of sentence positions of words, etc. Chen et al. (2018) compare

different configurations of Transformer or recurrent neural networks in the encoder and decoder, report that many of the different quality gains are due to a handful of training tricks, and show better results with a Transformer encoder and a RNN decoder. Dehghani et al. (2019) propose a variant, called Universal Transformers, that do not use a fixed number of processing layers, but an arbitrary long loop through a single processing layer.

Deeper Transformer Models

Naive implementations of deeper transformer models by just increasing number of encoder and decoder blocks leads to worse and sometimes catastrophic results. Wu et al. (2019) first train a model with n transformer blocks, then keep their parameters fixed and add m additional blocks. Bapna et al. (2018) argue that earlier encoder layers may be lost and connect all encoder layers to the attention computation of the decoder. Wang et al. (2019a) successfully train deep transformer models with up to 30 layers by relocating the normalization step to the beginning of the block and by adding residual connections to all previous layers, not just the directly preceding one.

document context ### Document Context

Maruf et al. (2018) consider the entire source document as context when translating a sentence. Attention is computed over all input sentences, and the sentences are weighted accordingly. Miculicich et al. (2018) extend this work with hierarchical attention, which first computes attention over sentences and then over words. Due to computational problems, this is limited to a window of surrounding sentences. Maruf et al. (2019) also use hierarchical attention but compute sentence-level attention over the entire document and filter out the most relevant sentences before extending attention over words. A gate distinguishes between words in the source sentence and words in the context sentences. Junczys-Dowmunt (2019) translates entire source documents (up to 1,000 words) at a time by concatenating all input sentences, showing significant improvements.

Chapter 12
Revisiting Words

In the beginning was the Word,
and the Word was with God,
and the Word was God.
John 1:1

The underlying assumption of our models is that language is made up of words as atomic units. But it is not that simple. Think of words such as *homework*, which is a word that seems to be composed of two words. Or consider the two words *cat* and *cats*—these are not really two different words, they are morphological variants of the same dictionary entry.

Other languages challenge our notion of words even more. Chinese writing does not place spaces between words, so defining what words are requires explicit linguistic analysis. Spoken language also does not pause between words, something that seems surprising, but very obvious when you listen to a foreign language that you do not understand. Most languages in the world have much richer morphology than English, with some languages such as German, Finnish, and Turkish famous for building monstrosities that stretch our English-centric understanding of words to an extreme.

In this chapter, I discuss solutions to practical challenges of large vocabularies and models that go one step further in breaking up sentences into words, by breaking up words into characters.

12.1 Word Embeddings

word embedding

To handle words in neural machine translation models, I introduced the notion of word embeddings in Chapter 7. Since neural networks operate on multidimensional real-numbered vector representations, discrete objects such as words pose a challenge. I introduced word embeddings as a lookup table, where each discrete word object is mapped to a vector representation. In our neural translation models, embeddings of source words are further processed in the encoder to contextualize them with their surrounding words and in the decoder as input to predict the next decoder state. When used in such way, word embeddings acquire through training useful properties, such as similar representations of semantically related (*cat* and *dog*) and morpho-syntactically related (*cat* and *cats*) words.

Word embeddings have been found to be very useful for core natural language processing steps (tagging, parsing, etc.), more advanced analysis (named entity detection, sentiment detection, etc.), and final applications (summarization, information retrieval). It has proven to be useful to have off-the-shelf word embeddings in place for these tasks. Such word pretrained word embeddings can be learned on massive amounts of text and then reused many times. In this section, I review some of the ways such general-purpose word embeddings are trained.

12.1.1 Latent Semantic Analysis

latent semantic analysis

The general idea of real-numbered word representations that have similar representations for semantically related words predates the current wave of deep learning and has been a mainstay of natural language processing for a long time. The key insight is that words that are similar occur in similar to contexts, e.g., you *pet a dog/cat*, you *feed a dog/cat*, you are a *dog/cat person*, you *post a picture of your cat/dog*.

By collecting statistics about the words that occur in the context of a word, especially the words just before and after its occurrence, already gives a good high-dimensional representation of that word (Figure 12.1). These scores are organized in a matrix X with a row for each word, and columns corresponding to context words.

However, such representations are quite sparse (many words will rarely or never occur in the context) and quite large. To obtain a more compact representation, **latent semantic analysis** transforms these raw co-occurrence statistics in two steps. First, each count value is replaced by its **point-wise mutual information** (PMI) score.

LSA

PMI

$$\text{PMI}(x; y) = \log \frac{p(x, y)}{p(x)p(y)}. \tag{12.1}$$

word	context				$\Longrightarrow$	word	context			
	cute	fluffy	dangerous	of			cute	fluffy	dangerous	of
dog	231	76	15	5,767		dog	9.4	6.3	0.2	1.1
cat	191	21	3	2,463		cat	8.3	3.1	0.1	1.0
lion	5	1	79	796		lion	0.1	0.0	12.1	1.0

Figure 12.1 Co-occurrence statistics, such as the word *cute* occurring 231 times in the context of *dog* (left table), are converted into point-wise mutual information scores (right table). Words with similar PMI vectors (rows in the right table) have similar syntactic and semantic properties.

PMI is a measure how much more often than chance the words co-occur. In the example in Figure 12.1, *cat* and *cute* occur together 8.3 times more often than chance while *cat* and *of* occur fairly independently of each other (PMI 1.1)—despite the fact that *cat* and *of* co-occur much more often than *cat* and *cute* (2,463 versus 191).

Next, we factorize the PMI matrix P using **singular value decomposition** (SVD) into two orthogonal matrices U and V (i.e., UU^T and VV^T are an identity matrix) and a diagonal matrix Σ (i.e., it only has non-zero values on the diagonal):

$$P = U\Sigma V^T. \tag{12.2}$$

Without going too much into detail, this reframes the matrix P into a rotation U, a stretching Σ, and another rotation V^T. The values on the diagonal of Σ are called the **singular values**, and by retaining only the largest of them (setting the lowest ones to zero), the resulting simplification $P' = U\Sigma'V^T$ is still a good approximation of P but with lower rank. To stay with the geometric interpretation: The stretching operation Σ compresses some dimensions, and flattening them completely does not make much difference (Figure 12.2).

For our purposes of context generalization, this may mean that context words like *cute* and *fluffy* are quite similar, so their dimensions can be combined into a single dimension of $0.4 \times cute + 0.7 \times fluffy$. Note that in real cases, each resulting dimension is a linear combination of all the context words.

12.1.2 Continuous Bag of Words

Continuous bag of words (CBOW) is similar to the n-gram neural language model that we first discussed when presenting word embeddings in Chapter 7. The method poses the task to predict a word w_t given the surrounding context words w_{t+j} in a window of size $2n$, i.e., $j \in \{-n, \ldots, -1, 1, \ldots, n\}$. However, it is stripped down to the bare essentials.

First, each context word (represented as a one hot vector) is mapped to its embedding Cw_{t+j} using an input word embedding matrix C. This

SVD

continuous bag of words

CBOW

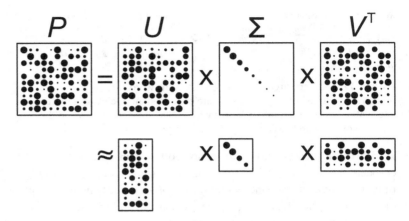

Figure 12.2 Intuition behind singular value decomposition used by latent semantic analysis. By reformulating a single matrix P into a rotation U, a diagonal matrix Σ, and another rotation V, we can remove the lowest singular values in the diagonal matrix (and thus corresponding columns and rows in U and V). When applied to co-occurrence matrices, the matrix U can be viewed as an embedding matrix, where each row corresponds to a vector representation of a word.

Figure 12.3 Continuous bag of words model (left) and skip gram model (right) to train word embeddings based on the surrounding words.

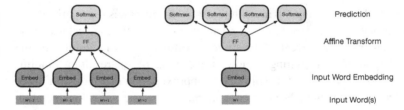

uses the same embedding matrix independent of the position of the context word j. These context word embeddings are then averaged, independent of their position (hence the term *bag of words*), resulting in a hidden layer representation h_t.

$$h_t = \frac{1}{2n} \sum_{j \in \{-n,\dots,-1,1,\dots,n\}} Cw_{t+j}. \tag{12.3}$$

This hidden layer representation h_t is then mapped into the prediction y_t of the targeted word w_t using a weight matrix U (Figure 12.3):

$$y_t = \text{softmax}(Uh_t). \tag{12.4}$$

The CBOW model looks similar to the n-gram language model, except that context words are not just the n previous words, but also the n words following the targeted word w_t.

12.1.3 Skip Gram

skip gram

The skip gram model reverses the idea of the CBOW model. Instead of predicting a word from its context, we now predict the context from a word.

Given a word w_t and its embedding Cw_t, we predict $2n$ context words using a weight matrix U. Since we again ignore the position of these context words, the prediction for all of these words is identical:

$$y_t = \text{softmax}(UCw_t). \tag{12.5}$$

During training this prediction is compared against the true context words w_{t+j}.

A couple of things worth noting here. Equation 12.5 contains the weight matrices C and U right next to each other, so what is gained from multiplying with two matrices (first C, then U), without a nonlinear activation function in the middle? Two words: dimensionality reduction. By reducing the representation from the one hot vector space of, say, 50,000 dimensions to a embedding space of, say, 500 dimensions we force the model to find a more compact representation that finds commonalities between words.

The parameters of the model are the weight matrices C and U, which can also be understood as input word embedding matrix and output word embedding matrix, respectively. For the input word w_t, a column is pulled from the matrix C, i.e., the input embedding v_t is looked up. For the prediction of an output context word, the column $\tilde{v}_{t+j}^T$ is multiplied against this vector v_t to obtain a prediction score for a particular context word. So, at the core of computing the relationship between the input word w_t and the output context word w_{t+j} is the vector product $\tilde{v}_{t+j}^T v_t$.

12.1.4 GloVe

GloVe

Instead of iterating through all the training sentences and each word in it, an alternative is to first aggregate the statistics about co-occurrences into a matrix X (as we did for latent semantic analysis in Section 12.1.1), and then train a model to predict these values.

This is the idea behind GloVe, short for global vectors (Pennington et al., 2014), named so because it is based on global (corpus-wide) statistics of word distributions. At its core, it aims to predict co-occurrence values X_{ij} from target word embeddings v_i and context word embeddings $\tilde{v}_j$. This score is computed by the vector product $\tilde{v}_j^T v_i$. The training objective is defined by the cost function (in very simplified form):

$$\text{cost} = \sum_i \sum_j \tilde{v}_j^T |v_i - \log X_{ij}|. \tag{12.6}$$

So, for training, we need to loop over all words, and then all their context words.

This basic idea is refined in a few ways. First, bias terms b and $\tilde{b}$ are introduced for each target and context word:

$$\text{cost} = \sum_i \sum_j |b_i + \tilde{b}_j + \tilde{v}_j^T v_i - \log X_{ij}|. \tag{12.7}$$

Then, there is a concern that most words pairs (i,j) have no relation with each other, especially if both i and j are rare. So, we would like to consider these training examples less strongly during training. On the other hand, X_{ij} may take on very large values that may overly impact the overall cost calculation, especially if one or both words involved are function words like *the* or *of*. We would also like to limit this during training.

The solution to that is a scaling factor for each word pair's cost calculation, defined as follows:

$$f(x) = \min(1, (x/x_{\max})^\alpha). \tag{12.8}$$

The choice of these particular hyper parameters, e.g., $\alpha = \frac{3}{4}$ and $x_{\max} = 200$, have been determined empirically and may be set differently for different data conditions.

Putting it all together, and using the square of the error, we have

$$\text{cost} = \sum_i \sum_j f(X_{ij})(b_i + \tilde{b}_j + \tilde{v}_j^T v_i - \log X_{ij})^2. \tag{12.9}$$

As a final note, we are free to compute the co-occurrence values X_{ij} in many different ways. Pennington et al. (2014) use a larger window (10 words) around each word, but also scale counts by the distance of the context word position.

GloVe word embeddings have been shown to outperform the previous approaches. Large inventories of word embeddings precomputed on large corpora have been made available[1] and are used in many applications.

12.1.5 ELMo

ELMo

When working on any natural language processing task, having a set of word embeddings on the shelf is a useful resource. However, word embeddings have some disadvantages, since they provide a fixed representation for each word, not adapted to their context at test time.

---

[1] https://nlp.stanford.edu/projects/glove.

This is especially a problem for ambiguous words that may have very different senses.

For this reason, neural machine translation models do not just use word embeddings as input representation, they pass it through additional processing steps in the encoder, such as recurrent neural language models. This allows us to contextualize and refine the word representations.

This insight has also been applied to other natural language processing tasks. An influential paper by Peters et al. (2018) contrasts the use of plain word embeddings and word embeddings that have been refined into the hidden states of multilayer recurrent neural language models for a large number of natural language applications (semantic role labeling, named entity recognition, sentiment classification, etc.). They call these embeddings ELMo, for *embeddings from language models* and show substantial improvements in all of them.

One interesting refinement is using the weighted average of representations at different layers of the recurrent neural language model and adjusting that weighting for the task. The authors observe that syntactic information is better represented in early layers but semantic information is better represented in deeper layers.

12.1.6 BERT

BERT

The latest method for obtaining contextualized word embeddings also takes lessons from advances in machine translation (Devlin et al., 2019). Bidirectional encoder representations from transformers (BERT) uses the Transformer model described in Section 11.5. BERT is pre-trained on plentiful monolingual data, and the resulting model is then fine-tuned toward the actual task at hand.

The pretraining task is also essentially a language modeling task. However, words are not predicted in a left-to-right sequence, as in ELMo, which uses recurrent neural networks. Instead, the self-attention mechanism (Section 11.2.4) enables the prediction of any word in the sentence given its surrounding words. This is called the **masked language model** task. A second pretraining task is next sentence prediction. Given a sentence, the task is to predict the words in the following sentence.

After pretraining on large amounts of monolingual data, the resulting model is then refined toward the targeted task, given the task-specific training data. Devlin et al. (2019) show superior results to ELMo on tasks such as answering questions for a scenario where the information is given in a paragraph of text or detecting that a follow-up sentence's meaning is entailed by the preceding sentence.

This is currently a very active field of research. For instance Yang et al. (2019) refine the BERT model by predicting one masked word at a time, with permutations on the order of the masked words (see also, multitask training in Section 14.3.3).

12.2 Multilingual Word Embeddings

multilingual word embedding

Word embeddings are often viewed as semantic representations of words. So, it is tempting to view these embedding spaces as language-independent meaning representations, where words that refer to the same concept, say *cat* (English), *gato* (Spanish), and *Katze* (German) are mapped to the same vector. Instead of overcoming the language barriers by machine translation between languages, it may be more promising to map languages into a common semantic space and come up with universal natural language applications that work for any language.

There may be also less ambitious reasons for having multilingual word embeddings, or at least the mapping between word embedding spaces of different languages. Consider that monolingual corpora will always be more copious than parallel corpora and there may be many words that only occur in a monolingual corpus, so we do not have any direct evidence of what they translate to in the other language. However, a monolingual corpus allows us to learn a word embedding for the word, which we can then map to the target word embedding space and find the closest matching word embedding of a target word.

There has been extensive work on multilingual word embedding; a recent comprehensive survey is presented by Ruder et al. (2017). This section covers basic ideas; please consult their paper for a more detail presentation.

12.2.1 Mapping between Language-Specific Word Embeddings

Most work in this area makes the assumption that we have sufficient amounts of monolingual data in both languages, and a bilingual dictionary that maps at least some of the words between the two languages.

This allows us to train, say, English word embeddings C_E and Spanish word embeddings C_S. An interesting observation is that the geometric relationships between words in English are very similar to the geometric relationships of the translation of these words in Spanish. See Figure 12.4 for an illustration taken from Mikolov et al. (2013b).

This motivates the idea that all we have to learn is a transformation matrix $W_{S \to E}$ that maps between the English embedding space C_E and the Spanish embedding space C_S. This can be framed as a optimization problem to minimize the distance between any embedding c_i^E of English

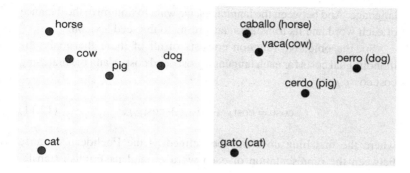

Figure 12.4 Word embedding spaces for words with the same meaning (English and Spanish), adapted from Mikolov et al. (2013b).

word w_i^E and the mapping the embedding c_i^S of its Spanish translation w_i^S, as defined, say, by the Euclidean distance:

$$\text{cost} = \sum_i ||W_{S \to E} \; c_i^S - c_i^E||. \qquad (12.10)$$

This cost can be optimized with gradient descent training, by looping over all the dictionary items as training data.

There are several refinements of this idea. The transformation matrix $W_{S \to E}$ should be orthogonal, i.e., just rotate the embedding spaces but not stretch any dimensions. Different choices for known word translations (also called the **seed lexicon**) have been explored. We may want to use only highly reliable lexicon entries, avoid ambiguous words with multiple translations, or—if we lack sufficient parallel data—use only cognates (say, English *electricity* and Spanish *electricidad*) or identically spelled words (say *internet* and *Washington*).

Another problem that has been identified and addressed is called **hubness**, meaning the tendency of some words being the nearest neighbor of many words. This is more likely to happen in highly dimensional spaces, but consider the four points at the ends and the one in the center of a plus ($+$) sign. The center is nearest neighbor to all the points on the edges. When looking to identify words based on a mapped embedding vector, we do not always want to end up with the same word.

12.2.2 Language-Independent Word Embeddings

language independent word embedding

Instead of having one word embedding space for each language, connected by a transformation matrix, another strategy is to aim for a single word embedding space for both languages—or even more than two languages, for that matter.

There are several aspects to training this shared embedding space. For each language, the words have to have the appropriate semantic relationships to each other. This is trained on monolingual text for each language. And between the languages, we want to minimize the distance of each word and its translation according to the seed lexicon.

So, the objective function consists of all of these the goals, the monolingual costs for each language (cost_E and cost_F), and the matching cost $\text{cost}_{E,F}$.

$$\text{cost} = \text{cost}_E + \text{cost}_F + \text{cost}_{E,F}, \tag{12.11}$$

where the matching cost may be defined as the Euclidean distance between the representation of each word c_i^F and its English translation c_i^E:

$$\text{cost}_{E,F} = \sum_i ||c_i^F - c_i^E||. \tag{12.12}$$

In its broad strokes, learning a language-independent embedding space is not all that different from learning monolingual embedding spaces first and then a mapping function. Training has to necessarily iterate through examples from the monolingual corpus for E, the monolingual corpus for F, and the bilingual seed lexicon (E, F). But we may see some benefits of frequently iterating over these different types of training data, which may mutually reinforce each other.

An interesting alternative idea for training language-independent embedding spaces is to take a sentence from the monolingual corpus in language E and randomly replace some of its words with their translation in language F, and vice versa. This treats words in the seed lexicon as completely interchangeable and thus anchors the training of the joint embedding space.

12.2.3 Using Only Monolingual Data

Mapping between the embedding spaces is commonly done using a transformation matrix $W_{S \rightarrow E}$ which is even often normalized to be orthogonal, i.e., it just rotates the spaces. This assumes that the geometric properties between words are the same across languages. This is intuitive for many words, i.e., the relationship between *dog*, *cat*, and *lion* should be the same no matter whether we use these English words or their Spanish or German translations.

Obviously, there are always words that are unique to a language (*Schadenfreude* is often cited as a uniquely German word), and some words may have slightly shifted meaning across languages (names of colors is an interesting example).

Nevertheless, if the assumption holds that words and their translation across languages have the same geometric relationships, no matter what

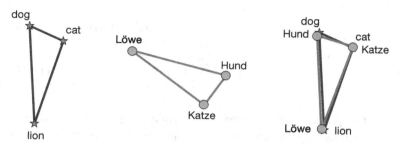

Figure 12.5 Matching up the geometric shape of embedding spaces. Unsupervised induction of the mapping between the spaces, revealing the translation pairs *dog/Hund, cat/Katze, lion/Löwe*.

language they are expressed in, then the task of matching the embedding spaces of each language is a task of rotating these embedding spaces so they line up with the best fit.

Think of the triangle of the words *dog*, *cat*, and *lion* (with *lion* more distant than the other two, but closer to *cat* than *dog*). This triangle exists in English word embedding space, and also in German embedding space for the corresponding words *Hund*, *Katze*, and *Löwe*. There is only one way to rotate the German embedding space, so that these triangles match up in the closest way possible, i.e., minimizing the distance the corners of the triangles. Having the German triangle rotated in this fashion, the corresponding corners reveal the discovered word mappings (Figure 12.5).

One idea for learning the transformation matrix $W_{\text{German}\rightarrow\text{English}}$ automatically just given the word embedding spaces C_{German} and C_{English}, is to use a cost metric that measures how well points in these spaces match up.

Instead, Lample et al. (2018a) propose to approach this problem with adversarial learning. If points in the German and English space do not match up, then it is possible to train a classifier that accurately predicts if a point corresponds to a German or a English word. So, the opponent in the adversarial setting (the so-called discriminator) aims to make this prediction. Formally, its learning objective is a classifier P that predicts mapped German word vectors g_i as German and English word vectors e_j as English, given a transformation matrix W:

$$\text{cost}_D(P|W) = -\frac{1}{n}\sum_{i=1}^{n}\log P(\text{German}|Wg_i)$$

$$-\frac{1}{m}\sum_{j=1}^{m}\log P(\text{English}|e_j). \qquad (12.13)$$

In contrast to that, the training objective of the unsupervised learner is to optimize the translation matrix W to minimize discriminator's the ability to make accurate predictions:

$$\text{cost}_L(W|P) = -\frac{1}{n}\sum_{i=1}^{n}\log P(\text{English}|Wg_i)$$

$$-\frac{1}{m}\sum_{j=1}^{m}\log P(\text{German}|e_j). \qquad (12.14)$$

Lample et al. (2018a) report good results comparable to supervised word embedding matching methods (which use a seed dictionary), with up to 80% accuracy for finding the translations for the 1,500 most frequent English words in Spanish and French word embedding spaces. While these are impressive numbers, it is not clear how useful these methods are for applications like machine translation. For instance, these methods do not work as well for the long tail of words that are less frequent. Prior experience has shown that even small amounts of parallel data have much bigger impact.

12.3 Large Vocabularies

vocabulary

Zipf's law tells us that words in a language are very unevenly distributed. So, there is always a large tail of rare words. New words come into the language all the time (e.g., *retweeting, website, woke, lit*), and we also have to deal with a very large inventory of names, including company names (e.g., *eBay, Yahoo, Microsoft*).

Neural methods are not well equipped to deal with such large vocabularies. The ideal representations for neural networks are continuous space vectors. This is why we first convert discrete objects such as words into vectors in such spaces, i.e., word embeddings.

However, ultimately the discrete nature of words shows up. On the input side, we need to train an embedding matrix that maps each word into its embedding. On the output side we predict a probability distribution over all output words. The latter is generally the bigger concern, since the amount of computation involved is linear with the size of the vocabulary, making this a very large matrix operation. Both the input word embedding matrix and the output softmax prediction matrix are very large, take up a lot of memory in the GPU, and cause computational challenges.

12.3.1 Special Treatment for Rare Words

rare word

Neural translation models typically restrict the vocabulary to, say, 20,000 to 80,000 words. Actual vocabulary sizes, especially for morphologically rich languages, are much larger than that.

In initial work on neural machine translation, only the most frequent words were used, and all others represented by an unknown token (*UNK*).

But whenever a rare (or actually unknown) word occurs in an input sentence, we still need to find a translation for it.

Assuming that during training, the model learns to map the unknown input word token *UNK* to the unknown output word token *UNK*, we can address this problem in postprocessing. The standard solution is to have a back-up dictionary obtained by traditional statistical machine translation methods, or other means. This is clearly an unsatisfying solution, and the subwords methods I discuss in the next section have replaced this approach.

However, it is worth noting that the majority of rare and unknown words, given sufficiently large training data, are names and numbers. Translation of these for most language pairs is quite straightforward. Names are typically unchanged (*Obama* is still *Obama* in Spanish and German). The same goes for numbers. There may be small differences that are easily addressed by simple rules (e.g., decimals such as *1.2* are written in German as *1,2*). There may be more complex problems such as number systems based on 10,000 (in Chinese the number 54,000 would be written as 5.4万, and the transliteration of names into different writing systems. But again, these may be better addressed with rule-based methods or specialized subcomponents.

So even today, special words such as names (e.g., *Obama*), numbers (e.g., *5.2 million*), dates (e.g., *August 3, 2019*), or measurement units (e.g., *25cm*) are replaced in some deployed real-word systems with special tokens that are copied into the output and replaced in postprocessing (which may even replace *25cm* with *10 inches*).

12.3.2 Byte Pair Encoding

The common approach to rare words today is to break them up into **subword units**. This may seem a bit crude but is actually very similar to standard approaches in statistical machine translation to handle compounds (recall *website → web + site*) and morphology (*unfollow → un + follow, convolutions → convolution + s*). It is even a decent approach to the problem of transliteration of names (Москва → *Moscow*), which are traditionally handled by a separate letter translation component.

A popular method for creating an inventory of subword units and legitimate words is **byte pair encoding**. This method is trained on the parallel corpus. First, the words in the corpus are split into characters (marking original spaces with a special space character). Then, the most frequent pair of characters is merged. This step is repeated for a fixed given number of times. Each of these steps increases the vocabulary by one, beyond the original inventory of single characters.

subword units

byte pair encoding

Consider this small toy corpus:

this ˍfat ˍcat ˍwith ˍthe ˍhat ˍis ˍin ˍthe ˍcave ˍof ˍthe ˍthin ˍbat

The most frequent pair here is *t h*, which occurs 6 times. So, we merge these two letters into a single token.

th is ˍfat ˍcat ˍwi th ˍth e ˍh at ˍis ˍin ˍth e ˍcave ˍof ˍth e ˍth in ˍb at

After this operation, the most frequent pair of tokens is *a t*, which occurs 4 times, so we merge it next.

th is ˍfat ˍc at ˍwi th ˍth e ˍh at ˍis ˍin ˍth e ˍcave ˍof ˍth e ˍth in ˍb at

Now the most frequent token pair is *th e*, which occurs 3 times. Merging these creates a full word.

th is ˍfat ˍc at ˍw i th ˍthe ˍh at ˍis ˍin ˍthe ˍcave ˍof ˍthe ˍth in ˍb at

The example mirrors quite well the behavior of the algorithm on real-world data sets. It starts with grouping together frequent letter combinations (*t+h*, *a+t*, *c+h*) and then joins frequent words (*the*, *in*, *of*). At the end of this process, the most frequent words will emerge as single tokens, while rare words consist of still unmerged subwords.

See Figure 12.6 for a real-world example, where subword units are indicated with two "at" symbols (@@). After 49,500 byte pair encoding operations, the vast majority of actually used words are intact, while rarer words are broken up (e.g., *critic@@ izes*, *destabil@@ izing*). Sometimes, the split seem to be morphologically motivated (e.g., *im@@ pending*), but mostly they are not (e.g., *stra@@ ined*). Note also the decomposition of the relatively rare name *Net@@ any@@ ahu*.

The number of byte pair encoding operations depends on the size of the training data. To have as many unsplit words as possible, a large number of byte pair operations are learned, resulting in as large a vocabulary as the memory on the GPU card allows. Typical values are 50,000–80,000. For low resource conditions, vocabulary sizes as low as 5,000 subword tokens have been used, avoiding tokens that occur only once in training and therefore cause sparse data problems. Furthermore, a common practice is to run byte encoding on the concatenation of the source side and target side of the corpus. This helps with the transliteration of names.

12.3.3 Sentence Piece

sentence piece A variant of byte pair encoding is called **sentence piece**. It is based
word piece on the same principle, i.e., assembling a vocabulary of subwords with the highest frequency. It frames this as maximizing unigram language

Obama receives Net@@ any@@ ahu

the relationship between Obama and Net@@ any@@ ahu is not
exactly friendly . the two wanted to talk about the implementation
of the international agreement and about Teheran 's destabil@@
izing activities in the Middle East . the meeting was also planned
to cover the conflict with the Palestinians and the disputed two
state solution . relations between Obama and Net@@ any@@
ahu have been stra@@ ined for years . Washington critic@@ izes
the continuous building of settlements in Israel and acc@@ uses
Net@@ any@@ ahu of a lack of initiative in the peace process .
the relationship between the two has further deteriorated because
of the deal that Obama negotiated on Iran 's atomic program .
in March , at the invitation of the Republic@@ ans , Net@@
any@@ ahu made a controversial speech to the US Congress ,
which was partly seen as an aff@@ ront to Obama . the speech
had not been agreed with Obama , who had rejected a meeting
with reference to the election that was at that time im@@ pending
in Israel .

Figure 12.6 Byte pair encoding applied to English (model used 49,500 BPE operations). Word splits are indicated with @@. Note that the data are also tokenized and true-cased in a preprocessing step.

model probability, but this is essentially the same criterion for merging character sequences.

One minor difference is the notation. While byte pair encoding would break up a word like *dog* into *dog@@* and *s*, sentence piece uses an explicit space symbol (represented by the underscore _). So, *dogs* would be broken up into *_dog* and *s*. There may be a subtle benefit to this notation. While byte pair encoding makes a difference between the single word occurrence of *dog* and the use as a prefix subword *dog@@*, it is the same for sentence piece (*_dig* in both cases). For languages that use suffixes for marking morphological variants, training data for common stems may be shared.

Since sentence piece explicitly marks space symbols, it may be used on raw text without prior tokenization. For example, the word *dog* followed by a end-of-sentence period, may be presented as *dog.* and the algorithm will likely learn to break it up into *_dog* and the period. While this does not make much of a difference for languages in Latin script for which simple tokenizers suffice, it means that the sentence piece algorithm may also be directly applied to languages such as Chinese, Japanese, and Thai that do mark word boundaries with spaces. For these languages tokenization (typically called word segmentation in this situation) is a much more complex problem, requiring word lists and other language statistics. But even for languages written in Latin script is has become popular lately to forgo tokenization and other preprocessing but instead just relying on sentence piece to do it all.

12.3.4 Training with Expectation Maximization

expectation maximization
EM algorithm

The greedy algorithm outlined in Section 12.3.2 may produce subwords that are frequent at the time but later get merged further, so becoming eventually rare. Consider an unusually spelled word such as *serendipity*, which may get slowly merged into subwords *seren*, *dipi*, and *ty*, then *serendipi* and *ty* and finally the full word. The intermediate subwords will rarely if ever occur by themselves after this, so there is no use in keeping them in the subword vocabulary, taking up valuable space in the embedding matrices.

Given a set of candidate subwords, either produced by the greedy algorithm or just the most frequent letter sequences, we may want to recompute their frequency in the training data and discard the rare ones. This is a process that consists of two steps: (1) splitting of the corpus with a given subword vocabulary with the goal of using the largest subwords with high frequency, and (2) counting the resulting subwords in the split data to obtain frequency counts. The default algorithm for such a two-step optimization problem is called **expectation maximization**. It alternates between the two steps, the first step being called the expectation step and the second step called the maximization step.

There are two conflicting goals for step (1): we want frequent subwords but we also want large subwords. Here, framing the training objective as a unigram language model comes in. Yes, the letters t, h, and e are frequent, but the joint probability of $p(t, h, e)$ with the independence assumption of the unigram language model is lower than the probability of the word $p(the)$, i.e., $p(t) \times p(h) \times p(e) < p(the)$. The result of the expectation step are all possible splits of words in the corpus, each with an associated probability $p(\text{split}|\text{word})$. The maximization step takes uses the probabilities to weight the counts for each subword. For example if the two possibilities are the split $t+h+e$ with probability 0.2, and the full word *the* with probability 0.8, then we collect the count of 0.2 for each of the three letters and 0.8 for the full word—in both times multiplied with the word count for *the*. With such counts in hand, we can reestimate the unigram language model probabilities.

The definition of the training objective as maximizing unigram language model probability over the corpus will prefer longer subwords over shorter, but it also allows us to compute how much we lose if we remove a subword from the vocabulary. So, we carry out the steps (1) and (2) for a few iterations, then remove the subwords with the least loss and repeat the process until we reach the specified vocabulary size.

12.3.5 Subword Regularization

subword regularization

Let us turn to another refinement that works for both byte pair encoding and sentence piece variants of subword generation. Let us say the morphological variants *recognize* and *recognizing* both occur in the corpus, but only *recognize* is frequent enough to become its own subword, but *recognizing* gets split up into *recogniz* and *ing*.

This means that *recognize* and *recogniz* are independent tokens that do not share any information. So even if *recognize* occurs frequently in many contexts, this does not help learning better how to translate *recognizing*.

A method called **subword regularization** proposes to not deterministically split up words into the biggest possible subwords but to sample different subword segmentations during training. This means that *recognize* is sometimes presented as the subword *recognize*, sometimes split up into *recogniz* and *e* or any other way. Whenever it is split up in this fashion, more can be learned about the syntactic and semantic context of the subword *recogniz* that will be useful for the rarer word *recognizing*. Sampling based on subword frequencies will still prefer maximal subwords, but will also often enough use the same training data to learn more general information about smaller subwords.

12.4 Character-Based Models

character-based model

In the onslaught of deep learning on natural language processing, the linguistic concept of the *word* has survived, even as concepts such as morphology and syntax have been relegated to be just latent properties of language that can be discovered automatically in the intermediate representations of neural network models. But even that may fall. Maybe the atomic unit of language should be just the consonant and vowels, or in their written form, a character in the writing system—a letter in Latin script, a logograph or even just a stroke in Chinese.

There are good reasons for breaking up words. The most obvious is the role morphology plays in language. Words like *cat* and *cats* are the singular and plural word form of the same word stem. The way plural forms of words are created follows clear morphological patterns that can be discovered from the character string. In English, this is *add an 's'* as the most basic rule (notwithstanding variants of that rule as in *baby/babies* or *dish/dishes*, and outright exceptions, e.g., *child/children*). If we treat all these words atomic units that are independent of each other, we do not allow the models to learn morphological patterns, such as that plurals are formed by adding an *s*, and thus generalize and induce the meaning of previously unseen morphological variants.

12.4.1 Character Sequence Models

A straightforward way to move from words to characters is to use the same exact model as before but just feed it strings of characters (including a special whitespace symbol) instead of strings of words. However, some of assumptions behind design decisions of that model architecture do not hold up well under this change. The most glaring one is the attention model. Attention to individual words as semantic units is well motivated, but attention over subsequences of characters is less so.

While such a character-sequence to character-sequence gives poor performance in practice (Ataman et al., 2018), there have been several efforts to use character-based representations at only the output layer. This mostly leaves the attention mechanism in place as before, but allows for more flexible generation of output, including the generation of novel words, especially morphological variants (Chung et al., 2016).

12.4.2 Character-Based Word Models

A less radical idea than dispensing with the concept of the word altogether is developing word representations that are based on their character strings. This may be done outside of a machine translation model. Consider the goal of learning word embeddings that are informed by their character sequence.

In this framing of the problem, we may first learn word embeddings for frequent words in the traditional way. Then, we obtain representations from character-based models for these words and map them into the same space. The character-based model is trained to predict the traditional word vector learned from the word's distributional properties. The character-based model can then also be applied to previously unseen words and hopefully yield an appropriate word embedding.

There are two main approaches to build character-based word models—using recurrent neural networks and using convolutional neural networks.

Recurrent Neural Networks – The use of recurrent neural networks over character sequences to obtain word representations is similar to the their use in the encoder of neural machine translation models.

Figure 12.7 shows a bidirectional recurrent neural network model over characters. A forward recurrent neural network starts at the first character and walks through the sequence, consuming one character at a time, terminating in a final state at the last letter. Conversely, a backward recurrent neural network starts at the last letter and terminates in a final state at the first letter. The two final states are concatenated and used to predict the word embedding.

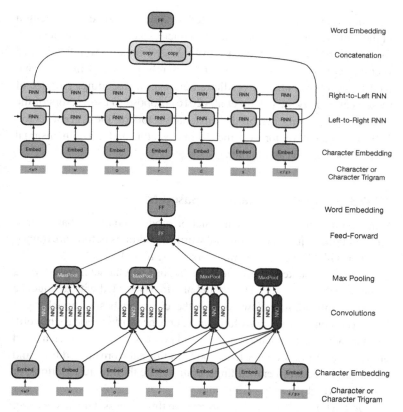

Figure 12.7 Word representation composed from a letter sequence using a bidirectional recurrent neural network. Instead of single letters, we may also use overlapping letter *n*-grams (here trigrams).

Figure 12.8 Word representation composed from a letter sequence using a convolutional neural network. Convolutions over 2-, 3-, 4-, and 5-letter *n*-grams are shown.

We do not have to base this model on single letters. We can also start with letter *n*-grams, typically trigrams. Using overlapping letter trigrams as input at every step provides richer input and has often shown to give better results.

Convolutional Neural Networks – Convolutional neural networks are the other popular design choice for character-based word models. The motivation is that a word may be made up of a stem and any number of affixes, and the full view of a word considers these parts equally, just like viewing an image considers different regions.

There are many ways to build convolutional neural networks over characters. Figure 12.8 shows the architecture used by Costa-jussà and Fonollosa (2016) for their machine translation model. It is based on convolutional layers that map sequences of a given length (say, three characters) into a single vector. Since there may be several character trigrams in a word, we typically obtain several such vectors. These are combined by a max pooling layer, which picks the highest value for each element across all the vectors. This results in a single fixed-sized vector independent of the length of the word.

Such vectors are not just computed for a single choice for the length of the input letter n-gram (say, three characters as suggested earlier), but for a range of lengths, say one to seven. So, we obtain seven fixed-sized vectors, which are concatenated and possibly processed in additional feed-forward layers before prediction the word embedding. The size of these vectors may vary. Kim et al. (2016) propose to use vectors of the size $\min(200, 50 * n)$, i.e., 50-dimensional vectors for the 1-gram vector, 100-dimensional vectors for the 2-gram vector, and 200-dimensional vectors for 4-grams and higher.

12.4.3 Integrating Character-Based Models

When used in neural machine translation models, character-based word representations, just like traditional word embeddings before, are trained together with all the other parameters of the model.

Let us first take a closer look at the use of character-based word models on the input side. This model previously started with a sequence of word embeddings. Now we use the character-based model (be it based on recurrent or convolutional neural networks). For each word, we start with the character sequence and process it into just such a word embedding. We may decide to use both traditional word embeddings and character-based word embeddings, concatenate their representations, or add them weighted by a gating unit.

On the output side, we have to reverse this process. Given a decoder state, we previously predicted a probability distribution over all output words using the softmax over a prediction layer. With character-based models, this process is more complex, because we have to carry out a search over possible character sequences to arrive at a word. To make this computationally tractable, it helps restrict the vocabulary to a set of known words. Then, we have only to compute scores for each word in the vocabulary, which can be efficiently parallelized. When combined with traditional predictions over output words, we may even limit this computation to words that have promising scores.

As a final note, let us contrast the ideas of subwords (as generated by byte pair encoding or other means) and character-based models. Both address the issue of very large vocabularies of natural languages, with the added benefit of being able to discover general properties of different words based on their spelling. Character-based models have more capacity to learn such generalizations but this comes with significant additional computational cost. But these two ideas do not have to stand in contrast, we can first break up words into subwords and then model these subwords with character-based models.

12.5 Further Readings

Special Handling of Rare Words

rare word

A significant limitation of neural machine translation models is the computational burden to support very large vocabularies. To avoid this, the vocabulary may be reduced to a shortlist of, say, 20,000 words, and the remaining tokens are replaced with the unknown word token *UNK*. To translate such an unknown word, Luong et al. (2015d) and Jean et al. (2015) resort to a separate dictionary. Arthur et al. (2016a) argue that neural translation models are worse for rare words and interpolate a traditional probabilistic bilingual dictionary with the prediction of the neural machine translation model. They use the attention mechanism to link each target word to a distribution of source words and weigh the word translations accordingly.

Source words such as names and numbers may also be directly copied into the target. Gulcehre et al. (2016) use a so-called switching network to predict either a traditional translation operation or a copying operation aided by a softmax layer over the source sentence. They preprocess the training data to change some target words into word positions of copied source words. Similarly, Gu et al. (2016) augment the word prediction step of the neural translation model to either translate a word or copy a source word. They observe that the attention mechanism is mostly driven by semantics and the language model in the case of word translation, but by location in case of copying.

Subwords

subword

Sennrich et al. (2016d) split up all words to subword units, using character *n*-gram models and a segmentation based on the byte pair encoding compression algorithm. Schuster and Nakajima (2012) developed a similar method originally for speech recognition, called word piece or sentence piece, that also starts with breaking up all words into character strings and joining them together to obtain a lower perplexity unigram language model trained on the data. Kudo and Richardson (2018) present a tool kit for the sentence piece method and describe it in more detail. Kudo (2018) proposes subword regularization that samples different subword segmentation during training to allow for richer data to learn smaller subword units. Morishita et al. (2018) use different granularities of subword segmentation (using 16,000, 1,000, and 300 operations) in the model and during decoding for the input words and the output word conditioning by summing up the different representations (a single subword from the large vocabulary may decompose into multiple subwords from the smaller vocabularies).

Ataman et al. (2017) propose a linguistically motivated vocabulary reduction method that models word formation as a sequence of stem and morphemes with a hidden Markov model, which can be optimized for a fixed target vocabulary size. Ataman and Federico (2018b) show that this method outperforms byte pair encoding for several morphologically rich language pairs. Banerjee and Bhattacharyya (2018) also note that morphologically inspired segmentation, as provided by a tool called Morfessor (Virpioja et al., 2013), sometimes gives better results than byte pair encoding, and that both methods combined may outperform either alone.

Nikolov et al. (2018) and Zhang and Komachi (2018) extend the idea of splitting up words to logographic languages such as Chinese by allowing the breaking up characters based on their Romanized version or decomposition into strokes.

character-based model ### *Character-Based Models*

Generating word representations from their character sequence has been originally proposed for machine translation by Costa-jussà et al. (2016). They use a convolutional neural network to encode input words, but Costa-jussà and Fonollosa (2016) also show success with character-based language models in reranking machine translation. Chung et al. (2016) propose using a recurrent neural network to encode target words and propose a biscale decoder, where a fast layer outputs a character at a time and a slow layer outputs a word at a time. Ataman et al. (2018); Ataman and Federico (2018a) show good results with a recurrent neural network over character trigrams for input words but not output words.

word embedding ### *Word Embeddings*

Word embeddings have become a common feature in current research in natural language processing. Mikolov et al. (2013c) propose the skip-gram method to obtain these representations. Mikolov et al. (2013a) introduce efficient training methods for the skip-gram and continuous bag of words models, which are used in the very popular word2vec implementation and publicly available word embedding sets for many languages.

Pennington et al. (2014) train word embedding models on the co-occurrence statistics of a word over the entire corpus.

Contextualized Word Embeddings

Peters et al. (2018) demonstrate that various natural language tasks can be improved by contextualizing word embeddings through bidirectional neural language model layers (called ELMo), just as it is done in encoders in machine translations. Devlin et al. (2019) show superior results with a method called BERT which pretrains word embeddings on a masked language model and next sentence prediction task using the transformer architecture. Yang et al. (2019) refine the BERT model by predicting one masked word at a time, with permutation of the order of the masked words. They call their variant XLNet.

Using Pretraining Word Embeddings

Xing et al. (2015) point out inconsistencies in the representation of word embeddings and the objective function for translation transforms between word embeddings, which they address with normalization. Hirasawa et al. (2019) de-bias word embeddings and show gains with pretrained word embeddings in a low resource setting.

Phrase Embeddings

phrase embeddings

Zhang et al. (2014) learn phrase embeddings using recursive neural networks and auto-encoders and a mapping between the input and output phrase to add an additional score to the phrase translations and to filter the phrase table. Hu et al. (2015a) use convolutional neural networks to encode the input and output phrase and pass them to matching that computes their similarity. They include the full input sentence context in the and use a learning strategy called curriculum learning, which first learns from the easy training examples and then the harder ones.

Multilingual Word Embeddings

Ruder et al. (2017) gives a comprehensive overview of work on cross-lingual word embeddings. The observation that word representations obtained from their distributional properties (i.e., how they are used in text) are similar across languages has been made long known, but Mikolov et al. (2013b) was among the first to observe this for the word embeddings generated by neural models and suggest that a simple linear transformation from word embeddings in one language to word embeddings in another language may be used to translate words.

multilingual word embeddings

Aligning Embedding Spaces

Mikolov et al. (2013b) learn the linear mapping between preexisting embedding spaces by minimizing the distance between a projected source word vector and a target word vector for a given seed lexicon. Xing et al. (2015) improve this method by requiring the mapping matrix to be orthogonal. Artetxe et al. (2016) refine this method further with mean centering. Faruqui and Dyer (2014) map monolingually generated word embeddings into a shared bilingual embedding state using canonical correlation analysis by maximizing the correlation of the two vectors for each word translation pair. Braune et al. (2018) point out that the accuracy of obtained bilingual lexicons is much lower for rare words, a problem that can be somewhat addressed with additional features such as representations built on letter *n*-grams and taking orthographic distance into account when mapping words. Heyman et al. (2019) learn a linear transform between embedding spaces based on an automatically generated seed lexicon and show improvements by incrementally adding languages and matching the spaces of newly added languages to all previous languages (multihub). Alqaisi and O'Keefe (2019) consider the problem of morphological-rich languages, for example Arabic, and demonstrate the importance of morphological analysis and word splitting.

Seed Lexicon

Supervised and semisupervised approaches to map embedding spaces require a seed lexicon of word translation pairs. These are most commonly generated with traditional statistical methods from parallel corpora (Faruqui and Dyer, 2014). Yehezkel Lubin et al. (2019) address the problem of noisy word pairs in such automatically generated lexicons, showing that they cause significant harm and develop a method that learns the noise level and finds noisy pairs. Søgaard et al. (2018) use identically spelled words in both languages as seeds. Shi et al. (2019) use off-the-shelf bilingual dictionaries and detail how such human-targeted dictionary definitions needs to be preprocessed. Artetxe et al. (2017) reduce the need for large seed dictionaries by starting with just 25 entries and iteratively increasing the dictionary based on the obtained mappings. Making do with weaker supervision, Gouws et al. (2015) learn directly from sentence pairs by predicting words in a target sentence from words in a source sentence. Coulmance et al. (2015) explore a variant of this idea. Vulić and Moens (2015) use pairs of Wikipedia document pairs, aiming to predict words in mixed-language documents. Zhou et al. (2019) use identically spelled words as seeds. Vulić and Korhonen (2016) compare different types and sizes of seed lexicons.

Unsupervised Methods

Miceli Barone (2016) suggests the idea of using auto-encoders and adversarial training to learn a mapping between monolingual alignment spaces without any parallel data or any other bilingual signal but does not report any results. Zhang et al. (2017b) demonstrate the effectiveness this idea, exploring both unidirectional and bidirectional mappings. Conneau et al. (2018) add a fine-tuning step based on a synthetic dictionary of high-confidence word pairs, achieving vastly better results. Mohiuddin and Joty (2019) extend this approach into a symmetric setup that learns mappings into both directions, with a discriminator for each language (called a CycleGAN), and reconstruction loss as a training objective component. Xu et al. (2018) propose a similar method, using Sinkhorn distance. Chen and Cardie (2018) extend the adversarial training approach to more than two languages.

Instead of using adversarial training, Zhang et al. (2017c) measure the difference between the two embedding spaces with earth mover's distance, defined as the sum of distances of how far each word vector has to be moved toward the nearest vector in the other language's embedding space. Hoshen and Wolf (2018) follow the same intuition but first reduce the complexity of the word vectors with principle component analysis (PCA) and align the spaces alongside the resulting axis first. Their iterative algorithm moves the projections of word vectors to the closest target-side vector in the projected space. Alvarez-Melis and Jaakkola (2018) draw parallels between this approach and optimal transport. In their method, they minimize the distance between a projected vector and all target-side vectors, measured by the L2 norm. Alaux et al. (2019) extend this to more than two languages, by mapping all languages into a common space and matching the word embedding distributions of any two languages at a time. Mukherjee et al. (2018) use squared-loss mutual information (SMI) as an optimization measure to match the monolingual distributions. Zhou et al. (2019) first learn a density distribution over the each of the monolingual word embedding spaces using Gaussian mixture models and then map those spaces so that word vectors in one language are mapped to vectors in the language space with similar density, measured with KL divergence.

Instead of learning a mapping between embedding spaces, Marie and Fujita (2019) learn a joint embedding space for multiple languages using a skip-gram model trained on mixed-language text. Their method is bootstrapped with unsupervised statistical machine translation. Wada et al. (2019) train a multilingual bidirectional language model with language-specific embeddings but shared state progression parameters. The resulting word embeddings are in a common space, with words close to their translations.

Properties of the Mapping

Methods that operate on fixed monolingual embedding spaces often learn a linear mapping between them, hence assuming that they are orthogonal. Nakashole and Flauger (2018) show that this assumption is less accurate when distant languages are involved. Søgaard et al. (2018) find the same when the languages are linguistically different, using a metric based on eigenvectors. They also note that the method works less well when the monolingual data are not drawn from the same domain or when different methods for monolingual word embedding training are used. Nakashole (2018) proposes to use linear mappings that are local to neighborhoods of words. Xing et al. (2015) argue that the mapping matrix should be orthogonal and show improvements when constraining it thus. Patra et al. (2019) relax orthogonality to a soft constraint in the training objective.

hubness ### Hubness Problem

An identified problem in finding the most similar word in another languages is the hubness problem. Some words are close to many other words and hence get more frequently identified as translations. Conneau et al. (2018) consider the average distance to neighboring words in the other language and scale the distance calculation accordingly. Joulin et al. (2018) use this adjustment during training. Smith et al. (2017) propose to normalize the distance matrix between input and output words. Given the distances of source word to every target word, the distances are normalized to add up to 1 using the softmax, and vice versa. Huang et al. (2019) formalize the underlying intuition behind this idea as an optimization problem to enforce both normalizations jointly and propose a gradient descent method to solve it.

sentence embeddings ### Multilingual Sentence Embeddings

Schwenk and Douze (2017) propose to obtain sentence embeddings from an LSTM-based neural machine translation models by adopting the final encoder state or max-pooling over all encoder states. Schwenk (2018) obtains better results by training a joint encoder for multiple languages and apply it to filter noisy parallel corpora. Similarly, España-Bonet et al. (2017) compute the sum of the encoder states to obtain sentence embeddings. Artetxe and Schwenk (2019) presented a encoder–decoder model built specifically to generate sentence embeddings, trained on parallel sentence pairs but with a single sentence embedding vector as the interface between encoder and decoder. Artetxe and Schwenk (2018) implemented this approach as a freely available tool kit called LASER. Schwenk et al. (2019) use it to extract large parallel corpora from Wikipedia. Ruiter et al. (2019) compute sentence embeddings as sum of word embeddings or encoder states of a neural machine translation model. They use these sentence embeddings to find parallel sentence pairs in a comparable corpus and iterate this process to improve the translation model and then find more and better sentence pairs.

document embeddings ### Multilingual Document Embeddings

With the aim to address the task of aligning bilingual documents, Guo et al. (2019) present a model to obtain document embeddings, built from word and sentence embeddings.

Chapter 13
Adaptation

adaptation

General wisdom in machine translation says that you need to build a system *adapted to a task* to get the best performance. Some of the training data may be more relevant for the task than others, and we need to have methods to emphasize the more relevant data. In machine translation, this adaptation is often called **domain adaptation**, with the stated goal of building a system for, say, the *information technology* domain. But we may also adapt a system for a particular deployment scenario or translation project, personalize it for a specific professional posteditor, or for just one particular document and even just on particular sentence.

domain adaptation

13.1 Domains

Before we go into domain adaptation, it is worth taking a closer look at what we mean by **domain**. Broadly, we can define it as a collection of text with similar topic, style, level of formality, etc. In practical terms, however, it typically means a corpus that comes from a specific source.

domain

Let us say, you want to build an Italian–English machine translation system. You first go to your favorite provider of publicly available parallel corpora, OPUS.[1] Figure 13.1 shows what you will get (at the time you are reading this, there may be even more data sources). There are a lot of data in the form of subtitles for movies and television shows as well as different institutions of the European Union, but also from Wikipedia and open source software documentation and localization.

---

[1] http://opus.nlpl.eu.

Figure 13.1 Available
parallel corpora on OPUS
website (Italian–English).

corpus	doc's	sent's	it tokens	en tokens	XCES/XML	raw	TMX	Moses
OpenSubtitles2018	48,746	37.8M	304.8M	284.5M	[xces en it]	[en it]	[tmx]	[moses]
EUbookshop	9,028	6.6M	268.7M	258.8M	[xces en it]	[en it]	[tmx]	[moses]
OpenSubtitles2016	35,299	28.7M	230.3M	214.9M	[xces en it]	[en it]	[tmx]	[moses]
DGT	26,880	3.2M	72.9M	64.0M	[xces en it]	[en it]	[tmx]	[moses]
Europarl	9,461	2.0M	59.9M	58.9M	[xces en it]	[en it]	[tmx]	[moses]
JRC-Acquis	12,042	0.8M	34.1M	34.5M	[xces en it]	[en it]	[tmx]	[moses]
Wikipedia	3	1.0M	26.5M	22.2M	[xces en it]	[en it]	[tmx]	[moses]
EMEA	1,920	1.1M	12.0M	13.9M	[xces en it]	[en it]	[tmx]	[moses]
ECB	1	0.2M	5.5M	5.8M	[xces en it]	[en it]	[tmx]	[moses]
GNOME	1,905	0.7M	3.8M	3.4M	[xces en it]	[en it]	[tmx]	[moses]
TED2013	1	0.2M	3.2M	2.7M	[xces en it]	[en it]	[tmx]	[moses]
Tanzil	15	0.1M	2.8M	2.4M	[xces en it]	[en it]	[tmx]	[moses]
Tatoeba	1	0.1M	3.6M	1.3M	[xces en it]	[en it]	[tmx]	[moses]
KDE4	1,957	0.3M	2.2M	2.3M	[xces en it]	[en it]	[tmx]	[moses]
GlobalVoices	3,220	81.3k	2.1M	2.0M	[xces en it]	[en it]	[tmx]	[moses]
News-Commentary11	1,423	45.9k	1.3M	1.0M	[xces en it]	[en it]	[tmx]	[moses]
Books	8	33.1k	0.9M	0.8M	[xces en it]	[en it]	[tmx]	[moses]
Ubuntu	452	0.1M	0.8M	0.6M	[xces en it]	[en it]	[tmx]	[moses]
News-Commentary	1	18.6k	0.5M	0.5M	[xces en it]	[en it]	[tmx]	[moses]
PHP	3,270	36.8k	0.5M	0.2M	[xces en it]	[en it]	[tmx]	[moses]
EUconst	47	10.2k	0.2M	0.2M	[xces en it]	[en it]	[tmx]	[moses]
OpenSubtitles	22	19.1k	0.2M	0.1M	[xces en it]	[en it]	[tmx]	[moses]
total	156,332	83.1M	1.0G	975.1M	83.1M		63.4M	77.4M

Clearly, some of these data will be more useful for you. How do you
decide what training data to include? How can you still get some use of
the less relevant data?

13.1.1 Differences in Corpora

Text differs in various aspects. Figure 13.2 provides short snippets from
publicly available parallel corpora, ranging from very official sources
such as Acquis Communitaire (the laws of the European Union) to
messages on Twitter.

Some of the commonly used dimensions to distinguish corpora are
the following:

Topic: The subject matter of the text, such as politics or sports.

Modality: How was this text originally created? Is this written text or transcribed
speech, and if speech, is it a formal presentation or an informal dialogue
full of incomplete and ungrammatical sentences?

Register: Level of politeness. In some languages, this is very explicit, such as
the use of the informal *Du* or the formal *Sie* for the personal pronoun *you*
in German.

Intent: Is the text a statement of fact, an attempt to persuade, or a communication
among multiple parties?

Style: Is it a terse informal text, full of emotional and flowery language?

In reality, we often do not have clear information about any of these
dimensions. A parallel corpus extracted from Wikipedia will span a
whole range of topics, although it will be fairly consistent in modality

EMEA *Abilify is a medicine containing the active substance aripiprazole. It is available as 5 mg, 10 mg, 15 mg and 30 mg tablets, as 10 mg, 15 mg and 30 mg orodispersible tablets (tablets that dissolve in the mouth), as an oral solution (1 mg/ml) and as a solution for injection (7.5 mg/ml).*

Software Localization *Default GNOME Theme*

OK

People

Literature *There was a slight noise behind her and she turned just in time to seize a small boy by the slack of his roundabout and arrest his flight.*

Law *Corrigendum to the Interim Agreement with a view to an Economic Partnership Agreement between the European Community and its Member States, of the one part, and the Central Africa Party, of the other part.*

Religion *This is The Book free of doubt and involution, a guidance for those who preserve themselves from evil and follow the straight path.*

News *The Facebook page of a leading Iranian leading cartoonist, Mana Nayestani, was hacked on Tuesday, 11 September 2012, by pro-regime hackers who call themselves "Soldiers of Islam".*

Movie subtitles *We're taking you to Washington, D.C.*

Do you know where the prisoner was transported to?

Uh, Washington.

Okay.

Twitter *Thank u @Starbucks & @Spotify for celebrating artists who #Give-Good with a donation to @BTWFoundation, and to great organizations by @Metallica and @ChanceTheRapper! Limited edition cards available now at Starbucks!*

Figure 13.2 Corpora differ. Snippets from various publicly available parallel corpora.

and style. Often, you have access to a corpus obtained from a broad crawl of the web where all bets are off about what it contains.

In practical terms this means, that you may want to enforce, say, a level of politeness in your machine translation system, but you will have a hard time obtaining data that are annotated with politeness levels. You will have to guess that official announcements from the European Union are more polite than movie subtitles.

An obvious consequence of differences in domains is that words have different meanings and hence different translations in different domains. The classic examples are *bat* which means something else in a baseball report than in a story about wildlife. But the difference in style etc. may be more relevant but harder to measure. It is a more severe mistake to address the CEO of your company with *What's up, dude?* instead of *Good morning, sir!*, even if it is not morning anymore.

Figure 13.3 Machine
translation systems for
different domains. Each is
trained on domain-specific
data, and input sentences are
routed to the matching
system.

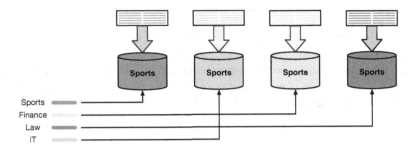

Given the amorphous nature of domains, adaptation is a hard-to-pin-
down problem. Data may differ narrowly (e.g., official publications from
the United Nations versus official announcements from the European
Union) or dramatically (e.g., chat room dialogs versus published laws).
The amounts of relevant and less relevant data differ. The data may be
cleanly separated by domain or just come in a massive disorganized
pile. Some of the data may be of higher translation quality than others,
which may be polluted by noise such as mistranslations, misalignments,
or even generated by a machine translation system.

13.1.2 Multiple Domain Scenario

multiple domains

Sometimes, we have multiple collections of data that are clearly identified by domain—typically categories such as sports, information technology, finance, and law. We can build specialized translation models
for each of these domains. For a given test sentence, we then select the
appropriate model. If we do not know the domain of the test sentence,
we first have to build a classifier that allows us to automatically make
this determination. Given the decision of the classifier, we then select
the most appropriate model. Figure 13.3 shows this process.

But we do not have to commit to a single domain. The classifier
may instead provide a distribution of relevance of the specific domain
models (say, 50% domain A, 30% domain B, 20% domain C), which
are then used as weights in an ensemble of domain-specific models. The
domain classification may done based on a whole document instead of
each individual sentence, which brings in more context to make a more
robust decision (more on this approach in Section 13.2).

13.1.3 In-Domain versus Out-of-Domain

Another view at the problem of optimizing machine translation for a spe-

in-domain

cific domain is to separate data into **in-domain** data and **out-of-domain**

out-of-domain

data. Typically there is much more out-of-domain data, compared to
in-domain data. We may be able to find a lot of parallel text for a specific
language pair, but only very little that match the task of translating, say,

Microsoft user manuals. Framed this way, the challenge is to properly balance both data sources, given more preference to in-domain data.

Why use out-of-domain data at all? Clearly, in-domain data are much more valuable, since they inform the correct translation choices, style, etc. However, since the amount of data is usually small, there are gaps. Some of the input words that we will have to translate during deployment of the system may not occur in the in-domain training data. Some of the input words may occur in the training data, but not with the correct translation. The out-of-domain data can fill these gaps. But we have to be careful that the out-of-domain data does not drown out the in-domain data.

13.1.4 Adaptation Effects

adaptation effects

Automatic scoring metrics such as BLEU are quite sensitive to adaptation effects. These metrics are very literal, so making the wrong word choices, even if they are synonyms, is counted as an error. So, adapting to the in-domain style and using the words common in that domain yield higher scores. This goes beyond single words. The type of language that is used, reflected in level of formality, register, terseness, etc., either matches the reference translation or not.

However, the BLEU score is a fairly blunt tool. To get a more detailed understanding of domain adaptation effects, Irvine et al. (2013) proposed the S^4 **metric**, which distinguishes between four different types of translation errors.

Seen: Is the input word translated incorrectly because it has not been seen in the parallel training data?

Sense: Does the word occur in the training data, but never in the sense of the input sentence and hence never with the translation that is needed to produce the correct translation?

Score: Has the input word been seen in the parallel training data with the correct translation, but the translation model scores another translation higher?

Search: Does the model prefer the correct translation for the input word, but beam search decoding fails to find it, generating a lower scoring faulty translation instead?

This metric is a useful tool to check if out-of-domain data improve coverage (fewer *seen* and *sense* errors), but leads to biasing the model too much toward the wrong translation choices (more *score* errors). However, due to the focus of the metric on single word translation, maybe even just content words like nouns, it does not capture well the style of the translations.

> **German source** *Verfahren und Anlage zur Durchführung einer exothermen Gasphasenreaktion an einem heterogenen partikelförmigen Katalysator*
> **Human reference translation** *Method and system for carrying out an exothermic gas phase reaction on a heterogeneous particulate catalyst*
> **General model translation** *Procedures and equipment for the implementation of an exothermen gas response response to a heterogeneous particle catalytic converter*
> **In-Domain model translation** *Method and system for carrying out an exothermic gas phase reaction on a heterogeneous particulate catalyst*

Figure 13.4 Differences between general and in-domain models (chemistry patents). Some of the improvements are stylistic (e.g., the use of the terms *method* and *system* instead of *procedures* and *equipment*), some resolve real word sense problems (e.g., *catalyst* instead of *catalytic converter*), and some are due to better coverage of the target language (e.g., the correct translation *exothermic gas phase reaction* instead of the mistranslation into *exothermen gas response response*).

Figure 13.4 shows an example of the difference between a general domain and in-domain model, in this case patents for chemistry. Words like the German *Verfahren* have several adequate translations, such as *procedures* and *method*, but only the latter is the correct terminology used in the patent domain. The ambiguous *Katalysator*, which is generally more often used for a part in a car (English *catalytic converter*), likely translates in the chemistry domain to *catalyst*. The general model also struggles with the very specific technical phrase *exothermen Gasphasenreaktion* (*exothermic gas phase reaction*).

13.1.5 Fair Warning

The problem of domain adaptation is somewhat amorphic, since the scenarios for adaptation differ in many dimensions. How much in-domain data are there in relation to out-of-domain data? Are there any in-domain data at all? Do we care about a singled targeted domain or multiple domains? How clear is the definition of domains? How different are in-domain and out-of-domain data? How heterogeneous is each type? Do we want to adapt on-demand and hence need fast methods? And so on.

There is a plethora of methods, and it is not often clear what is the most appropriate one for a given data condition. Moreover, these methods can be combined in any number of ways. In practice this means that a healthy dose of experimentation is required to obtain optimal results.

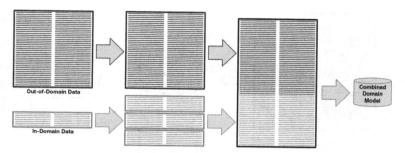

Figure 13.5 Data interpolation. To balance between in-domain and out-of-domain data, the in-domain data are duplicated by a chosen factor (here 3) in the training data set.

13.2 Mixture Models

mixture models

Let us take a look at the first family of methods that are based on the idea that we separate out the training data by domain, and optimize weights given to domain-specific models or data.

13.2.1 Data Interpolation

data interpolation

The default mode of training a machine translation system is to throw all the training together, no matter if relevant or not. Given that we typically have fewer in-domain data than out-of-domain data, the in-domain data are underrepresented. A straightforward fix is to duplicate the in-domain data multiple times when assembling the training data (also called **over-sampling**). This way, the training algorithm will encounter a specific in-domain sentence pair more often than any specific out-of-domain sentence pair (Figure 13.5).

oversampling

Since this is such a straightforward idea, it is often the first method that developers apply. Unfortunately, it is hard to optimize the factor with which the in-domain data are multiplied. A rough rule of thumb is that the in-domain data should make up half of the training data, but it is better to try out different factors and see what works best. However, since each factor value requires a full training run, this is computationally expensive.

13.2.2 Model Interpolation

model interpolation

If we divide up training data into in-domain and out-of-domain, we may also train two completely separate models for them. Instead of mixing the data, we then mix the models to make predictions. Their predictions are then combined, with appropriate weight given to the in-domain versus the out-of-domain model (Figure 13.6).

In Section 9.2 discussed the idea of assembling multiple neural models. There we talked about independently trained models on the

Figure 13.6 Model interpolation. Separate models are trained on in-domain and out-of-domain data. These are combined in order to give the in-domain model more weight, typically in the form of ensemble decoding, where the word predictions of the models are combined with a weighted sum.

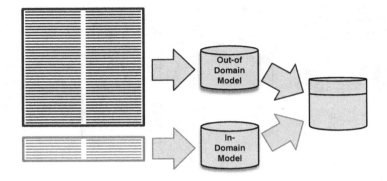

same data, now we are talking about models trained on different data sets. Apart from that, everything works the same way. During decoding, each model provides a probability distribution for the next word. We can then average these probability distributions and pick the best next word predictions from the averaged distribution. Beyond simple averaging, we may weight the models by a set of predefined weights. Instead of having to manually choose weight values for the models, we can find these weights automatically (recall Section 9.3.4).

So far, we discussed mixture models in the context of the in-domain versus out-of-domain scenario. But these methods also fit the multidomain scenario. If we trained separate models for, say, information technology, sports, and law, then the best translation system for any incoming sentence may be a combination of them. If test sentences are labeled by domain, we can determine optimal weights for each domain, as indicated above. If the test sentences have unknown domains, then we first need to build a domain classifier, and we may then use the prediction confidence for each domain as weights.

13.2.3 Domain-Aware Training

domain aware training

We just discussed the idea of an external domain classifier and multiple separately trained neural machine translation models. But why not combine all this into a single neural architecture?

domain token ***Domain Token***

A simple but effective way of adding domain information to the neural machine translation model is to add a domain token as the first word of the input sentence, without changing any of the model architecture (Sennrich et al., 2016a; Kobus et al., 2017). The domain token is an artificial word, such as <SPORTS>. This way, predicting words in the output is conditioned on the domain token via the attention mechanism.

The domain token also helps the encoder enrich the representation of the input words. The neural model automatically learns that the token is not a word that needs to be translated but a context feature that informs translation decisions.

The domain token may also be placed as the first word of the output sentence. If the domain is known, we insert the token before the decoding algorithm takes over to make decisions. If the domain is not known, we do not place the token, but let the decoder pick one based on the input sentence. If some of the training data are not tagged by domain, then we also allow output sentences to start without a domain token.

Domain Vector

domain vector

How about the case where the domain of input sentences is unknown? Then we do need to employ a domain classifier (which may be part of the neural architecture). It may predict the domain token, but it also may predict a domain classification vector where each element corresponds to a domain, and each value the relevance to that domain. This vector is added as a input component to the decoder (and maybe also the encoder) of the neural machine translation model. One way to do this is to add it as a conditioning context to the hidden state.

Since we have this classifier, we may also label the training data with it. This clearly helps if some of the training data do not have domain information. But even if we have clearly defined domains, there may be sentence pairs that cross over the domain boundaries. Think about a *sports* article that discusses a legal processes concerning a team's (or player's) rule violation. It has enough elements of *law* to benefit from the *law* domain model. If we add the predictions of the domain classifier to each training sentence pair, then these also have the same soft domain classification vectors that we will encounter during deployment.

Bias Term for Word Prediction

If we have a lot of different domains, such as the extreme case of personalization of the machine translation engine to thousands of translators (in a computer aided translation scenario) or authors (in a corpus where the authors are identified), these ideas may not scale well. There are very little training data for each person. In this case, we may want to focus on the output word prediction, where individual word choices are made.

One idea is to add a person-specific bias term to the output softmax. Recall that we compute the output word distribution t_i as a softmax over a feed-forward layer on the combination of previous hidden state (s_{i-1}), previous output word embedding (Ey_{i-1}), and input context (c_i):

$$t_i = \text{softmax}\big(W(Us_{i-1} + VEy_{i-1} + Cc_i) + b\big). \qquad (13.1)$$

The exact model architecture may differ, but what almost all neural machine translation systems share is the softmax over the feed-forward layer, parameterized by a weight matrix W and a bias term b, given some conditioning vector z_i:

$$t_i = \text{softmax}\left(Wz_i + b\right). \tag{13.2}$$

We now add an additional bias term β_p whose value is specific to a person p:

$$t_i = \text{softmax}\left(Wz_i + b + \beta_p\right). \tag{13.3}$$

Technically, the bias term is similar to word embeddings, in the way its parameters are a large matrix, from which we select one column associated with the current person (Michel and Neubig, 2018).

13.2.4 Topic Models

topic model

We already mentioned the word *topic* when discussing properties of domains, but technically **topic models** are models that automatically cluster a broad corpus into sets. Each of the set is understood as having a specific topic. So, topic models serve as an unsupervised way to introduce domain distinctions for a heterogenous corpus. With such breakdown by domain in hand, we then can use the domain adaptation techniques described earlier (Figure 13.7).

There are several techniques for obtaining such clustering of the data. One traditional one is latent Dirichlet allocation (LDA) (Blei et al., 2003) and some recent work uses sentence embeddings (Tars and Fishel, 2018). Note that we have to carry out this clustering on the input sentence alone, since this matches what is available when we have to translate a sentence during deployment.

Figure 13.7 Topic models automatically cluster sentence pairs based on the input sentence. Different topic machine translation models can be trained on each cluster.

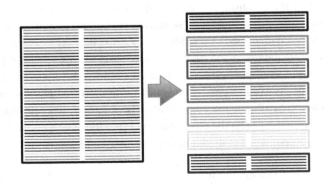

Latent Dirichlet Allocation

Formalized as a graphical model, LDA assumes that sentences belong to a fixed set of topics. The model first predicts a distribution over topics and then predicts words based on each topic. Training this generative process associates words with specific topics that typically correspond to notions of subject matter. For instance, the top words for one topic may be *European, political, policy, interests*, and for another *crisis, rate, financial, monetary* (Hasler et al., 2014).

Sentence Embeddings

Given the success of word embeddings, why stop there? Why not also embed sentences, paragraphs, or whole documents? Recall that word embeddings are typically trained by predicting them from their sur-rounding n words. We could train sentence embeddings similarly, but a much simpler method is to average the embeddings of the words in the sentence. While this is clearly problematic (*Joe kills the bear* and *the bear kills Joe* mean very different things), it may be sufficient for purposes such as classifying sentences by domain (both examples are sentences about killing and wildlife). Slightly more refined techniques also use embeddings for word n-grams or weight the individual embeddings when averaging.

Having the sentence embeddings is only the first step. We want to cluster the corpus into sets. Sentence embeddings represent the corpus as a highly dimensional space where each sentence is a point. Standard techniques as such as **k-means clustering** could be applied. In this step, we first randomly generate a number of points c_i (called **centroids**). Then we assign each data point in the space (here, a sentence embedding) to its closest centroid. We iterate this process by recomputing the value of the centroid as the mean of all its assigned data points, reassign data points, and so on.

k-means clustering

centroid

Once this process converges, we have a division of the space into subspaces defined by the proximity to the centroids. For our sentence embedding scenario, this means that each sentence is assigned to a domain that is defined by similarity to the domain's idealized typical sentence (the centroid in the space).

13.3 Subsampling

A common problem is that the amount of available in-domain data is very small, so just training on these data risks overfitting, i.e., very good performance on the seen data but poor performance on everything else. Large random collections of parallel text often contain data that closely

subsampling

Figure 13.8 Subsampling domain-relevant data from a larger pool of mostly out-of-domain data.

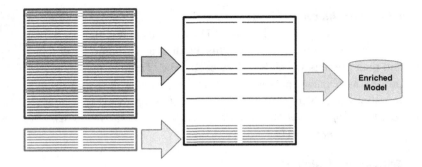

match the in-domain data. So, we may want to extract these in-domain data from the large collections of mainly out-of-domain data, and only then add that to our training corpus (Eetemadi et al., 2015; Figure 13.8).

13.3.1 Moore–Lewis: Language Model Cross-Entropy

Moore-Lewis cross-entropy

The general idea behind a variety of methods is to build two detectors: one in-domain detector trained on in-domain data and one out-of-domain detector trained on out-of-domain data. We then score each sentence pair in the out-of-domain data with both detectors and select sentence pairs that are preferred (or judged relatively relevant) by the in-domain detector.

The classic detectors are language models trained on the source and target side of the in-domain and out-of-domain data (Axelrod et al., 2011), resulting in a total of four language models: the source side in-domain model $\mathrm{LM}_f^{\mathrm{in}}$, the target side in-domain model $\mathrm{LM}_e^{\mathrm{in}}$, the source side out-of-domain model $\mathrm{LM}_f^{\mathrm{out}}$, and the target side out-of-domain model $\mathrm{LM}_e^{\mathrm{out}}$. Any given sentence pair from the out-of-domain data is then scored with these models.

This allows us to compute the entropy H for each sentence s scored by the language model:

$$H(s) = -\mathrm{LM}(s) \log \mathrm{LM}(s). \tag{13.4}$$

For each of the language model scores $\mathrm{LM}_e^{\mathrm{in}}$, $\mathrm{LM}_e^{\mathrm{out}}$, $\mathrm{LM}_f^{\mathrm{in}}$, and $\mathrm{LM}_f^{\mathrm{out}}$, we obtain entropy scores H_e^{in}, H_e^{out}, H_f^{in}, and H_f^{out}, which we combine into a relevance score:

$$\mathrm{relevance}_{e,f} = \left(H_e^{\mathrm{in}}(e) - H_e^{\mathrm{out}}(e) \right) + \left(H_f^{\mathrm{in}}(f) - H_f^{\mathrm{out}}(f) \right). \tag{13.5}$$

We may use traditional n-gram language models or neural recurrent language models. Some work suggests replacing open class words (nouns, verbs, adjectives, adverbs) with part-of-speech tags or word clusters—based on the idea that what matters more is the style of the sentences, not their actual content. We may even use in-domain and out-of-domain neural translation models to score sentence pairs instead of source and target side sentences in isolation.

13.3.2 Coverage-Based Methods

coverage-based methods

A concern with subsampling sentences based on their similarity to existing sentences is that we will not learn much new. But the motivation behind adding additional data was to increase the coverage of the model. So, when adding sentences from the out-of-domain corpus, we may want to keep track of how often words are covered in the existing pool of data. We add a new sentence pair only if it contains input or output words that have not been seen or were seen rarely.

Formally, we score each candidate sentence s_j that we have not yet added to the data by computing a word-based score:

$$\frac{1}{|s_i|} \sum_{w \in s} \text{score}(w, s_{1,\ldots,i-1}). \tag{13.6}$$

A simple scoring function checks if the word w occurred in the previously added sentences $s_1, \ldots, s_{i-1}$:

$$\text{score}(w, s_{1,\ldots,i-1}) = \begin{cases} 0 & \text{if } w \in s_1, \ldots, s_{i-1}. \\ 1 & \text{otherwise} \end{cases} \tag{13.7}$$

The sentence that scores highest (has the highest ratio of previously unseen words), will be added.

This method can be extended in several ways (Eck et al., 2005):

- Instead of just measuring coverage of words in isolation, we may also consider n-grams of words up to a certain length. So, we compute the score not just in terms of words, but over n-grams.

$$\frac{1}{|s_i| \times N} \sum_{n=0}^{N-1} \sum_{w_{j,\ldots,j+n} \in s} \text{score}(w_{j,\ldots,j+n}, s_{1,\ldots,i-1}). \tag{13.8}$$

- Once a word (or n-gram) occurs in one of the selected sentences, its score is 0 afterward, and it may not be added again. To learn good models, having seen a word frequently and in different contexts is essential. So, we may want to assign a score that decays with the frequency of the word in the corpus. An exponentially decaying function is a popular choice (Bicici and Yuret, 2011).

$$\text{score}(w, s_{1,\ldots,i-1}) = \text{frequency}(w, s_{1,\ldots,i-1}) \, e^{-\lambda \, \text{frequency}(w, s_{1,\ldots,i-1})}. \tag{13.9}$$

- The method treats obscure and rare words the same way as frequent words. We may want to see the frequent word represented appropriately. This requires augmenting scoring with a measure of the relationship between word (or *n*-gram) distributions in the full corpus and distributions in the selected sentences. It is not clear, if this is useful for domain subsampling, but it is more appropriate for the general goal of corpus size reduction.

Moreover, a computational concern with the method I just described is that it has quadratic run time. Given modern corpora of tens to hundreds of millions of sentences, this is a severe burden. Lewis and Eetemadi (2013) propose a method with linear run time. It defines a target count N of how often we would like to see each word in the corpus. We make one pass through the corpus. We keep count of how often each word in the sentence (or sentence pair) has been seen previously and add the sentence only if any of the words has not been seen as many times as the target count N.

Note that the order of the sentences matters. We can obtain this order with the Moore–Lewis subsampling method described in the previous section. So, we add sentences in preference of their relevance to the domain, but not if they do not add sufficiently new information.

13.3.3 Instance Weighting

instance weighting

We discussed the previous methods as a means to score the relevance of sentence pairs in the out-of-domain data. But using this score to include some of the data and discard the rest may be too harsh. Maybe there is utility to any sentence pair, but some should influence training more than others.

This is the idea behind instance weighting. We want to give more attention to relevant training data but still obtain some gain from the rest. For this, we first need a relevance score, typically in a range from 0 (least relevant) to 1 (most relevant). We then use this score during training to **scaling learing rate**   **scale the learning rate** (Chen et al., 2017).

Traditionally, computed gradients for weight updates are scaled based on a fixed or decaying learning rate whose value may depend on more complex optimization schemes such as Adagrad or Adam. Now, we further discount the learning rate by the relevance score. For the most relevant data (score equal 1), training is still done to full effect. But the less relevant the sentence pair, the less it will change model parameters.

The relevance score used in instance weighting may be a sentence-level score estimated by the methods we just described. But it may be anything, such as a corpus-level score for different domain corpora (hence, a different way to do data interpolation), or a score that takes the

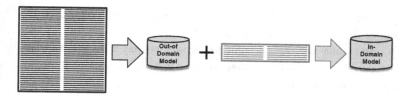

Figure 13.9 Online training of neural machine translation models allows a straightforward domain adaptation method. Having a general domain translation system trained on general-purpose data, a handful of additional training epochs on in-domain data allows for a domain-adapted system.

quality of the sentence pair into account (the likelihood that it is not the product of noisy preparation of the data).

13.4 Fine-Tuning

For neural machine translation, a fairly straightforward adaptation method has recently become popular. Called **fine-tuning** or **continued training**, this method divides training up into two stages. First, we train the model on all available data until convergence. Then, we run a few more iterations of training on the in-domain data only and stop training when performance on an in-domain validation set peaks (Figure 13.9). This way, the final model benefits from all the training data, but is still adapted to the in-domain data.

Practical experience with fine-tuning shows that the second in-domain training stage may converge very quickly. The amount of in-domain data is typically relatively small, and only a handful of training epochs is needed. There are however some tricky choices to be made about hyper parameters such as learning rate and optimization schemes (e.g., Adagrad and Adam, recall Section 10.3.2). These have to be resolved with experimentation.

13.4.1 Constraining Updates

The main concern with fine-tuning is that training on only a small in-domain corpus leads to overfitting and **catastrophic forgetting** of the general domain knowledge (not being able to translate general domain sentences anymore).

While the goal of adaptation is to perform well on in-domain data, we may also consider out-of-domain translation performance since it is a measure of the robustness of the model. So, while measuring and optimizing performance on an in-domain validation set, we may also track performance on an out-of-domain validation set. Some loss of

fine-tuning

continued training

constraining updates

catastrophic forgetting

performance of a few BLEU points is acceptable, total collapse on the out-of-domain test set should be avoided.

To combat such catastrophic forgetting, we may want to limit training during the fine-tuning stage in some way. A number of strategies have been proposed.

limited updates   *Updating Only Some Model Parameters*

We may want to update only some of the model parameters. Since we expect most of the impact of domain adaptation closer to the output side, we may want to focus on the decoder parameters, such as the weights impacting the hidden state progression, the output word prediction softmax, and the output word embeddings.

Limiting updates to a subset of the parameters constrains training to not depart too much the original model. However, selecting which parameters to update and which ones not, requires a fair bit of experimentation.

parameter   *Adding Adaptation Parameters*

Instead of updating the existing weights, we may add special adaptation parameters and update these only during the fine-tuning stage. One
LHUC   idea, called **learning hidden unit contribution (LHUC)**, is a layer
learning hidden unit   that postprocesses the hidden state h by scaling each of its node values
contribution   with a factor. Only these factors ρ are the trainable parameters during fine-tuning (Vilar, 2018).

Since we employ these factors to emphasize some values in the hidden state and turn off others, we may want to limit their values to a more narrow range, say between 0 and 2. This can be done with a variant of the softmax operation:

$$a(\rho) = \frac{2}{1 + e^\rho}.$$ (13.10)

We then use these scaled adaptaion values $a(\rho)$ to scale the values of the hidden state h:

$$h_{\text{LHUC}} = a(\rho) \circ h.$$ (13.11)

The advantage of this approach is that we can learn domain-specific adaptation vectors ρ at any time, swap them in when needed, and not use them to fall back to the unaltered general domain system.This makes it easy to perform incremental adaptation of the system, while not changing the behavior for domains for which no new training data arrive.

Regularized Training Objective

regularization   The stated goal of constraining updates is to not diverge too far from the original model that performed well on out-of-domain input. Hence, why not explicitly change the training objective to do well on the in-domain training data that are presented during the fine-tuning stage and so the predictions of the model are not too different from the originally trained out-of-domain model.

The classic training objective is to reduce the error on word predictions, indicated by the probability $t_i[y_i]$ given to the correct output word y_i at time step i (recall Equation 8.5):

$$\text{cost} = -\log t_i[y_i]. \tag{13.12}$$

To measure how much the current output word distribution t_i differs from the baseline model's output word distribution t_i^{BASE}, we may use the cross-entropy between the two distributions:

$$\text{cost}_{\text{REG}} = -\sum_{y \in V} t_i^{\text{BASE}}[y] \log t_i[y]. \tag{13.13}$$

Adding such additional terms to the cost function is called regularization (see also Section 10.4.1). A hyper parameter α defines the strengths of the regularization term cost_{REG}:

$$(1 - \alpha)\, \text{cost} + \alpha\, \text{cost}_{\text{REG}}. \tag{13.14}$$

The factor α in this formula allows us to bias fine-tuning toward either optimizing the in-domain data (low value for α) or preserving the original model predictions (high value for α). Suggested values are in the range of 0.001–0.1, so that the main objective is to adapt to the in-domain training data (Khayrallah et al., 2018b), but may also be as high as 0.9 to prevent as little deviation from the original model as possible (Dakwale and Monz, 2017).

13.4.2 Document-Level Adaptation

document-level adaptation

One application scenario for adaption is computer aided translation. Here, a professional translator interacts with machine translation either by postediting the draft translations of the machine translation system or by using more sophisticated methods such as interactive translation prediction (which functions more like the auto-complete function of mobile text entry systems, suggesting one word at a time).

While the translator works through a document, we would like to adapt the machine translation system to the choices of the translator. One obvious improvement is to the machine translation system to learn new vocabulary. If the machine translation system initially encounters a new word, it will unlikely have a good translation for it. However, the translator will correct the machine translation output and provide a good

Figure 13.10 Adaptation in a computer aided translation scenario. Machine translation provides a draft translation for sentences in a document, the professional translator corrects it. The resulting sentence pairs are used to adapt the machine translation system.

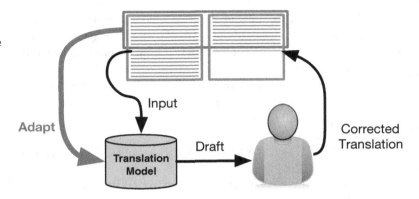

word translation. The next time, this word appears in the document, the machine translation should be able to return the translation provided by the professional translator (Figure 13.10).

The machine translation system should adapt not only to new vocabulary but also to translation choices (i.e., when the translator choses an alternative translation for an input word then the system originally suggests) and the more ephemeral style of the translator.

We can frame this problem as a fine-tuning task. A stream of new sentence pairs arrive (sentence translations confirmed by the professional translator), and we run model training on just these sentences. We may use any of the fine-tuning strategies described ealier (with higher learning rate, since the fine-tuning set is so small). Adding new vocabulary deserves special treatment. Providing the new input word and its translation as a training sentence pair has been shown to be effective, in addition to it being part of the new sentence pair (Kothur et al., 2018a).

13.4.3 Sentence-Level Adaptation

sentence-level adaptation

The most extreme case of fine-tuning is to adapt to a single sentence. In spirit, this is more similar to an established tool for professional translators: translation memories. Such a tool finds the most similar input sentence in an existing parallel corpus and returns it along with its translation. In many translation scenarios, where translators are tasked with translating very similar material (maybe even just updates to documents with existing translations), this is a very effective method.

If the sentence was translated before, why not just use the previous translation? Even if just a word or two has been changed (say, the product name), then fixing the previous translation is quite easy. The method for retrieving similar sentence pairs (based on the input sentence) is called **fuzzy matching** **fuzzy matching**, the retrieved sentence pair a fuzzy match. Typically, some variant of string edit distance is used.

The idea behind sentence-level adaptation is to prime the system for a specific sentence translation by fine-tuning to the fuzzy matches. This may be more than one sentence pair, but even just a single one seems to give good results. Since we are just adapting to a few sentence pairs, a fairly high learning rate has to be set and training is done just for one epoch (Farajian et al., 2017b).

13.4.4 Curriculum Training

curriculum learning

Recall the idea of curriculum learning that we described in Section 10.4.2. Learning may be easier when starting with the easy examples first and then moving to more realistic ones. We may apply this idea to the adaptation problem.

Let us assume that we have a large corpus of training data but a limited application domain. We can use the subsampling methods described in Section 13.3 to score each sentence pair in the training corpus by its domain relevance. This allows us to define subsets of the training data of different size, depending on the threshold we use for the domain relevance score.

We start training on the entire training corpus. Then we fine-tune the resulting model on smaller and smaller (and hence more and more relevant) subsets of the training corpus. We do not run any of the training stages until convergence but rather to a predefined curriculum, such as five epochs on all data, two epochs on subset A, two epochs on subset B, and so on (Van der Wees et al., 2017).

13.5 Further Readings

Domain adaptation has been widely studied in traditional statistical machine translation. These techniques have been adapted and new techniques have been applied to neural machine translation models to adapt them to domain or other stylistic aspects. There is often a domain mismatch between the bulk (or even all) of the training data for a translation and the test data during deployment. In addition to work on adaptation in neural machine translation, there is rich literature in traditional statistical machine translation on this topic that is still relevant.

Fine-Tuning

fine-tuning

A common approach for neural models is to first train on all available training data, and then run a few iterations on in-domain data only (Luong and Manning, 2015), as already pioneered in neural language model adaption (Ter-Sarkisov et al., 2015). Servan et al. (2016) demonstrate the effectiveness of this adaptation method with small in-domain sets consisting of as little as 500 sentence pairs. (Etchegoyhen et al., 2018) evaluate the quality of such domain-adapted systems using subjective assessment and posteditor productivity measures.

Chu et al. (2017) argue that given a small amount of in-domain data leads to overfitting and suggest mixing in-domain and out-of-domain data during adaption. Freitag and Al-Onaizan (2016) identify the same problem and suggest using an ensemble of baseline models and adapted models to avoid overfitting. Peris et al. (2017a) consider alternative training methods for the adaptation phase but do not find consistently better results than the traditional gradient descent training.

Vilar (2018) leaves the general model parameters fixed during fine-tuning and updates an adaption layer only in the recurrent states. Michel and Neubig (2018) update an additional bias term only in the output softmax. Thompson et al. (2018) explore which parameters (input embedding, recurrent state propagation, etc.) may be left unchanged while still obtaining good adaptation results.

Dakwale and Monz (2017) and Khayrallah et al. (2018a) regularize the training objective to include a term that penalizes departure from the word predictions of the unadapted baseline model. Miceli Barone et al. (2017a) use the L2 norm between baseline parameter values and adapted parameter values as regularizer in the objective function, in addition to drop-out techniques. Thompson et al. (2019) show superior results with a technique called elastic weight consolidation, which also tends to preserve model parameters that were important for general model translation quality.

curriculum learning ### Curriculum Training
Van der Wees et al. (2017) adopt curriculum training for the adaptation problem. They start with corpus consisting of all data and then train on smaller and smaller subsets that are increasingly in-domain, as determined by language model. Kocmi and Bojar (2017) employ curriculum training by first training on simpler sentence pairs, measured by the length of the sentences, the number of coordinating conjunctions, and the frequency of words. Platanios et al. (2019) show that a refined scheme that selects data of increasing difficulty based on the training progress converges faster and gives better performance for Transformer models. Zhang et al. (2019c) explored various other curriculum schedules based on difficulty, including training on the hard examples first. Kumar et al. (2019) learn a curriculum for data of different degrees of noisiness with reinforcement learning using gains on the validation set as rewards. Wang et al. (2018a) argue that sentence pairs that are already correctly predicted do not contribute to further improvement of the model and

increasingly remove sentence pairs that do not show improvement in their training objective cost between iterations.

Sentence-Level Adaptation to Fuzzy Match

Before translating a sentence, Farajian et al. (2017b) and Li et al. (2018) propose fetching a few similar sentences and their translations from a parallel corpus and adapt the neural translation model to this subsampled training set. Similarly, using only monolingual source side data, Chinea-Rios et al. (2017) subsample sentences similar to the sentences in a document to be translated and perform a self-training step. Self-training first translates the source text and then adapts the model to this synthetic parallel corpus. sentence-level adaptation

Gu et al. (2018c) modify the model architecture to include the retrieved sentence pairs. These sentence pairs are stored in a neural key-value memory, and words from these sentence pairs may be either copied over directly or fused with predictions of the baseline neural machine translation model. Zhang et al. (2018a) extract phrase pairs from the retrieved sentence pairs and add a bonus to hypotheses during search, if these contain them. Bapna and Firat (2019) retrieve similar sentence pairs from a domain-specific corpus at inference time and provide these as additional conditioning context. Similarly, Bulte and Tezcan (2019) add the target side of similar sentence pairs to the source sentence.

Sentence-Level Instant Updating

Kothur et al. (2018b) show that machine translation systems can be adapted instantly to the postedits of a translator working through a single document. They show gains with both fine-tuning to edited sentence pairs and adding new word translations via fine-tuning. Wuebker et al. (2018) build personalized translation models in a similar scenario. They modify the output layer predictions and use group lasso regularization to limit the divergence between the general model and the personalized models. Simianer et al. (2019) compare different sentence-level adaptation training methods in terms of how well they perform at translating words that occur once in an adaptation sentence pair as well as new words not yet encountered during the adaptation. They show that lasso-adaptation (Wuebker et al., 2018) improves on once-seen words while not degrading on previously unencountered words.

Subsampling and Instance Weighting

Inspired by domain adaptation work in statistical machine translation on subsampling, Wang et al. (2017a) augment the canonical neural translation model with a sentence embedding state that allows distinction subsampling
instance weighting between in-domain and out-of-domain sentences. It is computed as the sum of all input word representations and then used as the initial state of the decoder. This sentence embedding allows them to distinguish between in-domain and out-of-domain sentences, using the centroids of all in-domain and out-of-domain sentence embeddings, respectively. Out-of-domain sentences that are closer to the in-domain centroid are included in the training data. Chen et al. (2017) combine the idea of subsampling with sentence weighting. They build an in-domain versus out-of-domain classifier for sentence pairs in the training data and then use its prediction score to reduce the learning rate for sentence pairs that are out of domain. Wang et al. (2017b) also explore such sentence-level learning rate scaling and compare it against oversampling of in-domain data, showing similar results.

Farajian et al. (2017a) show that traditional statistical machine translation outperforms neural machine translation when training general-purpose machine translation systems on a collection of data and then testing on niche domains. The adaptation technique allows neural machine translation to catch up.

domain token ## Domain Tokens

A multidomain model may be trained and informed at run-time about the domain of the input sentence. Kobus et al. (2017) apply an idea initially proposed by Sennrich et al. (2016a)–to augment input sentences for register with a politeness feature token–to the domain adaptation problem. They add a domain token to each training and test sentence. Tars and Fishel (2018) give results that show domain tokens outperform fine-tuning and also explore word-level domain factors.

topic model ## Topic Models

If the data contain sentences from multiple domains but the composition is unknown, then automatically detecting different domains (then typically called topics) with methods such as LDA is an option. Zhang et al. (2016) apply such clustering and then compute for each word a topic distribution vector. It is used in addition to the word embedding to inform the encoder and decoder in a otherwise canonical neural translation model. Instead of word-level topic vectors, Chen et al. (2016b) encode the given domain membership of each sentence as an additional input vector to the conditioning context of word prediction layer. Tars and Fishel (2018) use sentence embeddings and k-means clustering to obtain topic clusters.

Noisy Data

Text to be translated by machine translation models may be noisy, either due to misspellings or creative language use that is common in social media text. Machine translation models may be adapted to such noise to be more robust. Vaibhav et al. (2019) add synthetic training data that contain types of noise similar to what has been seen in a test set of web discussion forum posts. Anastasopoulos et al. (2019) employ corpora from grammatical error correction tasks (sentences with errors from nonnative speakers alongside their corrections) to create synthetic input that mirrors the same type of errors. They compare translation quality between clean and noisy input and reduce the gap by adding similar synthetic noisy data to training.

Chapter 14
Beyond Parallel Corpora

Neural machine translation, like all supervised machine learning tasks, is trained on instances of labeled training examples, here sentences in the input languages labeled with their translation in the output language. But such parallel corpora are not the only data resource that can be used to train models.

Machine learning literature is rich in jargon to name the many ways data can be used to train models. **Supervised learning** implies that training examples that are of the same type as the test examples. If we want to label images with descriptions like *dog*, and *cat*, then we need to have training examples of such images with these labels. If we have only training examples without labels, this is called **unsupervised learning**. This means for machine translation that we have sentences in the source language (and maybe also sentences in the target language) that do not have translations. **Semisupervised learning** splits the difference. We have some labeled examples (a small parallel corpus), but typically much more unlabeled examples (monolingual corpora). **Self-training** is a semisupervised training method where we first train a model on the labeled data (the parallel corpus) and then generate additional training data by applying this model to unlabeled data (a monolingual corpus in the input language). The data generated in this fashion are added to the training data and the model is retrained.

What can we do with just unsupervised data? We can find patterns and generalizations. Word embeddings are a good example for that. We do not have any corpus where each word is labeled with a meaning representation, but by exploiting how words are distributed in text, such sense distinctions emerge.

supervised learning

unsupervised learning

semisupervised learning

self-training

transfer learning   **Transfer learning** is employed when we have much more similar data, such as a large corpus of French–English data, but we really want to translate Spanish to English. By pre-training the model on the French data, and then refining it on Spanish data, we are able to build on top of

zero shot   what we have already learned for a related language. **Zero-shot** learning takes this one step further for the case when we have only related data. In our example this would mean that we have French–English, French–German, and Spanish–German data, but no Spanish–English for which we want to build a system.

multitask   Finally, there is **Multitask** learning, where we train a model that performs many related tasks, each with its own training data, but with the hope that there are sufficient commonalities between the tasks so generalizations emerge that are broadly applicable.

This chapter explores how all these data conditions and learning methods have been applied to machine translation.

14.1 Using Monolingual Data

monolingual data

A key feature of statistical machine translation systems is language models that are trained on very large monolingual data sets. The larger the language model, the higher the translation quality. Language models trained on up to a trillion words crawled from the general web have been used. So, it is a surprise that the basic neural translation model does not use any additional monolingual data. Its language model aspect (the conditioning of the previous hidden decoder state and the previous output) is trained jointly with the translation model aspect (the conditioning on the input context), but it is only the target side of the parallel corpus that is used for this.

Two main ideas have been proposed for improving neural translation models with monolingual data. One is to integrate a language model as a component into the neural network architecture, and the other is to transform additional monolingual translation into parallel data by synthesizing the missing half of the data.

14.1.1 Adding a Language Model

Language models improve fluency of the output. Using larger amounts of monolingual data in the target language give the machine more evidence of what are common sequences of words and what are not.

We cannot simply use monolingual target side data during standard neural translation model training, since it is missing the source side. So the idea is to train a language model as a separate component of the neural translation model. We may first train a large language model

as a recurrent neural network on all available data, including the target
side of the parallel corpus. Then we combine this language model with
the neural translation model. Since both language model and translation
model predict output words, the natural point for connecting the two
models is joining them at that output prediction node in the network by
concatenating their conditioning contexts.

Recall the state progression in the decoder (Equation 8.3):

$$s_i = f(s_{i-1}, Ey_{i-1}, c_i). \tag{14.1}$$

The next decoder state s_i is conditioned on the previous decoder
state s^{i-1}, the embedding of the previous output word Ey_{i-1}, and the
source context c_i. As additional conditioning context, we add the hidden
state of the neural language model s_i^{LM}:

$$s_i = f(s_{i-1}, Ey_{i-1}, c_i, s_i^{LM}). \tag{14.2}$$

When training the combined model, we leave the parameters of the
large neural language model unchanged and update only the parameters of the translation model and the combination layer. The concern
is that otherwise the output side of the parallel corpus would overwrite the memory of the large monolingual corpus. In other words,
the language model would overfit to the parallel training data and be
less general.

One final question remains: how much weight should be given to the
translation model and how much weight should be given to the language
model? Equation 14.2 considers them in all instances the same way. But
there may be output words for which the translation model is more
relevant (e.g., the translation of content words with distinct meaning)
and output words where the language model is more relevant (e.g., the
introduction of relevant function words for fluency).

The balance between the translation model and the language model
can be achieved with a gate. The gate may be predicted solely from the
language model state s_i^{LM} and then used as a factor that is multiplied
with that language model state before it is used in the prediction of
Equation 14.2.

Formally, we first compute the gate $gate_i^{LM}$, a scalar number between
0 and 1:

$$gate_i^{LM} = f(s_i^{LM}). \tag{14.3}$$

This gate is then to scale the values of the language model state:

$$\bar{s}_i^{LM} = gate_i^{LM} \times s_i^{LM}. \tag{14.4}$$

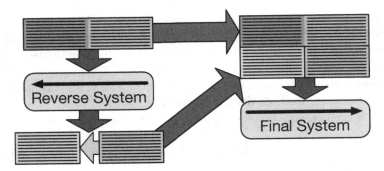

Figure 14.1 Creating synthetic parallel data from target-side monolingual data. (1) Train a system in reverse order, (2) use it to translate target-side monolingual data into the source language, and (3) combine the generated synthetic parallel data with the true parallel data in final system building.

We use this scaled state of the language model $\bar{s}_i^{\mathrm{LM}}$ in the translation model's decoder state progression:

$$s_i = f(s_{i-1},\ E y_{i-1}, c_i, \bar{s}_i^{\mathrm{LM}}). \tag{14.5}$$

14.1.2 Back Translation

back translation

We now take the view that monolingual data are parallel data that miss their other half. The idea is to just synthesize these data by **back translation**. Figure 14.1 shows the three steps involved.

1. Train a reverse system that translates from the intended target language into the source language. We typically use the same neural machine translation setup for this as for our final system, just with source and target flipped. But we may use any system, even traditional phrase-based systems.
2. Use the reverse system to translate the target-side monolingual data, creating a **synthetic parallel corpus**.

synthetic parallel corpus

3. Combine the generated synthetic parallel data with the true parallel data when building the final system.

It is an open question on how much synthetic parallel data should be used in relation to the amount of existing true parallel data. Typically, there are magnitudes more monolingual data available, but we also do not want to drown out the actual real data. Successful applications of this idea used equal amounts of synthetic and true data. We may also generate much more synthetic parallel data, but then ensure during training that we process equal amounts of each by oversampling the true parallel data.

Back translation may also be a useful method for addressing the problem of adapting the system to a specific domain (recall Chapter 13)

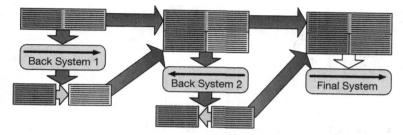

Figure 14.2 Iterative back translation. Taking the idea of back translation one step further. After training a system with back translated data (back system 2), it is used to create a synthetic parallel corpus for the final system.

in the case where we have only monolingual data in the target language, but no parallel data. Back translation then generates a synthetic in-domain corpus that helps produce output that matches the domain. In traditional statistical machine translation, much adaptation success has been achieved with just interpolating the language model, and this idea is the neural translation equivalent to that.

14.1.3 Iterative Back Translation

iterative back-translation

Take a closer look at the back translation setup. It allowed us to use monolingual target-side data. But how about monolingual data in the source language? It should tell us something about how words relate to each other in the source language.

With back translation, we already went through one direction of creating synthetic parallel data, so why not repeat this in the other direction (Figure 14.2). Here, we first start with building a system in the language direction of the intended final system. We use it to translate monolingual data in the input language, thus generating additional training data for the back translation system.

We do not have to stop at one iteration of repeated back translation. We can iterate training the two back translation systems multiple times. However, most of the gains are obtained from the first iteration. These gains can be attributed to the better machine translation system used to create the back translation model, hence the back translated data are better and lead to better final system quality.

14.1.4 Round Trip Training

round-trip training

Instead of iterating through parallel data creation through back translation and neural machine translation model training, there is a more principled approach to this idea of exploiting monolingual data, call **dual learning**. It sets up the idea of back translation as the goal of

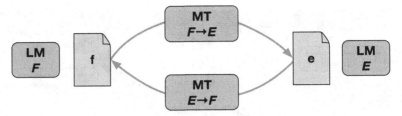

Figure 14.3 Round trip training. In addition to training two models $F \to E$ and $F \to E$, as done traditionally on parallel data, we also optimize both models to convert a sentence **f** into **e'** and then restore it back into **f**, using a monolingual sentence in language F. We may add a corresponding round trip starting with a monolingual sentence **e** in language E. Language models in language E and F are used to check if a translation is a valid sentence halfway through the round trip.

training two translation system, from language E to language F and in the reverse direction. Such a model can be trained so that a sentence in language F is first converted into language E and then back to language F.

Looking at the back translation idea from a strict machine learning perspective, we can see two learning objectives. One objective is to take a sentence **f** in one language F, translate it into a sentence **e'** in the other language E, and then translate it back into a sentence **f'** in language F, without any loss or distortion. We measure this by computing how well the original sentence **f** is reproduced from **e'**. However, there is one trick to fool such a training setup: if we do not alter the sentence at all (**e'** = **f**), when pretending to translate it, it is trivial to match the original sentence.

So, the other learning objective is to enforce that **e** is a valid sentence in E when first translating from F to E. Recall that we have no reference translation to check if that translation is accurate. But we can at least assess if a language model in language E considers **e'** a good sentence in that language (Figure 14.3).

There are two machine translation models. One that translates sentences in the language direction $F \to E$, the other in the opposite direction $E \to F$. These two models may be initially trained with traditional means, using a parallel corpus.

In this scenario, there are two objectives for model training.

- The translation **e'** of the given monolingual sentence **f** should be a valid sentence in the language E, as measured with a language model $\text{LM}_E(\mathbf{e'})$.
- The reconstruction of the translation **e'** back into the original language F is fairly straightforward, to be measured with the translation model $\text{MT}_{E \to F}(\mathbf{f}|\mathbf{e'})$ as in usual machine translation training.

These two objectives can be used to update model parameters in both translation models $MT_{F \to E}$ and $MT_{E \to F}$, while the language models remain static throughout.

Typically the model update is driven by the objective to make correct predictions of each word. In this round-trip scenario, the translation **e'** has to be computed first, before we can do the usual training of model $MT_{e \to f}$ with the given sentence pair (**e'**,**f**). To make better use of the training data, an n-best list of translations $\mathbf{e'}_1, \ldots, \mathbf{e'}_n$ is generated and model updates are computed for each of them.

We can also update the model $MT_{f \to e}$ with monolingual data in language f by scaling updates by the language model cost $LM_e(\mathbf{e'}_i)$ and the forward translation cost $MT_{f \to e}(\mathbf{e'}_i|\mathbf{f})$ for each of the translations $\mathbf{e'}_i$ in the n-best list.

To use monolingual data in language E, training is done in the reverse round trip direction.

14.2 Multiple Language Pairs

multiple language pairs

There are more than two languages in the world. And we also have training data for many language pairs. Sometimes it is highly overlapping (e.g., European Parliament proceedings in 24 languages), sometimes it is unique (e.g., Canadian Hansards in French and English). For some language pairs, a lot of training data are available (e.g., French–English). But for most language pairs, there are only very little, including commercially interesting language pairs such as Chinese–German snf Japanese–Spanish.

There is a long history of moving beyond specific languages and encoding meaning in a language-independent way, sometimes called an interlingua. In machine translation, the idea is to map the input language first into an interlingua and then map the interlingua into the output language. In such a system, we have to build just one mapping step into and one step out of the interlingua for each language. Then we can translate between it and all the other languages for which we have done the same.

Some researchers in deep learning do not hesitate to claim that intermediate states in neural translation models encode semantics or meaning. So, can we train a neural machine translation system that accepts text in any language as input and translates it into any other language, with a language-independent interlingual representation emerging in the middle?

Let us see, how we can slowly work toward this goal, starting with just multiple input languages.

14.2.1 Multiple Input Languages

Let us say, we have two parallel corpora, one for German–English, and one for French–English. We can train a neural machine translation model on both corpora at the same time by simply concatenating them. The input vocabulary contains both German and French words. Any input sentence will be quickly recognized as being either German or French, due to the sentence context, even disambiguating words such as *du* (*you* in German, *of* in French).

The combined model trained on both data sets has one advantage over two separate models. It is exposed to both English sides of the parallel corpora and hence can learn a better language model. There may be also be general benefits to having diversity in the data, leading to more robust models.

This setup has been shown to be successful, especially in low resources data conditions. If we do not have much training data for a specific language pair, training a system for it together with related language pairs has shown to improve translation quality. It does not seem to matter too much how related the input languages are.

14.2.2 Multiple Output Languages

We can do the same trick for the output language, by concatenating, say, a French–English and a French–Spanish corpus. But given a French input sentence during inference, how would the system know which output language to generate? A crude but effective way to signal this to the model is by adding a tag like [SPANISH] as first token of the input sentence.

[ENGLISH] *N'y a-t-il pas ici deux poids, deux mesures?*
⇒ *Is this not a case of double standards?*

[SPANISH] *N'y a-t-il pas ici deux poids, deux mesures?*
⇒ *¿No puede verse con toda claridad que estamos utilizando un doble rasero?*

Now let's take this a step further. If we train a system on the three corpora mentioned (German–English, French–English, and French–Spanish) we can also use it translate a sentence from German to Spanish, without having ever presenting a sentence pair in this language combination as training data to the system (Figure 14.4).

[SPANISH] *Messen wir hier nicht mit zweierlei Maß?*
⇒ *¿No puede verse con toda claridad que estamos utilizando un doble rasero?*

A single neural machine translation is trained on various parallel corpora in turn, resulting in a system that may translate between any seen

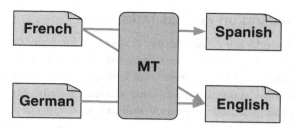

Figure 14.4 Multilanguage machine translation system trained on one language pair at a time, rotating through many of them. After training on French–English, French–Spanish, and German–English, it is possible to translate from German to Spanish.

input and output language. It is likely that increasingly deeper models (recall Section 8.4) may better serve as multilanguage translators, since their deeper layers compute more abstract representations of language.

For this to work, there has to be some representation of the meaning of the input sentence that is not tied to the input language and the output language. Surprisingly, experiments show that this actually does work, somewhat. To achieve good quality, however, some parallel data in the desired language pair is needed, but much less than for a standalone model (Johnson et al., 2017).

The method of marking the output language with a token such as [SPANISH] has been explored more widely in the context of systems for a single language pair. The token guides what kind of output is expected. Such tokens may represent the domain of the input sentence (Kobus et al., 2017) or the required level of politeness of the output sentence (Sennrich et al., 2016a).

14.2.3 Sharing Components

Instead of just throwing data at a generic neural machine translation model, we may want to more carefully consider which components may be shared among language-pair-specific models. The idea is to train one model per language pair, but some of the components are identical among these unique models.

- The encoder may be shared in models that have the same input language.
- The decoder may be shared in models that have the same output language.
- The attention mechanism may be shared in all models for all language pairs.

Sharing components means that the same parameter values (weight matrices, etc.) are used in these separate models. Updates to them when training a model for one language pair then also changes them for in the model for the other language pairs. There is no need to mark the output language, since each model is trained for a specific output language.

14.3 Training on Related Tasks

related tasks   Neural networks are a very flexible framework for many tasks. Since they make very few assumptions about the underlying problem, many of the architectures for different tasks look quite similar. For instance, the attentional sequence-to-sequence models initially explored for machine translation have been used with varying number of changes for quite different tasks, such as sentiment detection, grammar correction, semantic inference, summarization, question answering, and speech recognition.

The core components of neural machine translation models are quite general, such as encoding of the input words in word embeddings, refinement of their representation in the encoder to take sentence-level context into account, or the role of the decoder as an externally informed language model. Other tasks in natural language processing share these same components.

This raises the question, how much does training on related tasks help neural machine translation? The general idea is not to train separate models for all these different tasks, but to maybe train a general natural language processing model that is able to perform many tasks related to language. The hope is that such a system learns general facts about language that are informed by many different tasks and useful for many different tasks.

14.3.1 Pretraining Word Embeddings

pretraining   Neural machine translation models use word embeddings both to encode the input words as the first step of the encoder, and to encode output words to be used as conditioning context for the predictions of subsequent output words.

Word embeddings do not rely on parallel corpora but can be trained on vast amounts of monolingual data. Especially in low resource scenarios, when only small parallel corpora are available, an obvious solution is to first train word embeddings on monolingual data.

Standard methods for training word embeddings are described in some detail in Section 7.1.1. Generally speaking, the training objective for word embeddings is either to predict a word from its context or to predict the context a word appears in. Words that occur in similar contexts are deemed to have similar meaning and hence similar vector representations in the embedding space. This property of word embeddings is also useful for machine translation. In some contexts we prefer one word choice in the output over another. Being able to generalize these contexts and not rely on having seen the specific words next to each other during training helps with disambiguation.

Still, the training objective that produces word embeddings trained on monolingual data and the training objective for word embeddings for machine translation are different. So, it is generally not sufficient to just take the word embeddings trained on monolingual data and use them in machine translation models. When training the translation model, the word embeddings are typically used for initialization of the model, but then training is able to modify them to fit the task.

14.3.2 Pretraining the Encoder and Decoder

Other components of the neural machine translation model may be pretrained as well. We already mentioned that the decoder is an extension of a language model. It predicts output words based on previous output words (just like a language model), with additional guidance from the input sentence.

Just as we may pretrain word embeddings on monolingual data, we may pretrain the decoder on monolingual data, with the objective to do well as a language model. For this, we ignore the input context (typically just set it to zero). The training objective is unchanged: we measure how well we predict the next word, as measured by the probability mass given to it. After we trained the parameters related to the decoder in such a fashion, we use them as initial values before actual training on parallel data starts.

Moreover, the input encoder is also similar to a language model. So, we may pretrain the encoder layers with the objective to do well on predicting the next word in the sentence in the input language. Note that this training objective diverges from the purpose of the encoder for machine translation. For instance, for machine translation it is more important to disambiguate the meaning of each input word, especially if different senses lead to different output word predictions.

14.3.3 Multitask Training

Instead of initializing part of a neural machine translation model with **multitask training** pretrained components, the goal of multitask training is to train a combined model on multiple tasks at the same time. The combined model typically has shared components across tasks but may also be just a single model that can be configured to handle different tasks, depending on the input.

Training a single model on multiple language pairs at the same time can be viewed as a specific instance of multitask training. Here, we are looking at training completely different natural language processing tasks alongside neural machine translation. Tasks that have been explored in this setup are part-of-speech tagging, named entity recognition, and also syntactic parsing and semantic analysis.

All of these tasks can be framed as sequence-to-sequence problems. In the case of syntactic parsing or semantic analysis, this requires a representation of the output as a linearized sequence of words and special tokens (see Section 15.3.2 for details).

Just as we discussed in Section 14.2 on training with multiple language pairs, these tasks may share either some or all components and their parameters. Training iterates through batches of examples from different tasks. Better performance is typically obtain by concluding training by focusing on a specific task.

14.4 Further Readings

language model ***Integrating Language Models***
Traditional statistical machine translation models have a straightforward mechanism to integrate additional knowledge sources, such as a large out-of-domain language model. It is harder for end-to-end neural machine translation. Gülçehre et al. (2015) add a language model trained on additional monolingual data to this model, in form of a recurrently neural network that runs in parallel. They compare the use of the language model in reranking (or rescoring) against deeper integration, where a gated unit regulates the relative contribution of the language model and the translation model when predicting a word.

back translation ***Back Translation***
Sennrich et al. (2016c) back translate the monolingual data into the input language and use the obtained synthetic parallel corpus as additional training data. Hoang et al. (2018b) show that the quality of the machine translation system matters and can be improved by iterative back translation. Burlot and Yvon (2018) also show that back translation quality matters and carry out additional analysis. Edunov et al. (2018a) show better results with Monte Carlo search to generate the back translation data, i.e., randomly selecting word translations based on the predicted probability distribution. Imamura et al. (2018) and Imamura and Sumita (2018) also confirm that better translation quality can be obtained when back translating with such sampling and offer some refinements. Caswell et al. (2019) argue that the noise introduced by this type of stochastic search flags to the model that it consists of back translated data, something that can also be accomplished with an explicit special token, to the same effect.

Currey et al. (2017) show that in low resource conditions simple copying of target-side data to the source side also generates beneficial training data. Fadaee and Monz (2018) see gains with synthetic data generated by forward translation (also called self-training). They also report gains when subsampling back translation data to favor rare or difficult to generate words (words with high loss during training).

Dual Learning

He et al. (2016a) use monolingual data in a dual learning setup. Machine translation engines are trained in both directions, and in addition to regular model training from parallel data, monolingual data are translated in a round trip (**e** to **f** to **e**) and evaluated with a language model for language **f** and reconstruction match back to **e** as a cost function to drive gradient descent updates to the model. Tu et al. (2017) augment the translation model with a reconstruction step. The generated output is translated back into the input language and the training objective is extended to include not only the likelihood of the target sentence but also the likelihood to the reconstructed input sentence. Niu et al. (2018) simultaneously train a model in both translation directions (with the identity of the source language indicated by marker token. Niu et al. (2019) extend this work to round-trip translation training on monolingual data, allowing the forward translation and the reconstruction step to operate on the same model. They use Gumbel softmax to make the round trip differentiable.

dual learning

Unsupervised Machine Translation

The idea of back translation is also crucial for the ambitious goal of unsupervised machine translation, i.e., the training of machine translation systems with monolingual data only. These methods typically start with multilingual word embeddings, which may also be induced from monolingual data. Given such a word translation model, Lample et al. (2018a) propose translating sentences in one language with a simple word-by-word translation model into another language, using a shared encoder and decoder for both languages involved. They define three different objectives in their setup: the ability to reconstruct a source sentence form its intermediate representation, even with added noise (randomly dropping words), the ability to reconstruct a source sentence from its translation into the target language, and an adversarial component that attempts to classify the identity of the language from intermediate representation of a sentence in either language. Artetxe et al. (2018b) use a similar setup, with a shared encoder and language-specific decoder, relying on the idea of a denoising auto-encoder (just like the first objective given earlier), and the ability to reconstruct the source sentence from a translation into the target language. Sun et al. (2019) note that during training of the neural machine translation model, the bilingual word embedding deteriorates. They add the training objective

unsupervised machine translation

for the induction of the bilingual word embeddings into the objective function of neural machine translation training. Yang et al. (2018c) use language-specific encoders with some shared weights in a similar setup. Artetxe et al. (2018a) show better results when inducing phrase translations from phrase embeddings and use them in a statistical phrase-based machine translation model, which includes an explicit language model. They refine their model with synthetic data generated by iterative back translation. Lample et al. (2018b) combine unsupervised statistical and neural machine translation models. Their phrase-based model is initialized with word translations obtained from multilingual word embeddings and then iteratively refined into phrase translations. Ren et al. (2019) more closely tie together training of unsupervised statistical and neural machine translation systems by using the statistical machine translation model as a regularizer for the neural model training. Artetxe et al. (2019a) improve their unsupervised statistical machine translation model with a feature that favors similarly spelled translations and a unsupervised method to tune the weights for the statistical components. Circling back to bilingual lexicon induction, Artetxe et al. (2019b) use such an unsupervised machine translation model to synthesize a parallel corpus by translating monolingual data, process it with word alignment methods, and extract a bilingual dictionary using maximum likelihood estimation.

multilanguage training **Multilanguage Training**
Zoph et al. (2016) first train on a resource language pair and then adapt the resulting model toward a targeted low resource language, showing gains over just training on the low resource language. Nguyen and Chiang (2017) show better results when merging the vocabularies of the different input languages. Ha et al. (2016) prefix each input work with a language identifier (e.g., @en@dog, @de@Hund) and add monolingual data, both as source and target. Ha et al. (2017) observe that translation in multilanguage systems with multiple target languages may switch to the wrong language. They limit word predictions to words existing in the desired target language and add source-side language-identifying word factors. Lakew et al. (2018a) show that Transformer models perform better for multilanguage pair training than previous models based on recurrent neural networks. Lakew et al. (2018b) build one-to-many translation models for languages varieties, i.e., closely related dialects such Brazilian and European Portuguese or Croatian and Serbian. This requires language variety identification to separate out the training data. Lakew et al. (2018c) start with a model trained on a high-resource language pair and then incrementally add low-resource language pairs, including new vocabulary items. They show much faster

training convergence and slight quality gains over joint training. Neubig and Hu (2018) train a many-to-one model for 58 language pairs and fine-tune it toward each of them. Aharoni et al. (2019) scale multilanguage training up to 103 languages, training on language pairs with English on either side, measuring average translation performance from English and into English. They show that many-to-many systems improve over many-to-one system when translating into English but not over one-to-many systems when translating from English. They also see degradation when combining more than 5 languages. Murthy et al. (2019) identify a problem when a targeted language pair in the multilanguage setup is low resource and has different word order from the other language pair. They propose preordering the input to match the word order of the dominant language.

Zero Shot

zero shot

Johnson et al. (2017) explore how well a single canonical neural translation model is able to learn from multiple to multiple languages, by simultaneously training on on parallel corpora for several language pairs. They show small benefits for several input languages with the same output languages, mixed results for translating into multiple output languages (indicated by an additional input language token). The most interesting result is the ability for such a model to translate in language directions for which no parallel corpus is provided (zero-shot), thus demonstrating that some interlingual meaning representation is learned, although less well than using traditional pivot methods. Mattoni et al. (2017) explore zero-shot training for Indian languages with sparse training data, achieving limited success. Al-Shedivat and Parikh (2019) extend the training objective of zero-shot training in the scenario of English-*X* parallel corpora so that given an English–French sentence pair the translations French–Russian and English–Russian are consistent.

Multilanguage Training with Language-Specific Components

There have been a few suggestions to alter the model for multilanguage pair training. Dong et al. (2015) use different decoders for each target language. Firat et al. (2016a) support multilanguage input and output by training language-specific encoders and decoders and a shared attention mechanism. Firat et al. (2016b) evaluate how well this model works for zero-shot translation. Lu et al. (2018) add an additional interlingua layer between specialized encoders and decoders that is shared across all language pairs. Conversely, Blackwood et al. (2018) use shared encoders and decoders but language-pair-specific attention. Sachan and Neubig (2018) investigate which parameters in a Transformer model should be shared during one-to-many training and find that partial sharing of components outperforms no sharing or full sharing, although the best configuration depends on the languages involved. Wang et al. (2018b) add language-dependent positional embeddings and split the decoder state into a general and language-dependent part. Platanios et al. (2018) generate the language-pair specific parameters for the encoder and decoder with a parameter generator that takes embeddings of input and output language identifiers as input.

Gu et al. (2018b) frame the multilanguage training setup as meta learning, which they define as either learning a policy for updating model parameters or learning a good parameter initialization method for fast adaptation. Their approach falls under that second definition and is similar to multilanguage training with adaptation via fine-tuning, except for optimization during the first phase toward parameters that can be quickly adapted.

Gu et al. (2018a) focus on the problem of word representation in multilingual training. They map the tokens of every language into a universal embedding space, aided by monolingual data. Wang et al. (2019b) have the same goal in mind and use language-specific and language-independent character-based word representations to map to a shared word embedding space. This is done for input words in a 58-language to English translation model. Tan et al. (2019) change the training objective for multilanguage training. In addition to matching the training data for the language pairs, an additional training objective is to match the prediction of a "teacher" model that was trained on the corresponding single-language pair data. Malaviya et al. (2017) use the embedding associated with the language indicator token in massively multilanguage models to predict typological properties of a language. Ren et al. (2018) address the challenge of pivot translation (train an X–Z model by using a third language Y with large corpora X–Y and X–Z) in a neural model approach by setting up training objectives that match translation through the pivot path and the direct translation, and other paths in this language triangle.

multiple inputs   ### *Multiple Inputs*

Zoph and Knight (2016) augment a translation model to consume two meaning-equivalent sentences in different languages as input. Zhou et al. (2017) apply this idea to the task of system combination, i.e., obtaining a consensus translation from multiple machine translation outputs. Garmash and Monz (2016) train multiple single-language systems, feed each the corresponding meaning-equivalent input sentence and combine these predictions of the models in an ensemble approach during decoding. Nishimura et al. (2018b) explore how a multisource model works when input for some languages is missing. In their experiments, the multiencoder approach often works better than the ensemble. Nishimura et al. (2018a) fill in the missing sentences in the training data with (multisource) back translation. Dabre et al. (2017) concatenate the input sentences and also use training data in the same format (which requires intersecting overlapping parallel corpora).

Pretrained Word Embeddings

pretrained word embeddings

Gangi and Federico (2017) do not observe improvement when using monolingual word embeddings in a gated network that trains additional word embeddings purely on parallel data. Abdou et al. (2017) showed worse performance on a WMT news translation task with pretrained word embeddings. They argue, as Hill et al. (2014, 2017) did previously, that neural machine translation requires word embeddings that are based on semantic similarity of words (teacher and professor) rather than other kinds of relatedness (teacher and student), and demonstrate that word embeddings trained for translation score better on standard semantic similarity tasks. Artetxe et al. (2018b) use monolingually trained word embeddings in a neural machine translation system, without using any parallel corpus. Qi et al. (2018) show gains with pretrained word embeddings in low resource conditions, but note that benefits decrease with larger data sizes.

Multitask Training

Niehues and Cho (2017) tackle multiple tasks (translation, parts-of- multitask training speech tagging, and named entity identification) with shared components of a sequence-to-sequence model, showing that training on several tasks improves performance on each individual task. Zaremoodi and Haffari (2018) refine this approach with adversarial training that enforces task-independent representation in intermediate layers and applies to joint training with syntactic and semantic parsing. Li et al. (2019) add as auxiliary tasks the prediction of hierarchical word classes obtained by hierarchical Brown clustering. In the first layer of the decoder of a Transformer model, the coarsest word classes are predicted, and in later layers more fine-grained word classes are predicted. The authors argue that this increases generalization ability of intermediate representations and show improvements in translation quality.

Chapter 15
Linguistic Structure

One of the big debates in machine translation research is the question of whether the key to progress is to develop better, relatively generic, machine learning methods that implicitly learn the important features of language or to use linguistic insight to augment data and models.

Recent work in statistical machine translation has demonstrated the benefits of linguistically motivated models. The best statistical machine translation systems in major evaluation campaigns for language pairs such as Chinese–English and German–English are syntax-based. While they translate sentences, they also build up the syntactic structure of the output sentence. There have been serious efforts to move toward deeper semantics in machine translation.

The turn toward neural machine translation was at first a hard swing back toward better machine learning while ignoring linguistic insights. Neural machine translation views translation as a generic sequence to sequence task, which just happens to involve sequences of words in different languages. Methods such as byte pair encoding or character-based translation models even put the value of the concept of a word as a basic unit into doubt.

Hence neural machine translation models have to automatically learn from data all the linguistic insights that we already have. These are basic ideas such as that most output words have a one-to-one correspondence to a single input word; that we have to translate all the of the input, and all of it only once; or that words fall into classes such as nouns and verbs that behave different from each other, and are connected differently in different languages.

Linguistic research aims at finding core principles that are common across many if not all languages. This led computational linguistics to develop tools that analyze sentences into syntactic and semantic representation. Even if a sentence and its translation into a foreign language are quite different at the surface (e.g., different word order, different function words, etc.), they appear more similar in these deeper representations. A long-standing vision for machine translation research has been to develop methods that use such deeper linguistic representations as intermediate stages of processing.

Statistical machine translation research evolved over time toward more linguistically motivated models that used explicit representations of morphology, syntax, and even semantics. At the time of writing, neural machine translation models start this process again without any real linguistic annotation.

15.1 Guided Alignment Training

guided alignment training

The attention mechanism in neural machine translation models is motivated by the linguistic fact that each individual output word is often fully explained by a single word or at most a few relevant words in the input. Figure 15.1 shows an example of attention weights given to English input words for each German output word during the translation of a sentence. Most words in the output have a one-to-one correspondence to input words.

Statistical machine translation models that explicitly establish a many to many mapping between input and output words are part of the training pipeline. These originate in the earliest statistical machine translation models, the so-called IBM models. The attention values of neural machine translation models typically match up pretty well with the word alignments used in traditional statistical machine translation, obtained with tools such as GIZA++ or fast-align that implement variants of the IBM models.

There are several good uses for word alignments beyond their intrinsic value of improving the quality of translations. For instance in the next section, we look at using the attention mechanism to explicitly track coverage of the input. We may also want to override preferences of the neural machine translation model with prespecified translations of certain terminology or expressions such as numbers, dates, and measurements that are better handled by rule-based components; this requires to know when the neural model is about to translate a specific source word. But also the end user may be interested in alignment information—for example, translators using machine translation in a

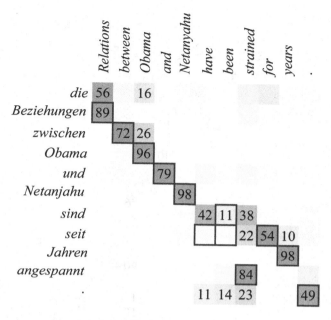

Figure 15.1 Alignment versus attention. In this example, alignment points from traditional word alignment methods are shown as squares, and attention states as shaded boxes depending on the alignment value (shown as percentage). They generally match up well, but note for instance that the prediction of the output auxiliary verb *sind* pays attention to the entire verb group *have been strained*.

computer aided translation tool may want to check the origin of an output word.

Hence, instead of trusting the attention mechanism to implicitly acquire the role as word aligner, we may enforce this role. The idea is to provide not just the parallel corpus as training data, but also precomputed word alignments using traditional means. Such additional information may even benefit the training of models to converge faster or overcome data sparsity under low resource conditions.

A straightforward way to add such given word alignment to the training process is to modify the training objective, and not the model. Typically, the goal of training neural machine translation models is to generate correct output words. We can also add to this goal to match a precomputed word alignment.

Formally, we assume to have access to an alignment matrix A that specifies alignment points A_{ij}, input words j, and output words i in a way that $\sum_j A_{ij} = 1$, i.e., each output word's alignment scores add up to 1. The model estimates attention scores α_{ij} that also add up to 1 for each output word: $\sum_j \alpha_{ij} = 1$ (recall Equation 8.7). The mismatch between given alignment scores A_{ij} and computed attention scores α_{ij} can be measured in several ways, such as cross-entropy:

$$\text{cost}_{\text{CE}} = -\frac{1}{I} \sum_{i=1}^{I} \sum_{j=1}^{J} A_{ij} \log \alpha_{ij} \qquad (15.1)$$

Figure 15.2 Examples of overgeneration and undergeneration. The input tokens around "*Social Housing*" are attended too much, leading to hallucinated output words (*das Unternehmen*, English: *the company*), while the end of the sentence *a fresh start* is not attended to and left untranslated.

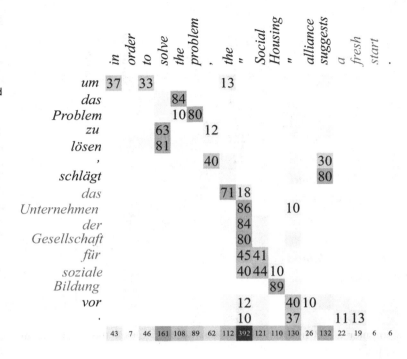

or mean squared error

$$\text{cost}_{\text{MSE}} = -\frac{1}{I} \sum_{i=1}^{I} \sum_{j=1}^{J} (A_{ij} - \alpha_{ij})^2. \tag{15.2}$$

This cost is added to the training objective and may be weighted.

15.2 Modeling Coverage

coverage

One impressive aspect of neural machine translation models is how well they are able to translate the entire input sentence, even when a lot of reordering is involved. But this aspect is not perfect; occasionally the model translates some input words multiple times, and sometimes it fails to translate some.

Figure 15.2 shows an actual neural machine translation system. The translation has two flaws related to misallocation of attention. The beginning of the phrase *"Social Housing" alliance* receives too much attention, resulting in a faulty translation with hallucinated words: *das Unternehmen der Gesellschaft für soziale Bildung*, or *the company of the society for social education*. At the end of the input sentence, the phrase *a fresh start* does not receive any attention and is thus untranslated in the output.

Hence an obvious idea is to more strictly model **coverage**. Given the attention model, a reasonable way to define coverage is by adding up the attention states. In a complete sentence translation, we roughly expect that each input word receives a similar amount of attention. If some input words never receive attention or receive too much attention that signals a problem with the translation.

15.2.1 Enforcing Coverage during Inference

We may enforce proper coverage during decoding. When considering multiple hypothesis in beam search, then we should discourage the ones that pay too much attention to some input words. And, once hypotheses are completed, we can penalize those that paid only little attention to some of the input. There are various ways to come up with scoring functions for overgeneration and undergeneration:

$$\text{coverage}(j) = \sum_i \alpha_{i,j}$$

$$\text{overgeneration} = \max\left(0, \sum_j \text{coverage}(j) - 1\right) \qquad (15.3)$$

$$\text{undergeneration} = \min\left(1, \sum_j \text{coverage}(j)\right).$$

The use of multiple scoring functions in the decoder is common practice in traditional statistical machine translation. For now, it is not in neural machine translation. A challenge is to give proper weight to the different scoring functions. If there are only two or three weights, these can be optimized with grid search over possible values. For more weights, we may borrow methods such as MERT or MIRA from statistical machine translation.

15.2.2 Coverage Models

coverage model

Instead of manipulating decoding, we may instead want to extend the underlying model. The vector that accumulates coverage of input words may be directly used to inform the attention model. Previously, the attention a given to a specific input word j at each time step i was conditioned on the previous state of the decoder s_{i-1} and the representation of the input word h_j. Now, we also add as conditioning context the accumulated attention given to the word (compare to Equation 8.6), parameterized by a weight matrix V^a:

$$a(s_{i-1}, h_j) = W^a s_{i-1} + U^a h_j + V^a \text{coverage}(j) + b^a. \qquad (15.4)$$

Coverage tracking may also be integrated into the training objective. Taking a page from guided alignment training (recall Section 15.1), we augment the training objective function with a coverage penalty with some weight λ:

$$\log \sum_i P(y_i|x) + \lambda \sum_j (1 - \text{coverage}(j))^2. \qquad (15.5)$$

Note that in general, it is problematic to add such additional functions to the learning objective, since it does distract from the main goal of producing good translations.

15.2.3 Fertility

fertility

So far, we described coverage as the need to cover all input words roughly evenly. However, even the earliest statistical machine translation models considered the **fertility** of a word, i.e., the number of output words that are generated from each input word. Consider the English *do not* construction: most other languages do not require an equivalent of *do* when negating a verb, so it does not lead to any output words being generated. Meanwhile, other words are translated into multiple output words. For instance, the German *natürlich* may be translated as *of course*, thus generating two output words.

We may augment models of coverage by adding a fertility components that predict the number of output words for each input word. Here is one example of a model that predicts the fertility Φ_j for each input word and uses it to normalize coverage statistics:

$$\Phi_j = N\sigma(W_j h_j)$$
$$\text{coverage}(j) = \frac{1}{\Phi_j} \sum_i \alpha_{i,j}. \qquad (15.6)$$

Fertility Φ_j is predicted with a neural network layer that is conditioned on the input word representation h_j and uses a sigmoid activation function (thus resulting in values from 0 to 1), which is scaled to a predefined maximum fertility of N.

15.2.4 Feature Engineering Versus Machine Learning

feature engineering

The work on modeling coverage in neural machine translation models is a nice example for contrasting between the engineering approach and trust in machine learning. From an engineering perspective, a good way to improve a system is to analyze its performance, find weak points, and consider changes to overcome them. Here, we notice overgeneration and undergeneration with respect to the input and add components to the model to overcome these problems. On the other hand, proper coverage is one of the properties of a good translation that machine learning should be able to get from the training data. If it is not able to do that, it may need deeper models, more robust estimation techniques, ways to fight overfitting or underfitting, or other adjustments to give it just the right amount of power needed for the problem.

It is hard to carry out the analysis needed to make generic machine learning adjustments, given the complexity of a task like machine translation. Still, the argument for deep learning is that it does not require feature engineering, such as adding coverage models. It remains to be seen how neural machine translation evolves over the next years, and if it moves more into a engineering or machine learning direction.

15.3 Adding Linguistic Annotation

linguistic annotation

However, recently there have been also attempts to add linguistic annotation into neural translation models and steps toward more linguistically motivated models. We will take a look at successful efforts (1) to integrate linguistic annotation to the input sentence, (2) to integrate linguistic annotation to the output sentence, and (3) to build linguistically structured models.

15.3.1 Linguistic Annotation of the Input

One of the great benefits of neural networks is their ability to cope with rich context. In the neural machine translation models we presented, each word prediction is conditioned on the entire input sentence and all previously generated output words. Even if, as is typically the case, a specific input sequence and partially generated output sequence have never been observed before during training, the neural model is able to generalize the training data and draw from relevant knowledge. In traditional statistical models, this required carefully chosen independence assumptions and back-off schemes.

So, adding more information to the conditioning context in neural translation models can be accommodated rather straightforwardly. First, what information would we like to add? The typical linguistic treasure chest contains part-of-speech tags, lemmas, morphological properties of words, syntactic phrase structure, syntactic dependencies, and maybe even some semantic annotation.

All of these can be formatted as annotations to individual input words. Sometimes, this requires a bit more work, such as syntactic and semantic annotation that spans multiple words (Figure 15.3). Let us walk

Words	*the*	*girl*	*watched*	*attentively*	*the*	*beautiful*	*fireflies*
Part of speech	DET	NN	VFIN	ADV	DET	JJ	NNS
Lemma	*the*	*girl*	*watch*	*attentive*	*the*	*beautiful*	*firefly*
Morphology	-	SING.	PAST	-	-	-	PLURAL
Noun phrase	BEGIN	CONT	OTHER	OTHER	BEGIN	CONT	CONT
Verb phrase	OTHER	OTHER	BEGIN	CONT	CONT	CONT	CONT
Syntactic dependency	*girl*	*watched*	-	*watched*	*fireflies*	*fireflies*	*watched*
Dependency relation	DET	SUBJ	-	ADV	DET	ADJ	OBJ
Semantic role	-	ACTOR	-	MANNER	-	MOD	PATIENT
Semantic type	-	HUMAN	VIEW	-	-	-	ANIMATE

Figure 15.3 Linguistic annotation of a sentence, formatted as word-level factored representation.

through the linguistic annotation of the word *girl* in the sentence: The girl watched attentively the beautiful fireflies.

- Part of speech is NN, a noun.
- Lemma is *girl*, the same as the surface form. The lemma differs for *watched* / *watch*.
- Morphology is singular.
- The word is the continuation (CONT) of the noun phrase that started with *the*.
- The word is not part of a verb phrase (OTHER).
- Its syntactic head is *watched*.
- The dependency relationship to the head is subject (SUBJ).
- Its semantic role is ACTOR.
- There are many schemes of semantic types. For instance *girl* could be classified as HUMAN.

Note how phrasal annotations are handled. The first noun phrase is *the girl*. It is common to use an annotation scheme that tags individual words in a phrasal annotation as BEGIN and CONTINUATION (or INTERMEDIATE), while labeling words outside such phrases as OTHER.

How do we encode such a word-level factored representation? Recall that words are initially represented as one hot vectors. Similarly, we can encode each factor in the factored representation as a one hot vector. The concatenation of these vectors is then used as input to the word embedding. Note that mathematically this means, that each factor of the representation is mapped to a embedding vector, and the final word embedding is the sum of the factor embeddings.

Since the input to the neural machine translation system is still a sequence of word embeddings, we do not have to change anything in the architecture of the neural machine translation model. We just provide richer input representations and hope that the model is able to learn how to take advantage of it.

Let us return to the debate about linguistics versus machine learning. All the linguistic annotation proposed here can arguable be learned automatically as part of the word embeddings (or contextualized word embeddings in the hidden encoder states). This may or may not work out in practice. But it does provide additional knowledge that comes from the tools that produce the annotation and that is particularly relevant if there are not enough training data to automatically induce it. Also, why make the job harder for the machine learning algorithm than needed? In other words, why force the machine learning to discover features that can be readily provided? Ultimately, these questions need to be resolved empirically by demonstrating what actually works in specific data conditions.

15.3.2 Linguistic Annotation of the Output

What we have done for input words could also be done for output words. Instead of discussing the fine points about what adjustments need to be made (e.g., separate softmax for each output factor), let us take a look at another annotation scheme for the output that has been successfully applied to neural machine translation.

The most successful syntax-based statistical machine translation models have focused on the output side. Traditional n-gram language models are good at promoting fluency among neighboring words. But they are not powerful enough to ensure overall grammaticality of the output sentence. By designing models that also produce and evaluate the syntactic parse structure for each output sentence, syntax-based models give the means to promote grammatically correct output.

The word-level annotation of phrase structure syntax suggested in Figure 15.3 is rather crude. The nature of language is recursive, and annotating nested phrases cannot be easily handled with a BEGIN/CONT/OTHER scheme. Instead, typically tree structures are used to represent syntax.

Figure 15.4 shows the phrase structure syntactic parse tree for our example sentence *The girl watched attentively the beautiful fireflies*. Generating a tree structure is generally a quite different process than

Sentence	*the girl watched attentively the beautiful fireflies*
Syntax tree	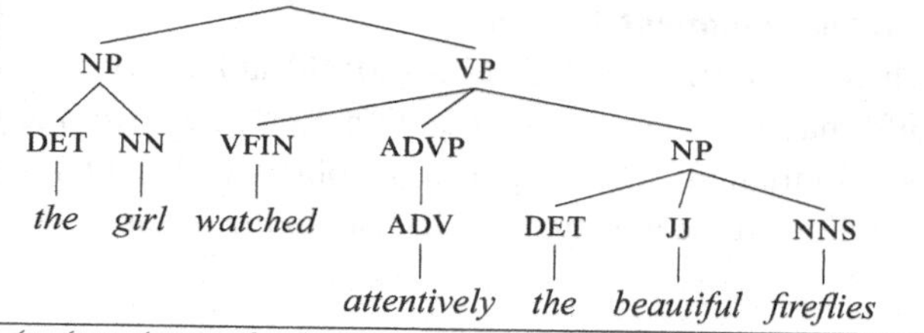
Linearized	(S (NP (DET *the*) (NN *girl*)) (VP (VFIN *watched*) (ADVP (ADV *attentively*)) (NP (DET *the*) (JJ *beautiful*) (NNS *fireflies*))))

Figure 15.4 Linearization of a phrase structure grammar tree into a sequence of words—e.g., *girl, watched*—and tags—e.g., (S, (NP,).

generating a sequence. It is typically built recursively bottom-up with algorithms such as chart parsing.

linearization of parse tree

However, we can **linearize** the parse tree into a sequence of words and structural tokens that indicate the beginning—e.g., "(NP"—and end—closing parenthesis ")"—of syntactic phrases. So, forcing syntactic parse tree annotations into our sequence-to-sequence neural machine translation model may be done by encoding the parse structure with additional output tokens. To be perfectly clear, the idea is to produce as the output of the neural translation system not just a sequence of words but a sequence of a mix of output words and special tokens.

The hope is that forcing the neural machine translation model to produce syntactic structures (even in a linearized form) encourages it to produce syntactically well-formed output. There is some evidence to support this hope, despite the simplicity of the approach.

15.3.3 Linguistically Structured Models

linguistically structured models

The field of syntactic parsing has not been left untouched by the recent wave of neural networks. The previous section suggests that syntactic parsing may be done as simply as framing it sequence to sequence with additional output tokens.

However, the best performing syntactic parsers use model structures that take the recursive nature of language to heart. They are either inspired by convolutional networks and build parse trees bottom-up or are neural versions of left-to-right push-down automata, which maintain a stack of opened phrases that any new word may extend or close or be pushed down the stack to start a new phrase.

There is some early work on integrating syntactic parsing and machine translation into a unified framework, but no consensus on best practices has emerged yet. At the time of writing, this is clearly still a challenge for future work.

15.4 Further Readings

guided alignment training

Guided Alignment Training
Chen et al. (2016b) and Liu et al. (2016b) add supervised word alignment information (obtained with traditional statistical word alignment methods) to training. They augment the objective function to also optimize matching of the attention mechanism to the given alignments.

coverage

Coverage
To better model coverage, Tu et al. (2016b) add coverage states for each input word by either (1) summing up attention values, scaled by a fertility

value predicted from the input word in context, or (2) learning a coverage update function as a feed-forward neural network layer. This coverage state is added as additional conditioning context for the prediction of the attention state. Feng et al. (2016) condition the prediction of the attention state also on the previous context state and introduce a coverage state (initialized with the sum of input source embeddings) that aims to subtract covered words at each step. Similarly, Meng et al. (2016) separate hidden states that keep track of source coverage and hidden states that keep track of produced output. Cohn et al. (2016) add a number of biases to model coverage, fertility, and alignment inspired by traditional statistical machine translation models. They condition the prediction of the attention state on absolute word positions, the attention state of the previous output word in a limited window, and coverage (added attention state values) over a limited window. They also add a fertility model and add coverage in the training objective.

Alkhouli et al. (2016) propose to integrate an alignment model that is similar to word-based statistical machine translation into a basic sequence-to-sequence translation model. This model is trained externally with traditional word alignment methods and informs predictions about which input word to translate next and bases the lexical translation decision on that word. Alkhouli and Ney (2017) combine such a alignment model with the more traditional attention model, showing improvements.

Linguistic Annotation

linguistic annotation

Wu et al. (2012) propose to use factored representations of words (using lemma, stem, and part of speech), with each factor encoded in a one hot vector, in the input to a recurrent neural network language model. Sennrich and Haddow (2016) use such representations in the input and output of neural machine translation models, demonstrating better translation quality. Aharoni and Goldberg (2017) encode syntax with special start-of-phrase and end-of-phrase tokens in a linearized sequence and use these both on the input and the output of traditional sequence-to-sequence models. Hirschmann et al. (2016) propose to tackle the problem of translating German compounds by splitting them into their constituent words. Huck et al. (2017) segment words based on morphological principles: separating prefixes and suffixes and splitting compounds, showing superior performance compared to the data-driven byte-pair encoding. Burlot et al. (2017) also detach morphemes from the lemma, but replace them with tags that indicate their morphological features. Tamchyna et al. (2017) use the same method for Czech, but with deterministic tags, avoiding a disambiguation postediting step. Nadejde et al. (2017) add syntactic CCG tags to each output word, thus encouraging the model to also produce proper syntactic structure alongside a fluent sequence of words. Pu et al. (2017) first train a word sense disambiguation model based WordNet senses, based on their sense description and then use it to augment the input sentence with sense tags. Rios et al. (2017) also perform word sense disambiguation and enrich the input with sense embeddings and semantically related words from previous input text. Ma et al. (2019a) compute the distance between source words in the syntax tree and use this information when attending to words. The prediction of the syntactic distance is done while translating, using it as a secondary training objective during training.

Chapter 16
Current Challenges

Neural machine translation has emerged as the most promising machine translation approach in recent years, showing superior performance on public benchmarks (Bojar et al., 2016) and rapid adoption in deployments by, e.g., Google (Wu et al., 2016), Systran (Crego et al., 2016), and WIPO (Junczys-Dowmunt et al., 2016). But there have also been reports of poor performance, such as the systems built under low-resource conditions.

In this chapter I review a number of challenges to neural machine translation and give empirical results on how well the technology currently holds up compared to traditional statistical machine translation. I show that, despite its recent successes, neural machine translation still has to overcome various challenges, most notably performance out of domain, under low resource conditions, and given noisy training data.

What a lot of these challenges have in common is that the neural translation models do not show robust behavior when confronted with data that differ significantly from training conditions, whether due to limited exposure to training data, unusual input in the case of out-of-domain test sentences, or unlikely initial word choices in a beam search. The solution to these problems may lie in a more general approach of training that steps outside optimizing single word predictions given perfectly matching prior sequences.

Another challenge, which we do not examine empirically: neural machine translation systems are much less interpretable. The answer to the question of why the training data lead these systems to decide on specific word choices during decoding is buried in large matrices of

Figure 16.1 Quality of systems (BLEU), when trained on one domain (rows) and tested on another domain (columns). Comparably, neural machine translation systems (left bars) show more degraded performance out of domain.

System ↓	Law	Medical	IT	Koran	Subtitles
All data	30.5 32.8	45.1 42.2	35.3 44.7	17.9 17.9	26.4 20.8
Law	31.1 34.4	12.1 18.2	3.5 6.9	1.3 2.2	2.8 6.0
Medical	3.9 10.2	39.4 43.5	2.0 8.5	0.6 2.0	1.4 5.8
IT	1.9 3.7	6.5 5.3	42.1 39.8	1.8 1.6	3.9 4.7
Koran	0.4 1.8	0.0 2.1	0.0 2.3	15.9 18.8	1.0 5.5
Subtitles	7.0 9.9	9.3 17.8	9.2 13.6	9.0 8.4	25.9 22.1

real-numbered values. There is a clear need to develop better analytics for neural machine translation, as discussed in the next chapter.

16.1 Domain Mismatch

domain mismatch

A known challenge in translation is that in different domains, words have different translations and meaning is expressed in different styles. Hence, a crucial step in developing machine translation systems targeted at a specific use case is domain adaptation (see Chapter 13).

Often, large amounts of training data are available only out of domain, but we still seek robust performance. To test how well neural machine translation and statistical machine translation hold up, we trained five different systems using different corpora obtained from OPUS (Tiedemann, 2012). An additional system was trained on all the training data. Note that these domains are quite distant from each other (Figure 16.1).

While the in-domain neural and statistical machine translation systems are similar (neural machine translation is better for IT and subtitles, statistical machine translation is better for law, medical, and the Koran), the out-of-domain performance for the neural machine translation systems is worse in almost all cases, sometimes dramatically so. For instance the medical system leads to a BLEU score of 3.9 (neural machine translation) versus 10.2 (statistical machine translation) on the law test set.

When translating the sentence *Schaue um dich herum* (reference: *Look around you*) from the subtitles corpus, we see mostly nonsensical and completely unrelated output from the neural machine translation systems (Figure 16.2). For instance, the translation from the IT system is *Switches to paused*.

Source	Schaue um dich herum.
Reference	Look around you.
All	NMT: Look around you.
	SMT: Look around you.
Law	NMT: Sughum gravecorn.
	SMT: In order to implement dich Schaue .
Medical	NMT: EMEA / MB / 049 / 01-EN-Final Work progamme for 2002
	SMT: Schaue by dich around .
IT	NMT: Switches to paused.
	SMT: To Schaue by itself . \t \t
Koran	NMT: Take heed of your own souls.
	SMT: And you see.
Subtitles	NMT: Look around you.
	SMT: Look around you .

Figure 16.2 Examples for the translation of a sentence from the subtitles corpus, when translated with systems trained on different corpora. Performance out of domain is dramatically worse for neural machine translation.

Note that the output of the neural machine translation system is typically quite fluent (e.g., *Take heed of your own souls.*) but completely unrelated to the input, while the statistical machine translation output betrays its difficulties with coping with the out-of-domain input by leaving some words untranslated (e.g., *Schaue by dich around.*). This is of particular concern when MT is used for information gisting; the user will be mislead by hallucinated content in the neural machine translation output.

16.2 Amount of Training Data

amount of training data

A well-known property of statistical systems is that increasing amounts of training data lead to better results. In statistical machine translation systems, doubling the amount of training data typically gives a fixed increase in BLEU scores. This holds true for both parallel and monolingual data.

How do the data needs of statistical machine translation and neural machine translation compare? Neural machine translation promises both to generalize better (exploiting word similarity in embeddings) and to condition on larger context (entire input and all prior output words).

We built English–Spanish systems using about 400 million English words paired with Spanish. To obtain a learning curve, we used $\frac{1}{1024}$, $\frac{1}{512}$, ..., $\frac{1}{2}$, and all of the data. For statistical machine translation, the language model was trained on the Spanish part of each subset, respectively. In addition to a neural and statistical machine translation system trained on each subset, we also used all additionally provided monolingual data for a big language model in contrastive statistical machine translation systems (Figure 16.3).

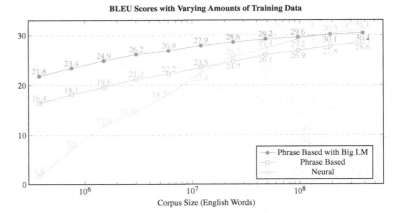

Figure 16.3 BLEU scores for English–Spanish systems trained on 0.4 million to 385.7 million words of parallel data. Quality for neural machine translation starts much lower, outperforms statistical machine translation at about 15 million words, and even beats a statistical machine translation system with a big 2-billion-word in-domain language model (LM) under high-resource conditions.

Neural machine translation exhibits a much steeper learning curve, starting with abysmal results (BLEU score of 1.6 versus 16.4 for $\frac{1}{1024}$ of the data), outperforming statistical machine translation 25.7 versus 24.7 with $\frac{1}{16}$ of the data (24.1 million words), and even beating the statistical machine translation system with a big language model with the full data set (31.1 for neural machine translation, 28.4 for statistical machine translation, 30.4 for statistical with a big language model).

The contrast between the neural and statistical machine translation learning curves is quite striking. While neural machine translation is able to exploit increasing amounts of training data more effectively, it is unable to get off the ground with training corpus sizes of a few million words or less.

To visualize this, see Figure 16.4. With $\frac{1}{1024}$ of the training data, the output is completely unrelated to the input, some key words are properly translated with $\frac{1}{512}$ and $\frac{1}{256}$ of the data (*estrategia* for *strategy*, *elección* or *elecciones* for *election*), and starting with $\frac{1}{64}$ the translations become respectable.

16.3 Rare Words

rare word

Several researcher have reported that neural machine translation models perform particularly poorly on rare words (Luong et al., 2015c; Sennrich et al., 2016e; Arthur et al., 2016b). We examine this claim by comparing

Ratio	Words	Source: *A Republican strategy to counter the reelection of Obama*
		Reference: *Una estrategia republicana para obstaculizar la reelección de Obama*
$\frac{1}{1024}$	0.4 million	*Un órgano de coordinación para el anuncio de libre determinación*
$\frac{1}{512}$	0.8 million	*Lista de una estrategia para luchar contra la elección de hojas de Ohio*
$\frac{1}{256}$	1.5 million	*Explosión realiza una estrategia divisiva de luchar contra las elecciones de autor*
$\frac{1}{128}$	3.0 million	*Una estrategia republicana para la eliminación de la reelección de Obama*
$\frac{1}{64}$	6.0 million	*Estrategia siria para contrarrestar la reelección del Obama .*
$\frac{1}{32}+$	12.0 million	*Una estrategia republicana para contrarrestar la reelección de Obama*

Figure 16.4 Translations of the first sentence of the test set using neural machine translation system trained on varying amounts of training data. Under low resource conditions, neural machine translation produces fluent output unrelated to the input.

performance on rare word translation between NMT and SMT systems of similar quality for German–English and find that NMT systems actually outperform SMT systems on translation of very infrequent words. However, both NMT and SMT systems continue to have difficulty translating some infrequent words, particularly those belonging to highly inflected categories.

Both models have case-sensitive BLEU scores of 34.5 on the WMT 2016 news test set. We pursue the following approach for examining the effect of source word frequency on translation accuracy.

- First, we automatically align the source sentence and the machine translation output.
- Each source word is either unaligned ("dropped") or aligned to one or more target language words.
- For each target word to which the source word is aligned, we check if that target word appears in the reference translation.

  - If the target word appears the same number of times in the MT output as in the reference, we award that alignment a score of 1.
  - If the target word appears more times in the MT output than in the reference, we award a fractional credit.
  - If the target word does not appear in the reference, we award 0 credit.

- We then average these scores over the full set of target words aligned to the given source word to compute the precision for that source word. Source words can then be binned by frequency and average translation precisions can be computed.

The overall average precision is quite similar between the NMT and SMT systems, with the SMT system scoring 70.1% overall and the NMT

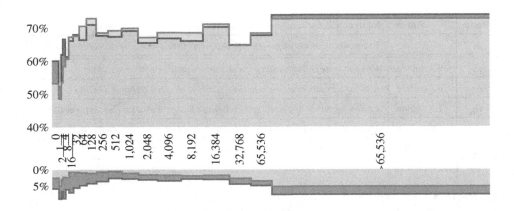

Figure 16.5 Precision of translation and deletion rates by source words type. SMT (light blue) and NMT (dark green). The horizontal axis represents the corpus frequency of the source types, with the axis labels showing the upper end of the bin. Bin width is proportional to the number of word types in that frequency range. The upper part of the graph shows the precision averaged across all word types in the bin. The lower part shows the proportion of source tokens in the bin that were deleted.

system scoring 70.3%. This reflects the similar overall quality of the MT systems. Figure 16.5 gives a detailed breakdown.

The neural machine translation system has an overall higher proportion of deleted words. An interesting observation is what happens with unknown words (words that were never observed in the training corpus). The SMT system translates these correctly 53.2% of the time, while the NMT system translates them correctly 60.1% of the time.

Both SMT and NMT systems actually have their worst performance on words that were observed a single time in the training corpus, dropping to 48.6% and 52.2%, respectively; even worse than for unobserved words. The most common unknown word types are named entities and nouns. The named entities can often be passed through unchanged (for example, the surname *Elabdellaoui* is broken into *E@ @ lab@ @ d@ @ ell@ @ a@ @ oui* by byte-pair encoding and is correctly passed through unchanged by both the NMT and SMT systems). Unsurprisingly, there are many numbers that were unobserved in the training data; these tend to be translated correctly (with occasional errors due to formatting of commas and periods, resolvable by postprocessing).

While there remains room for improvement, NMT systems (at least those using byte-pair encoding) perform better on very low frequency words then SMT systems do. Byte-pair encoding is sometimes sufficient (much like stemming or compound splitting) to allow the successful translation of rare words even though it does not necessarily split words at

Table 16.1 Adding noisy web-crawled data (raw data from `paracrawl.eu`) to a WMT 2017 German–English statistical system obtains small gains (+1.2 BLEU). A neural system falls apart (−9.9 BLEU).

	NMT	SMT
WMT17	27.2	24.0
+ noisy corpus	17.3 (−9.9)	25.2 (+1.2)

morphological boundaries. As with the fluent-sounding but semantically inappropriate examples from domain mismatch, NMT may sometimes fail similarly when it encounters unknown words even in-domain.

16.4 Noisy Data

Another challenge to neural machine translation are noisy parallel data. **noisy data** As a motivating example, consider the numbers in Table 16.1. Here, we add an equally sized noisy web-crawled corpus to high-quality training data. This addition leads to a 1.2 BLEU point increase for the statistical machine translation system, but degrades the neural machine translation system by 9.9 BLEU.

The maxim *more data are better* that holds true for statistical machine translation seems to come with some caveats for neural machine translation. The added data cannot be too noisy. But what kind of noise harms neural machine translation models?

In this chapter, I explore several types of noise and assess the impact by adding synthetic noise to an existing parallel corpus. We find that for almost all types of noise, neural machine translation systems are harmed more than statistical machine translation systems. We discovered that one type of noise, copied source language segments, has a catastrophic impact on neural machine translation quality, leading it to learn a copying behavior that it then exceedingly applies.

16.4.1 Real-World Noise

What types of noise are prevalent in crawled web data? We manually **real-world noise** examined 200 sentence pairs of the Paracrawl corpus and classified them into several error categories. Obviously, the results of such a study depend very much on how crawling and extraction is executed, but the results (Table 16.2) give some indication of what noise to expect.

We classified any pairs of German and English sentences that are not translations of each other as misaligned sentences. These may be caused by any problem in alignment processes (at the document level

Table 16.2 Noise in the raw Paracrawl corpus.

Type of Noise	Count (%)
Okay	23
Misaligned sentences	41
One or both sentences in a third language	3
Both sentences in English	10
Both sentences in German	10
Untranslated sentences	4
Short segments ($\leq$2 tokens)	1
Short segments (3–5 tokens)	5
Nonlinguistic characters	2

or the sentence level) or by forcing the alignment of content that is not in fact parallel. Such misaligned sentences are the biggest source of error (41%).

There are three types of wrong language content (totaling 23%): one or both sentences may be in a language different from German and English (3%), both sentences may be German (10%), or both may be English (10%).

Of the sentence pairs, 4% are untranslated, i.e., source and target are identical. Another 2% consists of random byte sequences, only HTML markup, or Javascript. A number of sentence pairs have very short German or English sentences, containing at most 2 tokens (1%) or 5 tokens (5%).

Since it is a very subjective value judgment of what constitutes disfluent language, we do not classify these as errors. However, consider the following sentence pairs that we did count as okay, although they contain mostly untranslated names and numbers.

German: *Anonym 2 24.03.2010 um 20:55 314 Kommentare*
English: *Anonymous 2 2010-03-24 at 20:55 314 Comments*

German: *< < erste < zurück Seite 3 mehr > letzte > >*
English: *< < first < prev. page 3 next > last > >*

At first sight, some types of noise seem to be easier to automatically identify than others. However, consider, for instance, content in a wrong language. While there are established methods for language identification (typically based on character *n*-grams), these do not work well on a sentence-level basis, especially for short sentences. Or, take the apparently obvious problem of untranslated sentences. If they are completely identical, that is easy to spot. However, there are many degrees of near-identical content of unclear utility.

16.4.2 Synthetic Noise

Since it is too expensive to annotate large corpora by noise type, we instead simulate them. By creating artificial noisy data, we are able to study their impact when added to the training data.

synthetic noise

Misaligned Sentences

As has been shown, a common source of noise in parallel corpora is faulty document or sentence alignment. This results in sentences that are not matched to their translation. Such noise is rare in corpora such as Europarl where strong clues about debate topics and speaker turns reduce the alignment task to the scope of paragraph pairs, but more common in the alignment of less structured websites. We artificially create misaligned sentence data by randomly shuffling the order of sentences on one side of the original clean parallel training corpus.

Misordered Words

Language may be disfluent in many ways. This may be the product of machine translation, poor human translation, or heavily specialized language use, such as bullet points in product descriptions (recall also the earlier examples). We consider one extreme case of disfluent language: sentences from the original corpus where the words are reordered randomly. We do this on the source or target side.

Wrong Language

A parallel corpus may be polluted by text in a third language, say French in a German–English corpus. This may occur on the source or target side of the parallel corpus. To simulate this, we add French–English (bad source) or German–French (bad target) data to a German–English corpus.

Untranslated Sentences

Especially in parallel corpora crawled from the web, there are often sentences that are untranslated from the source in the target. Examples are navigational elements or copyright notices in the footer. Purportedly multilingual websites may be only partially translated, while some original text is copied. Again, this may show up on the source or the target side. We take sentences from either the source or target side of the original parallel corpus and simply copy them to the other side.

Short Segments

Sometimes additional data come in the form of bilingual dictionaries. Can we simply add them as additional sentence pairs, even if they consist of single words or short phrases? We simulate these kind of data by subsubsampling a parallel corpus to include only sentences of maximum length 2 or 5.

16.4.3 Impact on Translation Quality

noise impac

The study used state-of-the-art statistical and neural machine translation systems. We translate from German to English. For MISALIGNEDSENTENCE and MISORDEREDWORD noise, we use the clean corpus and perturb the data.

We sample the noisy corpus in an amount equal to 5%, 10%, 20%, 50%, and 100% of the clean corpus. This reflects the realistic situation where there is a clean corpus, and one would like to add additional data that have the potential to be noisy. For each experiment, we use the target side of the parallel corpus to train the SMT language model, including the noisy text.

Table 16.3 shows the effect of adding each type of noise to the clean corpus. For some types of noise NMT is harmed more than SMT: MISALIGNED SENTENCES, MISORDERED WORDS (source), WRONG LANGUAGE (target). The noise types SHORT SEGMENTS, UNTRANSLATED SOURCE SENTENCES and WRONG SOURCE LANGUAGE have little impact on either. MISORDERED TARGET WORDS decreases BLEU scores for both SMT and NMT by just over 1 point when adding 100% noise.

The most dramatic difference is UNTRANSLATED TARGET SENTENCE noise. When added at 5% of the original data, it degrades NMT performance by 9.6 BLEU, from 27.2 to 17.6. Adding this noise at 100% of the original data degrades performance by 24.0 BLEU, dropping the score from 27.2 to 3.2. In contrast, the SMT system drops only 2.9 BLEU, from 24.0 to 21.1.

Since the noise type when the target side is a copy of the source has such a big impact, we examine the system output in more detail. We report the percent of sentences in the evaluation set that are identical to the source for the UNTRANSLATED TARGET SENTENCE and RAW CRAWL data in Figure 16.6 (solid bars). The SMT systems output 0 or 1 sentences that are exact copies. However, with just 20% of the UNTRANSLATED TARGET SENTENCE noise, 60% of the NMT output sentences are identical to the source.

This suggests that the NMT systems learn to copy, which may be useful for named entities. However, with even a small amount of these data, it is doing far more harm than good.

Figure 16.6 shows the percent of sentences that have a worse TER score against the reference than against the source (shaded bars). This means that it would take fewer edits to transform the sentence into the

Table 16.3 Results from adding different amounts of noise (ratio of original clean corpus) for various types of noise in German–English Translation. Generally neural machine translation (left green bars) is harmed more than statistical machine translation (right blue bars). The worst type of noise are segments in the source language copied untranslated into the target.

	5%	10%	20%	50%	100%
MISALIGNED SENTENCES	26.5 24.0 -0.7 -0.0	26.5 24.0 -0.7 -0.0	26.3 23.9 -0.9 -0.1	26.1 23.9 -1.1 -0.1	25.3 23.4 -1.9 -0.6
MISORDERED WORDS (SOURCE)	26.9 24.0 -0.3 -0.0	26.6 23.6 -0.6 -0.4	26.4 23.9 -0.8 -0.1	26.6 23.6 -0.6 -0.4	25.5 23.7 -1.7 -0.3
MISORDERED WORDS (TARGET)	27.0 24.0 -0.2 -0.0	26.8 24.0 -0.4 -0.0	26.4 23.4 -0.8 -0.6	26.7 23.2 -0.5 -0.8	26.1 22.9 -1.1 -1.1
WRONG LANGUAGE (FRENCH SOURCE)	26.9 24.0 -0.3 -0.0	26.8 23.9 -0.4 -0.1	26.8 23.9 -0.4 -0.1	26.8 23.9 -0.4 -0.1	26.8 23.8 -0.4 -0.2
WRONG LANGUAGE (FRENCH TARGET)	26.7 24.0 -0.5 -0.0	26.6 23.9 -0.6 -0.1	26.7 23.8 -0.5 -0.2	26.2 23.5 -1.0 -0.5	25.0 23.4 -2.2 -0.6
UNTRANSLATED (ENGLISH SOURCE)	27.2 23.9 -0.0 -0.1	27.0 23.9 -0.2 -0.1	26.7 23.6 -0.5 -0.4	26.8 23.7 -0.4 -0.3	26.9 23.5 -0.3 -0.5
UNTRANSLATED (GERMAN TARGET)	17.6 23.8 -0.2 -9.8	11.2 23.9 -0.1 -16.0	5.6 23.8 -0.2 -21.6	3.2 23.4 -0.6 -24.0	3.2 21.1 -2.9 -24.0
SHORT SEGMENTS (max 2)	27.1 24.1 -0.1 +0.1	26.5 23.9 -0.7 -0.1	26.7 23.8 -0.5 -0.2		
SHORT SEGMENTS (max 5)	27.8 24.2 +0.6 +0.2	27.6 24.5 +0.4 +0.5	28.0 24.5 +0.8 +0.5	26.6 24.2 -0.6 +0.2	
RAW CRAWL DATA	27.4 24.2 +0.2 +0.2	26.6 24.2 -0.6 +0.2	24.7 24.4 +0.4 -2.5	20.9 24.8 +0.8 -6.3	17.3 25.2 +1.2 -9.9

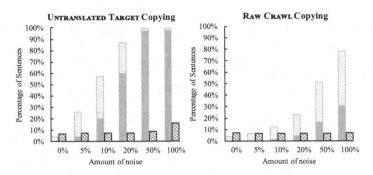

Figure 16.6 Copied sentences in the UNTRANSLATED (TARGET) (left) and
RAW CRAWL (right) experiments. NMT is the left green bars, SMT is the right
blue bars. Sentences that are exact matches to the source are the solid bars,
sentences that are more similar to the source than the target are the shaded bars.

source than it would to transform it into the target. When just 10%
UNTRANSLATED TARGET SENTENCE data are added, 57% of the sentences
are more similar to the source than to the reference, indicating partial
copying.

This suggests that the NMT system is overfitting the copied portion
of the training corpus.

beam search

16.5 Beam Search

The task of decoding is to find the full-sentence translation with the highest probability. Heuristic search techniques explore the most promising
subset of the space of possible translations. A common feature of these
search techniques is a beam size parameter that limits the number of
partial translations maintained per input word.

In statistical machine translation, there is typically a straightforward
relationship between this beam size parameter and the model score of
resulting translations and also their quality score (e.g., BLEU). While
there are diminishing returns for increasing the beam parameter, typically improvements in these scores can be expected with larger beams.

In neural translation models decoding, we maintain the best scoring
words in a list of partial translations when predicting each output word.
We record with each partial translation the word translation probabilities (obtained from the softmax), extend each partial translation with
subsequent word predictions, and accumulate these scores. Since the
number of partial translation explodes exponentially with each new
output word, we prune them down to a beam of highest scoring partial
translations.

As in traditional statistical machine translation decoding, increasing
the beam size allows us to explore a larger set of the space of possible
translation and hence find translations with better model scores.

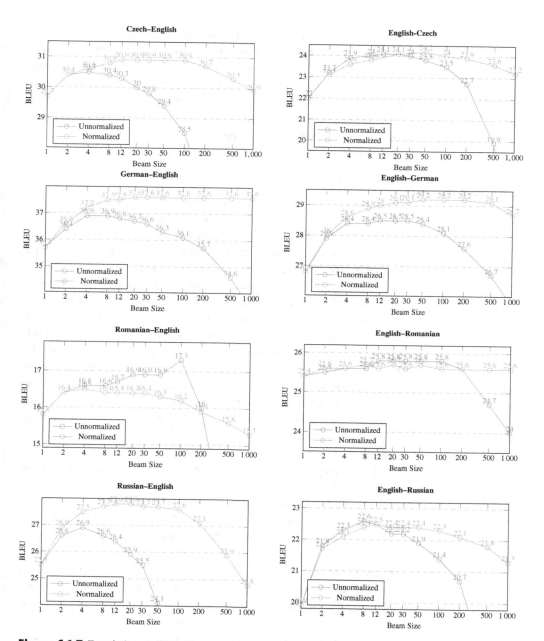

Figure 16.7 Translation quality with varying beam sizes. For large beams, quality decreases, especially when not normalizing scores by sentence length.

However, as Figure 16.7 illustrates, increasing the beam size does not consistently improve translation quality. In fact, in almost all cases, worse translations are found beyond an optimal beam size setting (we are using again Edinburgh's WMT 2016 systems). The optimal beam size varies from 4 (e.g., Czech–English) to around 30 (English–Romanian).

Normalizing sentence-level model scores by length of the output alleviates the problem somewhat and leads to better optimal quality in most cases (5 of the 8 language pairs investigated). Optimal beam sizes are in the range of 30–50 in almost all cases, but quality still drops with larger beams. The main cause of deteriorating quality is shorter translations under wider beams. The search often terminates early after improbable word choices that appear to confuse the decoder.

16.6 Word Alignment

word alignment

The key contribution of the attention model in neural machine translation (Bahdanau et al., 2015) was the imposition of an alignment of the output words to the input words. This takes the shape of a probability distribution over the input words, which is used to weigh them in a bag-of-words representation of the input sentence.

Arguably, this attention model does not functionally play the role of a word alignment between the source in the target, at least not in the same way as its analog in statistical machine translation. While in both cases, alignment is a latent variable that is used to obtain probability distributions over words or phrases, arguably the attention model has a broader role. For instance, when translating a verb, attention may also be paid to its subject and object since these may disambiguate it. To further complicate matters, the word representations are products of bidirectional gated recurrent neural networks that have the effect that each word representation is informed by the entire sentence context.

But an alignment mechanism between source and target words has many useful applications. For instance, prior work used the alignments provided by the attention model to interpolate word translation decisions with traditional probabilistic dictionaries (Arthur et al., 2016a), for the introduction of coverage and fertility models (Tu et al., 2016b), etc.

But is the attention model in fact the proper means? To examine this, we compare the soft alignment matrix (the sequence of attention vectors) with word alignments obtained by traditional word alignment methods. We use incremental fast align (Dyer et al., 2013) to align the input and output of the neural machine system.

In Figure 16.8a, we compare the word attention states (green boxes) with the word alignments obtained with fast align (blue outlines). For most words, these match up pretty well. Both attention states and fast-align alignment points are a bit fuzzy around the function words *have-been/sind*.

However, the attention model may settle on alignments that do not correspond with our intuition or alignment points obtained with fast

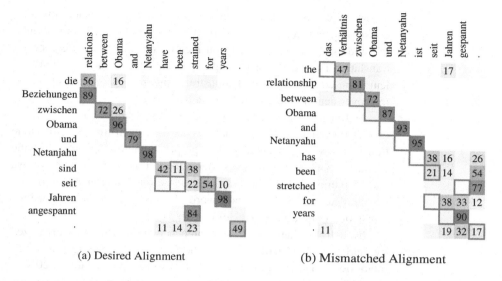

Figure 16.8 Word alignment for English–German, comparing the attention model states (green boxes with probability in percent if over 10) with alignments obtained from fast-align (blue outlines).

align. Figure 16.8b shows the reverse language direction, German–English. All the alignment points appear to be off by one position. We are not aware of any intuitive explanation for this divergent behavior—the translation quality is high for both systems.

16.7 Further Readings

Other studies have looked at the comparable performance of neural and statistical machine translation systems. Bentivogli et al. (2016) considered different linguistic categories for English–German and Toral and Sánchez-Cartagena (2017) compared different broad aspects such as fluency and reordering for nine language directions.

Noisy Data

noise

There is a robust body of work on filtering out noise in parallel data. For example, Taghipour et al. (2011) use an outlier detection algorithm to filter a parallel corpus; Xu and Koehn (2017) generate synthetic noisy data (inadequate and nonfluent translations) and use these data to train a classifier to identify good sentence pairs from a noisy corpus; and Cui et al. (2013) use a graph-based random walk algorithm and extract phrase pair scores to weight the phrase translation probabilities to bias toward more trustworthy ones.

Most of this work was done in the context of statistical machine translation, but more recent work (Carpuat et al., 2017) targets neural models. That work focuses on identifying semantic differences in translation pairs using cross-lingual textual entailment and additional length-based features, and demonstrates that removing such sentences improves neural machine translation performance.

As Rarrick et al. (2011) point out, one problem of parallel corpora extracted from the web is translations that have been created by machine translation. Venugopal et al. (2011) propose a method to watermark the output of machine translation systems to aid this distinction. Antonova and Misyurev (2011) report that rule-based machine translation output can be detected due to certain word choices, and statistical machine translation output due to lack of reordering.

In 2016, a shared task on sentence pair filtering was organized by Barbu et al. (2016), albeit in the context of cleaning translation memories, which tend to be cleaner than web-crawled data. In 2018, a shared task explored filtering techniques for neural machine translation (Koehn et al., 2018).

Belinkov and Bisk (2017) investigate noise in neural machine translation, but they focus on creating systems that can *translate* the kinds of orthographic errors (typos, misspellings, etc.) that humans can comprehend. In contrast, we address noisy *training* data and focus on types of noise occurring in web-crawled corpora.

There is a rich literature on data selection that aims at subsampling parallel data relevant for a task-specific machine translation system (Axelrod et al., 2011). Van der Wees et al. (2017) find that the existing data selection methods developed for statistical machine translation are less effective for neural machine translation. This is different from our goals of handling noise since those methods tend to discard perfectly fine sentence pairs (say, about cooking recipes) that are just not relevant for the targeted domain (say, software manuals). Our work is focused on noise that is harmful for all domains.

Since we begin with a clean parallel corpus and add potentially noisy data to it, this work can be seen as a type of data augmentation. Sennrich et al. (2016c) incorporate monolingual corpora into NMT by first translating it using an NMT system trained in the opposite direction. While such a corpus has the potential to be noisy, the method is very effective. Currey et al. (2017) create additional parallel corpora by copying monolingual corpora in the target language into the source, and find it improves over back translation for some language pairs. Fadaee et al. (2017) improve NMT performance in low-resource settings by altering existing sentences to create training data that include rare words in different contexts.

Copy Noise

Other work has also considered copying in NMT. Currey et al. (2017) add copied data and back-translated data to a clean parallel corpus. They report improvements on EN ↔ RO when adding as much back-translated and copied data as they have parallel (1:1:1 ratio). For EN↔TR and EN↔DE, they add twice as much back translated and copied data as parallel data (1:2:2 ratio), and report improvements on EN↔TR but not on EN↔DE. However, their EN↔DE systems trained with the copied corpus did not perform worse than baseline systems. Ott et al. (2018b) found that while copied training sentences represent less than 2.0% of their training data (WMT 14 EN↔DE and EN↔FR), copies are overrepresented in the output of beam search. Using a subset of training data from WMT 17, they replace a subset of the true translations with a copy of the input. They analyze varying amounts of copied noise and a variety of beam sizes. Larger beams are more affected by this kind of noise; however, for all beam sizes performance degrades completely with 50% copied sentences.

Chapter 17
Analysis and Visualization

Deep neural networks have been proven to be a powerful machine learning approach for many tasks, such as machine translation. Multiple layers of processing allow the automatic discovery of relevant features to make the right predictions. However, while the networks discover such features, it is not clear what they are. The models hide them in a sea of numbers that are have no obvious meaning to the human eye.

This is all fine, to some degree, when things go right and we benefit from high translation quality. But it does give little guidance when the quality is not good enough. There are no obvious knobs to turn and kinks to straighten.

Moreover, it is somewhat unsatisfying to have built a machine that is pretty good at the given task of translation but that does not provide any insight into the problem of translation, e.g., what linguistic properties are relevant, what human and machine processes are at work when meaning is expressed in different languages, and so on.

Hence, the analysis of the behavior of neural networks and the visualization and inspection of their internal structure is a key challenge and a very active field of research. New ways have been explored to look at the output and inner workings of these models that allow us to gain some insight into how neural machine translation actually works.

17.1 Error Analysis

Let us start with a close look at the output of neural machine translation models. As a engineering strategy, the field has done very well by measuring the quality of machine translation systems with automatic metrics such as the BLEU score. An improved BLEU score is a pretty good indicator that we indeed have better machine translation.

But a single number is quite reductive. What kind of translation mistakes does the model make? What kind of problems are too difficult to overcome? A closer look at the output would be helpful.

17.1.1 Typical Errors of Neural Machine Translation

Let us first walk through an example sentence and how it is translated by different neural machine translation systems. The following sentence is taken from the WMT 2016 news test set, to be translated from German to English:

Bei der Begegnung soll es aber auch um den Konflikt mit den Palästinensern und die diskutierte Zwei-Staaten-Lösung gehen.

Its human reference translation is:

The meeting was also planned to cover the conflict with the Palestinians and the disputed two-state solution.

In early stages of training, some basic facts about language are discovered by the neural machine translation model. These are core properties such as the length of the output sentence relative to the input, or what the most frequent output words are. The very early output of the model may be just repetitions of the word *the*.

Here is translation after 10,000 training steps in a training run:

However, the government has been able to have been able to have been able to have been able to have been able to be the same.

This output has little to do with the input, maybe just that it has about the right length. It seems to settle on a loop of repeating the phrase *have been able to*, a common phrase in English. This type of output is also not unusual for a fully trained neural machine translation model under low resource conditions or when tested out of domain. It ignores the input and settles on output that is has observed frequently in training. This problem of **hallucinated output** is a severe problem for neural machine translation. The habit to sometimes produce fluent but completely wrong output is very problematic for applications such as information retrieval and for document triage to see what a foreign text is generally about.

When training progresses under ideal conditions (large amounts of in-domain data), translation quality improves. Here is a snapshot of a training run after 20,000 training steps:

But the meeting is also to go to the conflict with the Palestinians and to go two states solution.

This does contain some of the right content, such as *the meeting, the Palestinians*, and *two states solution* but does not tie these elements together into a correct or even just coherent sentence.

Here now the output of the best system that participated in the WMT 2016 evaluation campaign, from the University of Edinburgh:

> At the meeting, however, it is also a question of the conflict with the Palestinians and the two-state solution that is being discussed.

The translation has the faulty wording *it is also a question*, which is clumsy in English and also wrong. It is understandable that the neural translation model is struggling here. The German input has the discontinuous construction *soll es ... um ... gehen*. A literal gloss of this is roughly *it should go about*, which the human translator rendered as *was ... planned to cover*. This is a tough challenge for machine translation: common words with many meanings (even the main verb *gehen*, in English *go*), spread out throughout the sentence that form a semantic unit.

However, it is apparently not an unsurmountable problem. Here is the output of a more recent system, trained with the same data:

> However, the meeting should also focus on the conflict with the Palestinians and the discussed two-state solution.

This is a fine translation, even if it is different from the human reference translation.

17.1.2 Linguistic Error Categories

It is very educating to peruse the output of neural machine translation models and to compare it to the input and human reference translations. What kind of errors occur? What linguistic challenges are tricky? Meaning is often encoded in phrasal constructions, and translating them may require a drastic change of sentence structure. How are ambiguous words handled? How about information that is implicit in the input language but has to be expressed explicitly in the output language? **linguistic error categories**

While an unstructured examination of translation output is informative, it is not clear how to summarize any findings to communicate to others. One should also be careful to not extrapolate too much from what has been seen. A translation problem that occurs frequently in the first 100 sentences may show up only rarely later.

There is a clear need for a systematic approach for error analysis that informs decisions on the architecture and training of machine translation models. Typically, this is done by defining a set of linguistically informed error categories and counting how many errors of each type occur.

We may broadly distinguish between word choice errors, word order errors, and disfluencies such as grammatical agreement errors. We may want to distinguish between those occurring with function words and those with content words like nouns, verbs, or adjectives.

A good strategy is to first edit the output of the machine translation system into an acceptable translation.

Consider the following wrong translation that should have the more likely meaning of the dog being the aggressor:

The man bit the dog.

A human evaluator would now first correct this translation with the intended meaning:

The dog bit the man.

Then, the evaluator can look at this correction and label this as a reordering error—all the words are still the same, just the two noun phrases have switched position.

But there are also other ways to fix the translation, for instance by changing the verb from active to passive voice:

The man was bitten by the dog.

Given this correction, the translation error would be labeled as a verb morphology error (*bitten* instead of *bit*), maybe additionally counting the insertion of function words *was* and *by*.

So, there will be always disagreement between annotators on how to correct translations and which error types to assign. Even with strong guidance and instruction on making only minimum corrections, evaluators will vary a lot in their assessments.

To give a real-word example, consider the translation from the previous section:

At the meeting, however, it is also a question of the conflict with the Palestinians and the two-state solution that is being discussed.

We may want to correct this translation into:

~~At~~ *the meeting, however,* **should** *also* **address the** *question of the conflict with the Palestinians and the two-state solution that is being discussed.*

While trying to stick to minimal edits, we did make several changes:

- removing the leading *at* to turn this prepositional phrase into the subject noun phrase,
- changing the verb construction *it is* to *should address*, and
- changing the indefinite article *a* into the definite article *the*.

All these are somewhat related. The change of the verb construction forced change of the syntactic role of the leading prepositional phrase. Arguable the change from *a question* to *the question* is also a consequence of the choice of verb and its argument structure. A human posteditor may also decide the drop *a question* completely since it is not required to bring the meaning of the sentence across.

17.1.3 Example of a Real-World Study

Despite concerns about variance of human annotations of translation errors, these do provide useful indications what the most pressing problems in the output of machine translation systems are.

Bentivogli et al. (2018) carried out a study on several neural machine translation systems for English–French and English–German. Their evaluation protocol roughly matched what I described earlier. It involved human posteditors, in this case professional translators, who corrected the output of machine translation systems. The initial goal of their work was to assess the quality of the different systems based on how many words needed to be edited (human translation edit rate), as part of the IWSLT evaluation campaign on the machine translation of TED talks.

Given the machine translation output and the human corrections, each edit was then automatically classified, aided by a part-of-speech tagger and a morphological analyzer. The study's broad error categories were

- Lexical errors: Words that were changed, added or deleted.
- Morphological errors: Words that were changed in their morphological inflection.
- Reordering errors: Words that were moved with respect to neighboring words.

For each of the error categories, a more detailed breakdown was done based on the part of speech of the words involved. Table 17.1 shows an adapted summary of their findings. The predominant error category is lexical errors (13.8 per 100 words for English–French, 17.1 per 100 words for English–German). Reordering errors are rare, although twice as frequent for English–German (2.0 per 100 words) than for English–French (1.0 per 100 words), which is not surprising given that German word order differs more strongly from English than French order does. There are also relatively few morphological errors, although both French and German are only moderately morphologically rich languages.

Broken down by part of speech, there is a relatively high number of lexical translation errors involving verbs (2.9 for English–French and 3.5 for English–German), especially considering that these are less frequent

Table 17.1 Errors per 100 words for output from neural machine translation (neural systems translating TED talks as part of the IWSLT evaluation campaign). Adapted from Bentivogli et al. (2018).

Category	English–French	English–German
Lexical	13.8	17.1
... adjective	0.8	0.8
... adverb	0.8	1.5
... article	1.0	1.5
... named entity	0.2	0.3
... noun	2.1	3.1
... preposition	2.2	1.6
... pronoun	2.3	1.8
... verb	2.9	3.5
... other	1.5	3.0
Morphology only	2.3	2.4
Reordering only	1.0	2.2
Morphology and reordering	0.3	0.6

in text than nouns (2.1 errors per 100 words for English–French, 3.1 errors per 100 words for English–German). But also prepositions and pronouns are among the main sources of error. These numbers suggest that lexical choice, caused by ambiguous word senses, as well as complex semantic relationships, as expressed in prepositions and pronouns, are still a major concern for machine translation today.

17.1.4 Targeted Test Sets

targeted test set

Instead of inspecting translation errors in view of suspected linguistic error categories, researchers also looked into directly assessing how well machine translation systems cope with presumed linguistic challenges. If, for instance, we assume that long-distance morphological agreement is a concern in the generation of the output sentence, then why not challenge set   construct a number of test sentences where this problem shows up?

Challenge Set – Isabelle et al. (2017) propose constructing a challenge set for machine translation in which a variety of hard problems show up, and then evaluating the output of the machine translation systems in terms of how well they addressed the specific challenge.

Figure 17.1 provides an example. French requires subject–verb agreement for count, meaning that singular and plural subjects require different verb inflection—just as English in the present tense (say, *he eats* versus *they eat*). Language generation systems deal with this rather

Source	*The repeated calls from his mother* **should** *have alerted us.*
Reference	*Les appels répétés de sa mère* **auraient** *dû nous alerter.*
System	*Les appels répétés de sa mère* **devraient** *nous avoir alertes.*
	Is the subject–verb agreement correct (y/n)? **Yes**

Figure 17.1 Challenge set. A difficult translation problem is posed to the machine translation system (long-distance subject–verb agreement in count between the translation of *calls* and *should*), and a human annotator assesses if the translation solved it.

well when subject and verb are right next to each other but it is more difficult if other words intervene.

In Figure 17.1, the subject noun is *calls* and the auxiliary verb is *should*, while the prepositional phrase *from his mother* separates the two. Note why this is a challenge: the English *should* is not inflected for count, it is the same for singular and plural. The noun just in front of the verb, *mother*, is singular while the subject noun is plural. A French translation cannot draw information from the input verb and is also misled by the directly preceding noun.

The French translation in the example is correct, *should* is translated as *devraient* which is the correct plural form. The singular form the verb is *devrait*. So, a human evaluator would look at the translation and mark it as correct.

Isabelle et al. (2017) identify a number of translation problems, such as polarity (retaining negation) or translation of verbs that require switching of subject and object. In their study, a neural machine translation system was able to address 53% of the examples in their test set.

contrastive translation pairs

Contrastive Translation Pairs – The challenge set evaluation protocol outlined here is very labor-intensive. It not only requires a person with linguistic skill to devise categories and example sentences that exhibit them, each time a machine translation system is evaluated this way, an human evaluator has to inspect each translation and judge if the challenge was addressed correctly.

Sennrich (2017) propose an alternative that automates some of this work. It relies on the ability of neural machine translation systems to score any output sequence. If presented with an output sequence that is a correct translation and one that is altered to include a translation mistake, the model should assign the correct translation a higher score.

In his study, similar translation challenges such as one mentioned earlier are presented. Typically, these require a change to only a single word. This is the case for the agreement example that we encountered in Figure 17.1. Here, we would use the given reference translation and then alter it by replacing the word *auraient* with its singular form *aurait*.

- Candidate translation 1: *Les appels répétés de sa mère* **auraient** *dû nous alerter.*
- Candidate translation 2: *Les appels répétés de sa mère* **aurait** *dû nous alerter.*

The neural machine translation system should give the correct candidate translation a higher score.

Such test sets can be automatically constructed by taking a typical test set of input sentences and human reference translation and automatically changing, say, all singular verbs into plural verbs. Depending on the linguistic problem to be addressed, these changes require morphological analyzers and syntactic parsers as well as somewhat complex processing of reference translation to produce the erroneous translation. But then the test sentence pairs can be automatically scored by any neural machine translation model.

Here are some examples for the translation challenges posed by Sennrich (2017):

- Noun phrase agreement: *... these interesting proposals ...* versus *... this interesting proposals ...*
- Subject–verb agreement in subclauses: *... the idea whose time has come ...* versus *... the idea whose time have come ...*
- Separable verb prefix: *... switch the light on ...* versus *... switch the light by ...*
- Preservation of polarity: *... have no idea ...* versus *... have an idea ...*

The study was carried out for English–German where there are more long-distance agreement challenges due to nested construction and the placement of the verb in the sentence. Nevertheless, the neural systems preferred the correct translation 93–98% of the time, with the lowest number for the deletion of negation words.

17.1.5 Synthetic Languages

synthetic language

We may also test the ability of neural machine translation models on more formal grounds. For example, linguistic construction such as long-distance agreement or nested relative clauses require some kind of memory in the state of the decoder. What are the limits to such memory?

One idea is to test this by training the models on synthetic languages. Synthetic languages allow us to focus on some aspect of language without having to deal with all the complex interdependencies of the many types of ambiguity and vagaries of natural language. This has been explored more often for language models but also to test certain syntactic constructions in machine translation.

Consider the example of a language that consists of different kinds of brackets where opening and closing brackets have to match up. Some valid sentences in this language are:

- *({ })*
- *({ } { ( ) })*
- *{ ({ } ({ })) ({ }) }*

When processing such strings with a model trained on randomly generated examples, we can test how often the model makes the right prediction at each time step: closing the right kind of bracket, or opening any new one. We can test how well the model performs, depending on sequence length, nesting depth, amount of training data, etc.

17.2 Visualization

visualization

Error analysis gives us some idea *what* kind of errors a given machine translation system makes, but not much insight into *why* it makes them. For this, we need to look inside the models.

In statistical machine translation, this was a complex but doable undertaking. Why a particular output word was chosen by the system could be tracked down to the model components (probabilities of the language model and the translation tables) and even their roots in the data (e.g., that a particular word choice was observed more frequently as a translation of a given input word).

This is much harder for neural machine translation, since the model parameters have been modified by millions of training updates. But we do not have to give up hope in the face of this sea of numbers unmoored from the original training data. There are increasing efforts to shed light on them from many different angles. Let us first consider ways to visualize the model parameters and node values during inference.

17.2.1 Word Embeddings

word embedding

One visual representation that we have already encountered in this book, is the display of word embeddings, as shown in Figure 17.2. Word embeddings are highly dimensional continuous space representations of words, but in the figure the high number of dimensions (say, 500) is reduced to 2 to be placed on a flat sheet of paper, using **t-distributed stochastic neighbor embedding** (t-SNE).

We can examine word embeddings to check if semantically similar words have indeed similar vector representations. This is the most striking observation at first glance. Words like *growing* and *developing* are next to each other. But also words with opposite meaning, such as *left*

Figure 17.2 Word embeddings projected into two dimensions using (t-SNE). Semantically similar words occur close to each other. (Illustration by James Le, used with permission.)

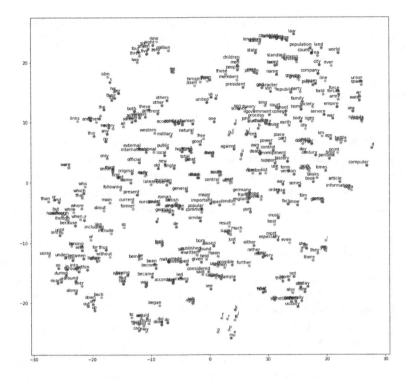

and *right*, *winning* and *losing*, and *reading* and *writing* are close. We can check more closely, if these pairs differ in a consistent way.

Word embeddings have been demonstrated to display consistent patterns for morpho-syntactic relationships between words. For instance, the difference between singular and plural forms are quite similar across words. How well does this hold up for words that have been seen only rarely in the training data? The answer may give us a clue about how often words need to occur in training to learn robust representations for them and hence to be able to translate them well.

17.2.2 Encoder State: Word Sense

word sense

The main role of the encoder is to refine the representation of each word from the fixed embedding parameters in the context of the sentence it occurs in. One of the core problems of translation are words with multiple meanings, such as the word *right* which may have a legal, political, directional sense, among others. Different senses of a word may have different translations. For instance, *right* in sense of *correct* translates as *richtig* in German, while in the sense of the opposite of *left*, it translates as *rechts*.

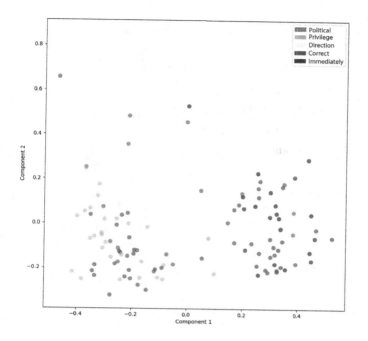

Figure 17.3 Word sense disambiguation in the encoder. Different occurrences of the word *right* receive different encoder representations due to their sentence context. Plotting each encoder state after applying principle component analysis reveals sense clusters.

Just as humans recognize the right sense from context, we expect that neural translation models use processing in encoder layers to yield different representations for the different senses of a word, especially if this implies different translations.

While the word embeddings are parameters of the model that are fixed after training, the encoder states are the values of the nodes in the encoder layers and differ for each input sentence that is being processed. Still, the way we set up encoders, there is still a vector associated with each input word. For deep encoders, there are also multiple layers of processing. We may look at values at any of the layers.

Figure 17.3 plots encoding layer representations of occurrences of the word *right* in sentences that are translated into French. These are originally 500-dimensional vectors that are projected down to two dimensions with principle component analysis (PCA).

Some of the senses appear to form clusters, such as the sense *immediately*, as in *he joined right before me*, while others are less distinct, such as the political sense. This may have something to do with the syntactic roles the word can take. In the sense *immediately*, it is placed almost always in an adverbial position, while in the political sense it can be a noun or an adjective. Note that such syntactic patterns are also visible in the word embedding plot. Verb forms ending in-*ing* are close to each other, suggesting a syntactic cluster more than a semantic one.

Figure 17.4 Visualization of attention weights. The prediction of output words is more strongly influenced by input words that can be considered their literal translation (*Obama/Obama* or *Beziehungen/relations*), while sometimes other words may help with disambiguation (the English preposition *for* has many possible translations, but its word sense in the input sentence is clarified by the preceding word *strained* and the following word *years*, giving it a clear temporal sense which leads to the translation *seit*, instead of the much more frequent translation *für*).

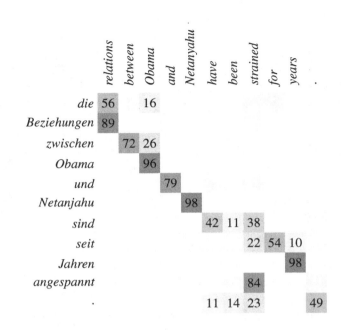

Given the fuzzy definition of semantics, it is not always clear what such plots really reveal. But we can take the same stance as we took for word embedding. Encoder states may help with error analysis. If a word was translated in the wrong sense, was its encoder state more similar to the encoder states with the right sense or the wrong sense? If so, how can the encoder be improved to better disambiguate word senses?

17.2.3 Attention

attention

Attention, the next processing step in neural translation models also has an intuitive explanation: it determines how important an input word's encoder state is for the prediction of an output word. So it plays a similar role as word alignment played in statistical machine translation.

Recall the illustration of attention weights in Figure 17.4 that we already encountered in this book. The immediate impression from such a plot of attention weights is that it links output words to input words that have direct word-to-word correspondences. This is most striking for words that have clear translations, such as the translation of the word *Obama*, where 96% of the attention weight is given to the German occurrence of the same name. But it also shows up with output words that appear to be the result of simple word-by-word translation, such as the word *Beziehungen* which attends 89% its English equivalent *relations*.

But attention does not only appear to establish links between words that have the same meaning. The most suggestive example in the figure is the generation of the word *seit*. This German preposition is linked most strongly to the corresponding English word *for* but only with 54% of the attention weight. The preposition *for*, like most prepositions is highly ambiguous in its translation. In this sentence, it plays a temporal role, which is not its most common meaning. The temporal role is clearly identifiable by the following word *years*, and to some degree by the preceding word *strained*. Both of these words receive significant amounts of attention (10% and 22%, respectively), an indication of their role in disambiguating the preposition *for*.

Recall that we already pointed to attention weights as a diagnostic tools to detect untranslated input words (which are hardly attended to at any decoding state and hence do not result in any output words) and overtranslation (resulting from repeated attention to the same input word). Section 15.2 proposed modifications to the decoding algorithm and the model that kept track of attention values during the output sequence generation.

As a diagnostic tool, attention weights also play a clear role. Why was a particular output word generated? Consulting the attention weights and the input words they point to will be the first step in such an investigation.

17.2.4 Multihead Attention

One advancement of recent models, initially proposed for the Transformer model is multihead attention (recall Section 11.2.2). As a consequence, we do not have a single scalar attention weight anymore but a vector of attention weights.

multihead attention

In their introduction of multihead attention, Vaswani et al. (2017) explore the unique role of each attention head. They focus their inspection to self-attention in the encoder. They observe that there is often consensus among the heads on where to focus attention, as shown in Figure 17.5. In that example, the representation of the verb *making* is refined by paying attention to *more difficult*, the other part of this phrasal verb construction, and six of the eight heads turn their attention there.

Some attention heads seem to play special roles. For instance, when enriching the representation of pronouns, the authors observe that two of the heads pay attention to the relevant antecedent.

Many attention heads play roles that relate to linguistic notions of syntactic phrase constructions and dependencies. Figure 17.6 shows another example of an attention head. Its role seems to refine the representation of words in basic phrases (e.g., noun phrases like *the law* or verb–adjective construction like *be perfect* or *be just*) by paying attention to their semantic heads.

Figure 17.5 Multihead attention 1. In this self-attention example (Vaswani et al., 2017), the meaning of the verb *making* is refined by *more difficult*, as 6 of the 8 attention heads turn their attention there.

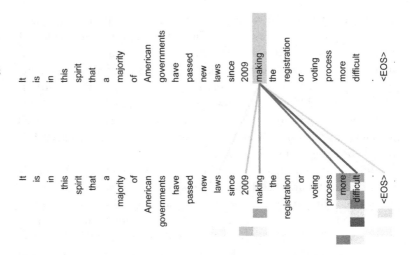

Figure 17.6 Multihead attention 2. Visualization of one of the attention heads (Vaswani et al., 2017). The authors note that, "Many of the attention heads exhibit behavior that seems related to the structure of the sentence."

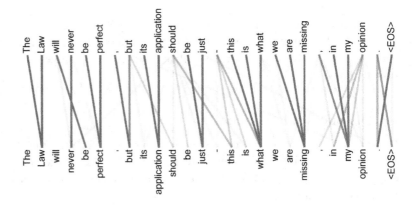

It has been observed that multihead attention in the decoder corresponds less to our notion of word alignment, i.e., averaged attention over the multiple heads does not point to the input word that is a lexical translation of the output word. Since such a property is useful for many applications, modifications have been proposed (Alkhouli et al., 2018; Zenkel et al., 2019).

17.2.5 Memory in Language Model Predictions

memory

Moving on to the decoder in neural machine translations, the first point to stress is that the decoder combines two sources of information: the most recently produced output words and an attention-focused view of the input sentence. The former plays a similar role to that of a language model in traditional statistical machine translation models. It ensures that the generated output sequence is fluent in the language.

Language model decisions are mainly driven by a narrow context. The most recently generated output words are most predictive for the next output word to be predicted. In fact, traditional language models in statistical machine translation cut off the view to previously generated words to a very narrow window. Typically 5-gram language models are used, so only the last four output words are considered. However, certain linguistic problems that are relevant for the generation of fluent output require a broader view. Examples of that are long-distance agreement (e.g., between the subject inflection and the verb conjugation), keeping track of the subcategorization frame of a verb, separable prefixes of verbs (e.g., *switch ... on*), or nested constructions such as relative clauses that create more distance in the main clause.

The promise of recurrent neural networks is that they do not limit the view to a narrow window of a few words but are informed by the entire previously generated output sequence. But how well do they handle the type of long distance that we just listed? We hope that relevant information will be stored and transferred between decoder states, but it is not obvious how to identify that information.

Tran et al. (2016) propose recurrent memory networks for language modeling that work like traditional LSTM language models, with an added attention mechanism over the stored sequence of hidden decoder states. So, besides what is hidden in the LSTM decoder state, there is now an explicit memory mechanism that identifies relevant previously generated output words. This allows the visualization of the attention weights, as shown in Figure 17.7.

The figure shows three examples, where the next word depends on previously generated words that are quite a bit away. The first German example shows a separable prefix verb (*hängt ... ab*, English: *depends*)

Figure 17.7 Recurrent memory networks: Recurrent neural networks for language models (Tran et al., 2016), with an added attention mechanism highlighting what previously generated words are most relevant for the prediction of the next word: (1) separable prefix depends on its verb: *hängt ... ab*, (2) verb depends on object: *schlüsselrolle ... spielen*, (3) object depends on verb: *insignito ... titolo*.

where some attention is also paid to its object (*Annahmen*, English: assumptions). The second German example shows a verb in the final sentence position (*spielen*, English: *play*), where most attention is paid to its object (*Schlüsselrolle*, English: *key role*). The Italian example shows that the object (*titolo*, English: *title*) depends mostly on the verb (*insignito*, English: *awarded*).

Note that this idea of attention over previous words is the self-attention idea discussed in Section 11.2.4. So a similar inspection can be carried out in neural machine translation models that use self-attention.

17.2.6 Decoder States

decoding

As just remarked, the decoder state is a confluence of several flows of information. Hence plots of these states are not obvious to interpret. Strobelt et al. (2019) offer an alternative way to inspect them. They compare a decoder state when translating a test sentence to decoder states seen in training. The most similar states are returned and the corresponding training sentence pair and output word position are displayed to the user.

Recall that during training, inference is carried out in the forward pass of back-propagation. Hence the computations carried out are identical to inference at test time. So a decoder state encountered when translating a test sentence should be similar to a decoder state when processing a similar training example (Figure 17.8).

When translating the following sentence:

die längsten Reisen fangen an, wenn es auf den Straßen dunkel wird,

decoding the generated the sequence

the longest journey begins, when it gets ...

Figure 17.8 Similar decoder states. Strobelt et al. (2019) present a inspection tool that maps a decoder state to the most similar states encountered during training. On the left, a two-dimensional plot of the states is shown; on the right, the target sides of the training examples are shown, highlighting the word being predicted from the state. (Illustration used with permission from Hendrik Strobelt.)

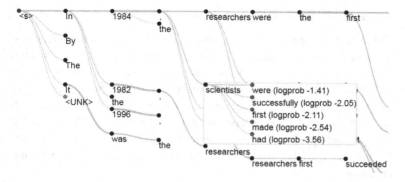

Figure 17.9 An inspection tool for beam search (Lee et al., 2017) shows what promising alternative paths were explored and why they were discarded.

predicts the word *to*, although *dark* would be a better choice (to complete the translation with *... dark on the streets*).

The most similar states encountered during training are shown in the figure. In most cases, the word *dark* is predicted, and sometimes the last generated word is *gets* or a morphological variant. This suggests there are sufficient training examples that support the right decision here and the current decoder state is quite appropriate.

17.2.7 Beam Search

beam search

Finally, we can inspect the behavior of beam search. Fortunately, we are dealing here with few discrete objects, the hypotheses representing partial translations and the connections between them as the result of expansion steps.

Figure 17.9 plots the search graph for a sentence. It takes the form of a tree with paths branching out when hypotheses are expanded and terminating when they fall out of the beam. For each hypothesis we may be also interested what the other, lower scoring options were to expand it. The tool presented by Lee et al. (2017), as shown in the figure, allows for this. The user can drive the decisions of hypothesis expansion to explore the construction of a high-quality but still high-scoring construction. The user may even probe what happens when some computed values, like attention, are changed.

What all these inspection and visualization tools allow is to glean some insight into neural machine translation models. Hopefully this dispels some misconceptions and provides some inspiration on how to refine them. However, human inspection is always able to view only a limited set of examples, which may be not representative and may be quite misleading. Also, the human ability to see patters where there may not be any may lead to overconfidence of any impressions. So, inspection tools are often just a starting point to formulate questions that can be studied with more rigorous methods.

17.3 Probing Representations

probing representations

When linguists analyze language, they find it useful to employ categories such as *verbs* and *adjectives*, groupings such as *noun phrases*, and linking words in relationships such as *verb–subject dependencies*.

verb–subject dependency

What do machines do when confronted with a natural language processing task? Is what happens in the layers of the encoder and decoder similar to what is happening in linguistic analysis? Do categories like parts-of-speech tags or syntactic dependencies emerge as useful features in models, just as they are useful concepts for explaining language?

17.3.1 Classifier Approach

To answer these questions, we may probe the intermediate representations (such as encoder and decoder states) by checking if the information that is contained in them reveal the kind of morphological, syntactic, or semantic properties that are thought to be useful from a linguistic perspective. One way to do this to set this up as a classification problem. The inputs are the intermediate representations and the outputs are linguistic properties associated them.

To give one example: parts-of-speech tags. Some words are ambiguous in their part of speech, for example *fly* (noun or verb?) or *like* (preposition, verb, interjection, or even noun?) . Disambiguating them should be useful for translation, *like* translates very different as a preposition than as a verb.

Predicting the part of speech of a word from its word embedding will not get us very far. The embedding for a word is the same, no matter how it is used in a sentence, so a classifier would always make the same prediction. However, the encoder layers refine word representations by taking the sentence context into account, enabling the disambiguation decisions that are essential for reaching a correct translation. So taking these contextualized word representations, we would hope to make better predictions for each occurrence of a word.

To set up a classifier, we need labeled data. On the input side for the classifier, we need to translate some sentences, which gives us the intermediate word representations. On the output side for the classifier, we need the correct tags. We may use hand-labeled corpora for this purpose but we may also rely on linguistic tools such as part-of-speech taggers, morphological analyzers, and syntactic or semantic parsers that are trained to make highly accurate decisions in view of the entire sentence.

Given pairs of, say, an intermediate word representation and a part-of-speech tag, we can now train a classifier on the labeled data.

We may use a simple linear classifier or other standard machine learning methods, such as support vector machines or multilayer feed-forward networks.

When we test the classifier on test sentences not seen in training, we obtain a measure on how well the linguistic information is encoded in the intermediate layer. This gives us some indication, if the neural model has "discovered" properties such as part-of-speech tags.

17.3.2 Findings

Belinkov et al. (2017a) use the classifier approach to predict part-of-speech tags and morphological properties such as tense, count, and gender. They find that representations in the early encoder layers are better at predicting part-of-speech and morphological features, outperforming predictions from input word embeddings. They show better performance with encoders that start with character-based representations, especially for previously unseen input words.

Belinkov et al. (2017b) confirm these findings on parts-of-speech tags for deeper encoders. They also look at semantic tagging tasks, such as the distinction of an emphasizing role of a pronoun, such as in *Sarah herself bought a book*, versus an reflexive role, such as in *Sarah bought herself a book*. They show slightly stronger gains for semantic tags in deeper layers than for parts-of-speech tags, especially for tags related to discourse relationships.

Shi et al. (2016b) find that the encoder layers learn syntactic properties such as voice (active or passive) and top-level sentence structure almost as well from a translation task as from a parsing task, i.e., a task that has to "translate" a sequence of words into a bracketed syntax structure, for instance, mapping *I like it* into *(S (NP PRP)$_{NP}$ (VP VBP (NP PRP)$_{NP}$)$_{VP}$).)$_S$*.

Also note that the investigation into word sense disambiguation discussed in Section 17.2.2 could be also set up as a tagging task and measured in a similar way.

17.4 Identifying Neurons

identifying neurons

So far, we have looked at different methods to cluster and probe the values of neurons in a layer. What will we see if we look at individual neurons?

17.4.1 Cognitive Theories

cognitive theory

The fundamental question on how information is encoded has already been asked about the biological inspiration for neural networks: the brain. When we think of our pet dog, is there one individual neuron that fires? When we consider the 100 billion neurons in the brain, we then could store 100 billion facts. However, as computer scientists we know that 100 billion bits of memory allows us to represent $2^{100 \text{ billion}}$ different numbers. So is the pet dog just one of these numbers?

Neuroscience proposes three different ideas about how information is stored.

Specificity coding: proposes that memory of, say, a specific person is encoded in the activation of a single neuron. So we have one neuron for Bill, one neuron for Mary, etc.

Population coding: proposes that a specific memory is stored as a pattern over all the neurons. This is the other extreme, Bill is encoded as activation of neuron 2, 5, 9, ..., etc. while Mary is encoded as the activation of neuron 2, 4, 7, ... etc.

Sparse coding: proposes that a specific memory is stored as a pattern over a small subset of neurons. For instance all memories of persons may use the same subset of neurons, which are activated as in a unique pattern for each person, while even in these patterns most neurons are not activated.

Technology has not evolved to the point that we can look at all the individual neurons in the human brain. Methods like magnetic resonance imaging (MRI) rely on increased blood flow as result of neural activity and have a resolution of thousands of neurons grouped together. Inspecting the brain this way found that different regions in the brain seem to be responsible for different functions, such as language, vision, etc. Any specific activity or thought process (for instance, looking at a tree in a picture) correlates with activation patterns in one or more of these regions.

17.4.2 Individual Neurons

individual neuron Artificial neural networks have the nice advantage that we can indeed inspect them down to the level of individual neurons. There are also no ethical quarrels with probing and even changing them in any way possible.

Shi et al. (2016a) inspected the neurons in an encoder–decoder recurrent neural network without attention, with this question in mind: how does the network manage to produce translations with the right output length? As Figure 17.10 shows, they found two neurons that correlate with the input and output length. For each, its absolute value increases when input tokens are consumed, and then decreases when output tokens are generated. Once a sufficient number of output tokens is generated, the probability of generating the end-of-sentence token skyrockets.

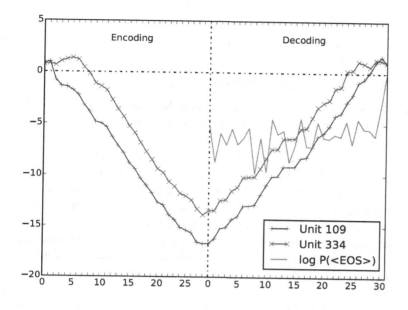

Figure 17.10 Individual neurons correlated with length (Shi et al., 2016a). Their values decrease when input tokens are consumed (left half of curve) and then increases when output tokens are generated (right half of curve). Once their values are positive, the probability of generating the end-of-sentence token <EOS> becomes close to 1.

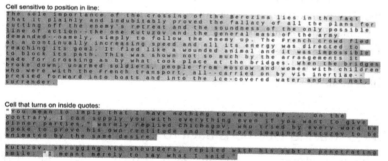

Figure 17.11 Values for two cells in a character-based LSTM neural language model (Karpathy et al., 2016). The first tracks the position in the line, increasing the probability of creating a newline character. The second flips on quotes, indicating if the current state is within or outside the quotes. Similar nodes exist for flagging brackets.

Karpathy et al. (2016) inspect individual neurons in a character-based neural language model. Figure 17.11 shows the behavior of two neurons they discovered. The first tracks the line position, helping anticipate a line break that is encoded as the newline character. The second turns on quotation marks, keeping track if the current character position is inside or outside of quotes.

They also investigate the behavior of language models trained on computer source code, finding neurons that track bracketing structure, e.g., turning on when an opening bracket "*{*" is encountered and turning off with its corresponding closing bracket "*}*".

Plotting the vast majority of neurons in this fashion, however, does not reveal any discernible pattern.

17.4.3 Discovering Neurons

discovering neurons The examples from the previous section show that at least some of the relevant information is stored in individual neurons, as specificity coding theory predicts.

We can find such neurons with correlation studies. We may be interested in a property such as the position of a word in the sentence, if a word is a noun or a verb, positioned inside a subordinate clause, or part of a direct object noun phrase. Then we look at all the values for each neuron when processing a large corpus of sentence pairs (or just a plain sentence when considering only language models). For each neuron, we can compute the correlation between the node value and the value of the property (which may be an integer, a Boolean value, or a real-valued number).

Shi et al. (2016a) propose using the least squares method to fit the data points (say, sentence position and node value) to a line that minimizes the distance between the data points and the line. While they find the striking examples shown in Figure 17.10, they also point out that better correlation can be found with the values of a small groups of neurons.

17.5 Tracing Decisions Back to Inputs

tracing decisions Often the goal of analysis and visualization is to answer the question *Why did this happen?* when confronted with an error in the translation output. What we would like is to track back what contributed to a decision. Which of the input values had the biggest impact? This may be any of the input words, any of the previously produced output words, or intermediate states.

We will take a look at two methods that have been recently proposed to aid such an investigation, layer-wise relevance propagation and saliency. Both methods have been borrowed from vision research. There, the corresponding question would be, say, where in the image did the model see a *dog*? The answer should be a heat map over the relevant pixels. In machine translation, we do not deal with pixels in an input image but the sources of information that drive the prediction of a specific output word, mainly the input words and the previously produced output words.

17.5.1 Layer-Wise Relevance Propagation

Let us first take a look at a method called **layer-wise relevance propagation**. During machine translation decoding, a particular output word is picked because its corresponding value in the softmax prediction layer is the highest. The idea behind relevance propagation is to compute backward what contributed to this high value.

layer-wise relevance propagation

Typically, a value in a neural network layer is the sum of input values multiplied with weights, followed by an activation function. For the purposes of relevance propagation, the activation function is ignored, so this leaves the values and the weights.

We now want to identify the neurons in the preceding layer that contributed most to the output value under inspection. In other words, we want to compute the **relevance value** R of these neurons. The impact of a neuron on an output value is the neuron's value and the strength of the weight between the neuron and the output value.

Formally, the value of an output node y_k is computed from the preceding hidden layer values h_j (for each neuron j) and weights u_{kj} by a weighted sum:

$$y_k = \sum_j h_j u_{kj}. \tag{17.1}$$

We now want to backtrack to what contributed to a specific output value y_k. Intuitively, these are neurons j that have high values h_j and strong connections u_{kj}. Hence we can compute relevance values for each of the neurons in the preceding layer as the product of its value and the value of the weight pointing to the high-value output node.

Formally, we propagate the relevance R_{h_j} of each hidden node j from the relevance value $R_{y_k} = 1$ for the targeted output node k:

$$R_{h_j} = \sum_j R_{y_k} u_{kj}. \tag{17.2}$$

Given the relevance values R_{h_j} for nodes in that hidden layer, we can now recurse the process until we reach input layers. In other words, we are computing the answer to the question of what in a layer contributed to the high relevance values in the subsequent layer. Note that the relevance values are not normalized during this computation. This computation is repeated until input values are reached.

Figure 17.12 illustrates a simple feed-forward neural network. Relevance propagation concludes that the third input node is most responsible for the high value of the output node with the highest value.

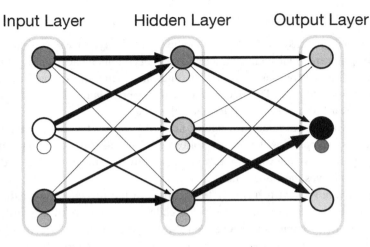

Figure 17.12 Computation relevance of input nodes for the value of an output node. Shading of nodes correspond to node values and thickness of lines correspond to weight values in the forward computation resulting in the middle output node receiving the highest value. Layer-wise relevance propagation backward tracks the contribution of hidden nodes (small circles below nodes) and then the input nodes. In the hidden layer, the bottom node has the highest relevance, since it has the highest activation value and strongest connection to the selected output node. The other two have the same connection weight but the upper one is slightly more relevant since it has an higher activation value.

17.5.2 Relevance Propagation for Machine Translation

Figure 17.13 shows the relevance of some of the input words and previously generated output words for the states in a neural machine translation model, when translating a Chinese sentence into English. The model here is a sequence-to-sequence model with attention but with only a single encoder and a single decoder layer. For each state in the network, layer-wise relevance propagation is used to compute relevance values, starting with the word prediction and backtracking to the input and output word embeddings.

There are two examples in Figure 17.13. The left example examines just the encoder. It shows relevance values for what lead to the encoder states of the third input word (*nian*, English: *years*), breaking it down into the forward recurrent state ($\overrightarrow{h_3}$), the backward recurrent state ($\overleftarrow{h_3}$), and the combination of them (h_3). So, each time, we are asking which input word embeddings contributed most to the values in each of these states.

- The forward recurrent state ($\overrightarrow{h_3}$) is mostly informed by the word itself (*nian*) and the directly preceding word (*liang*, English: *two*).

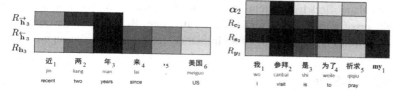

Figure 17.13 Relevance propagation determines which input words and previously generated output words had the biggest impact on computing the values for intermediate and final states of the neural network (Ding et al., 2017). The left the example shows the relevance values for each input word for encoder states for the third input word *nian*, the right example shows the relevance values for some of the input and output words for the decoder states for the second output word *visit*. For instance, the prediction of the second output word *visit* (y_2) is mostly driven by the previously generated output word *my* and the second input word (*canbai*, which has the dictionary translation *visit*), as shown in row R_{y_2}.

- The backward recurrent state ($\overleftarrow{h}_3$) is also mostly informed by the word itself (*nian*), with subsequent words becoming less relevant the more distant they are.
- The relevance of each input word for the encoder representation (h_3) reflects the relevance for these two states.

The right example in the figure shows relevance for the decoder representations when predicting the second output word *visit*. So here we are asking which input and output word embeddings contributed most to these values in each of these states.

- The figure also shows attention values (α_2) that concentrated on the input word *canbai* (English: *visit*).
- The relevance of input words for the input context (c_2), while still centered around *canbai*, has a smoother distribution, reflecting the fact each encoder representation corresponding to an input word is not just informed by that word but also by the surrounding context. Note that these differ somewhat from the attention values; their distribution is less spiked, a reflection that input word encoder states are informed by more than the corresponding input word.
- The decoder state s_2 is informed by both input words and output words. In the example, the relevance appears more evenly distributed among all these words, with the least relevance on the most distant input word *qiqiu* (English: *pray*).
- Ultimately, the output word prediction y_2 is mostly driven by the previous output word *my* and the second input word (*canbai*, English: *visit*).

Ding et al. (2017) observe that the relevance of input and output words often varies significantly across different layers of hidden states and also differs from attention weights. They use relevance propagation for error analysis and find that, for instance, that target-side context sometimes has too strong of an influence, leading to translation errors.

17.5.3 Saliency

Another method for tracing decisions back to inputs is called **saliency**. The method also originated in computer vision. Saliency is used to determine which inputs where important for making the decision by an approach that is similar to back-propagation of errors during training.

The intuition behind saliency is as follows: if a decision changes a lot if a specific input value changes, then that input is more relevant. If a change in the input value has no impact on the decision, then it is less relevant.

Mathematically, we consider the relationship between an input value x_0 and a given output value y_0. The probability that the output value y_0 is obtained given the input value x_0 denoted $p(y_0|x_0)$. If we assume this to be a linear relationship (which is approximately true locally), then the slope of the line can be computed by the derivative. Hence we define the derivative as our saliency measure:

$$\text{saliency}(x, y) = \frac{\partial p(x|y)}{\partial x}. \tag{17.3}$$

We can compute the actual value for this derivative at any given point by back-propagation.

If our question is which input word had the most influence on an output word prediction, then we are not so much interested in the role of each individual neuron in the input word embedding—we are interested in their overall impact. We could just average the salience values for all the values in the embedding vector. Ding et al. (2019a) argue that a more principled way to weight the salience values is by the embedding value.

Ding et al. (2019a) also show that salience is a practical means for establishing word alignments between input and output words. Figure 17.14 shows that their method outperforms the attention mechanism on a word alignment benchmark, providing evidence that saliency is indeed attributing the right input words for output word predictions.

In general, assessing if methods like saliency and layer-wise relevance propagation are revealing the reasons behind decisions of neural networks is a difficult supposition. In the case of word alignment, our human intuition of what inputs *should* matter for a model may not match what inputs *do* matter for a model. Staying with the example of word alignment: yes, the English word *bank* is most responsible for producing

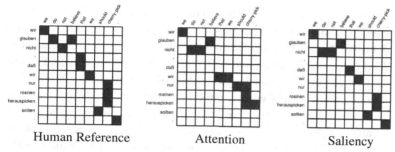

Figure 17.14 Word alignment established with saliency, a method for tracing the impact of input values to output decisions. The figure contrasts which words correspond to each other as determined by human annotators (left), which words the attention mechanism in a recurrent neural network focused on (middle), and what the saliency method revealed (right). (Illustration from Ding et al. (2019a).)

the German output word *Bank*, but other English words in a sentence, say, *credit* or *account* may be crucial for word sense disambiguation and hence also play a role. Other words may provide clues that the word is a noun in the sentence and not a verb, etc.

17.6 Further Readings

Detailed Quality Assessments

With the advent of neural machine translation and its better quality in terms of automatic metrics such as BLEU and human ranking of translation quality (Bojar et al., 2016), researchers and users of machine translation were initially interested in more fine-grained assessment of the differences of these two technologies. Bentivogli et al. (2016, 2018) considered different automatically assessed linguistic categories when comparing the performance of neural verus statistical machine translation systems for English–German. Klubička et al. (2017) use multidimensional quality metrics (MQM) for a manual error analysis to compare two statistical and one neural system for English–Croatian. Burchardt et al. (2017) pose difficult linguistic challenges to assess several statistical, neural, and rule-based systems for German–English and English–German, showing better performance for the rule-based system for verb tense and valency but better performance for the neural system for many other categories, such as handling of composition, function words, multiword expressions, and subordination. Harris et al. (2017) extend this analysis to English–Latvian and English–Czech. Popović (2017) uses similar manual annotation of different linguistic error categories to compare a neural and statistical system for these language pairs. Parida and Bojar (2018) compare a phrase-based

quality assessment

statistical model, a recurrent neural translation model, and a transformer model for the task of translation of short English-to-Hindi segments, with the transformer model coming out on top. Toral and Sánchez-Cartagena (2017) compared different broad aspects such as fluency and reordering for nine language directions. Castilho et al. (2017a) use automatic scores when comparing neural and statistical machine translation for different domains (e-commerce, patents, educational content), showing better performance for the neural systems, except for patent abstracts and e-commerce. They followed this up (Castilho et al., 2017b) with a more detailed human assessment of linguistic aspects for the educational content. They find better performance for the neural model across categories such as inflectional morphology, word order, omission, addition and mistranslation for four languages. Cohn-Gordon and Goodman (2019) examine how sentences are translated that are ambiguous in one language due to underspecification.

Addressing the use of machine translation, Martindale and Carpuat (2018) highlight that the typically fluent output of neural machine translation systems may lead to unwarranted high level of trust. They show that exposure to bad translations reduces users' trust, but more so for disfluent than misleading translations. Castilho and Guerberof (2018) carry out a task-based comparative evaluation between a neural and a statistical machine translation system for three language pairs. The human evaluators read the translation and answered questions about the content, allowing for measurement of reading speed and correctness of answers, as well as solicitation of feedback.

The claim of human parity for Chinese–English news translation (Hassan et al., 2018) has triggered a number of responses. Toral et al. (2018) call this claim into question by observing the impact of using test sets created in the reverse order (translated from the target side to the source side, opposite to the machine translation direction and the skill of human evaluators. Läubli et al. (2018) present results that show annotators gave machine translation higher scores on adequacy than human translations, but only on the sentence level, not the document level, and also that human translations are ranked higher in terms of fluency.

Targeted Test Sets

targeted test set   Isabelle et al. (2017) pose a challenge set of manually crafted French sentences for a number of linguistic categories that pose hard problems for translations, such as long-distance agreement or preservation of polarity. Sennrich (2017) developed an automatic method for detecting specific morphosyntactic errors. First a test set is created by taking sentence pairs, and modifying the target sentence to exhibit specific types of error, such as wrong gender of determiners, wrong particles for verbs, wrong transliteration. Then a neural translation model is evaluated by how often it scores the correct translation higher then the faulty translations. The paper compares byte-pair encoding against character-based models for rare and unknown words. Rios et al. (2017) use this method to create contrastive translation pairs to address the problem of translating ambiguous nouns. Burlot and Yvon (2017) use it to create a test set for selecting the correct morphological variant in a morphologically rich target language, Latvian. Müller et al. (2018) created a test set to evaluate the translation of pronouns, although Guillou and Hardmeier (2018) point out that automatic evaluation of pronoun translation is tricky and may not correlate well with human judgment. Shao et al. (2018) propose evaluating the translation of idioms with a blacklist method: if words that are part of a literal translation of the idiomatic phrase occur in the output, they are flagged as incorrect.

Visualization

visualization

It is common to plot word embeddings (van der Maaten and Hinton, 2008) or attention weights (Koehn and Knowles, 2017; Vaswani et al., 2017) for inspection of parameters and model states. Marvin and Koehn (2018) plot embedding states for words marked with their senses. Ghader and Monz (2017) more closely examine attention states, in comparison to traditional word alignments. Tran et al. (2016) integrate an attention mechanism into a language model and show which previous words had the most influence on predictions of the next word. Stahlberg et al. (2018) add additional markup to the target side of the parallel corpus and hence the output of the translation model that flags translation decisions.

Lee et al. (2017) developed an interactive tool that allows exploration of the behavior of beam search. Strobelt et al. (2019) present the more comprehensive tool Seq2seq-Vis that also allows the plotting and comparison of encoder and decoder states to neighbor states seen during training. Neubig et al. (2019) present the tool compare-MT that allows more fine-grained error analysis by comparing the output of two systems in terms of automatic scores, breakdowns by word frequency, parts-of-speech tags, and others, as well as identification of source words with strongly divergent translation quality. Schwarzenberg et al. (2019) train a classifier using a convolutional neural network to distinguish between human and machine translations and use the contribution of word-based features to identify words that drive this decision.

Predicting Properties from Internal Representations

probing representations

To probe intermediate representations, such as encoder and decoder states, a strategy is to use them as input to a classifier that predicts specific, mostly linguistic, properties. Belinkov et al. (2017a) predict the parts of speech and morphological features of words linked to encoder and decoder states, showing better performance of character-based models, but not much difference for deeper layers. Belinkov et al. (2017b) also consider semantic properties. Shi et al. (2016b) find that basic syntactic properties are learned by translation models. Poliak et al. (2018) probe if sentence embeddings (the first and last state of the RNN encoder) have sufficient semantic information to serve as input to semantic entailment tasks.

Raganato and Tiedemann (2018) assess the encoder states of the transformer model. They develop four syntactic probing tasks (parts-of-speech tagging, chunking, named entity recognition, and semantic dependency) and find that the earlier layers contain more syntactic information (e.g., parts-of-speech tagging) while later layer contain more semantic information (e.g., semantic dependencies). Tang et al. (2018) examine the role of the attention mechanism when handling ambiguous nouns. Contrary to their intuition, the decoder pays more attention to the word itself instead of context words in the case of ambiguous nouns compared to nouns in general. This is the case both for RNN-based and transformer-based translation models. They suspect that word sense disambiguation already takes place in the encoder.

A number of studies of internal representation focus on just language modeling. Linzen et al. (2016) propose the task of subject–verb agreement, especially when interrupted by other nouns, as a challenge to sequence models that have to preserve agreement information. Gulordava et al. (2018) extend this idea into several other hierarchical language problems. Giulianelli et al. (2018) build classifiers to predict the verb agreement information from the internal states at different layers of an LSTM language model and go even a step further and demonstrate that changing the decoder states based on insight gained from the classifiers allows them to make better decisions. Tran et al. (2018) compare how well fully attentional (transformer) models compare against recurrent neural networks when it comes to decisions depending of hierarchical structure. Their experiments show that recurrent neural networks perform better at tasks such as subject–verb agreement separated by recursive phrases. Zhang and Bowman (2018) show that states obtained from bidirectional language models are a better at parts of speech tagging and supertagging tasks than the encoder states of a neural translation model. Dhar and Bisazza (2018) explore if multilingual language training leads to generalizing a more general syntax but find only small improvement on agreement tasks when completely separating the vocabularies.

Role of Individual Neurons

Karpathy et al. (2016) inspect individual neurons in a character-based   **individual neuron**
language model and find single neurons that appear to keep track of
position in the line (expecting a line break character) and the opening
of brackets. Shi et al. (2016a) correlated activation values of specific
nodes in the state of a simple LSTM encoder–decoder translation model
(without attention) with the length of the output and discovered nodes
that count the number of words to ensure proper output length.

Tracing Decisions Back to Prior States

tracing decisions

Ding et al. (2017) propose using layer-wise relevance feedback to measure which of the input states or intermediate states had the biggest
influence on prediction decisions. Tackling the same problem, Ding
et al. (2019b) propose using saliency, a method that measures the impact
of input states based on how much small changes in their values (as
indicated by the gradients) impact prediction decisions. Ma et al. (2018)
examine the relative role of source context and prior decoder states on
output word predictions. Knowles and Koehn (2018) explore what drives
decisions of the model to copy input words such as names. They show
the impact of both the context and properties of the word (such as cap-
italization). Wallace et al. (2018) change the way predictions are made
in neural models. Instead of a softmax prediction layer, final decoder
states are compared to states during training, providing examples that
explain the decision of the network.

Bibliography

Mostafa Abdou, Vladan Gloncak, and Ondřej Bojar. 2017. Variable mini-batch sizing and pre-trained embeddings. In *Proceedings of the Second Conference on Machine Translation. Volume 2: Shared Task Papers*. Association for Computational Linguistics, Copenhagen, pages 680–686. www.aclweb.org/anthology/W17-4780.

Roee Aharoni and Yoav Goldberg. 2017. Towards string-to-tree neural machine translation. In *Proceedings of the 55th Annual Meeting of the Association for Computational Linguistics. Volume 2: Short Papers*. Association for Computational Linguistics, Vancouver, BC, pages 132–140. http://aclweb.org/anthology/P17-2021.

Roee Aharoni, Melvin Johnson, and Orhan Firat. 2019. Massively multilingual neural machine translation. In *Proceedings of the 2019 Conference of the North American Chapter of the Association for Computational Linguistics: Human Language Technologies. Volume 1: Long and Short Papers*. Association for Computational Linguistics, Minneapolis, MN, pages 3874–3884. www.aclweb.org/anthology/N19-1388.

Maruan Al-Shedivat and Ankur Parikh. 2019. Consistency by agreement in zero-shot neural machine translation. In *Proceedings of the 2019 Conference of the North American Chapter of the Association for Computational Linguistics: Human Language Technologies. Volume 1: Long and Short Papers*. Association for Computational Linguistics, Minneapolis, MN, pages 1184–1197. www.aclweb.org/anthology/N19-1121.

Jean Alaux, Edouard Grave, Marco Cuturi, and Armand Joulin. 2019. Unsupervised hyper-alignment for multilingual word embeddings. In *International Conference on Learning Representations (ICLR)*. New Orleans, LA. http://arxiv.org/pdf/1811.01124.pdf.

Ashkan Alinejad, Maryam Siahbani, and Anoop Sarkar. 2018. Prediction improves simultaneous neural machine translation. In *Proceedings of the 2018 Conference on Empirical Methods in Natural Language Processing*. Association for Computational Linguistics, Brussels, pages 3022–3027. www.aclweb.org/anthology/D18-1337.

Tamer Alkhouli, Gabriel Bretschner, and Hermann Ney. 2018. On the alignment problem in multi-head attention-based neural machine translation. In *Proceedings of the Third Conference on Machine Translation. Volume 1: Research Papers*. Association for Computational Linguistics, Brussels, pages 177–185. www.aclweb.org/anthology/W18-6318.

Tamer Alkhouli, Gabriel Bretschner, Jan-Thorsten Peter, Mohammed Hethnawi, Andreas Guta, and Hermann Ney. 2016. Alignment-based neural machine translation. In *Proceedings of the First Conference on Machine Translation*. Association for Computational Linguistics, Berlin, pages 54–65. www.aclweb.org/anthology/W/W16/W16-2206.

Tamer Alkhouli and Hermann Ney. 2017. Biasing attention-based recurrent neural networks using external alignment information. In *Proceedings of the Second Conference on Machine Translation. Volume 1: Research Papers*. Association for Computational Linguistics, Copenhagen, pages 108–117. www.aclweb.org/anthology/W17-4711.

Robert B. Allen. 1987. Several studies on natural language and back-propagation. *Proceedings of the IEEE First International Conference on Neural Networks* 2(5):335–341. http://boballen.info/RBA/PAPERS/NL-BP/nl-bp.pdf.

Taghreed Alqaisi and Simon O'Keefe. 2019. En-ar bilingual word embeddings without word alignment: Factors effects. In *Proceedings of the Fourth Arabic Natural Language Processing Workshop*. Association for Computational Linguistics, Florence, pages 97–107. www.aclweb.org/anthology/W19-4611.

David Alvarez-Melis and Tommi Jaakkola. 2018. Gromov-Wasserstein alignment of word embedding spaces. In *Proceedings of the 2018 Conference on Empirical Methods in Natural Language Processing*. Association for Computational Linguistics, Brussels, pages 1881–1890. https://doi.org/10.18653/v1/D18-1214.

Antonios Anastasopoulos, Alison Lui, Toan Q. Nguyen, and David Chiang. 2019. Neural machine translation of text from non-native speakers. In *Proceedings of the 2019 Conference of the North American Chapter of the Association for Computational Linguistics: Human Language Technologies*. Volume 1: *Long and Short Papers*. Association for Computational Linguistics, Minneapolis, MN, pages 3070–3080. www.aclweb.org/anthology/N19-1311.

Peter Anderson, Basura Fernando, Mark Johnson, and Stephen Gould. 2017. Guided open vocabulary image captioning with constrained beam search. In *Proceedings of the 2017 Conference on Empirical Methods in Natural Language Processing*. Association for Computational Linguistics, Copenhagen, pages 936–945. www.aclweb.org/anthology/D17-1098.

Alexandra Antonova and Alexey Misyurev. 2011. Building a web-based parallel corpus and filtering out machine-translated text. In *Proceedings of the 4th Workshop on Building and Using Comparable Corpora: Comparable Corpora and the Web*. Association for Computational Linguistics, Portland, OR, pages 136–144. www.aclweb.org/anthology/W11-1218.

Arturo Argueta and David Chiang. 2019. Accelerating sparse matrix operations in neural networks on graphics processing units. In *Proceedings of the 57th Conference of the Association for Computational Linguistics*. Association for Computational Linguistics, Florence, pages 6215–6224. www.aclweb.org/anthology/P19-1626.

Naveen Arivazhagan, Colin Cherry, Wolfgang Macherey, Chung-Cheng Chiu, Semih Yavuz, Ruoming Pang, Wei Li, and Colin Raffel. 2019. Monotonic infinite lookback attention for simultaneous machine translation. In *Proceedings of the 57th Conference of the Association for Computational Linguistics*. Association for Computational Linguistics, Florence, pages 1313–1323. www.aclweb.org/anthology/P19-1126.

Mikel Artetxe, Gorka Labaka, and Eneko Agirre. 2016. Learning principled bilingual mappings of word embeddings while preserving monolingual invariance. In *Proceedings of the 2016 Conference on Empirical Methods in Natural Language Processing*. Association for Computational Linguistics, Austin, TX, pages 2289–2294. https://aclweb.org/anthology/D16-1250.

Mikel Artetxe, Gorka Labaka, and Eneko Agirre. 2017. Learning bilingual word embeddings with (almost) no bilingual data. In *Proceedings of the 55th Annual Meeting of the Association for Computational Linguistics*. Volume 1: *Long Papers*. Association for Computational Linguistics, Vancouver, BC, pages 451–462. https://doi.org/10.18653/v1/P17-1042.

Mikel Artetxe, Gorka Labaka, and Eneko Agirre. 2018a. Unsupervised statistical machine translation. In *Proceedings of the 2018 Conference on Empirical Methods in Natural Language Processing*. Association for Computational Linguistics, Brussels, pages 3632–3642. www.aclweb.org/anthology/D18-1399.

Mikel Artetxe, Gorka Labaka, and Eneko Agirre. 2019a. Bilingual lexicon induction through unsupervised machine translation. In *Proceedings of the 57th Conference of the Association for Computational Linguistics*. Association for Computational Linguistics, Florence, pages 5002–5007. www.aclweb.org/anthology/P19-1494.

Mikel Artetxe, Gorka Labaka, and Eneko Agirre. 2019b. An effective approach to unsupervised machine translation. In *Proceedings of the 57th Conference of the Association for Computational Linguistics*. Association for Computational Linguistics, Florence, pages 194–203. www.aclweb.org/anthology/P19-1019.

Mikel Artetxe, Gorka Labaka, Eneko Agirre, and Kyunghyun Cho. 2018b. Unsupervised neural machine translation. In *International Conference on Learning Representations*. Vancouver, BC. https://openreview.net/forum?id=Sy2ogebAW.

Mikel Artetxe and Holger Schwenk. 2018. Massively multilingual sentence embeddings for zero-shot cross-lingual transfer and beyond. Ithaca, NY: Cornell University abs/1812.10464. http://arxiv.org/abs/1812.10464.

Mikel Artetxe and Holger Schwenk. 2019. Margin-based parallel corpus mining with multilingual sentence embeddings. In *Proceedings of the 57th Conference of the Association for Computational Linguistics*. Association for Computational Linguistics, Florence, pages 3197–3203. www.aclweb.org/anthology/P19-1309.

Philip Arthur, Graham Neubig, and Satoshi Nakamura. 2016a. Incorporating discrete translation lexicons into neural machine translation. In *Proceedings of the 2016 Conference on Empirical Methods in Natural Language Processing*. Association for Computational Linguistics, Austin, TX, pages 1557–1567. https://aclweb.org/anthology/D16-1162.

Philip Arthur, Graham Neubig, and Satoshi Nakamura. 2016b. Incorporating discrete translation lexicons into neural machine translation. In *Proceedings of the 2016 Conference on Empirical Methods in Natural Language Processing*. Association for Computational Linguistics, Austin, TX, pages 1557–1567. https://aclweb.org/anthology/D16-1162.

Duygu Ataman and Marcello Federico. 2018a. Compositional representation of morphologically-rich input for neural machine translation. In *Proceedings of the 56th Annual Meeting of the Association for Computational Linguistics*. Volume 2: *Short Papers*. Association for Computational Linguistics, Melbourne, pages 305–311. http://aclweb.org/anthology/P18-2049.

Duygu Ataman and Marcello Federico. 2018b. An evaluation of two vocabulary reduction methods for neural machine translation. In *Annual Meeting of the Association for Machine Translation in the Americas (AMTA)*. Boston, MA. www.aclweb.org/anthology/W18-1810.

Duygu Ataman, Mattia Antonino Di Gangi, and Marcello Federico. 2018. Compositional source word representations for neural machine translation. In *Proceedings of the 21st Annual Conference of the European Association for Machine Translation*. Melbourne. https://arxiv.org/pdf/1805.02036.pdf.

Duygu Ataman, Matteo Negri, Marco Turchi, and Marcello Federico. 2017. Linguistically motivated vocabulary reduction for neural machine translation from Turkish to English. *The Prague Bulletin of Mathematical Linguistics* 108:331–342. https://ufal.mff.cuni.cz/pbml/108/art-ataman-negri-turchi-federico.pdf.

Amittai Axelrod, Xiaodong He, and Jianfeng Gao. 2011. Domain adaptation via pseudo in-domain data selection. In *Proceedings of the 2011 Conference on Empirical Methods in Natural Language Processing*. Association for Computational Linguistics, Edinburgh, pages 355–362. www.aclweb.org/anthology/D11-1033.

Dzmitry Bahdanau, Kyunghyun Cho, and Yoshua Bengio. 2015. Neural machine translation by jointly learning to align and translate. In *ICLR*. San Diego, CA. http://arxiv.org/pdf/1409.0473v6.pdf.

Paul Baltescu and Phil Blunsom. 2015. Pragmatic neural language modelling in machine translation. In *Proceedings of the 2015 Conference of the North American Chapter of the Association for Computational Linguistics: Human Language Technologies*. Association for Computational Linguistics, Denver, CO, pages 820–829. www.aclweb.org/anthology/N15-1083.

Paul Baltescu, Phil Blunsom, and Hieu Hoang. 2014. Oxlm: A neural language modelling framework for machine translation. *The Prague Bulletin of Mathematical Linguistics* 102:81–92. http://ufal.mff.cuni.cz/pbml/102/art-baltescu-blunsom-hoang.pdf.

Tamali Banerjee and Pushpak Bhattacharyya. 2018. Meaningless yet meaningful: Morphology grounded subword-level nmt. In *Proceedings of the Second Workshop on Subword/Character LEvel Models*. Association for Computational Linguistics, New Orleans, LA, pages 55–60. https://doi.org/10.18653/v1/W18-1207.

Ankur Bapna, Mia Chen, Orhan Firat, Yuan Cao, and Yonghui Wu. 2018. Training deeper neural machine translation models with transparent attention. In *Proceedings of the 2018 Conference on Empirical Methods in Natural Language Processing*. Association for Computational Linguistics, Brussels, pages 3028–3033. www.aclweb.org/anthology/D18-1338.

Ankur Bapna and Orhan Firat. 2019. Non-parametric adaptation for neural machine translation. In *Proceedings of the 2019 Conference of the North American Chapter of the Association for Computational Linguistics: Human Language Technologies*. Volume 1: *Long and Short Papers*. Association for Computational Linguistics, Minneapolis, MN, pages 1921–1931. www.aclweb.org/anthology/N19-1191.

Eduard Barbu, Carla Parra Escartín, Luisa Bentivogli, Matteo Negri, Marco Turchi, Constantin Orasan, and Marcello Federico. 2016. The first automatic translation memory cleaning shared task. *Machine Translation* 30(3):145–166. https://doi.org/10.1007/s10590-016-9183-x.

Yonatan Belinkov and Yonatan Bisk. 2017. Synthetic and natural noise both break neural machine translation. Ithaca, NY: Cornell University, abs/1711.02173. http://arxiv.org/abs/1711.02173.

Yonatan Belinkov, Nadir Durrani, Fahim Dalvi, Hassan Sajjad, and James Glass. 2017a. What do neural machine translation models learn about morphology?

In *Proceedings of the 55th Annual Meeting of the Association for Computational Linguistics*. Volume 1: *Long Papers*. Association for Computational Linguistics, Vancouver, BC, pages 861–872. http://aclweb.org/anthology/P17-1080.

Yonatan Belinkov, Lluís Màrquez, Hassan Sajjad, Nadir Durrani, Fahim Dalvi, and James Glass. 2017b. Evaluating layers of representation in neural machine translation on part-of-speech and semantic tagging tasks. In *Proceedings of the Eighth International Joint Conference on Natural Language Processing.* Volume 1: *Long Papers*. Asian Federation of Natural Language Processing, Taipei, pages 1–10. www.aclweb.org/anthology/I17-1001.

Yoshua Bengio, Réjean Ducharme, Pascal Vincent, and Christian Jauvin. 2003. A neural probabilistic language model. *Journal of Machine Learning Research* 3:1137–1155.

Luisa Bentivogli, Arianna Bisazza, Mauro Cettolo, and Marcello Federico. 2016. Neural versus phrase-based machine translation quality: A case study. In *Proceedings of the 2016 Conference on Empirical Methods in Natural Language Processing*. Association for Computational Linguistics, Austin, TX, pages 257–267. https://aclweb.org/anthology/D16-1025.

Luisa Bentivogli, Arianna Bisazza, Mauro Cettolo, and Marcello Federico. 2018. Neural versus phrase-based MT quality: An in-depth analysis on English–German and English–French. *Computer Speech and Language* 49:52–70. https://doi.org/10.1016/j.csl.2017.11.004.

Ergun Bicici and Deniz Yuret. 2011. Instance selection for machine translation using feature decay algorithms. In *Proceedings of the Sixth Workshop on Statistical Machine Translation*. Association for Computational Linguistics, Edinburgh, pages 272–283. www.aclweb.org/anthology/W11-2131.

Graeme Blackwood, Miguel Ballesteros, and Todd Ward. 2018. Multilingual neural machine translation with task-specific attention. In *Proceedings of the 27th International Conference on Computational Linguistics*. Association for Computational Linguistics, Santa Fe, NM, pages 3112–3122. www.aclweb.org/anthology/C18-1263.

Frédéric Blain, Lucia Specia, and Pranava Madhyastha. 2017. Exploring hypotheses spaces in neural machine translation. In *Machine Translation Summit XVI*. Nagoya, Japan. www.doc.ic.ac.uk/pshantha/papers/mtsummit17.pdf.

David M Blei, Andrew Y Ng, and Michael I Jordan. 2003. Latent Dirichlet allocation. *Journal of Machine Learning Research* 3:993–1022.

Ondřej Bojar, Rajen Chatterjee, Christian Federmann, Yvette Graham, Barry Haddow, Matthias Huck, Antonio Jimeno Yepes, Philipp Koehn, Varvara Logacheva, Christof Monz, Matteo Negri, Aurelie Neveol, Mariana Neves, Martin Popel, Matt Post, Raphael Rubino, Carolina Scarton, Lucia Specia, Marco Turchi, Karin Verspoor, and Marcos Zampieri. 2016. Findings of the 2016 conference on machine translation. In *Proceedings of the First Conference on Machine Translation*. Association for Computational Linguistics, Berlin, pages 131–198. www.aclweb.org/anthology/W/W16/W16-2301.

Fabienne Braune, Viktor Hangya, Tobias Eder, and Alexander Fraser. 2018. Evaluating bilingual word embeddings on the long tail. In *Proceedings of the 2018 Conference of the North American Chapter of the Association for Computational Linguistics: Human Language Technologies*. Volume 2: *Short Papers*. Association for Computational Linguistics, New Orleans, LA, pages 188–193. http://aclweb.org/anthology/N18-2030.

Bram Bulte and Arda Tezcan. 2019. Neural fuzzy repair: Integrating fuzzy matches into neural machine translation. In *Proceedings of the 57th Conference of the Association for Computational Linguistics*. Association for Computational Linguistics, Florence, pages 1800–1809. www.aclweb.org/anthology/P19-1175.

Aljoscha Burchardt, Vivien Macketanz, Jon Dehdari, Georg Heigold, Jan-Thorsten Peter, and Philip Williams. 2017. A linguistic evaluation of rule-based, phrase-based, and neural MT engines. *The Prague Bulletin of Mathematical Linguistics* 108:159–170. https://doi.org/10.1515/pralin-2017-0017.

Franck Burlot, Mercedes García-Martínez, Loïc Barrault, Fethi Bougares, and François Yvon. 2017. Word representations in factored neural machine translation. In *Proceedings of the Second Conference on Machine Translation*. Volume 1: *Research Papers*. Association for Computational Linguistics, Copenhagen, pages 20–31. www.aclweb.org/anthology/W17-4703.

Franck Burlot and François Yvon. 2017. Evaluating the morphological competence of machine translation systems. In *Proceedings of the Second Conference on Machine Translation*. Volume 1: *Research Paper.*

Association for Computational Linguistics, Copenhagen, pages 43–55. www.aclweb.org/anthology/W17-4705.

Franck Burlot and François Yvon. 2018. Using monolingual data in neural machine translation: a systematic study. In *Proceedings of the Third Conference on Machine Translation: Research Papers*. Association for Computational Linguistics, Belgium, pages 144–155. www.aclweb.org/anthology/W18-6315.

Chris Callison-Burch, Philipp Koehn, Christof Monz, Kay Peterson, Mark Przybocki, and Omar Zaidan. 2010. Findings of the 2010 joint workshop on statistical machine translation and metrics for machine translation. In *Proceedings of the Joint Fifth Workshop on Statistical Machine Translation and MetricsMATR*. Association for Computational Linguistics, Uppsala, pages 17–53. www.aclweb.org/anthology/W10-1703.

Marine Carpuat, Yogarshi Vyas, and Xing Niu. 2017. Detecting cross-lingual semantic divergence for neural machine translation. In *Proceedings of the First Workshop on Neural Machine Translation*. Association for Computational Linguistics, Vancouver, BC, pages 69–79. www.aclweb.org/anthology/W17-3209.

M. Asunción Castaño, Francisco Casacuberta, and Enrique Vidal. 1997. Machine translation using neural networks and finite-state models. In *Theoretical and Methodological Issues in Machine Translation*, Santa Fe, NM, pages 160–167. www.mt-archive.info/TMI-1997-Castano.pdf.

Sheila Castilho and Ana Guerberof. 2018. Reading comprehension of machine translation output: What makes for a better read? In *Proceedings of the 21st Annual Conference of the European Association for Machine Translation*. Melbourne. https://rua.ua.es/dspace/bitstream/10045/76032/1/EAMT2018-Proceedings_10.pdf.

Sheila Castilho, Joss Moorkens, Federico Gaspari, Iacer Calixto, John Tinsley, and Andy Way. 2017a. Is neural machine translation the new state of the art? *The Prague Bulletin of Mathematical Linguistics* 108:109–120. https://doi.org/10.1515/pralin-2017-0013.

Sheila Castilho, Joss Moorkens, Federico Gaspari, Rico Sennrich, Vilelmini Sosoni, Panayota Georgakopoulou, Pintu Lohar, Andy Way, Antonio Valerio Miceli Barone, and Maria Gialama. 2017b. A comparative quality evaluation of PBSMT and NMT using professional translators. In *Machine Translation Summit XVI*. Nagoya, Japan.

Isaac Caswell, Ciprian Chelba, and David Grangier. 2019. Tagged back-translation. In *Proceedings of the Fourth Conference on Machine Translation*. Association for Computational Linguistics, Florence, pages 53–63. www.aclweb.org/anthology/W19-5206.

Mauro Cettolo, Marcello Federico, Luisa Bentivogli, Jan Niehues, Sebastian Stüker, Katsuitho Sudoh, Koichiro Yoshino, and Christian Federmann. 2017. Overview of the IWSLT 2017 evaluation campaign. In *International Workshop on Spoken Language Translation*. Tokyo, pages 2–14.

Rajen Chatterjee, Matteo Negri, Marco Turchi, Marcello Federico, Lucia Specia, and Frédéric Blain. 2017. Guiding neural machine translation decoding with external knowledge. In *Proceedings of the Second Conference on Machine Translation,* Volume 1: *Research Paper*. Association for Computational Linguistics, Copenhagen, pages 157–168. www.aclweb.org/anthology/W17-4716.

Boxing Chen, Colin Cherry, George Foster, and Samuel Larkin. 2017. Cost weighting for neural machine translation domain adaptation. In *Proceedings of the First Workshop on Neural Machine Translation*. Association for Computational Linguistics, Vancouver, BC pages 40–46. www.aclweb.org/anthology/W17-3205.

Jianmin Chen, Rajat Monga, Samy Bengio, and Rafal Jozefowicz. 2016a. Revisiting distributed synchronous SGD. In *International Conference on Learning Representations Workshop Track*. https://arxiv.org/abs/1604.00981.

Mia Xu Chen, Orhan Firat, Ankur Bapna, Melvin Johnson, Wolfgang Macherey, George Foster, Llion Jones, Mike Schuster, Noam Shazeer, Niki Parmar, Ashish Vaswani, Jakob Uszkoreit, Lukasz Kaiser, Zhifeng Chen, Yonghui Wu, and Macduff Hughes. 2018. The best of both worlds: Combining recent advances in neural machine translation. In *Proceedings of the 56th Annual Meeting of the Association for Computational Linguistics*. Volume 1: *Long Papers*. Association for Computational Linguistics, Melbourne, pages 76–86. http://aclweb.org/anthology/P18-1008.

Wenhu Chen, Evgeny Matusov, Shahram Khadivi, and Jan-Thorsten Peter. 2016b. Guided alignment training for topic-aware neural machine translation. Ithaca, NY: Cornell University, abs/1607.01628. https://arxiv.org/pdf/1607.01628.pdf.

Xilun Chen and Claire Cardie. 2018. Unsupervised multilingual word embeddings. In *Proceedings of the 2018 Conference on Empirical Methods in Natural*

Language Processing. Association for Computational Linguistics, Brussels, pages 261–270. www.aclweb.org/anthology/D18-1024.

Yong Cheng, Zhaopeng Tu, Fandong Meng, Junjie Zhai, and Yang Liu. 2018. Towards robust neural machine translation. In *Proceedings of the 56th Annual Meeting of the Association for Computational Linguistics*. Volume 1: *Long Papers*. Association for Computational Linguistics, Melbourne, pages 1756–1766. http://aclweb.org/anthology/P18-1163.

Mara Chinea-Rios, Álvaro Peris, and Francisco Casacuberta. 2017. Adapting neural machine translation with parallel synthetic data. In *Proceedings of the Second Conference on Machine Translation*. Volume 1: *Research Paper*. Association for Computational Linguistics, Copenhagen, pages 138–147. www.aclweb.org/anthology/W17-4714.

Kyunghyun Cho. 2016. Noisy parallel approximate decoding for conditional recurrent language model. Ithaca, NY, Cornell University, abs/1605.03835. http://arxiv.org/abs/1605.03835.

Kyunghyun Cho and Masha Esipova. 2016. Can neural machine translation do simultaneous translation? Ithaca, NY, Cornell University, abs/1606.02012. http://arxiv.org/abs/1606.02012.

Kyunghyun Cho, Bart van Merrienboer, Dzmitry Bahdanau, and Yoshua Bengio. 2014. On the properties of neural machine translation: Encoder–decoder approaches. In *Proceedings of SSST-8, Eighth Workshop on Syntax, Semantics and Structure in Statistical Translation*. Association for Computational Linguistics, Doha, Qatar, pages 103–111. www.aclweb.org/anthology/W14-4012.

Heeyoul Choi, Kyunghyun Cho, and Yoshua Bengio. 2018. Fine-grained attention mechanism for neural machine translation. *Neurocomputing* 284:171–176.

Jan Chorowski and Navdeep Jaitly. 2017. Towards better decoding and language model integration in sequence to sequence models. In *Interspeech*. Stockholm, pages 523–527.

Chenhui Chu, Raj Dabre, and Sadao Kurohashi. 2017. An empirical comparison of domain adaptation methods for neural machine translation. In *Proceedings of the 55th Annual Meeting of the Association for Computational Linguistics*. Volume 2: *Short Papers*. Association for Computational Linguistics, Vancouver, BC, pages 385–391. http://aclweb.org/anthology/P17-2061.

Junyoung Chung, Kyunghyun Cho, and Yoshua Bengio. 2016. A character-level decoder without explicit segmentation for neural machine translation.

In *Proceedings of the 54th Annual Meeting of the Association for Computational Linguistics*. Volume 1: *Long Papers*. Association for Computational Linguistics, Berlin, pages 1693–1703. www.aclweb.org/anthology/P16-1160.

Kenneth W. Church and Eduard H. Hovy. 1993. Good applications for crummy machine translation. *Machine Translation* 8(4):239–258. www.isi.edu/natural-language/people/hovy/papers/93churchhovy.pdf.

Trevor Cohn, Cong Duy Vu Hoang, Ekaterina Vymolova, Kaisheng Yao, Chris Dyer, and Gholamreza Haffari. 2016. Incorporating structural alignment biases into an attentional neural translation model. In *Proceedings of the 2016 Conference of the North American Chapter of the Association for Computational Linguistics: Human Language Technologies*. Association for Computational Linguistics, San Diego, CA, pages 876–885. www.aclweb.org/anthology/N16-1102.

Reuben Cohn-Gordon and Noah Goodman. 2019. Lost in machine translation: A method to reduce meaning loss. In *Proceedings of the 2019 Conference of the North American Chapter of the Association for Computational Linguistics: Human Language Technologies*. Volume 1: *Long and Short Papers*. Association for Computational Linguistics, Minneapolis, MN, pages 437–441. www.aclweb.org/anthology/N19-1042.

Alexis Conneau, Guillaume Lample, Marc'Aurelio Ranzato, Ludovic Denoyer, and Hervé Jégou. 2018. Word translation without parallel data. In *International Conference on Learning Representations*. Vancouver, BC. https://openreview.net/pdf?id=H196sainb.

Marta R. Costa-jussà, Cristina España Bonet, Pranava Madhyastha, Carlos Escolano, and José A. R. Fonollosa. 2016. The TALP–UPC Spanish–English WMT biomedical task: Bilingual embeddings and char-based neural language model rescoring in a phrase-based system. In *Proceedings of the First Conference on Machine Translation*. Association for Computational Linguistics, Berlin, pages 463–468. www.aclweb.org/anthology/W/W16/W16-2336.

Marta R. Costa-jussà and José A. R. Fonollosa. 2016. Character-based neural machine translation. In *Proceedings of the 54th Annual Meeting of the Association for Computational Linguistics*. Volume 2: *Short Papers*. Association for Computational Linguistics, Berlin, pages 357–361. http://anthology.aclweb.org/P16-2058.

Jocelyn Coulmance, Jean-Marc Marty, Guillaume Wenzek, and Amine Benhalloum. 2015. Trans-gram, fast cross-lingual word-embeddings. In *Proceedings of the 2015 Conference on Empirical Methods in Natural Language Processing*. Association for Computational Linguistics, Lisbon, pages 1109–1113. `http://aclweb.org/anthology/D15-1131`.

Josep Maria Crego, Jungi Kim, Guillaume Klein, Anabel Rebollo, Kathy Yang, Jean Senellart, Egor Akhanov, Patrice Brunelle, Aurelien Coquard, Yongchao Deng, Satoshi Enoue, Chiyo Geiss, Joshua Johanson, Ardas Khalsa, Raoum Khiari, Byeongil Ko, Catherine Kobus, Jean Lorieux, Leidiana Martins, Dang-Chuan Nguyen, Alexandra Priori, Thomas Riccardi, Natalia Segal, Christophe Servan, Cyril Tiquet, Bo Wang, Jin Yang, Dakun Zhang, Jing Zhou, and Peter Zoldan. 2016. Systran's pure neural machine translation systems. Ithaca, NY: Cornell University, abs/1610.05540. `http://arxiv.org/abs/1610.05540`.

Lei Cui, Dongdong Zhang, Shujie Liu, Mu Li, and Ming Zhou. 2013. Bilingual data cleaning for SMT using graph-based random walk. In *Proceedings of the 51st Annual Meeting of the Association for Computational Linguistics*. Volume 2: *Short Papers*. Association for Computational Linguistics, Sofia, Bulgaria, pages 340–345. `www.aclweb.org/anthology/P13-2061`.

Anna Currey, Antonio Valerio Miceli Barone, and Kenneth Heafield. 2017. Copied monolingual data improves low-resource neural machine translation. In *Proceedings of the Second Conference on Machine Translation*. Volume 1: *Research Paper*. Association for Computational Linguistics, Copenhagen, pages 148–156. `http://www.aclweb.org/anthology/W17-4715`.

Raj Dabre, Fabien Cromieres, and Sadao Kurohashi. 2017. Enabling multi-source neural machine translation by concatenating source sentences in multiple languages. In *Machine Translation Summit XVI*. Nagoya, Japan `https://arxiv.org/pdf/1702.06135.pdf`.

Praveen Dakwale and Christof Monz. 2017. Fine-tuning for neural machine translation with limited degradation across in- and out-of-domain data. In *Machine Translation Summit XVI*.

Fahim Dalvi, Nadir Durrani, Hassan Sajjad, and Stephan Vogel. 2018. Incremental decoding and training methods for simultaneous translation in neural machine translation. In *Proceedings of the 2018 Conference of the North American Chapter of the Association for Computational Linguistics: Human Language Technologies,* Volume 2: *Short Papers*. Association for

Computational Linguistics, New Orleans, LA, pages 493–499. `http://aclweb.org/anthology/N18-2079`.

Adrià de Gispert, Gonzalo Iglesias, and Bill Byrne. 2015. Fast and accurate preordering for SMT using neural networks. In *Proceedings of the 2015 Conference of the North American Chapter of the Association for Computational Linguistics: Human Language Technologies*. Association for Computational Linguistics, Denver, CO, pages 1012–1017. `www.aclweb.org/anthology/N15-1105`.

Mostafa Dehghani, Stephan Gouws, Oriol Vinyals, Jakob Uszkoreit, and Lukasz Kaiser. 2019. Universal transformers. In *International Conference on Learning Representations (ICLR)*. New Orleans, LA. `https://openreview.net/pdf?id=HyzdRiR9Y7`.

Florian Dessloch, Thanh-Le Ha, Markus Müller, Jan Niehues, Thai Son Nguyen, Ngoc-Quan Pham, Elizabeth Salesky, Matthias Sperber, Sebastian Stüker, Thomas Zenkel, and Alex Waibel. 2018. Kit lecture translator: Multilingual speech translation with one-shot learning. In *Proceedings of the 27th International Conference on Computational Linguistics: System Demonstrations*. Association for Computational Linguistics, Santa Fe, NM, pages 89–93. `www.aclweb.org/anthology/C18-2020`.

Jacob Devlin. 2017. Sharp models on dull hardware: Fast and accurate neural machine translation decoding on the CPU. In *Proceedings of the 2017 Conference on Empirical Methods in Natural Language Processing*. Association for Computational Linguistics, Copenhagen, pages 2810–2815. `http://aclweb.org/anthology/D17-1300`.

Jacob Devlin, Ming-Wei Chang, Kenton Lee, and Kristina Toutanova. 2019. BERT: Pre-training of deep bidirectional transformers for language understanding. In *Proceedings of the 2019 Conference of the North American Chapter of the Association for Computational Linguistics: Human Language Technologies*. Volume 1: *Long and Short Papers*. Association for Computational Linguistics, Minneapolis, MN, pages 4171–4186. `www.aclweb.org/anthology/N19-1423`.

Jacob Devlin, Rabih Zbib, Zhongqiang Huang, Thomas Lamar, Richard Schwartz, and John Makhoul. 2014. Fast and robust neural network joint models for statistical machine translation. In *Proceedings of the 52nd Annual Meeting of the Association for Computational Linguistics*. Volume 1: *Long Papers*.

Association for Computational Linguistics, Baltimore, MD, pages 1370–1380. www.aclweb.org/anthology/P14-1129.

Prajit Dhar and Arianna Bisazza. 2018. Does syntactic knowledge in multilingual language models transfer across languages? In *Proceedings of the 2018 EMNLP Workshop BlackboxNLP: Analyzing and Interpreting Neural Networks for NLP*. Association for Computational Linguistics, Brussels, pages 374–377. www.aclweb.org/anthology/W18-5453.

Shuoyang Ding, Hainan Xu, and Philipp Koehn. 2019a. Salience-driven word alignment interpretation for neural machine translation. In *Proceedings of the Conference on Machine Translation (WMT)*. Florence.

Shuoyang Ding, Hainan Xu, and Philipp Koehn. 2019b. Saliency-driven word alignment interpretation for neural machine translation. In *Proceedings of the Fourth Conference on Machine Translation*. Association for Computational Linguistics, Florence, pages 1–12.

Yanzhuo Ding, Yang Liu, Huanbo Luan, and Maosong Sun. 2017. Visualizing and understanding neural machine translation. In *Proceedings of the 55th Annual Meeting of the Association for Computational Linguistics. Volume 1: Long Papers*. Association for Computational Linguistics, Vancouver, BC, pages 1150–1159. http://aclweb.org/anthology/P17-1106.

Georgiana Dinu, Prashant Mathur, Marcello Federico, and Yaser Al-Onaizan. 2019. Training neural machine translation to apply terminology constraints. In *Proceedings of the 57th Conference of the Association for Computational Linguistics*. Association for Computational Linguistics, Florence, pages 3063–3068. www.aclweb.org/anthology/P19-1294.

Daxiang Dong, Hua Wu, Wei He, Dianhai Yu, and Haifeng Wang. 2015. Multi-task learning for multiple language translation. In *Proceedings of the 53rd Annual Meeting of the Association for Computational Linguistics and the 7th International Joint Conference on Natural Language Processing. Volume 1: Long Papers*. Association for Computational Linguistics, Beijing, pages 1723–1732. https://doi.org/10.3115/v1/P15-1166.

John Duchi, Elad Hazan, and Yoram Singer. 2011. Adaptive subgradient methods for online learning and stochastic optimization. *Journal of Machine Learning Research* 12:2121–2159. Nagoya, Japan

Chris Dyer, Victor Chahuneau, and Noah A. Smith. 2013. A simple, fast, and effective reparameterization of IBM model 2. In *Proceedings of the 2013 Conference of the North American Chapter of the Association for Computational Linguistics: Human Language Technologies*. Association for Computational Linguistics, Atlanta, GA, pages 644–648. www.aclweb.org/anthology/N13-1073.

Matthias Eck, Stephan Vogel, and Alex Waibel. 2005. Low cost portability for statistical machine translation based on n-gram frequency and TF-IDF. In *Proceedings of the International Workshop on Spoken Language Translation*. Pittsburgh, PA. http://20.210-193-52.unknown.qala.com.sg/archive/iwslt_05/papers/slt5_061.pdf.

Sergey Edunov, Myle Ott, Michael Auli, and David Grangier. 2018a. Understanding back-translation at scale. In *Proceedings of the 2018 Conference on Empirical Methods in Natural Language Processing*. Association for Computational Linguistics, Brussels, pages 489–500. www.aclweb.org/anthology/D18-1045.

Sergey Edunov, Myle Ott, Michael Auli, David Grangier, and Marc'Aurelio Ranzato. 2018b. Classical structured prediction losses for sequence to sequence learning. In *Proceedings of the 2018 Conference of the North American Chapter of the Association for Computational Linguistics: Human Language Technologies. Volume 1: Long Papers*. Association for Computational Linguistics, New Orleans, LA, pages 355–364. http://aclweb.org/anthology/N18-1033.

Sauleh Eetemadi, William Lewis, Kristina Toutanova, and Hayder Radha. 2015. Survey of data-selection methods in statistical machine translation. *Machine Translation* 29(3–4):189–223.

Bradley Efron and Robert J. Tibshirani. 1993. *An Introduction to the Bootstrap*. Boca Raton, FL: Chapman & Hall.

C. España-Bonet, Á'. C. Varga, A. Barrón-Cedeño, and J. van Genabith. 2017. An empirical analysis of NMT-derived interlingual embeddings and their use in parallel sentence identification. *IEEE Journal of Selected Topics in Signal Processing* 11(8):1340–1350. https://doi.org/10.1109/JSTSP.2017.2764273.

Thierry Etchegoyhen, Anna Fernández Torné, Andoni Azpeitia, Eva Martínez Garcia, and Anna Matamala. 2018. Evaluating domain adaptation for machine translation across scenarios. In *Proceedings of the Eleventh International Conference on Language Resources and Evaluation (LREC 2018)*. European

Language Resources Association (ELRA), Miyazaki, Japan, pages 6–18.

Marzieh Fadaee, Arianna Bisazza, and Christof Monz. 2017. Data augmentation for low-resource neural machine translation. In *Proceedings of the 55th Annual Meeting of the Association for Computational Linguistics. Volume 2: Short Papers.* Association for Computational Linguistics, Vancouver, BC, pages 567–573. http://aclweb.org/anthology/P17-2090.

Marzieh Fadaee and Christof Monz. 2018. Back-translation sampling by targeting difficult words in neural machine translation. In *Proceedings of the 2018 Conference on Empirical Methods in Natural Language Processing.* Association for Computational Linguistics, Brussels, pages 436–446. www.aclweb.org/anthology/D18-1040.

M. Amin Farajian, Marco Turchi, Matteo Negri, Nicola Bertoldi, and Marcello Federico. 2017a. Neural vs. phrase-based machine translation in a multi-domain scenario. In *Proceedings of the 15th Conference of the European Chapter of the Association for Computational Linguistics. Volume 2: Short Papers.* Association for Computational Linguistics, Valencia, Spain, pages 280–284. www.aclweb.org/anthology/E17-2045.

M. Amin Farajian, Marco Turchi, Matteo Negri, and Marcello Federico. 2017b. Multi-domain neural machine translation through unsupervised adaptation. In *Proceedings of the Second Conference on Machine Translation. Volume 1: Research Paper.* Association for Computational Linguistics, Copenhagen, pages 127–137. www.aclweb.org/anthology/W17-4713.

Manaal Faruqui and Chris Dyer. 2014. Improving vector space word representations using multilingual correlation. In *Proceedings of the 14th Conference of the European Chapter of the Association for Computational Linguistics.* Association for Computational Linguistics, Gothenburg, Sweden, pages 462–471. www.aclweb.org/anthology/E14-1049.

Shi Feng, Shujie Liu, Nan Yang, Mu Li, Ming Zhou, and Kenny Q. Zhu. 2016. Improving attention modeling with implicit distortion and fertility for machine translation. In *Proceedings of COLING 2016, the 26th International Conference on Computational Linguistics: Technical Papers.* The COLING 2016 Organizing Committee, Osaka, pages 3082–3092. http://aclweb.org/anthology/C16-1290.

Andrew Finch, Paul Dixon, and Eiichiro Sumita. 2012. Rescoring a phrase-based machine transliteration system with recurrent neural network language models. In *Proceedings of the 4th Named Entity Workshop (NEWS) 2012.* Association for Computational Linguistics, Jeju, Korea, pages 47–51. www.aclweb.org/anthology/W12-4406.

Orhan Firat, Kyunghyun Cho, and Yoshua Bengio. 2016a. Multi-way, multilingual neural machine translation with a shared attention mechanism. In *Proceedings of the 2016 Conference of the North American Chapter of the Association for Computational Linguistics: Human Language Technologies.* Association for Computational Linguistics, San Diego, CA, pages 866–875. http://www.aclweb.org/anthology/N16-1101.

Orhan Firat, Baskaran Sankaran, Yaser Al-Onaizan, Fatos T. Yarman Vural, and Kyunghyun Cho. 2016b. Zero-resource translation with multi-lingual neural machine translation. In *Proceedings of the 2016 Conference on Empirical Methods in Natural Language Processing.* Association for Computational Linguistics, Austin, TX, pages 268–277. https://aclweb.org/anthology/D16-1026.

Mikel L. Forcada and Ramón P. Ñeco. 1997. Recursive hetero-associative memories for translation. In *Biological and Artificial Computation: From Neuroscience to Technology*, Lanzarote, Canary Islands, pages 453–462.

Markus Freitag and Yaser Al-Onaizan. 2016. Fast domain adaptation for neural machine translation. Ithaca, NY: Cornell University, abs/1612.06897. http://arxiv.org/abs/1612.06897.

Markus Freitag and Yaser Al-Onaizan. 2017. Beam search strategies for neural machine translation. In *Proceedings of the First Workshop on Neural Machine Translation.* Association for Computational Linguistics, Vancouver, BC. pages 56–60. www.aclweb.org/anthology/W17-3207.

Christian Fügen, Alex Waibel, and Muntsin Kolss. 2007. Simultaneous translation of lectures and speeches. *Machine Translation* 21(4):209–252.

Mattia Antonino Di Gangi and Marcello Federico. 2017. Monolingual embeddings for low resourced neural machine translation. In *Proceedings of the International Workshop on Spoken Language Translation (IWSLT).* Stockholm. http://workshop2017.iwslt.org/downloads/P05-Paper.pdf.

Ekaterina Garmash and Christof Monz. 2016. Ensemble learning for multi-source neural machine translation. In *Proceedings of COLING 2016, the 26th International Conference on Computational Linguistics: Technical Papers.* The COLING 2016

Organizing Committee, Osaka, Japan, pages 1409–1418.
http://aclweb.org/anthology/C16-1133.

Jonas Gehring, Michael Auli, David Grangier, Denis Yarats, and Yann N. Dauphin. 2017. Convolutional sequence to sequence learning. Ithaca, NY: Cornell University, abs/1705.03122.
http://arxiv.org/abs/1705.03122.

Mevlana Gemici, Chia-Chun Hung, Adam Santoro, Greg Wayne, Shakir Mohamed, Danilo Jimenez Rezende, David Amos, and Timothy P. Lillicrap. 2017. Generative temporal models with memory. arXiv:1702.04649. Cornell University, Ithaca, NY.
http://arxiv.org/abs/1702.04649.

Xinwei Geng, Xiaocheng Feng, Bing Qin, and Ting Liu. 2018. Adaptive multi-pass decoder for neural machine translation. In *Proceedings of the 2018 Conference on Empirical Methods in Natural Language Processing*. Association for Computational Linguistics, Brussels, pages 523–532.
www.aclweb.org/anthology/D18-1048.

Hamidreza Ghader and Christof Monz. 2017. What does attention in neural machine translation pay attention to? In *Proceedings of the Eighth International Joint Conference on Natural Language Processing.* Volume 1: *Long Papers.* Asian Federation of Natural Language Processing, Taipei, pages 30–39.
www.aclweb.org/anthology/I17-1004.

Mario Giulianelli, Jack Harding, Florian Mohnert, Dieuwke Hupkes, and Willem Zuidema. 2018. Under the hood: Using diagnostic classifiers to investigate and improve how language models track agreement information. In *Proceedings of the 2018 EMNLP Workshop BlackboxNLP: Analyzing and Interpreting Neural Networks for NLP.* Association for Computational Linguistics, Brussels, pages 240–248.
www.aclweb.org/anthology/W18-5426.

Xavier Glorot and Yoshua Bengio. 2010. Understanding the difficulty of training deep feedforward neural networks. In *Proceedings of the 13th International Conference on Artificial Intelligence and Statistics (AISTATS).* Sardinia.

Yoav Goldberg. 2017. *Neural Network Methods for Natural Language Processing.* Volume 37: *Synthesis Lectures on Human Language Technologies.* Morgan & Claypool, San Rafael, CA. https://doi.org/10.2200/S00762ED1V01Y201703HLT037.

Ian Goodfellow, Yoshua Bengio, and Aaron Courville. 2016. *Deep Learning.* MIT Press, Boston.
www.deeplearningbook.org.

Stephan Gouws, Yoshua Bengio, and Greg Corrado. 2015. Bilbowa: Fast bilingual distributed representations without word alignments. In *Proceedings of the 32nd International Conference on International Conference on Machine Learning*, Volume 37. JMLR.org, ICML'15, Lille, France, pages 748–756.
http://arxiv.org/pdf/1410.2455.pdf.

Jiatao Gu, Kyunghyun Cho, and Victor O.K. Li. 2017a. Trainable greedy decoding for neural machine translation. In *Proceedings of the 2017 Conference on Empirical Methods in Natural Language Processing.* Association for Computational Linguistics, Copenhagen, pages 1958–1968.
http://aclweb.org/anthology/D17-1210.

Jiatao Gu, Hany Hassan, Jacob Devlin, and Victor O.K. Li. 2018a. Universal neural machine translation for extremely low resource languages. In *Proceedings of the 2018 Conference of the North American Chapter of the Association for Computational Linguistics: Human Language Technologies.* Volume 1: *Long Papers.* Association for Computational Linguistics, New Orleans, LA, pages 344–354.
http://aclweb.org/anthology/N18-1032.

Jiatao Gu, Zhengdong Lu, Hang Li, and Victor O.K. Li. 2016. Incorporating copying mechanism in sequence-to-sequence learning. In *Proceedings of the 54th Annual Meeting of the Association for Computational Linguistics.* Volume 1: *Long Papers.* Association for Computational Linguistics, Berlin, pages 1631–1640.
www.aclweb.org/anthology/P16-1154.

Jiatao Gu, Graham Neubig, Kyunghyun Cho, and Victor O.K. Li. 2017b. Learning to translate in real-time with neural machine translation. In *Proceedings of the 15th Conference of the European Chapter of the Association for Computational Linguistics.* Volume 1: *Long Papers.* Association for Computational Linguistics, Valencia, Spain, pages 1053–1062.
www.aclweb.org/anthology/E17-1099.

Jiatao Gu, Yong Wang, Yun Chen, Victor O. K. Li, and Kyunghyun Cho. 2018b. Meta-learning for low-resource neural machine translation. In *Proceedings of the 2018 Conference on Empirical Methods in Natural Language Processing.* Association for Computational Linguistics, Brussels, pages 3622–3631.
www.aclweb.org/anthology/D18-1398.

Jiatao Gu, Yong Wang, Kyunghyun Cho, and Victor O.K. Li. 2018c. Search engine guided non-parametric neural machine translation. In *Proceedings of the American*

Association for Artificial Intelligence. Monterey, CA. https://arxiv.org/pdf/1705.07267.

Liane Guillou and Christian Hardmeier. 2018. Automatic reference-based evaluation of pronoun translation misses the point. In *Proceedings of the 2018 Conference on Empirical Methods in Natural Language Processing*. Association for Computational Linguistics, Brussels, pages 4797–4802. www.aclweb.org/anthology/D18-1513.

Caglar Gulcehre, Sungjin Ahn, Ramesh Nallapati, Bowen Zhou, and Yoshua Bengio. 2016. Pointing the unknown words. In *Proceedings of the 54th Annual Meeting of the Association for Computational Linguistics*. Volume 1: *Long Papers*. Association for Computational Linguistics, Berlin, pages 140–149. www.aclweb.org/anthology/P16-1014.

Çaglar Gülçehre, Orhan Firat, Kelvin Xu, Kyunghyun Cho, Loïc Barrault, Huei-Chi Lin, Fethi Bougares, Holger Schwenk, and Yoshua Bengio. 2015. On using monolingual corpora in neural machine translation. Ithaca, NY: Cornell University, abs/1503.03535. http://arxiv.org/abs/1503.03535.

Kristina Gulordava, Piotr Bojanowski, Edouard Grave, Tal Linzen, and Marco Baroni. 2018. Colorless green recurrent networks dream hierarchically. In *Proceedings of the 2018 Conference of the North American Chapter of the Association for Computational Linguistics: Human Language Technologies*. Volume 1: *Long Papers*. Association for Computational Linguistics, New Orleans, LA, pages 1195–1205. https://doi.org/10.18653/v1/N18-1108.

Mandy Guo, Yinfei Yang, Keith Stevens, Daniel Cer, Heming Ge, Yun-hsuan Sung, Brian Strope, and Ray Kurzweil. 2019. Hierarchical document encoder for parallel corpus mining. In *Proceedings of the Fourth Conference on Machine Translation*. Association for Computational Linguistics, Florence, pages 64–72. www.aclweb.org/anthology/W19-5207.

Thanh-Le Ha, Jan Niehues, and Alex Waibel. 2016. Toward multilingual neural machine translation with universal encoder and decoder. In *Proceedings of the International Workshop on Spoken Language Translation (IWSLT)*. Seattle, WA. http://workshop2016.iwslt.org/downloads/IWSLT_2016_paper_5.pdf.

Thanh-Le Ha, Jan Niehues, and Alex Waibel. 2017. Effective strategies in zero-shot neural machine translation. In *Proceedings of the International Workshop on Spoken Language Translation (IWSLT)*.

Tokyo. http://workshop2017.iwslt.org/downloads/P06-Paper.pdf.

Kim Harris, Lucia Specia, and Aljoscha Burchardt. 2017. Feature-rich NMT and SMT post-edited corpora for productivity and evaluation tasks with a subset of MQM-annotated data. In *Machine Translation Summit XVI*. Nagoya, Japan.

Kazuma Hashimoto and Yoshimasa Tsuruoka. 2019. Accelerated reinforcement learning for sentence generation by vocabulary prediction. In *Proceedings of the 2019 Conference of the North American Chapter of the Association for Computational Linguistics: Human Language Technologies*. Volume 1: *Long and Short Papers*. Association for Computational Linguistics, Minneapolis, MN, pages 3115–3125. www.aclweb.org/anthology/N19-1315.

Eva Hasler, Phil Blunsom, Philipp Koehn, and Barry Haddow. 2014. Dynamic topic adaptation for phrase-based MT. In *Proceedings of the 14th Conference of the European Chapter of the Association for Computational Linguistics*. Association for Computational Linguistics, Gothenburg, pages 328–337. www.aclweb.org/anthology/E14-1035.

Eva Hasler, Adrià Gispert, Gonzalo Iglesias, and Bill Byrne. 2018. Neural machine translation decoding with terminology constraints. In *Proceedings of the 2018 Conference of the North American Chapter of the Association for Computational Linguistics: Human Language Technologies*. Volume 2: *Short Papers*. Association for Computational Linguistics, New Orleans, LA, pages 506–512. http://aclweb.org/anthology/N18-2081.

Hany Hassan, Anthony Aue, Chang Chen, Vishal Chowdhary, Jonathan Clark, Christian Federmann, Xuedong Huang, Marcin Junczys-Dowmunt, William Lewis, Mu Li, Shujie Liu, Tie-Yan Liu, Renqian Luo, Arul Menezes, Tao Qin, Frank Seide, Xu Tan, Fei Tian, Lijun Wu, Shuangzhi Wu, Yingce Xia, Dongdong Zhang, Zhirui Zhang, and Ming Zhou. 2018. Achieving human parity on automatic chinese to English news translation. Ithaca, NY: Cornell University abs/1803.05567. http://arxiv.org/abs/1803.05567.

Di He, Yingce Xia, Tao Qin, Liwei Wang, Nenghai Yu, Tieyan Liu, and Wei-Ying Ma. 2016a. Dual learning for machine translation. In D. D. Lee, M. Sugiyama, U. V. Luxburg, I. Guyon, and R. Garnett, editors, *Advances in Neural Information Processing Systems 29*, Barcelona, pages 820–828.

http://papers.nips.cc/paper/6469-dual-learning-for-machine-translation.pdf.

Wei He, Zhongjun He, Hua Wu, and Haifeng Wang. 2016b. Improved neural machine translation with SMT features. In *Proceedings of the Thirtieth AAAI Conference on Artificial Intelligence*. Phoenix, AZ, pages 151–157.

Geert Heyman, Bregt Verreet, Ivan Vulić, and Marie-Francine Moens. 2019. Learning unsupervised multilingual word embeddings with incremental multilingual hubs. In *Proceedings of the 2019 Conference of the North American Chapter of the Association for Computational Linguistics: Human Language Technologies*. Volume 1: *Long and Short Papers*. Association for Computational Linguistics, Minneapolis, MN, pages 1890–1902. www.aclweb.org/anthology/N19-1188.

Felix Hill, Kyunghyun Cho, Sébastien Jean, and Yoshua Bengio. 2017. The representational geometry of word meanings acquired by neural machine translation models. *Machine Translation* 31(1-2):3–18. https://doi.org/10.1007/s10590-017-9194-2.

Felix Hill, Kyunghyun Cho, Sébastien Jean, Coline Devin, and Yoshua Bengio. 2014. Embedding word similarity with neural machine translation. Ithaca, NY: Cornell University, abs/1412.6448. http://arxiv.org/abs/1412.6448.

Tosho Hirasawa, Hayahide Yamagishi, Yukio Matsumura, and Mamoru Komachi. 2019. Multimodal machine translation with embedding prediction. In *Proceedings of the 2019 Conference of the North American Chapter of the Association for Computational Linguistics: Student Research Workshop*. Association for Computational Linguistics, Minneapolis, MN, pages 86–91. www.aclweb.org/anthology/N19-3012.

Fabian Hirschmann, Jinseok Nam, and Johannes Fürnkranz. 2016. What makes word-level neural machine translation hard: A case study on english-german translation. In *Proceedings of COLING 2016, the 26th International Conference on Computational Linguistics: Technical Papers*. The COLING 2016 Organizing Committee, Osaka, pages 3199–3208. http://aclweb.org/anthology/C16-1301.

Cong Duy Vu Hoang, Gholamreza Haffari, and Trevor Cohn. 2017. Towards decoding as continuous optimisation in neural machine translation. In *Proceedings of the 2017 Conference on Empirical Methods in Natural Language Processing*. Association for Computational

Linguistics, Copenhagen, pages 146–156. http://aclweb.org/anthology/D17-1014.

Hieu Hoang, Tomasz Dwojak, Rihards Krislauks, Daniel Torregrosa, and Kenneth Heafield. 2018a. Fast neural machine translation implementation. In *Proceedings of the 2nd Workshop on Neural Machine Translation and Generation*. Association for Computational Linguistics, Melbourne, pages 116–121. http://aclweb.org/anthology/W18-2714.

Vu Cong Duy Hoang, Philipp Koehn, Gholamreza Haffari, and Trevor Cohn. 2018b. Iterative back-translation for neural machine translation. In *Proceedings of the 2nd Workshop on Neural Machine Translation and Generation*. Association for Computational Linguistics, Melbourne, pages 18–24. http://aclweb.org/anthology/W18-2703.

Chris Hokamp and Qun Liu. 2017. Lexically constrained decoding for sequence generation using grid beam search. In *Proceedings of the 55th Annual Meeting of the Association for Computational Linguistics*. Volume 1: *Long Papers*. Association for Computational Linguistics, Vancouver, BC, pages 1535–1546. http://aclweb.org/anthology/P17-1141.

Kurt Hornik, Maxwell Stinchcombe, and Halbert White. 1989. Multilayer feedforward networks are universal approximators. *Neural Networks* 2:359–366.

Yedid Hoshen and Lior Wolf. 2018. Non-adversarial unsupervised word translation. In *Proceedings of the 2018 Conference on Empirical Methods in Natural Language Processing*. Association for Computational Linguistics, Brussels, pages 469–478. www.aclweb.org/anthology/D18-1043.

Baotian Hu, Zhaopeng Tu, Zhengdong Lu, Hang Li, and Qingcai Chen. 2015a. Context-dependent translation selection using convolutional neural network. In *Proceedings of the 53rd Annual Meeting of the Association for Computational Linguistics and the 7th International Joint Conference on Natural Language Processing*. Volume 2: *Short Papers*. Association for Computational Linguistics, Beijing, pages 536–541. www.aclweb.org/anthology/P15-2088.

J. Edward Hu, Huda Khayrallah, Ryan Culkin, Patrick Xia, Tongfei Chen, Matt Post, and Benjamin Van Durme. 2019. Improved lexically constrained decoding for translation and monolingual rewriting. In *Proceedings of the 2019 Conference of the North American Chapter of the Association for Computational Linguistics: Human Language Technologies*. Volume 1: *Long and Short Papers*. Association for Computational Linguistics, Minneapolis, MN, pages 839–850. www.aclweb.org/anthology/N19-1090.

Xiaoguang Hu, Wei Li, Xiang Lan, Hua Wu, and Haifeng Wang. 2015b. Improved beam search with constrained softmax for nmt. In *Machine Translation Summit XV*. Miami, FL, pages 297–309.
`www.mt-archive.info/15/MTS-2015-Hu.pdf`.

Jiaji Huang, Qiang Qiu, and Kenneth Church. 2019. Hubless nearest neighbor search for bilingual lexicon induction. In *Proceedings of the 57th Conference of the Association for Computational Linguistics*. Association for Computational Linguistics, Florence, pages 4072–4080.
`www.aclweb.org/anthology/P19-1399`.

Liang Huang, Kai Zhao, and Mingbo Ma. 2017. When to finish? optimal beam search for neural text generation (modulo beam size). In *Proceedings of the 2017 Conference on Empirical Methods in Natural Language Processing*. Association for Computational Linguistics, Copenhagen, pages 2134–2139.
`https://doi.org/10.18653/v1/D17-1227`.

Matthias Huck, Simon Riess, and Alexander Fraser. 2017. Target-side word segmentation strategies for neural machine translation. In *Proceedings of the Second Conference on Machine Translation*. Volume 1: *Research Paper*. Association for Computational Linguistics, Copenhagen, pages 56–67.
`www.aclweb.org/anthology/W17-4706`.

Gonzalo Iglesias, William Tambellini, Adrià Gispert, Eva Hasler, and Bill Byrne. 2018. Accelerating NMT batched beam decoding with lmbr posteriors for deployment. In *Proceedings of the 2018 Conference of the North American Chapter of the Association for Computational Linguistics: Human Language Technologies*. Volume 3: *Industry Papers*. Association for Computational Linguistics, New Orleans, LA, pages 106–113.
`http://aclweb.org/anthology/N18-3013`.

Kenji Imamura, Atsushi Fujita, and Eiichiro Sumita. 2018. Enhancement of encoder and attention using target monolingual corpora in neural machine translation. In *Proceedings of the 2nd Workshop on Neural Machine Translation and Generation*. Association for Computational Linguistics, Melbourne, pages 55–63.
`http://aclweb.org/anthology/W18-2707`.

Kenji Imamura and Eiichiro Sumita. 2018. Nict self-training approach to neural machine translation at NMT-2018. In *Proceedings of the 2nd Workshop on Neural Machine Translation and Generation*. Association for Computational Linguistics, Melbourne, pages 110–115.
`http://aclweb.org/anthology/W18-2713`.

Ann Irvine, John Morgan, Marine Carpuat, Hal Daume III, and Dragos Munteanu. 2013. Measuring machine translation errors in new domains. In *Transactions of the Association for Computational Linguistics (TACL)*. 1, pages 429–440.
`www.transacl.org/wp-content/uploads/2013/10/paperno35.pdf`.

Pierre Isabelle, Colin Cherry, and George Foster. 2017. A challenge set approach to evaluating machine translation. In *Proceedings of the 2017 Conference on Empirical Methods in Natural Language Processing*. Association for Computational Linguistics, Copenhagen, pages 2476–2486.
`http://aclweb.org/anthology/D17-1262`.

Sébastien Jean, Kyunghyun Cho, Roland Memisevic, and Yoshua Bengio. 2015. On using very large target vocabulary for neural machine translation. In *Proceedings of the 53rd Annual Meeting of the Association for Computational Linguistics and the 7th International Joint Conference on Natural Language Processing*. Volume 1: *Long Papers*. Association for Computational Linguistics, Beijing, pages 1–10.
`www.aclweb.org/anthology/P15-1001`.

Melvin Johnson, Mike Schuster, Quoc Le, Maxim Krikun, Yonghui Wu, Zhifeng Chen, Nikhil Thorat, Fernanda Viegas, Martin Wattenberg, Greg Corrado, Macduff Hughes, and Jeffrey Dean. 2017. Google's multilingual neural machine translation system: Enabling zero-shot translation. *Transactions of the Association for Computational Linguistics* 5:339–351.
`https://transacl.org/ojs/index.php/tacl/article/view/1081`.

Armand Joulin, Piotr Bojanowski, Tomas Mikolov, Hervé Jégou, and Edouard Grave. 2018. Loss in translation: Learning bilingual word mapping with a retrieval criterion. In *Proceedings of the 2018 Conference on Empirical Methods in Natural Language Processing*. Association for Computational Linguistics, Brussels, pages 2979–2984.
`www.aclweb.org/anthology/D18-1330`.

Marcin Junczys-Dowmunt. 2019. Microsoft translator at wmt 2019: Towards large-scale document-level neural machine translation. In *Proceedings of the Fourth Conference on Machine Translation. Shared Task Papers*. Association for Computational Linguistics, Florence.

Marcin Junczys-Dowmunt, Tomasz Dwojak, and Hieu Hoang. 2016. Is neural machine translation ready for deployment? A case study on 30 translation directions. In *Proceedings of the International Workshop on Spoken Language Translation (IWSLT)*. Seattle, WA.
`http://workshop2016.iwslt.org/downloads/IWSLT_2016_paper_4.pdf`.

Nal Kalchbrenner and Phil Blunsom. 2013. Recurrent continuous translation models. In *Proceedings of the 2013 Conference on Empirical Methods in Natural Language Processing*. Association for Computational Linguistics, Seattle, pages 1700–1709. www.aclweb.org/anthology/D13-1176.

Shin Kanouchi, Katsuhito Sudoh, and Mamoru Komachi. 2016. Neural reordering model considering phrase translation and word alignment for phrase-based translation. In *Proceedings of the 3rd Workshop on Asian Translation (WAT2016)*. The COLING 2016 Organizing Committee, Osaka, pages 94–103. aclweb.org/anthology/W16-4607.

Andrej Karpathy, Justin Johnson, and Fei-Fei Li. 2016. Visualizing and understanding recurrent networks. In *International Conference on Learning Representations (ICLR)*. San Juan, Puerto Rico. https://arxiv.org/pdf/1506.02078.

Huda Khayrallah, Gaurav Kumar, Kevin Duh, Matt Post, and Philipp Koehn. 2017. Neural lattice search for domain adaptation in machine translation. In *Proceedings of the Eighth International Joint Conference on Natural Language Processing*. Volume 2: *Short Papers*. Asian Federation of Natural Language Processing, Taipei, pages 20–25. www.aclweb.org/anthology/I17-2004.

Huda Khayrallah, Brian Thompson, Kevin Duh, and Philipp Koehn. 2018a. Regularized training objective for continued training for domain adaptation in neural machine translation. In *Proceedings of the 2nd Workshop on Neural Machine Translation and Generation*. Association for Computational Linguistics, Melbourne, pages 36–44. http://aclweb.org/anthology/W18-2705.

Huda Khayrallah, Brian Thompson, Kevin Duh, and Philipp Koehn. 2018b. Regularized training objective for continued training for domain adaption in neural machine translation. In *Proceedings of the Second Workshop on Neural Machine Translation and Generation*. Association for Computational Linguistics. Melbourne.

Yuta Kikuchi, Graham Neubig, Ryohei Sasano, Hiroya Takamura, and Manabu Okumura. 2016. Controlling output length in neural encoder-decoders. In *Proceedings of the 2016 Conference on Empirical Methods in Natural Language Processing*. Association for Computational Linguistics, Austin, TX, pages 1328–1338. https://aclweb.org/anthology/D16-1140.

Yoon Kim, Yacine Jernite, David Sontag, and Alexander M. Rush. 2016. Character-aware neural language models.

In *Proceedings of the Thirtieth AAAI Conference on Artificial Intelligence*. AAAI Press, AAAI'16, Pheonix, AZ, pages 2741–2749. http://dl.acm.org/citation.cfm?id=3016100.3016285.

Diederik P. Kingma and Jimmy Ba. 2015. Adam: A method for stochastic optimization. Paper presented at the 3rd International Conference on Learning Representations, San Diego, CA. https://arxiv.org/pdf/1412.6980.pdf.

Filip Klubička, Antonio Toral, and Víctor M. Sánchez-Cartagena. 2017. Fine-grained human evaluation of neural versus phrase-based machine translation. *The Prague Bulletin of Mathematical Linguistics* 108:121–132. https://doi.org/10.1515/pralin-2017-0014.

Rebecca Knowles and Philipp Koehn. 2016. Neural interactive translation prediction. In *Proceedings of the Conference of the Association for Machine Translation in the Americas (AMTA)*. Austin, TX.

Rebecca Knowles and Philipp Koehn. 2018. Context and copying in neural machine translation. In *Proceedings of the 2018 Conference on Empirical Methods in Natural Language Processing*. Association for Computational Linguistics, Brussels, pages 3034–3041. www.aclweb.org/anthology/D18-1339.

Rebecca Knowles, Marina Sanchez-Torron, and Philipp Koehn. 2019. A user study of neural interactive translation prediction. *Machine Translation* 33(1):135–154. https://doi.org/10.1007/s10590-019-09235-8.

Catherine Kobus, Josep Crego, and Jean Senellart. 2017. Domain control for neural machine translation. In *Proceedings of the International Conference Recent Advances in Natural Language Processing, RANLP 2017*. INCOMA Ltd., Varna, Bulgaria, pages 372–378. https://doi.org/10.26615/978-954-452-049-6_049.

Tom Kocmi and Ondřej Bojar. 2017. Curriculum learning and minibatch bucketing in neural machine translation. In *Proceedings of the International Conference Recent Advances in Natural Language Processing, RANLP 2017*. INCOMA Ltd., Varna, Bulgaria, pages 379–386. https://doi.org/10.26615/978-954-452-049-6_050.

Philipp Koehn. 2010. *Statistical Machine Translation*. Cambridge: Cambridge University Press.

Philipp Koehn, Huda Khayrallah, Kenneth Heafield, and Mikel L. Forcada. 2018. Findings of the wmt 2018 shared task on parallel corpus filtering. In *Proceedings of the Third Conference on Machine Translation*.

Association for Computational Linguistics, Belgium, pages 739–752. www.aclweb.org/anthology/W18-64081.

Philipp Koehn and Rebecca Knowles. 2017. Six challenges for neural machine translation. In *Proceedings of the First Workshop on Neural Machine Translation*. Association for Computational Linguistics, Vancouver, BC, pages 28–39. www.aclweb.org/anthology/W17-3204.

Philipp Koehn and Christof Monz. 2005. Shared task: Statistical machine translation between European languages. In *Proceedings of the ACL Workshop on Building and Using Parallel Texts*. Association for Computational Linguistics, Ann Arbor, MI, pages 119–124. www.aclweb.org/anthology/W/W05/W05-0820.

Sachith Sri Ram Kothur, Rebecca Knowles, and Philipp Koehn. 2018a. Document-level adaptation for neural machine translation. In *Proceedings of the Second Workshop on Neural Machine Translation and Generation*. Association for Computational Linguistics. Melbourne.

Sachith Sri Ram Kothur, Rebecca Knowles, and Philipp Koehn. 2018b. Document-level adaptation for neural machine translation. In *Proceedings of the 2nd Workshop on Neural Machine Translation and Generation*. Association for Computational Linguistics, Melbourne, pages 64–73. http://aclweb.org/anthology/W18-2708.

Taku Kudo. 2018. Subword regularization: Improving neural network translation models with multiple subword candidates. In *Proceedings of the 56th Annual Meeting of the Association for Computational Linguistics*. Volume 1: *Long Papers*. Association for Computational Linguistics, Melbourne, pages 66–75. http://aclweb.org/anthology/P18-1007.

Taku Kudo and John Richardson. 2018. Sentencepiece: A simple and language independent subword tokenizer and detokenizer for neural text processing. In *Proceedings of the 2018 Conference on Empirical Methods in Natural Language Processing: System Demonstrations*. Association for Computational Linguistics, Brussels, pages 66–71. www.aclweb.org/anthology/D18-2012.

Gaurav Kumar, George Foster, Colin Cherry, and Maxim Krikun. 2019. Reinforcement learning based curriculum optimization for neural machine translation. In *Proceedings of the 2019 Conference of the North American Chapter of the Association for Computational Linguistics: Human Language Technologies*. Volume 1: *Long and Short Papers*.

Association for Computational Linguistics, Minneapolis, MN, pages 2054–2061. www.aclweb.org/anthology/N19-1208.

Surafel Melaku Lakew, Mauro Cettolo, and Marcello Federico. 2018a. A comparison of transformer and recurrent neural networks on multilingual neural machine translation. In *Proceedings of the 27th International Conference on Computational Linguistics*. Association for Computational Linguistics, Santa Fe, NM, pages 641–652. www.aclweb.org/anthology/C18-1054.

Surafel Melaku Lakew, Aliia Erofeeva, and Marcello Federico. 2018b. Neural machine translation into language varieties. In *Proceedings of the Third Conference on Machine Translation: Research Papers*. Association for Computational Linguistics, Belgium, pages 156–164. www.aclweb.org/anthology/W18-6316.

Surafel Melaku Lakew, Aliia Erofeeva, Matteo Negri, Marcello Federico, and Marco Turchi. 2018c. Transfer learning in multilingual neural machine translation with dynamic vocabulary. In *Proceedings of the International Workshop on Spoken Language Translation (IWSLT)*. Bruge, Belgium. https://arxiv.org/pdf/1811.01137.pdf.

Guillaume Lample, Alexis Conneau, Ludovic Denoyer, and Marc'Aurelio Ranzato. 2018a. Unsupervised machine translation using monolingual corpora only. In *International Conference on Learning Representations*. Vancouver, BC. https://openreview.net/forum?id=rkYTTf-AZ.

Guillaume Lample, Myle Ott, Alexis Conneau, Ludovic Denoyer, and Marc'Aurelio Ranzato. 2018b. Phrase-based & neural unsupervised machine translation. In *Proceedings of the 2018 Conference on Empirical Methods in Natural Language Processing*. Association for Computational Linguistics, Brussels, pages 5039–5049. www.aclweb.org/anthology/D18-1549.

Samuel Läubli, Rico Sennrich, and Martin Volk. 2018. Has machine translation achieved human parity? A case for document-level evaluation. In *Proceedings of the 2018 Conference on Empirical Methods in Natural Language Processing*. Association for Computational Linguistics, Brussels, pages 4791–4796. www.aclweb.org/anthology/D18-1512.

Yann LeCun, B. Boser, J. Denker, D. Henderson, R. Howard, W. Hubbard, and L. Jackel. 1989. Backpropagation applied to handwritten zip code recognition. *Neural Computation* 1(4):541–551.

Jaesong Lee, Joong-Hwi Shin, and Jun-Seok Kim. 2017. Interactive visualization and manipulation of attention-based neural machine translation. In *Proceedings of the 2017 Conference on Empirical Methods in Natural Language Processing: System Demonstrations*. Association for Computational Linguistics, Copenhagen, pages 121–126. http://aclweb.org/anthology/D17-2021.

J. Lei Ba, J. R. Kiros, and Geoffrey Hinton. 2016. Layer normalization. Ithaca, NY: Cornell University, ArXiv e-prints.

William Lewis and Sauleh Eetemadi. 2013. Dramatically reducing training data size through vocabulary saturation. In *Proceedings of the Eighth Workshop on Statistical Machine Translation*. Association for Computational Linguistics, Sofia, Bulgaria, pages 281–291. www.aclweb.org/anthology/W13-2235.

Guanlin Li, Lemao Liu, Xintong Li, Conghui Zhu, Tiejun Zhao, and Shuming Shi. 2019. Understanding and improving hidden representations for neural machine translation. In *Proceedings of the 2019 Conference of the North American Chapter of the Association for Computational Linguistics: Human Language Technologies. Volume 1: Long and Short Papers*. Association for Computational Linguistics, Minneapolis, MN, pages 466–477. www.aclweb.org/anthology/N19-1046.

Jiwei Li and Dan Jurafsky. 2016. Mutual information and diverse decoding improve neural machine translation. Ithaca, NY: Cornell University, abs/1601.00372. http://arxiv.org/abs/1601.00372.

Jiwei Li, Will Monroe, and Dan Jurafsky. 2016. A simple, fast diverse decoding algorithm for neural generation. Ithaca, NY: Cornell University, abs/1611.08562. http://arxiv.org/abs/1611.08562.

Peng Li, Yang Liu, Maosong Sun, Tatsuya Izuha, and Dakun Zhang. 2014. A neural reordering model for phrase-based translation. In *Proceedings of COLING 2014, the 25th International Conference on Computational Linguistics: Technical Papers*. Dublin City University and Association for Computational Linguistics, Dublin, pages 1897–1907. www.aclweb.org/anthology/C14-1179.

Xiaoqing Li, Jiajun Zhang, and Chengqing Zong. 2018. One sentence one model for neural machine translation. In *Proceedings of the Eleventh International Conference on Language Resources and Evaluation (LREC 2018)*. European Language Resources Association (ELRA), Miyazaki, Japan.

Tal Linzen, Emmanuel Dupoux, and Yoav Goldberg. 2016. Assessing the ability of LSTMs to learn syntax-sensitive dependencies. *Transactions of the Association for Computational Linguistics* 4:521–535. https://doi.org/10.1162/tacl_a_00115.

P. Lison and Jörg Tiedemann. 2016. Opensubtitles2016: Extracting large parallel corpora from movie and TV subtitles. In *Proceedings of the 10th International Conference on Language Resources and Evaluation (LREC 2016)*. European Language Resources Association (ELRA), Portorož, Slovenia.

Lemao Liu, Masao Utiyama, Andrew Finch, and Eiichiro Sumita. 2016a. Agreement on target-bidirectional neural machine translation. In *Proceedings of the 2016 Conference of the North American Chapter of the Association for Computational Linguistics: Human Language Technologies*. Association for Computational Linguistics, San Diego, CA, pages 411–416. www.aclweb.org/anthology/N16-1046.

Lemao Liu, Masao Utiyama, Andrew Finch, and Eiichiro Sumita. 2016b. Neural machine translation with supervised attention. In *Proceedings of COLING 2016, the 26th International Conference on Computational Linguistics: Technical Papers*. The COLING 2016 Organizing Committee, Osaka, pages 3093–3102. http://aclweb.org/anthology/C16-1291.

Shixiang Lu, Zhenbiao Chen, and Bo Xu. 2014. Learning new semi-supervised deep auto-encoder features for statistical machine translation. In *Proceedings of the 52nd Annual Meeting of the Association for Computational Linguistics. Volume 1: Long Papers*. Association for Computational Linguistics, Baltimore, MD, pages 122–132. www.aclweb.org/anthology/P14-1012.

Yichao Lu, Phillip Keung, Faisal Ladhak, Vikas Bhardwaj, Shaonan Zhang, and Jason Sun. 2018. A neural interlingua for multilingual machine translation. In *Proceedings of the Third Conference on Machine Translation: Research Papers*. Association for Computational Linguistics, Belgium, pages 84–92. www.aclweb.org/anthology/W18-6309.

Minh-Thang Luong and Christopher Manning. 2015. Stanford neural machine translation systems for spoken language domains. In *Proceedings of the International Workshop on Spoken Language Translation (IWSLT)*. Da Nang, Vietnam, pages 76–79. www.mt-archive.info/15/IWSLT-2015-luong.pdf.

Thang Luong, Michael Kayser, and Christopher D. Manning. 2015a. Deep neural language models for machine translation. In *Proceedings of the Nineteenth*

Conference on Computational Natural Language Learning. Association for Computational Linguistics, Beijing, pages 305–309. www.aclweb.org/anthology/K15-1031.

Thang Luong, Hieu Pham, and Christopher D. Manning. 2015b. Effective approaches to attention-based neural machine translation. In *Proceedings of the 2015 Conference on Empirical Methods in Natural Language Processing*. Association for Computational Linguistics, Lisbon, pages 1412–1421. http://aclweb.org/anthology/D15-1166.

Thang Luong, Ilya Sutskever, Quoc Le, Oriol Vinyals, and Wojciech Zaremba. 2015c. Addressing the rare word problem in neural machine translation. In *Proceedings of the 53rd Annual Meeting of the Association for Computational Linguistics and the 7th International Joint Conference on Natural Language Processing*. Volume 1: *Long Papers*. Association for Computational Linguistics, Beijing, pages 11–19. www.aclweb.org/anthology/P15-1002.

Thang Luong, Ilya Sutskever, Quoc V. Le, Oriol Vinyals, and Wojciech Zaremba. 2015d. Addressing the rare word problem in neural machine translation. In *Proceedings of the 53rd Annual Meeting of the Association for Computational Linguistics and the 7th International Joint Conference on Natural Language Processing*. Volume 1: *Long Papers*. Association for Computational Linguistics, Beijing, pages 11–19. www.aclweb.org/anthology/P15-1002.

Chunpeng Ma, Akihiro Tamura, Masao Utiyama, Eiichiro Sumita, and Tiejun Zhao. 2019a. Improving neural machine translation with neural syntactic distance. In *Proceedings of the 2019 Conference of the North American Chapter of the Association for Computational Linguistics: Human Language Technologies*. Volume 1: *Long and Short Papers*. Association for Computational Linguistics, Minneapolis, MN, pages 2032–2037. www.aclweb.org/anthology/N19-1205.

Mingbo Ma, Liang Huang, Hao Xiong, Renjie Zheng, Kaibo Liu, Baigong Zheng, Chuanqiang Zhang, Zhongjun He, Hairong Liu, Xing Li, Hua Wu, and Haifeng Wang. 2019b. STACL: Simultaneous translation with implicit anticipation and controllable latency using prefix-to-prefix framework. In *Proceedings of the 57th Conference of the Association for Computational Linguistics*. Association for Computational Linguistics, Florence, pages 3025–3036. www.aclweb.org/anthology/P19-1289.

Mingbo Ma, Renjie Zheng, and Liang Huang. 2019c. Learning to stop in structured prediction for neural machine translation. In *Proceedings of the 2019 Conference of the North American Chapter of the Association for Computational Linguistics: Human Language Technologies*. Volume 1: *Long and Short Papers*. Association for Computational Linguistics, Minneapolis, MN, pages 1884–1889. www.aclweb.org/anthology/N19-1187.

Xutai Ma, Ke Li, and Philipp Koehn. 2018. An analysis of source context dependency in neural machine translation. In *Proceedings of the 21st Annual Conference of the European Association for Machine Translation*. Melbourne.

Chaitanya Malaviya, Graham Neubig, and Patrick Littell. 2017. Learning language representations for typology prediction. In *Proceedings of the 2017 Conference on Empirical Methods in Natural Language Processing*. Association for Computational Linguistics, Copenhagen, pages 2529–2535. http://aclweb.org/anthology/D17-1268.

Christopher D. Manning. 2015. Computational linguistics and deep learning. *Computational Linguistics* 41(4):701–707.

Benjamin Marie and Atsushi Fujita. 2019. Unsupervised joint training of bilingual word embeddings. In *Proceedings of the 57th Conference of the Association for Computational Linguistics*. Association for Computational Linguistics, Florence, pages 3224–3230. www.aclweb.org/anthology/P19-1312.

Marianna J. Martindale and Marine Carpuat. 2018. Fluency over adequacy: A pilot study in measuring user trust in imperfect MT. In *Annual Meeting of the Association for Machine Translation in the DAmericas (AMTA)*. Boston. https://arxiv.org/pdf/1802.06041.pdf.

Sameen Maruf, André F. T. Martins, and Gholamreza Haffari. 2018. Contextual neural model for translating bilingual multi-speaker conversations. In *Proceedings of the Third Conference on Machine Translation: Research Papers*. Association for Computational Linguistics, Belgium, pages 101–112. www.aclweb.org/anthology/W18-6311.

Sameen Maruf, André F. T. Martins, and Gholamreza Haffari. 2019. Selective attention for context-aware neural machine translation. In *Proceedings of the 2019 Conference of the North American Chapter of the Association for Computational Linguistics: Human Language Technologies*. Volume 1: *Long and Short*

Papers. Association for Computational Linguistics, Minneapolis, MN, pages 3092–3102. www.aclweb.org/anthology/N19-1313.

Rebecca Marvin and Philipp Koehn. 2018. Exploring word sense disambiguation abilities of neural machine translation systems. In *Annual Meeting of the Association for Machine Translation in the Americas (AMTA)*. Boston, MA.

Giulia Mattoni, Pat Nagle, Carlos Collantes, and Dimitar Shterionov. 2017. Zero-shot translation for low-resource Indian languages. In *Machine Translation Summit XVI*. Nagoya, Japan.

S. McCulloch and W. Pitts. 1943. A logical calculus of the ideas immanent in nervous activity. *The Bulletin of Mathematical Biophysics* 5(4):115–133.

Fandong Meng, Zhengdong Lu, Hang Li, and Qun Liu. 2016. Interactive attention for neural machine translation. In *Proceedings of COLING 2016, the 26th International Conference on Computational Linguistics: Technical Papers*. The COLING 2016 Organizing Committee, Osaka, pages 2174–2185. http://aclweb.org/anthology/C16-1205.

Haitao Mi, Zhiguo Wang, and Abe Ittycheriah. 2016. Vocabulary manipulation for neural machine translation. In *Proceedings of the 54th Annual Meeting of the Association for Computational Linguistics. Volume 2: Short Papers*. Association for Computational Linguistics, Berlin, pages 124–129. http://anthology.aclweb.org/P16-2021.

Antonio Valerio Miceli Barone. 2016. Towards cross-lingual distributed representations without parallel text trained with adversarial autoencoders. In *Proceedings of the 1st Workshop on Representation Learning for NLP*. Association for Computational Linguistics, Berlin, pages 121–126. https://doi.org/10.18653/v1/W16-1614.

Antonio Valerio Miceli Barone, Barry Haddow, Ulrich Germann, and Rico Sennrich. 2017a. Regularization techniques for fine-tuning in neural machine translation. In *Proceedings of the 2017 Conference on Empirical Methods in Natural Language Processing*. Association for Computational Linguistics, Copenhagen, pages 1490–1495. http://aclweb.org/anthology/D17-1156.

Antonio Valerio Miceli Barone, Jindřich Helcl, Rico Sennrich, Barry Haddow, and Alexandra Birch. 2017b. Deep architectures for neural machine translation. In *Proceedings of the Second Conference on Machine Translation, Volume 1: Research Paper*. Association

for Computational Linguistics, Copenhagen, pages 99–107. www.aclweb.org/anthology/W17-4710.

Paul Michel and Graham Neubig. 2018. Extreme adaptation for personalized neural machine translation. In *Proceedings of the 55th Annual Meeting of the Association for Computational Linguistics. Volume 2: Short Papers*. Association for Computational Linguistics. Vancouver, BC.

Lesly Miculicich, Dhananjay Ram, Nikolaos Pappas, and James Henderson. 2018. Document-level neural machine translation with hierarchical attention networks. In *Proceedings of the 2018 Conference on Empirical Methods in Natural Language Processing*. Association for Computational Linguistics, Brussels, pages 2947–2954. www.aclweb.org/anthology/D18-1325.

Tomas Mikolov. 2012. Statistical language models based on neural networks. PhD thesis, Brno University of Technology. www.fit.vutbr.cz/ imikolov/rnnlm/thesis.pdf.

Tomas Mikolov, Kai Chen, Greg Corrado, and Jeffrey Dean. 2013a. Efficient estimation of word representations in vector space. Ithaca, NY: Cornell University, abs/1301.3781. http://arxiv.org/abs/1301.3781.

Tomas Mikolov, Quoc V. Le, and Ilya Sutskever. 2013b. Exploiting similarities among languages for machine translation. Ithaca, NY: Cornell University, abs/1309.4168. http://arxiv.org/abs/1309.4168.

Tomas Mikolov, Ilya Sutskever, Kai Chen, Greg Corrado, and Jeffrey Dean. 2013c. Distributed representations of words and phrases and their compositionality. Ithaca, NY: Cornell University, abs/1310.4546. http://arxiv.org/abs/1310.4546.

Tomas Mikolov, Wen-tau Yih, and Geoffrey Zweig. 2013d. Linguistic regularities in continuous space word representations. In *Proceedings of the 2013 Conference of the North American Chapter of the Association for Computational Linguistics: Human Language Technologies*. Association for Computational Linguistics, Atlanta, GA, pages 746–751. www.aclweb.org/anthology/N13-1090.

Marvin Minsky and Seymour Papert. 1969. *Perceptrons. An Introduction to Computational Geometry*. MIT Press, Cambridge, MA.

Tasnim Mohiuddin and Shafiq Joty. 2019. Revisiting adversarial autoencoder for unsupervised word translation with cycle consistency and improved training. In *Proceedings of the 2019 Conference of the North American Chapter of the Association for Computational Linguistics: Human Language Technologies*. Volume 1: *Long and Short Papers*. Association for Computational Linguistics, Minneapolis, MN, pages 3857–3867. www.aclweb.org/anthology/N19-1386.

Makoto Morishita, Jun Suzuki, and Masaaki Nagata. 2018. Improving neural machine translation by incorporating hierarchical subword features. In *Proceedings of the 27th International Conference on Computational Linguistics*. Association for Computational Linguistics, Santa Fe, NM, pages 618–629. www.aclweb.org/anthology/C18-1052.

Tanmoy Mukherjee, Makoto Yamada, and Timothy Hospedales. 2018. Learning unsupervised word translations without adversaries. In *Proceedings of the 2018 Conference on Empirical Methods in Natural Language Processing*. Association for Computational Linguistics, Brussels, pages 627–632. www.aclweb.org/anthology/D18-1063.

Mathias Müller, Annette Rios, Elena Voita, and Rico Sennrich. 2018. A large-scale test set for the evaluation of context-aware pronoun translation in neural machine translation. In *Proceedings of the Third Conference on Machine Translation: Research Papers*. Association for Computational Linguistics, Belgium, pages 61–72. www.aclweb.org/anthology/W18-6307.

Kenton Murray and David Chiang. 2018. Correcting length bias in neural machine translation. In *Proceedings of the Third Conference on Machine Translation: Research Papers*. Association for Computational Linguistics, Belgium, pages 212–223. www.aclweb.org/anthology/W18-6322.

Rudra Murthy, Anoop Kunchukuttan, and Pushpak Bhattacharyya. 2019. Addressing word-order divergence in multilingual neural machine translation for extremely low resource languages. In *Proceedings of the 2019 Conference of the North American Chapter of the Association for Computational Linguistics: Human Language Technologies*. Volume 1: *Long and Short Papers*. Association for Computational Linguistics, Minneapolis, MN, pages 3868–3873. www.aclweb.org/anthology/N19-1387.

Maria Nadejde, Siva Reddy, Rico Sennrich, Tomasz Dwojak, Marcin Junczys-Dowmunt, Philipp Koehn, and Alexandra Birch. 2017. Predicting target language CCG supertags improves neural machine translation. In *Proceedings of the Second Conference on Machine Translation*. Volume 1: *Research Papers*. Association

for Computational Linguistics, Copenhagen, pages 68–79. www.aclweb.org/anthology/W17-4707.

Ndapa Nakashole. 2018. Norma: Neighborhood sensitive maps for multilingual word embeddings. In *Proceedings of the 2018 Conference on Empirical Methods in Natural Language Processing*. Association for Computational Linguistics, Brussels, pages 512–522. www.aclweb.org/anthology/D18-1047.

Ndapa Nakashole and Raphael Flauger. 2018. Characterizing departures from linearity in word translation. In *Proceedings of the 56th Annual Meeting of the Association for Computational Linguistics*. Volume 2: *Short Papers*. Association for Computational Linguistics, Melbourne, pages 221–227. http://aclweb.org/anthology/P18-2036.

Graham Neubig. 2016. Lexicons and minimum risk training for neural machine translation: Naist-CMU at wat2016. In *Proceedings of the 3rd Workshop on Asian Translation (WAT2016)*. The COLING 2016 Organizing Committee, Osaka, pages 119–125. http://aclweb.org/anthology/W16-4610.

Graham Neubig, Zi-Yi Dou, Junjie Hu, Paul Michel, Danish Pruthi, and Xinyi Wang. 2019. compare-mt: A tool for holistic comparison of language generation systems. In *Proceedings of the 2019 Conference of the North American Chapter of the Association for Computational Linguistics (Demonstrations)*. Association for Computational Linguistics, Minneapolis, MN, pages 35–41. www.aclweb.org/anthology/N19-4007.

Graham Neubig and Junjie Hu. 2018. Rapid adaptation of neural machine translation to new languages. In *Proceedings of the 2018 Conference on Empirical Methods in Natural Language Processing*. Association for Computational Linguistics, Brussels, pages 875–880. www.aclweb.org/anthology/D18-1103.

New navy device learns by doing; psychologist shows embryo of computer designed to read and grow wiser. 1958. *New York Times*. www.nytimes.com/1958/07/08/archives/new-navy-device-learns-by-doing-psychologist-shows-embryo-of.html.

Toan Q. Nguyen and David Chiang. 2017. Transfer learning across low-resource, related languages for neural machine translation. In *Proceedings of the Eighth International Joint Conference on Natural Language Processing*. Volume 2: *Short Papers*. Asian Federation of Natural Language Processing, Taipei, pages 296–301. www.aclweb.org/anthology/I17-2050.

Jan Niehues and Eunah Cho. 2017. Exploiting linguistic resources for neural machine translation using multi-task learning. In *Proceedings of the Second Conference on Machine Translation*. Volume 1: *Research Papers*. Association for Computational Linguistics, Copenhagen, pages 80–89. http://www.aclweb.org/anthology/W17-4708.

Jan Niehues, Eunah Cho, Thanh-Le Ha, and Alex Waibel. 2016. Pre-translation for neural machine translation. In *Proceedings of COLING 2016, the 26th International Conference on Computational Linguistics: Technical Papers*. The COLING 2016 Organizing Committee, Osaka, Japan, pages 1828–1836. http://aclweb.org/anthology/C16-1172.

Jan Niehues, Eunah Cho, Thanh-Le Ha, and Alex Waibel. 2017. Analyzing neural MT search and model performance. In *Proceedings of the First Workshop on Neural Machine Translation*. Association for Computational Linguistics, Vancouver, BC, pages 11–17. www.aclweb.org/anthology/W17-3202.

Nikola Nikolov, Yuhuang Hu, Mi Xue Tan, and Richard H.R. Hahnloser. 2018. Character-level Chinese-English translation through ascii encoding. In *Proceedings of the Third Conference on Machine Translation: Research Papers*. Association for Computational Linguistics, Belgium, pages 10–16. www.aclweb.org/anthology/W18-6302.

Yuta Nishimura, Katsuhito Sudoh, Graham Neubig, and Satoshi Nakamura. 2018a. Multi-source neural machine translation with data augmentation. In *Proceedings of the International Workshop on Spoken Language Translation (IWSLT)*. Bruges, Belgium. https://arxiv.org/pdf/1810.06826.pdf.

Yuta Nishimura, Katsuhito Sudoh, Graham Neubig, and Satoshi Nakamura. 2018b. Multi-source neural machine translation with missing data. In *Proceedings of the 2nd Workshop on Neural Machine Translation and Generation*. Association for Computational Linguistics, Melbourne, pages 92–99. http://aclweb.org/anthology/W18-2711.

Xing Niu, Michael Denkowski, and Marine Carpuat. 2018. Bi-directional neural machine translation with synthetic parallel data. In *Proceedings of the 2nd Workshop on Neural Machine Translation and Generation*. Association for Computational Linguistics, Melbourne, pages 84–91. http://aclweb.org/anthology/W18-2710.

Xing Niu, Weijia Xu, and Marine Carpuat. 2019. Bi-directional differentiable input reconstruction for low-resource neural machine translation. In *Proceedings of the 2019 Conference of the North American Chapter of the Association for Computational Linguistics: Human Language Technologies*. Volume 1: *Long and Short Papers*. Association for Computational Linguistics, Minneapolis, MN, pages 442–448. www.aclweb.org/anthology/N19-1043.

Myle Ott, Michael Auli, David Grangier, and Marc'Aurelio Ranzato. 2018a. Analyzing uncertainty in neural machine translation. In Jennifer Dy and Andreas Krause, editors, *Proceedings of the 35th International Conference on Machine Learning*. Volume 80: *Proceedings of Machine Learning Research*. PMLR, StockholmsmÄ¤ssan, Stockholm, pages 3956–3965. http://proceedings.mlr.press/v80/ott18a/ott18a.pdf.

Myle Ott, Michael Auli, David Grangier, and Marc'Aurelio Ranzato. 2018b. Analyzing uncertainty in neural machine translation. Ithaca, NY: Cornell University, abs/1803.00047. http://arxiv.org/abs/1803.00047.

Myle Ott, Sergey Edunov, David Grangier, and Michael Auli. 2018c. Scaling neural machine translation. In *Proceedings of the Third Conference on Machine Translation: Research Papers*. Association for Computational Linguistics, Belgium, pages 1–9. www.aclweb.org/anthology/W18-6301.

Shantipriya Parida and Ondřej Bojar. 2018. Translating short segments with NMT: A case study in English-to-Hindi. In *Proceedings of the 21st Annual Conference of the European Association for Machine Translation*. Melbourne, https://rua.ua.es/dspace/bitstream/10045/76083/1/EAMT2018-Proceedings_25.pdf.

Razvan Pascanu, Tomas Mikolov, and Yoshua Bengio. 2013. On the difficulty of training recurrent neural networks. In *Proceedings of the 30th International Conference on Machine Learning, ICML*. Atlanta, GA, pages 1310–1318. http://proceedings.mlr.press/v28/pascanu13.pdf.

Barun Patra, Joel Ruben Antony Moniz, Sarthak Garg, Matthew R. Gormley, and Graham Neubig. 2019. Bilingual lexicon induction with semi-supervision in non-isometric embedding spaces. In *Proceedings of the 57th Conference of the Association for Computational Linguistics*. Association for Computational Linguistics, Florence, pages 184–193. www.aclweb.org/anthology/P19-1018.

Jeffrey Pennington, Richard Socher, and Christopher Manning. 2014. Glove: Global vectors for word representation. In *Proceedings of the 2014 Conference on Empirical Methods in Natural Language Processing (EMNLP)*. Association for Computational Linguistics, Doha, Qatar, pages 1532–1543. www.aclweb.org/anthology/D14-1162.

Álvaro Peris and Francisco Casacuberta. 2019. A neural, interactive-predictive system for multimodal sequence to sequence tasks. In *Proceedings of the 57th Conference of the Association for Computational Linguistics: System Demonstrations*. Association for Computational Linguistics, Florence, pages 81–86. www.aclweb.org/anthology/P19-3014.

Álvaro Peris, Luis Cebrián, and Francisco Casacuberta. 2017a. Online learning for neural machine translation post-editing. Ithaca, NY: Cornell University, abs/1706.03196. http://arxiv.org/abs/1706.03196.

Ivaro Peris, Miguel Domingo, and Francisco Casacuberta. 2017b. Interactive neural machine translation. *Computer Speech Language* 45(C):201–220. https://doi.org/10.1016/j.csl.2016.12.003.

Matthew Peters, Mark Neumann, Mohit Iyyer, Matt Gardner, Christopher Clark, Kenton Lee, and Luke Zettlemoyer. 2018. Deep contextualized word representations. In *Proceedings of the 2018 Conference of the North American Chapter of the Association for Computational Linguistics: Human Language Technologies*. Volume 1: *Long Papers*. Association for Computational Linguistics, New Orleans, LA, pages 2227–2237. http://aclweb.org/anthology/N18-1202.

Emmanouil Antonios Platanios, Mrinmaya Sachan, Graham Neubig, and Tom Mitchell. 2018. Contextual parameter generation for universal neural machine translation. In *Proceedings of the 2018 Conference on Empirical Methods in Natural Language Processing*. Association for Computational Linguistics, Brussels, pages 425–435. www.aclweb.org/anthology/D18-1039.

Emmanouil Antonios Platanios, Otilia Stretcu, Graham Neubig, Barnabas Poczos, and Tom Mitchell. 2019. Competence-based curriculum learning for neural

machine translation. In *Proceedings of the 2019 Conference of the North American Chapter of the Association for Computational Linguistics: Human Language Technologies*. Volume 1: *Long and Short Papers*. Association for Computational Linguistics, Minneapolis, MN, pages 1162–1172. www.aclweb.org/anthology/N19-1119.

Mirko Plitt and Francois Masselot. 2010. A productivity test of statistical machine translation post-editing in a typical localisation context. *The Prague Bulletin of Mathematical Linguistics* 94:7–16. http://ufal.mff.cuni.cz/pbml/93/art-plitt-masselot.pdf.

Adam Poliak, Yonatan Belinkov, James Glass, and Benjamin Van Durme. 2018. On the evaluation of semantic phenomena in neural machine translation using natural language inference. In *Proceedings of the 2018 Conference of the North American Chapter of the Association for Computational Linguistics: Human Language Technologies*. Volume 2: *Short Papers*. Association for Computational Linguistics, New Orleans, LA, pages 513–523. http://aclweb.org/anthology/N18-2082.

Maja Popović. 2017. Comparing Language Related Issues for NMT and PBMT between German and English. *The Prague Bulletin of Mathematical Linguistics* 108:209–220. https://doi.org/10.1515/pralin-2017-0021.

Matt Post and David Vilar. 2018. Fast lexically constrained decoding with dynamic beam allocation for neural machine translation. In *Proceedings of the 2018 Conference of the North American Chapter of the Association for Computational Linguistics: Human Language Technologies*. Volume 1: *Long Papers*. Association for Computational Linguistics, New Orleans, LA, pages 1314–1324. http://aclweb.org/anthology/N18-1119.

Xiao Pu, Nikolaos Pappas, and Andrei Popescu-Belis. 2017. Sense-aware statistical machine translation using adaptive context-dependent clustering. In *Proceedings of the Second Conference on Machine Translation*. Volume 1: *Research Papers*. Association for Computational Linguistics, Copenhagen, pages 1–10. www.aclweb.org/anthology/W17-4701.

Ye Qi, Devendra Sachan, Matthieu Felix, Sarguna Padmanabhan, and Graham Neubig. 2018. When and why are pre-trained word embeddings useful for neural machine translation? In *Proceedings of the 2018 Conference of the North American Chapter of the Association for Computational Linguistics: Human*

Language Technologies. Volume 2: *Short Papers.*
Association for Computational Linguistics, New
Orleans, LA, pages 529–535.
`http://aclweb.org/anthology/N18-2084`.

Alessand ro Raganato and Jörg Tiedemann. 2018. An
analysis of encoder representations in
transformer-based machine translation. In *Proceedings
of the 2018 EMNLP Workshop BlackboxNLP:
Analyzing and Interpreting Neural Networks for NLP.*
Association for Computational Linguistics, Brussels,
pages 287–297.
`www.aclweb.org/anthology/W18-5431`.

Spencer Rarrick, Chris Quirk, and Will Lewis. 2011. MT
detection in web-scraped parallel corpora. In
*Proceedings of the 13th Machine Translation Summit
(MT Summit XIII).* International Association for
Machine Translation, Xiamen, China, pages 422–430.
`www.mt-archive.info/
MTS-2011-Rarrick.pdf`.

Shuo Ren, Wenhu Chen, Shujie Liu, Mu Li, Ming Zhou, and
Shuai Ma. 2018. Triangular architecture for rare
language translation. In *Proceedings of the 56th Annual
Meeting of the Association for Computational
Linguistics.* Volume 1: *Long Papers.* Association for
Computational Linguistics, Melbourne, pages 56–65.
`http://aclweb.org/anthology/P18-1006`.

Shuo Ren, Zhirui Zhang, Shujie Liu, Ming Zhou, and Shuai
Ma. 2019. Unsupervised neural machine translation
with SMT as posterior regularization. In *Proceedings
of the AAAI Conference on Artificial Intelligence.*
Honolulu, HI, pages 241–248.
`https://doi.org/10.1609/
aaai.v33i01.3301241`.

Annette Rios, Laura Mascarell, and Rico Sennrich. 2017.
Improving word sense disambiguation in neural
machine translation with sense embeddings. In
*Proceedings of the Second Conference on Machine
Translation.* Volume 1: *Research Papers.* Association
for Computational Linguistics, Copenhagen,
pages 11–19.
`www.aclweb.org/anthology/W17-4702`.

Frank Rosenblatt. 1957. The perceptron, a perceiving and
recognizing automaton. Technical report, Buffalo, NY:
Cornell Aeronautical Laboratory.

Sebastian Ruder, Ivan Vulić, and Anders Søgaard. 2017. A
survey of cross-lingual embedding models. Ithaca, NY:
Cornell University, abs/1706.04902.
`http://arxiv.org/abs/1706.04902`.

Dana Ruiter, Cristina España-Bonet, and Josef van
Genabith. 2019. Self-supervised neural machine

translation. In *Proceedings of the 57th Conference of
the Association for Computational Linguistics.*
Association for Computational Linguistics, Florence,
pages 1828–1834.
`www.aclweb.org/anthology/P19-1178`.

David E. Rumelhart, Geoffrey E. Hinton, and Ronald J.
Williams. 1986. Learning internal representations by
error propagation. *Parallel Distributed Processing:
Explorations in the Microstructure of Cognition*
1:318–362.

Devendra Sachan and Graham Neubig. 2018. Parameter
sharing methods for multilingual self-attentional
translation models. In *Proceedings of the Third
Conference on Machine Translation: Research Papers.*
Association for Computational Linguistics, Belgium,
pages 261–271.
`www.aclweb.org/anthology/W18-6327`.

Marina Sanchez-Torron and Philipp Koehn. 2016. Machine
translation quality and post-editor productivity. In
*Proceedings of the Conference of the Association for
Machine Translation in the Americas (AMTA).*
Austin, TX.

Harsh Satija and Joelle Pineau. 2016. Simultaneous machine
translation using deep reinforcement learning. In
*Abstraction in Reinforcement Learning (ICML
Workshop).* New York.
`http://docs.wixstatic.com/ugd/3195dc_
538b63de8e2644b782db920c55f74650.pdf`.

M. Schuster and K. Nakajima. 2012. Japanese and korean
voice search. In *2012 IEEE International Conference
on Acoustics, Speech and Signal Processing (ICASSP).*
Toronto, pages 5149–5152. `https://doi.org/
10.1109/ICASSP.2012.6289079`.

Robert Schwarzenberg, David Harbecke, Vivien Macketanz,
Eleftherios Avramidis, and Sebastian Möller. 2019.
Train, sort, explain: Learning to diagnose translation
models. In *Proceedings of the 2019 Conference of the
North American Chapter of the Association for
Computational Linguistics (Demonstrations).*
Association for Computational Linguistics,
Minneapolis, MN, pages 29–34.
`https://www.aclweb.org/
anthology/N19-4006`.

Holger Schwenk. 2007. Continuous space language models.
Computer Speech and Language 3(21):492–518.
`https://wiki.inf.ed.ac.uk/twiki/pub/
CSTR/ListenSemester2_2009_10/
sdarticle.pdf`.

Holger Schwenk. 2010. Continuous-space language models
for statistical machine translation. *The Prague Bulletin*

of *Mathematical Linguistics* 93:137–146.
`http://ufal.mff.cuni.cz/pbml/93/`
`art-schwenk.pdf`.

Holger Schwenk. 2012. Continuous space translation models for phrase-based statistical machine translation. In *Proceedings of COLING 2012: Posters*. The COLING 2012 Organizing Committee, Mumbai, pages 1071–1080.
`www.aclweb.org/anthology/C12-2104`.

Holger Schwenk. 2018. Filtering and mining parallel data in a joint multilingual space. In *Proceedings of the 56th Annual Meeting of the Association for Computational Linguistics*. Volume 2: *Short Papers*. Association for Computational Linguistics, Melbourne, pages 228–234.
`http://aclweb.org/anthology/P18-2037`.

Holger Schwenk, Vishrav Chaudhary, Shuo Sun, Hongyu Gong, and Francisco Guzmán. 2019. Wikimatrix: Mining 135m parallel sentences in 1620 language pairs from wikipedia. Ithaca, NY: Cornell University, abs/1907.05791.
`http://arxiv.org/abs/1907.05791`.

Holger Schwenk, Daniel Dechelotte, and Jean-Luc Gauvain. 2006. Continuous space language models for statistical machine translation. In *Proceedings of the COLING/ACL 2006 Main Conference Poster Sessions*. Association for Computational Linguistics, Sydney, Australia, pages 723–730.
`www.aclweb.org/anthology/P/`
`P06/P06-2093`.

Holger Schwenk and Matthijs Douze. 2017. Learning joint multilingual sentence representations with neural machine translation. In *Proceedings of the 2nd Workshop on Representation Learning for NLP*. Association for Computational Linguistics, Vancouver, BC, pages 157–167.
`https://doi.org/10.18653/v1/W17-2619`.

Holger Schwenk, Anthony Rousseau, and Mohammed Attik. 2012. Large, pruned or continuous space language models on a GPU for statistical machine translation. In *Proceedings of the NAACL-HLT 2012 Workshop: Will We Ever Really Replace the N-gram Model? On the Future of Language Modeling for HLT*. Association for Computational Linguistics, Montréal, pages 11–19.
`www.aclweb.org/anthology/W12-2702`.

Jean Senellart, Dakun Zhang, Bo WANG, Guillaume KLEIN, Jean-Pierre Ramatchandirin, Josep Crego, and Alexander Rush. 2018. Opennmt system description for wnmt 2018: 800 words/sec on a single-core cpu. In *Proceedings of the 2nd Workshop on Neural Machine Translation and Generation*. Association for

Computational Linguistics, Melbourne, pages 122–128.
`http://aclweb.org/anthology/W18-2715`.

Rico Sennrich. 2017. How grammatical is character-level neural machine translation? Assessing MT quality with contrastive translation pairs. In *Proceedings of the 15th Conference of the European Chapter of the Association for Computational Linguistics. Volume 2: Short Papers*. Association for Computational Linguistics, Valencia, Spain, pages 376–382.
`www.aclweb.org/anthology/E17-2060`.

Rico Sennrich and Barry Haddow. 2016. Linguistic input features improve neural machine translation. In *Proceedings of the First Conference on Machine Translation*. Association for Computational Linguistics, Berlin, pages 83–91.
`www.aclweb.org/anthology/W/`
`W16/W16-2209`.

Rico Sennrich, Barry Haddow, and Alexandra Birch. 2016a. Controlling politeness in neural machine translation via side constraints. In *Proceedings of the 2016 Conference of the North American Chapter of the Association for Computational Linguistics: Human Language Technologies*. Association for Computational Linguistics, San Diego, CA, pages 35–40.
`www.aclweb.org/anthology/N16-1005`.

Rico Sennrich, Barry Haddow, and Alexandra Birch. 2016b. Edinburgh neural machine translation systems for wmt 16. In *Proceedings of the First Conference on Machine Translation*. Association for Computational Linguistics, Berlin, pages 371–376.
`www.aclweb.org/anthology/W/`
`W16/W16-2323`.

Rico Sennrich, Barry Haddow, and Alexandra Birch. 2016c. Improving neural machine translation models with monolingual data. In *Proceedings of the 54th Annual Meeting of the Association for Computational Linguistics. Volume 1: Long Papers*. Association for Computational Linguistics, Berlin, pages 86–96.
`www.aclweb.org/anthology/P16-1009`.

Rico Sennrich, Barry Haddow, and Alexandra Birch. 2016d. Neural machine translation of rare words with subword units. In *Proceedings of the 54th Annual Meeting of the Association for Computational Linguistics. Volume 1: Long Papers*. Association for Computational Linguistics, Berlin, pages 1715–1725.
`www.aclweb.org/anthology/P16-1162`.

Rico Sennrich, Barry Haddow, and Alexandra Birch. 2016e. Neural machine translation of rare words with subword units. In *Proceedings of the 54th Annual Meeting of the Association for Computational Linguistics. Volume 1:*

Long Papers. Association for Computational Linguistics, Berlin, pages 1715–1725. www.aclweb.org/anthology/P16-1162.

Christophe Servan, Josep Maria Crego, and Jean Senellart. 2016. Domain specialization: A post-training domain adaptation for neural machine translation. Ithaca, NY: Cornell University, abs/1612.06141. http://arxiv.org/abs/1612.06141.

Yutong Shao, Rico Sennrich, Bonnie Webber, and Federico Fancellu. 2018. Evaluating machine translation performance on chinese idioms with a blacklist method. In *Proceedings of the Eleventh International Conference on Language Resources and Evaluation (LREC 2018)*. European Language Resources Association (ELRA), Miyazaki, Japan. https://arxiv.org/pdf/1711.07646.pdf.

Ehsan Shareghi, Matthias Petri, Gholamreza Haffari, and Trevor Cohn. 2016. Fast, small and exact: Infinite-order language modelling with compressed suffix trees. *Transactions of the Association for Computational Linguistics* 4:477–490. https://transacl.org/ojs/index.php/tacl/article/view/865.

Shiqi Shen, Yong Cheng, Zhongjun He, Wei He, Hua Wu, Maosong Sun, and Yang Liu. 2016. Minimum risk training for neural machine translation. In *Proceedings of the 54th Annual Meeting of the Association for Computational Linguistics. Volume 1: Long Papers*. Association for Computational Linguistics, Berlin, pages 1683–1692. www.aclweb.org/anthology/P16-1159.

Weijia Shi, Muhao Chen, Yingtao Tian, and Kai-Wei Chang. 2019. Learning bilingual word embeddings using lexical definitions. In *Proceedings of the 4th Workshop on Representation Learning for NLP (RepL4NLP-2019)*. Association for Computational Linguistics, Florence, pages 142–147. www.aclweb.org/anthology/W19-4316.

Xing Shi and Kevin Knight. 2017. Speeding up neural machine translation decoding by shrinking run-time vocabulary. In *Proceedings of the 55th Annual Meeting of the Association for Computational Linguistics. Volume 2: Short Papers*. Association for Computational Linguistics, Vancouver, BC, pages 574–579. http://aclweb.org/anthology/P17-2091.

Xing Shi, Kevin Knight, and Deniz Yuret. 2016a. Why neural translations are the right length. In *Proceedings of the 2016 Conference on Empirical Methods in Natural Language Processing*. Association for

Computational Linguistics, Austin, TX, pages 2278–2282. https://aclweb.org/anthology/D16-1248.

Xing Shi, Inkit Padhi, and Kevin Knight. 2016b. Does string-based neural MT learn source syntax? In *Proceedings of the 2016 Conference on Empirical Methods in Natural Language Processing*. Association for Computational Linguistics, Austin, TX, pages 1526–1534. https://aclweb.org/anthology/D16-1159.

Raphael Shu and Hideki Nakayama. 2018. Improving beam search by removing monotonic constraint for neural machine translation. In *Proceedings of the 56th Annual Meeting of the Association for Computational Linguistics. Volume 2: Short Papers*. Association for Computational Linguistics, Melbourne, pages 339–344. http://aclweb.org/anthology/P18-2054.

Patrick Simianer, Joern Wuebker, and John DeNero. 2019. Measuring immediate adaptation performance for neural machine translation. In *Proceedings of the 2019 Conference of the North American Chapter of the Association for Computational Linguistics: Human Language Technologies. Volume 1: Long and Short Papers*. Association for Computational Linguistics, Minneapolis, MN, pages 2038–2046. www.aclweb.org/anthology/N19-1206.

Samuel L. Smith, David H. P. Turban, Steven Hamblin, and Nils Y. Hammerla. 2017. Offline bilingual word vectors, orthogonal transformations and the inverted softmax. In *Proceedings of the International Conference on Learning Representations (ICLR)*. Toulon, France.

Matthew Snover, Bonnie J. Dorr, Richard Schwartz, Linnea Micciulla, and John Makhoul. 2006. A study of translation edit rate with targeted human annotation. In *5th Conference of the Association for Machine Translation in the Americas (AMTA)*. Boston. http://mt-archive.info/AMTA-2006-Snover.pdf.

Anders Søgaard, Sebastian Ruder, and Ivan Vulić. 2018. On the limitations of unsupervised bilingual dictionary induction. In *Proceedings of the 56th Annual Meeting of the Association for Computational Linguistics. Volume 1: Long Papers*. Association for Computational Linguistics, Melbourne, pages 778–788. https://doi.org/10.18653/v1/P18-1072.

Kai Song, Yue Zhang, Heng Yu, Weihua Luo, Kun Wang, and Min Zhang. 2019. Code-switching for enhancing NMT with pre-specified translation. In *Proceedings of the 2019 Conference of the North American Chapter of* the *Association for Computational Linguistics: Human Language Technologies*. Volume 1: *Long and Short Papers*. Association for Computational Linguistics, Minneapolis, MN, pages 449–459. `www.aclweb.org/anthology/N19-1044`.

Nitish Srivastava, Geoffrey Hinton, Alex Krizhevsky, Ilya Sutskever, and Ruslan Salakhutdinov. 2014. Dropout: A simple way to prevent neural networks from overfitting. *Journal of Machine Learning Research* 15:1929–1958. `http://jmlr.org/papers/v15/srivastava14a.html`.

Felix Stahlberg, Adrià de Gispert, Eva Hasler, and Bill Byrne. 2017. Neural machine translation by minimising the Bayes-risk with respect to syntactic translation lattices. In *Proceedings of the 15th Conference of the European Chapter of the Association for Computational Linguistics*. Volume 2: *Short Papers*. Association for Computational Linguistics, Valencia, Spain, pages 362–368. `www.aclweb.org/anthology/E17-2058`.

Felix Stahlberg, Danielle Saunders, and Bill Byrne. 2018. An operation sequence model for explainable neural machine translation. In *Proceedings of the 2018 EMNLP Workshop BlackboxNLP: Analyzing and Interpreting Neural Networks for NLP*. Association for Computational Linguistics, Brussels, pages 175–186. `www.aclweb.org/anthology/W18-5420`.

Hendrik Strobelt, Sebastian Gehrmann, Michael Behrisch, Adam Perer, Hanspeter Pfister, and Alexander M Rush. 2019. Seq2seq-vis: A visual debugging tool for sequence-to-sequence models. *IEEE Transactions on Visualization and Computer Graphics* 25(1):353–363.

Haipeng Sun, Rui Wang, Kehai Chen, Masao Utiyama, Eiichiro Sumita, and Tiejun Zhao. 2019. Unsupervised bilingual word embedding agreement for unsupervised neural machine translation. In *Proceedings of the 57th Conference of the Association for Computational Linguistics*. Association for Computational Linguistics, Florence, pages 1235–1245. `www.aclweb.org/anthology/P19-1119`.

Martin Sundermeyer, Ilya Oparin, Jean-Luc Gauvain, Ben Freiberg, Ralf Schlüter, and Hermann Ney. 2013. Comparison of feedforward and recurrent neural network language models. In *IEEE International Conference on Acoustics, Speech, and Signal Processing*. Vancouver, BC, pages 8430–8434. `www.eu-bridge.eu/downloads/_Comparison_of_Feedforward_and_Recurrent_Neural_Network_Language_Models.pdf`.

Ilya Sutskever, Oriol Vinyals, and Quoc V. Le. 2014. Sequence to sequence learning with neural networks. In Z. Ghahramani, M. Welling, C. Cortes, N. D. Lawrence, and K. Q. Weinberger, editors, *Advances in Neural Information Processing Systems 27*. Barcelona, pages 3104–3112. `http://papers.nips.cc/paper/5346-sequence-to-sequence-learning-with-neural-networks.pdf`.

Kaveh Taghipour, Shahram Khadivi, and Jia Xu. 2011. Parallel corpus refinement as an outlier detection algorithm. In *Proceedings of the 13th Machine Translation Summit (MT Summit XIII)*. International Association for Machine Translation, Xiamen, China, pages 414–421. `www.mt-archive.info/MTS-2011-Taghipour.pdf`.

Aleš Tamchyna, Marion Weller-Di Marco, and Alexander Fraser. 2017. Modeling target-side inflection in neural machine translation. In *Proceedings of the Second Conference on Machine Translation*. Volume 1: *Research Papers*. Association for Computational Linguistics, Copenhagen, pages 32–42. `www.aclweb.org/anthology/W17-4704`.

Xu Tan, Yi Ren, Di He, Tao Qin, Zhou Zhao, and Tie-Yan Liu. 2019. Multilingual neural machine translation with knowledge distillation. In *International Conference on Learning Representations (ICLR)*. New Orleans, LA. `https://openreview.net/pdf?id=S1gUsoR9YX`.

Gongbo Tang, Rico Sennrich, and Joakim Nivre. 2018. An analysis of attention mechanisms: The case of word sense disambiguation in neural machine translation. In *Proceedings of the Third Conference on Machine Translation: Research Papers*. Association for Computational Linguistics, Belgium, pages 26–35. `www.aclweb.org/anthology/W18-6304`.

Sander Tars and Mark Fishel. 2018. Multi-domain neural machine translation. In *Proceedings of the 21st Annual Conference of the European Association for Machine Translation*. Melbourne.

Alex Ter-Sarkisov, Holger Schwenk, Fethi Bougares, and Loïc Barrault. 2015. Incremental adaptation strategies for neural network language models. In *Proceedings of the 3rd Workshop on Continuous Vector Space Models and their Compositionality*. Association for Computational Linguistics, Beijing, pages 48–56. `www.aclweb.org/anthology/W15-4006`.

Brian Thompson, Jeremy Gwinnup, Huda Khayrallah, Kevin Duh, and Philipp Koehn. 2019. Overcoming catastrophic forgetting during domain adaptation of neural machine translation. In *Proceedings of the 2019*

Conference of the North American Chapter of the Association for Computational Linguistics: Human Language Technologies. Volume 1: *Long and Short Papers.* Association for Computational Linguistics, Minneapolis, MN, pages 2062–2068. www.aclweb.org/anthology/N19-1209.

Brian Thompson, Huda Khayrallah, Antonios Anastasopoulos, Arya D. McCarthy, Kevin Duh, Rebecca Marvin, Paul McNamee, Jeremy Gwinnup, Tim Anderson, and Philipp Koehn. 2018. Freezing subnetworks to analyze domain adaptation in neural machine translation. In *Proceedings of the Third Conference on Machine Translation: Research Papers.* Association for Computational Linguistics, Belgium, pages 124–132. www.aclweb.org/anthology/W18-6313.

Jörg Tiedemann. 2012. Parallel data, tools and interfaces in opus. In Nicoletta Calzolari, Khalid Choukri, Thierry Declerck, Mehmet Uğur Doğan, Bente Maegaard, Joseph Mariani, Jan Odijk, and Stelios Piperidis, editors, *Proceedings of the Eighth International Conference on Language Resources and Evaluation (LREC-2012).* European Language Resources Association (ELRA), Istanbul, pages 2214–2218. ACL Anthology Identifier: L12-1246. www.lrec-conf.org/proceedings/lrec2012/pdf/463_Paper.pdf.

Antonio Toral, Sheila Castilho, Ke Hu, and Andy Way. 2018. Attaining the unattainable? reassessing claims of human parity in neural machine translation. In *Proceedings of the Third Conference on Machine Translation: Research Papers.* Association for Computational Linguistics, Belgium, pages 113–123. www.aclweb.org/anthology/W18-6312.

Antonio Toral and Víctor M. Sánchez-Cartagena. 2017. A multifaceted evaluation of neural versus phrase-based machine translation for 9 language directions. In *Proceedings of the 15th Conference of the European Chapter of the Association for Computational Linguistics.* Volume 1: *Long Papers.* Association for Computational Linguistics, Valencia, Spain, pages 1063–1073. www.aclweb.org/anthology/E17-1100.

Ke Tran, Arianna Bisazza, and Christof Monz. 2016. Recurrent memory networks for language modeling. In *Proceedings of the 2016 Conference of the North American Chapter of the Association for Computational Linguistics: Human Language Technologies.* Association for Computational Linguistics, San Diego, CA, pages 321–331. www.aclweb.org/anthology/N16-1036.

Ke Tran, Arianna Bisazza, and Christof Monz. 2018. The importance of being recurrent for modeling hierarchical structure. In *Proceedings of the 2018 Conference on Empirical Methods in Natural Language Processing.* Association for Computational Linguistics, Brussels, pages 4731–4736. www.aclweb.org/anthology/D18-1503.

Zhaopeng Tu, Yang Liu, Zhengdong Lu, Xiaohua Liu, and Hang Li. 2016a. Context gates for neural machine translation. Ithaca, NY: Cornell University, abs/1608.06043. http://arxiv.org/abs/1608.06043.

Zhaopeng Tu, Yang Liu, Lifeng Shang, Xiaohua Liu, and Hang Li. 2017. Neural machine translation with reconstruction. In *Proceedings of the 31st AAAI Conference on Artificial Intelligence.* San Francisco. http://arxiv.org/abs/1611.01874.

Zhaopeng Tu, Zhengdong Lu, Yang Liu, Xiaohua Liu, and Hang Li. 2016b. Modeling coverage for neural machine translation. In *Proceedings of the 54th Annual Meeting of the Association for Computational Linguistics.* Volume 1: *Long Papers.* Association for Computational Linguistics, Berlin, pages 76–85. www.aclweb.org/anthology/P16-1008.

Vaibhav Vaibhav, Sumeet Singh, Craig Stewart, and Graham Neubig. 2019. Improving robustness of machine translation with synthetic noise. In *Proceedings of the 2019 Conference of the North American Chapter of the Association for Computational Linguistics: Human Language Technologies.* Volume 1: *Long and Short Papers).* Association for Computational Linguistics, Minneapolis, MN, pages 1916–1920. www.aclweb.org/anthology/N19-1190.

L. J. P. van der Maaten and Geoffrey Hinton. 2008. Visualizing data using t-SNE. *Journal of Machine Learning Research* 9:2579–2605. http://jmlr.org/papers/volume9/vandermaaten08a/vandermaaten08a.pdf.

Marlies van der Wees, Arianna Bisazza, and Christof Monz. 2017. Dynamic data selection for neural machine translation. In *Proceedings of the 2017 Conference on Empirical Methods in Natural Language Processing.* Association for Computational Linguistics, Copenhagen, pages 1411–1421. http://aclweb.org/anthology/D17-1147.

Ashish Vaswani, Noam Shazeer, Niki Parmar, Jakob Uszkoreit, Llion Jones, Aidan N Gomez, Ł ukasz Kaiser, and Illia Polosukhin. 2017. Attention is all you need. In I. Guyon, U. V. Luxburg, S. Bengio, H. Wallach, R. Fergus, S. Vishwanathan, and R. Garnett, editors, *Advances in Neural Information*

Processing Systems 30. Barcelona, pages 5998–6008. http://papers.nips.cc/paper/ 7181-attention-is-all-you-need.pdf.

Ashish Vaswani, Yinggong Zhao, Victoria Fossum, and David Chiang. 2013. Decoding with large-scale neural language models improves translation. In *Proceedings of the 2013 Conference on Empirical Methods in Natural Language Processing*. Association for Computational Linguistics, Seattle, WA, pages 1387–1392. www.aclweb.org/anthology/D13-1140.

Bernard Vauquois. 1968. Structures profondes et traduction automatique. le système du ceta. *Revue Roumaine de linguistique* 13(2):105–130.

Ashish Venugopal, Jakob Uszkoreit, David Talbot, Franz Och, and Juri Ganitkevitch. 2011. Watermarking the outputs of structured prediction with an application in statistical machine translation. In *Proceedings of the 2011 Conference on Empirical Methods in Natural Language Processing*. Association for Computational Linguistics, Edinburgh, pages 1363–1372. www.aclweb.org/anthology/D11-1126.

David Vilar. 2018. Learning hidden unit contribution for adapting neural machine translation models. In *Proceedings of the 2018 Conference of the North American Chapter of the Association for Computational Linguistics: Human Language Technologies. Volume 2: Short Papers*. Association for Computational Linguistics, New Orleans, LA, pages 500–505. http://aclweb.org/anthology/N18-2080.

Sami Virpioja, Peter Smit, Stig-Arne Grönroos, and Mikko Kurimo. 2013. Morfessor 2.0: Python implementation and extensions for Morfessor baseline. Technical Report 25, Espoo, Finland: Aalto University.

Ivan Vulić and Anna Korhonen. 2016. On the role of seed lexicons in learning bilingual word embeddings. In *Proceedings of the 54th Annual Meeting of the Association for Computational Linguistics. Volume 1: Long Papers*. Association for Computational Linguistics, Berlin, pages 247–257. www.aclweb.org/anthology/P16-1024.

Ivan Vulić and Marie-Francine Moens. 2015. Bilingual word embeddings from non-parallel document-aligned data applied to bilingual lexicon induction. In *Proceedings of the 53rd Annual Meeting of the Association for Computational Linguistics and the 7th International Joint Conference on Natural Language Processing*. Volume 2: *Short Papers*. Association for Computational Linguistics, Beijing, pages 719–725. www.aclweb.org/anthology/P15-2118.

Takashi Wada, Tomoharu Iwata, and Yuji Matsumoto. 2019. Unsupervised multilingual word embedding with limited resources using neural language models. In *Proceedings of the 57th Conference of the Association for Computational Linguistics*. Association for Computational Linguistics, Florence, pages 3113–3124. www.aclweb.org/anthology/P19-1300.

Alex Waibel, A. N. Jain, A. E. McNair, H. Saito, A. G. Hauptmann, and J. Tebelskis. 1991. Janus: A speech-to-speech translation system using connectionist and symbolic processing strategies. In *Proceedings of the 1991 International Conference on Acoustics, Speech and Signal Processing (ICASSP)*. Toronto, pages 793–796.

Eric Wallace, Shi Feng, and Jordan Boyd-Graber. 2018. Interpreting neural networks with nearest neighbors. In *Proceedings of the 2018 EMNLP Workshop BlackboxNLP: Analyzing and Interpreting Neural Networks for NLP*. Association for Computational Linguistics, Brussels, pages 136–144. www.aclweb.org/anthology/W18-5416.

Qiang Wang, Bei Li, Tong Xiao, Jingbo Zhu, Changliang Li, Derek F. Wong, and Lidia S. Chao. 2019a. Learning deep transformer models for machine translation. In *Proceedings of the 57th Conference of the Association for Computational Linguistics*. Association for Computational Linguistics, Florence, pages 1810–1822. www.aclweb.org/anthology/P19-1176.

Rui Wang, Andrew Finch, Masao Utiyama, and Eiichiro Sumita. 2017a. Sentence embedding for neural machine translation domain adaptation. In *Proceedings of the 55th Annual Meeting of the Association for Computational Linguistics. Volume 2: Short Papers*. Association for Computational Linguistics, Vancouver, BC, pages 560–566. http://aclweb.org/anthology/P17-2089.

Rui Wang, Masao Utiyama, Isao Goto, Eiichro Sumita, Hai Zhao, and Bao-Liang Lu. 2013. Converting continuous-space language models into n-gram language models for statistical machine translation. In *Proceedings of the 2013 Conference on Empirical Methods in Natural Language Processing*. Association for Computational Linguistics, Seattle, WA, pages 845–850. www.aclweb.org/anthology/D13-1082.

Rui Wang, Masao Utiyama, Lemao Liu, Kehai Chen, and Eiichiro Sumita. 2017b. Instance weighting for neural machine translation domain adaptation. In *Proceedings of the 2017 Conference on Empirical Methods in*

Natural Language Processing. Association for Computational Linguistics, Copenhagen pages 1483–1489.
http://aclweb.org/anthology/D17-1155.

Rui Wang, Masao Utiyama, and Eiichiro Sumita. 2018a. Dynamic sentence sampling for efficient training of neural machine translation. In *Proceedings of the 56th Annual Meeting of the Association for Computational Linguistics.* Volume 2: *Short Papers.* Association for Computational Linguistics, Melbourne, pages 298–304.
http://aclweb.org/anthology/P18-2048.

Rui Wang, Hai Zhao, Bao-Liang Lu, Masao Utiyama, and Eiichiro Sumita. 2014. Neural network based bilingual language model growing for statistical machine translation. In *Proceedings of the 2014 Conference on Empirical Methods in Natural Language Processing (EMNLP).* Association for Computational Linguistics, Doha, Qatar, pages 189–195.
www.aclweb.org/anthology/D14-1023.

Xinyi Wang, Hieu Pham, Philip Arthur, and Graham Neubig. 2019b. Multilingual neural machine translation with soft decoupled encoding. In *International Conference on Learning Representations (ICLR).* New Orleans, LA.
https://openreview.net/pdf?id=Skeke3C5Fm.

Yining Wang, Jiajun Zhang, Feifei Zhai, Jingfang Xu, and Chengqing Zong. 2018b. Three strategies to improve one-to-many multilingual translation. In *Proceedings of the 2018 Conference on Empirical Methods in Natural Language Processing.* Association for Computational Linguistics, Brussels, pages 2955–2960.
www.aclweb.org/anthology/D18-1326.

Warren Weaver. 1947. Letter to Norbert Wiener. Translated in 1949 and reprinted in Locke and Booth (1955).

Hao-Ran Wei, Shujian Huang, Ran Wang, Xin-yu Dai, and Jiajun Chen. 2019. Online distilling from checkpoints for neural machine translation. In *Proceedings of the 2019 Conference of the North American Chapter of the Association for Computational Linguistics: Human Language Technologies.* Volume 1: *Long and Short Papers.* Association for Computational Linguistics, Minneapolis, MN, pages 1932–1941.
www.aclweb.org/anthology/N19-1192.

Sam Wiseman and Alexander M. Rush. 2016. Sequence-to-sequence learning as beam-search optimization. In *Proceedings of the 2016 Conference on Empirical Methods in Natural Language Processing.* Association for Computational Linguistics, Austin, TX, pages 1296–1306.
https://aclweb.org/anthology/D16-1137.

Lijun Wu, Xu Tan, Di He, Fei Tian, Tao Qin, Jianhuang Lai, and Tie-Yan Liu. 2018. Beyond error propagation in neural machine translation: Characteristics of language also matter. In *Proceedings of the 2018 Conference on Empirical Methods in Natural Language Processing.* Association for Computational Linguistics, Brussels, pages 3602–3611.
www.aclweb.org/anthology/D18-1396.

Lijun Wu, Yiren Wang, Yingce Xia, Fei Tian, Fei Gao, Tao Qin, Jianhuang Lai, and Tie-Yan Liu. 2019. Depth growing for neural machine translation. In *Proceedings of the 57th Conference of the Association for Computational Linguistics.* Association for Computational Linguistics, Florence, pages 5558–5563.
www.aclweb.org/anthology/P19-1558.

Lijun Wu, Yingce Xia, Li Zhao, Fei Tian, Tao Qin, Jianhuang Lai, and Tie-Yan Liu. 2017. Adversarial neural machine translation. Ithaca, NY: Cornell University, abs/1704.06933.
https://arxiv.org/pdf/1704.06933.pdf.

Yonghui Wu, Mike Schuster, Zhifeng Chen, Quoc V. Le, Mohammad Norouzi, Wolfgang Macherey, Maxim Krikun, Yuan Cao, Qin Gao, Klaus Macherey, Jeff Klingner, Apurva Shah, Melvin Johnson, Xiaobing Liu, Lukasz Kaiser, Stephan Gouws, Yoshikiyo Kato, Taku Kudo, Hideto Kazawa, Keith Stevens, George Kurian, Nishant Patil, Wei Wang, Cliff Young, Jason Smith, Jason Riesa, Alex Rudnick, Oriol Vinyals, Greg Corrado, Macduff Hughes, and Jeffrey Dean. 2016. Google's neural machine translation system: Bridging the gap between human and machine translation. Ithaca, NY: Cornell University, abs/1609.08144.
http://arxiv.org/abs/1609.08144.pdf.

Youzheng Wu, Hitoshi Yamamoto, Xugang Lu, Shigeki Matsuda, Chiori Hori, and Hideki Kashioka. 2012. Factored recurrent neural network language model in TED lecture transcription. In *Proceedings of the Seventh International Workshop on Spoken Language Translation (IWSLT).* Hong Kong, pages 222–228.
www.mt-archive.info/IWSLT-2012-Wu.pdf.

Joern Wuebker, Spence Green, John DeNero, Sasa Hasan, and Minh-Thang Luong. 2016. Models and inference for prefix-constrained machine translation. In *Proceedings of the 54th Annual Meeting of the Association for Computational Linguistics.* Volume 1: *Long Papers.* Association for Computational Linguistics, Berlin, pages 66–75.
www.aclweb.org/anthology/P16-1007.

Joern Wuebker, Patrick Simianer, and John DeNero. 2018. Compact personalized models for neural machine translation. In *Proceedings of the 2018 Conference on Empirical Methods in Natural Language Processing*. Association for Computational Linguistics, Brussels, pages 881–886. www.aclweb.org/anthology/D18-1104.

Chao Xing, Dong Wang, Chao Liu, and Yiye Lin. 2015. Normalized word embedding and orthogonal transform for bilingual word translation. In *Proceedings of the 2015 Conference of the North American Chapter of the Association for Computational Linguistics: Human Language Technologies*. Association for Computational Linguistics, Denver, CO, pages 1006–1011. www.aclweb.org/anthology/N15-1104.

Hainan Xu and Philipp Koehn. 2017. Zipporah: A fast and scalable data cleaning system for noisy web-crawled parallel corpora. In *Proceedings of the 2017 Conference on Empirical Methods in Natural Language Processing*. Association for Computational Linguistics, Copenhagen, pages 2935–2940. http://aclweb.org/anthology/D17-1318.

Ruochen Xu, Yiming Yang, Naoki Otani, and Yuexin Wu. 2018. Unsupervised cross-lingual transfer of word embedding spaces. In *Proceedings of the 2018 Conference on Empirical Methods in Natural Language Processing*. Association for Computational Linguistics, Brussels, pages 2465–2474. https://doi.org/10.18653/v1/D18-1268.

Weijia Xu, Xing Niu, and Marine Carpuat. 2019. Differentiable sampling with flexible reference word order for neural machine translation. In *Proceedings of the 2019 Conference of the North American Chapter of the Association for Computational Linguistics: Human Language Technologies*. Volume 1: *Long and Short Papers*. Association for Computational Linguistics, Minneapolis, MN, pages 2047–2053. www.aclweb.org/anthology/N19-1207.

Yilin Yang, Liang Huang, and Mingbo Ma. 2018a. Breaking the beam search curse: A study of (re-)scoring methods and stopping criteria for neural machine translation. In *Proceedings of the 2018 Conference on Empirical Methods in Natural Language Processing*. Association for Computational Linguistics, Brussels, pages 3054–3059. www.aclweb.org/anthology/D18-1342.

Zhen Yang, Wei Chen, Feng Wang, and Bo Xu. 2018b. Improving neural machine translation with conditional sequence generative adversarial nets. In *Proceedings of the 2018 Conference of the North American Chapter of the Association for Computational Linguistics: Human Language Technologies*. Volume 1: *Long Papers*. Association for Computational Linguistics, New Orleans, LA, pages 1346–1355. http://aclweb.org/anthology/N18-1122.

Zhen Yang, Wei Chen, Feng Wang, and Bo Xu. 2018c. Unsupervised neural machine translation with weight sharing. In *Proceedings of the 56th Annual Meeting of the Association for Computational Linguistics*. Volume 1: *Long Papers*. Association for Computational Linguistics, Melbourne, pages 46–55. http://aclweb.org/anthology/P18-1005.

Zhilin Yang, Zihang Dai, Yiming Yang, Jaime G. Carbonell, Ruslan Salakhutdinov, and Quoc V. Le. 2019. Xlnet: Generalized autoregressive pretraining for language understanding. Ithaca, NY: Cornell University, abs/1906.08237. http://arxiv.org/abs/1906.08237.

Noa Yehezkel Lubin, Jacob Goldberger, and Yoav Goldberg. 2019. Aligning vector-spaces with noisy supervised lexicon. In *Proceedings of the 2019 Conference of the North American Chapter of the Association for Computational Linguistics: Human Language Technologies*. Volume 1: *Long and Short Papers*. Association for Computational Linguistics, Minneapolis, MN, pages 460–465. www.aclweb.org/anthology/N19-1045.

Poorya Zaremoodi and Gholamreza Haffari. 2018. Neural machine translation for bilingually scarce scenarios: A deep multi-task learning approach. In *Proceedings of the 2018 Conference of the North American Chapter of the Association for Computational Linguistics: Human Language Technologies*. Volume 1: *Long Papers*. Association for Computational Linguistics, New Orleans, LA, pages 1356–1365. http://aclweb.org/anthology/N18-1123.

Matthew D. Zeiler. 2012. ADADELTA: An adaptive learning rate method. Ithaca, NY: Cornell University, abs/1212.5701. http://arxiv.org/abs/1212.5701.

Thomas Zenkel, Joern Wuebker, and John DeNero. 2019. Adding interpretable attention to neural translation models improves word alignment. In *arXiv*. https://arxiv.org/pdf/1901.11359.

Jiajun Zhang, Shujie Liu, Mu Li, Ming Zhou, and Chengqing Zong. 2014. Bilingually-constrained phrase embeddings for machine translation. In *Proceedings of the 52nd Annual Meeting of the Association for Computational Linguistics*. Volume 1: *Long Papers*.

Association for Computational Linguistics, Baltimore, MD, pages 111–121. www.aclweb.org/anthology/P14-1011.

Jian Zhang, Liangyou Li, Andy Way, and Qun Liu. 2016. Topic-informed neural machine translation. In *Proceedings of COLING 2016, the 26th International Conference on Computational Linguistics: Technical Papers*. The COLING 2016 Organizing Committee, Osaka, pages 1807–1817. http://aclweb.org/anthology/C16-1170.

Jingyi Zhang, Masao Utiyama, Eiichro Sumita, Graham Neubig, and Satoshi Nakamura. 2017a. Improving neural machine translation through phrase-based forced decoding. In *Proceedings of the Eighth International Joint Conference on Natural Language Processing. Volume 1: Long Papers*. Asian Federation of Natural Language Processing, Taipei, pages 152–162. www.aclweb.org/anthology/I17-1016.

Jingyi Zhang, Masao Utiyama, Eiichro Sumita, Graham Neubig, and Satoshi Nakamura. 2018a. Guiding neural machine translation with retrieved translation pieces. In *Proceedings of the 2018 Conference of the North American Chapter of the Association for Computational Linguistics: Human Language Technologies. Volume 1: Long Papers*. Association for Computational Linguistics, New Orleans, LA, pages 1325–1335. http://aclweb.org/anthology/N18-1120.

Kelly Zhang and Samuel Bowman. 2018. Language modeling teaches you more than translation does: Lessons learned through auxiliary syntactic task analysis. In *Proceedings of the 2018 EMNLP Workshop BlackboxNLP: Analyzing and Interpreting Neural Networks for NLP*. Association for Computational Linguistics, Brussels, pages 359–361. www.aclweb.org/anthology/W18-5448.

Longtu Zhang and Mamoru Komachi. 2018. Neural machine translation of logographic language using sub-character level information. In *Proceedings of the Third Conference on Machine Translation: Research Papers*. Association for Computational Linguistics, Belgium, pages 17–25. www.aclweb.org/anthology/W18-6303.

Meng Zhang, Yang Liu, Huanbo Luan, and Maosong Sun. 2017b. Adversarial training for unsupervised bilingual lexicon induction. In *Proceedings of the 55th Annual Meeting of the Association for Computational Linguistics. Volume 1: Long Papers*. Association for Computational Linguistics, Vancouver, BC, pages 1959–1970. https://doi.org/10.18653/v1/P17-1179.

Meng Zhang, Yang Liu, Huanbo Luan, and Maosong Sun. 2017c. Earth mover's distance minimization for unsupervised bilingual lexicon induction. In *Proceedings of the 2017 Conference on Empirical Methods in Natural Language Processing*. Association for Computational Linguistics, Long Beach, CA, pages 1924–1935. www.aclweb.org/anthology/D17-1207.

Pei Zhang, Niyu Ge, Boxing Chen, and Kai Fan. 2019a. Lattice transformer for speech translation. In *Proceedings of the 57th Conference of the Association for Computational Linguistics*. Association for Computational Linguistics, Florence, pages 6475–6484. www.aclweb.org/anthology/P19-1649.

Wen Zhang, Yang Feng, Fandong Meng, Di You, and Qun Liu. 2019b. Bridging the gap between training and inference for neural machine translation. In *Proceedings of the 57th Conference of the Association for Computational Linguistics*. Association for Computational Linguistics, Florence, pages 4334–4343. www.aclweb.org/anthology/P19-1426.

Wen Zhang, Liang Huang, Yang Feng, Lei Shen, and Qun Liu. 2018b. Speeding up neural machine translation decoding by cube pruning. In *Proceedings of the 2018 Conference on Empirical Methods in Natural Language Processing*. Association for Computational Linguistics, Brussels, pages 4284–4294. www.aclweb.org/anthology/D18-1460.

Xuan Zhang, Pamela Shapiro, Gaurav Kumar, Paul McNamee, Marine Carpuat, and Kevin Duh. 2019c. Curriculum learning for domain adaptation in neural machine translation. In *Proceedings of the 2019 Conference of the North American Chapter of the Association for Computational Linguistics: Human Language Technologies. Volume 1: Long and Short Papers*. Association for Computational Linguistics, Minneapolis, MN, pages 1903–1915. www.aclweb.org/anthology/N19-1189.

Zhisong Zhang, Rui Wang, Masao Utiyama, Eiichiro Sumita, and Hai Zhao. 2018c. Exploring recombination for efficient decoding of neural machine translation. In *Proceedings of the 2018 Conference on Empirical Methods in Natural Language Processing*. Association for Computational Linguistics, Brussels, pages 4785–4790. www.aclweb.org/anthology/D18-1511.

Baigong Zheng, Renjie Zheng, Mingbo Ma, and Liang Huang. 2019. Simultaneous translation with flexible policy via restricted imitation learning. In *Proceedings of the 57th Conference of the Association for Computational Linguistics*. Association for Computational Linguistics, Florence, pages 5816–5822. www.aclweb.org/anthology/P19-1582.

Chunting Zhou, Xuezhe Ma, Di Wang, and Graham Neubig. 2019. Density matching for bilingual word embedding. In *Proceedings of the 2019 Conference of the North American Chapter of the Association for Computational Linguistics: Human Language Technologies*. Volume 1: *Long and Short Papers*. Association for Computational Linguistics, Minneapolis, MN, pages 1588–1598. www.aclweb.org/anthology/N19-1161.

Long Zhou, Wenpeng Hu, Jiajun Zhang, and Chengqing Zong. 2017. Neural system combination for machine translation. In *Proceedings of the 55th Annual Meeting of the Association for Computational Linguistics*.

Volume 2: *Short Papers*. Association for Computational Linguistics, Vancouver, BC, pages 378–384. http://aclweb.org/anthology/P17-2060.

Barret Zoph and Kevin Knight. 2016. Multi-source neural translation. In *Proceedings of the 2016 Conference of the North American Chapter of the Association for Computational Linguistics: Human Language Technologies*. Association for Computational Linguistics, San Diego, CA, pages 30–34. www.aclweb.org/anthology/N16-1004.

Barret Zoph, Deniz Yuret, Jonathan May, and Kevin Knight. 2016. Transfer learning for low-resource neural machine translation. In *Proceedings of the 2016 Conference on Empirical Methods in Natural Language Processing*. Association for Computational Linguistics, Austin, TX, pages 1568–1575. https://aclweb.org/anthology/D16-1163.

Author Index

Index